East West Central

East West Central
Re-Building Europe, 1950–1990

Edited by Ákos Moravánszky, Torsten Lange,
Judith Hopfengärtner, Karl R. Kegler

Ákos Moravánszky, Torsten Lange (Eds.)

Re-Framing Identities

Architecture's Turn to History, 1970–1990

East West Central
Re-Building Europe
1950–1990
Vol. 3

Birkhäuser
Basel

Editors
Prof. Dr. Ákos Moravánszky
Department of Architecture, ETH Zurich, Switzerland

Dr. Torsten Lange
Department of Architecture, ETH Zurich, Switzerland
torsten.lange@gta.arch.ethz.ch

Editors' proofreading: Alan Lockwood, PL-Warsaw
Publishers' proofreading: Alun Brown, A-Vienna
Project and production management: Angelika Heller, Birkhäuser Verlag, A-Vienna
Layout and typography: Ekke Wolf, typic.at, A-Vienna
Cover design: Martin Gaal, A-Vienna
Printing and binding: Holzhausen Druck GmbH, A-Wolkersdorf

Library of Congress Cataloging-in-Publication data
A CIP catalog record for this book has been applied for at the Library of Congress.

Bibliographic information published by the German National Library
The German National Library lists this publication in the Deutsche Nationalbibliografie; detailed bibliographic data are available on the Internet at http://dnb.dnb.de.

This publication is also available as an e-book (ISBN PDF 978-3-0356-0815-1).

P.O. Box 44, 4009 Basel, Switzerland
Part of Walter de Gruyter GmbH, Berlin/Boston

Printed on acid-free paper produced from chlorine-free pulp. TCF ∞

Printed in Austria

ISBN 978-3-0356-1015-4 Volume 1
ISBN 978-3-0356-1016-1 Volume 2
ISBN 978-3-0356-1017-8 Volume 3
ISBN 978-3-0356-1014-7 Set Volume 1–3

9 8 7 6 5 4 3 2 1

www.birkhauser.com

Contents

Ákos Moravánszky

Foreword

East West Central: Re-Building Europe

The Iron Curtain stood for the static immutability of the status quo. "From Stettin in the Baltic to Trieste in the Adriatic, an iron curtain has descended across the Continent" – Winston Churchill told his audience in a famous speech on March 5, 1946. Like most metaphors, the term Iron Curtain has imprinted itself into the perception of reality and was associated with the fortified border, erected to block the movement of people and information between East and West. Architectural historiography followed suit, presenting the history of modernization and modernism in Europe from a perspective determined – and limited – by this political boundary. The imagery produced by the dissolution of the Soviet Union: the "fall," the "lifting" or the "raising" of the curtain, the "breaching" of the wall, is a sign of confusion – regarding not only metaphors, but also underlying assumptions, methods and categories of architectural historiography.

Writing in the 1920s, art historian Erwin Panofsky famously referred to the perspective as a symbolic form. By this he meant that representing reality by means of a cohesive set of rules and symbols would give shape to a specific worldview. The exchange of views between cultures can therefore be studied using examples of visual representations, based on differing concepts of the relationship between observer and reality. When Panofsky gave his seminal lecture on Western perspective, Russian philosopher-physicist-inventor-priest Pavel Florensky wrote a study on the "reverse perspective" used in icon painting. He compared it to Renaissance representations of space in order to point out the differences between the two types of visual representation and their respective philosophical and theological underpinnings.

The exchange of glances as expressed in the German word *Blickwechsel* is a suggestive image: we are invited to switch between the viewpoints of the observer and the observed, so that our image of the world is suddenly no longer taken for granted. The metaphor of the Iron Curtain, however, suggests that after WWII the boundary between the two halves of Europe was hermetic and impermeable, even to the gaze. Western and Eastern Europe regarded each other as their own dark "others": communism and capitalism, divided by the Iron Curtain, were the "Twin Empires" on the mythical map of Europe. Yet, the perfect symmetry of the image eschewed the evidently more complex reality. As an image, the Iron Curtain was able to trigger both Western fear and desire, but actually it was far from being impenetrable. Rather, the Iron Curtain's semi-permeability, which turned it into an osmotic membrane, refuted the supposed symmetry of the East-West division. Contrary to the widespread identification in the West with the concept of Western Europe and its corresponding values, the idea of a shared Eastern European identity has never been popular among the inhabitants of this region. Architects in the East were generally very well informed about the latest developments in Western architecture. One could hardly survive as an architect without having browsed the latest issues of *L'Architecture d'Aujourd'hui, The Architectural Review* or the magazines from Scandinavian countries, all of which were available in the libraries of the large state-owned design offices. The optical metaphor, however, held true: images were floating around but remained disembodied signifiers, as they weren't grounded in personal experience. At the same time, travels of architects and professional organizations from the West to the East intensified during 1970s and 1980s. The lessons that participants drew from such exchanges more often than not depended on their respective viewpoints of the perspective.

The discrepancy between the bipolarity of block-thinking and the more complex and heterogeneous civilizational and political reality of Europe has led historians to develop different concepts to describe the historical identity of European regions more adequately than the East-West dichotomy. The term *Mitteleuropa* has never been merely a geographical term. It was a political one as well, just as East and West were connected with distinct political ideas or concepts. With the active support of intellectuals from the United States and England in the 1980s, Central Europe became a program to affirm a particular identity of the region: politically part of the Eastern Bloc, but without losing its Western cultural orientation – a result of the region's specific historical development and its political affiliations before the war. "The phrase, a peculiar one, a hybrid of sorts, hearkened back to the Cold War period; while it reflected a certain deference to the ideas of Milan Kundera and others, it avoided the outright suggestion that the notion of Eastern Europe was outmoded, essentially a fabrication of the age of Stalin, that it brought together in a single category societies that remained significantly different" – wrote Stephen R. Graubard, editor of *Daedalus*, the journal of the American Academy of Arts and Sciences in 1990, in his introduction for the issue "Eastern Europe… Central Europe… Europe." The title suggested a development of concepts: the first term referred to the Cold War period, the second was the "preferred word of certain individuals and groups in the 1960s, 1970s, and 1980s," while the third was the "word of the moment." From the contemporary perspective of more than two decades later, the question about what might be further stages in this progression is at the heart of heated debates.

Ironically, it was exactly the abolishment of state socialism and the new freedom of movement that have lessened the urgency to cross borders intellectually. In 1987, the idea of a joint international exhibition to take place in Budapest and Vienna in 1995 was embraced with much enthusiasm, only to be abandoned in its advanced stage. The "bridges into the future" – the motto of Expo'95 – literally lost their appeal after the Pan-European Picnic in August 1989.

Today, as block thinking and block-politics are reemerging, the category of the Central promises to be a useful tool for investigating European architecture between two moments of "re-building": the postwar reconstruction and the start of shifting the "curtain" (which is not less "irony" today than before) more and more toward the East. We decided to use the word Central not only because it was a buzzword during the decades that are the focus of our investigation, but because the "thirding" that is implicit in the term opposes a bipolar narrative that regards modernization and globalization as Westernization and regards Eastern European developments as secondary or non-authentic, never questioning the constructs that legitimate these interpretations.

An investigation into issues such as housing, the exporting of knowledge to the Third World, building for education and for leisure between the two re-buildings of Europe would be impossible if one resorted to the narrative of the Iron Curtain. Rather than this dualistic concept, we have to consider among others competitions, cooperation, critical transformation, and knowledge transfer as more adequate frameworks for investigating these more dynamic conditions. The critique of self-serving dichotomizations of cultural phenomena in line with the East/West dispositive (marginal/central, modern/traditional, authentic/copy etc.) does not mean that, in this process of explaining the changing urban and architectural conditions over the course of the last seventy years, the diverse cultural landscape of Europe needs to be flattened.

The re-mapping of the European historiography of the postwar decades is an urgent task in the face of the paradoxical perpetuation of the Cold War discourse. One of the reasons behind its endurance is the imbalance between the ongoing institutionalization of archives of postwar architectural production in Western Europe vis-à-vis the disappearance of archival sources in the East. To lend visibility to the architectural discourse in former socialist countries, it is important to give voice to protagonists and witnesses. The failure to do this would not only reinforce already existing blind spots in the architectural historiography of the postwar period, but would also distort the perception of Western-European architecture culture from the 1960s onward. This includes the concept of the welfare state as being restricted to the Western social-democratic project and posited in contrast to state socialism, rather than recognizing parallel development in the post-Stalinist socialist countries and its architecture revolving around issues of consumption, leisure, mass housing and the emergence of new collective subjectivities such as "users," "inhabitants," or "consumers." Another example could be the reduction of current processes of globalization to their earlier stages, presenting globalization as "Americanization," thus forgetting the multiple, vibrant and heterogeneous processes of the internationalization of architecture and planning practices between socialist and post-colonial countries.

Three international conferences organized by the Chair of Architectural Theory at the ETH Zurich prepared the ground for this re-mapping. The topic of our first East West Central conference in May 2014 was *Re-Humanizing Architecture: New Forms of Community, 1950–1970*. Our intention was to show that the rhetoric of humanism provided an ideal common ground for liberal and socialist positions in the postwar years. With the second conference *Re-Scaling the Environment: New Landscapes of Design, 1960–1980*, held in November 2014, we abandoned the metaphor of the "human scale" as the natural way of viewing the world for a larger, superhuman, geographic or territorial scale. The theme of the third conference in *Re-Framing Identities: Architecture's Turn to History, 1970–1990* in September 2015 shows another overlap by a decade. This does not mean that the themes of humanism and scale disappear; even postmodernism is regarded by some historians as a project of re-humanization. While we investigate these altogether four decades from three different perspectives, the themes of humanism, scale and identity remain relevant categories throughout the entire time period 1950–1990.

We could not have gotten started on this project without the generous and long-term support of the Department of Architecture of the ETH Zurich and its Institut gta (Institute for the History and Theory of Architecture). The Swiss National Science Foundation (SNF) has provided us with financial assistance for the organization of the conferences. The book has been made possible only by the contributions of our authors; we owe them all a debt of gratitude. We would also like to thank the persons and institutions who gave their permission for the illustrations. We owe a considerable debt to everybody at Birkhäuser Verlag who helped in the production of the book; most of all David Marold and Angelika Heller. We also would like to express our gratitude to our student assistants Josephine Eigner and Laure Nashed for their help.

Torsten Lange

Introduction

A specter is haunting architecture – the specter of postmodernism. Walking down the corridors and studio spaces of international architecture schools today, one easily notes just how preoccupied the discipline is, again, with postmodern aesthetics. This resurging interest within contemporary design practice is met by the topic's prominence in architectural discourse. Among the seemingly unending wave of publications and popular exhibitions[1] that try to grapple with postmodernism as an aesthetic and intellectual phenomenon which has defined the end of the twentieth century, and in the midst of current debates about postmodernism's "topicality,"[2] one might ask: what will another book on the subject be able to add to the already very dense picture?

The answer is simple. Familiar mainstream narratives about the emergence of postmodernism in architecture and urban design since the mid-1960s, and its rise in the following two decades – evident foremost in the increasingly critical attitude toward functionalist modernism and a growing concern for historicism, symbolism and meaning that was paralleled and sustained by a proliferation of architectural theory, influenced in particular by phenomenology and semiotics – have tended to focus on developments in North America. Moreover, they have often sidelined the political aspects of postmodernity in favor of foregrounding postmodern aesthetics.[3]

Yet, as a global cultural phenomenon postmodernism has transcended disciplinary and geographical boundaries. Its impact can be detected in many places. Aided not least by the general climate of steadily improving and intensifying political and economic relations between the Communist Bloc and the West in the wake of late-1960s *Ostpolitik* and the Helsinki Accords of 1975, its reach went beyond the Cold War geopolitics of the East and West. During the 1980s, several state-socialist countries in Eastern Europe witnessed processes of liberalization and economic reforms that would eventually lead to the overthrow of authoritarian state leaderships in 1989/90, the disintegration of the Eastern Bloc, and the end of Europe's political division. These processes not only resonated, but also intersected with the spread of postmodernist aesthetics. Architecture was viewed and utilized as a means for re-framing identities. As forgotten or neglected historical relationships were being reconsidered, for example, built heritage and preservation became inevitably politicized. Questioning the modern project on the level of aesthetics thus went hand in hand with rethinking its wider political premises (and future promises).

Taking this specific dynamic into account, then, the diverse contributions assembled in this book attempt to overcome the prevalent geographical and thematic bias by offering a complex analysis of postmodernism's development in Europe (and beyond) to reflect its heterogeneous nature.[4] The resulting picture is thus necessarily kaleidoscopic and fragmentary. Nevertheless, the different authors in this volume share the ambition of examining "architecture's turn to history" in the 1970s and 1980s as a transnational cultural legacy in relation to fundamental and far-reaching socio-economic and political transformations. Parallel developments in architecture and urban design in Western and Eastern Europe are therefore discussedon equal terms and side by side, asking for interrelationships as well as mechanisms of exchange and translation. At the same time, contributions remain sensitive to locally specific manifestations and their discrete contexts – be they social, intellectual, ideological, political, or economic. One of the questions that emerges from the articles, for example, is that there appears to be a discrepancy between subversion, play, irony, and pastiche as the tools, strategies, and characteristics with which Western postmodernism is usually associated and some of the more serious attempts to locate, restore and imagine regional or national traditions in Eastern Europe.

The ambition of this collection lies not primarily in revising the established narratives of postmodern architecture's history – this would in many ways be futile, given that this "recent history" remains very much in flux – but to expand these narratives by asking different questions as well as increasing the scope and breadth of the enquiry. In recent years, scholars have traced the influence of phenomenological thought on architectural culture after WWII[5]; explored the uneasy relationship between postmodernity, architecture and utopia[6]; or investigated architectural history's role in feeding the notion of an eternal present that has become so characteristic of the latter part of the twentieth century.[7] Moreover, research has begun to document and analyze the role and significance of key protagonists such as Aldo Rossi, both locally and internationally.[8] Other important actors beyond the narrow frame of the architectural profession such as the German art historian and architectural theorist Heinrich Klotz, founding director of the DAM in Frankfurt/Main, have also received some attention.[9]

However, parallel developments in, and exchanges with, Eastern Europe have thus far played only a marginal role and have not received the same amount of attention.[10] Foregrounding politicized modes of action in opposition to the authoritarian socialist state and party leadership and official discourse, historiography has often followed art historical and visual culture research, adopting terms and concepts advanced within this type of scholarship.[11] Narratives of dissent and critique thus also characterize some of the recent scholarship on architecture in Eastern European countries in the 1970s and 1980s, in particular when this work focuses on practices at the intersection of art and architecture; for example speculative designs and paper architecture.[12] The limitations of such an approach seem obvious; narratives of critiquing communist ideology might apply to singular cases, yet they can't be sustained, as numerous other examples exemplify how postmodern ideas concerning subjectivity, experience, historicity, heritage, regional identity and urbanity were, in fact, quickly absorbed by official discourse and the policies of the state-led construction system – even if their widespread practical implementation remained relatively slow.[13] Until now, only a few studies have moved beyond national boundaries to consider the significance of transnational exchanges through work in post-colonial contexts in the global south; in particular, in facilitating the spread of a postmodern aesthetic.[14]

The articles in this collection oscillate between the three larger topics of identity, history and the city, with the "turn to history" forming a central connecting thread – a common denominator and vanishing point. The different contributions trace the chronology of the turn to history in architecture and urban design in different European countries; ask how terms and concepts such as modernism and postmodernism were discussed by architects and theorists in East and West; examine the role played by questions of heritage and identity in architectural practice, the impact of historicism and postmodernism on the development of cities, and the specific forms this took in various contexts; and investigate the mechanisms of international exchange and transfer that allowed postmodernism to become a global phenomenon.

Part I: Identity Construct(ion)s

The first part of this book, "Identity Construct(ion)s," investigates the notion of identity on three different levels: first, the identities produced by larger geographical and geopolitical constructs in the second half of the twentieth century; second, cross-cultural exchanges brought about by the globalization of building; and third, the ideological dimension of architectural discourses on identity in the contexts of late capitalist, late socialist and postsocialist societies.

Opening this section is the article by Ákos Moravánszky. Recounting memories and personal experiences, the author asks whether the intensification of contacts between architects in the East and West that resulted from the increasing permeability of the Wall after 1970 led to more exchange and understanding, or whether participants in these encounters with "the Other" merely ended up projecting their own desires on their counterparts. Moravánszky shows not only how, during those years, the Wall served as a border rather than a boundary – becoming a space for "inter-action" rather than posing a strict limit[15] – but also how the mobilization of a libidinal economy across the Cold War geopolitical divide depended on the former's physical presence. The Wall's disintegration in 1990 thus also meant the waning of willingness to engage. In their contribution, Georgi Stanishev (senior) and Georgi Stanishev (junior) also develop a broader cultural-geographical perspective. Their analysis of the processes of modernization – and postmodernization – in Central and East European countries rests upon a dynamic center-periphery model. In this model two ideological "constructions" are at play, constantly working against one another in the fabrication of identity: while the first one understands Central Eastern European cultures as an internal periphery to both Soviet and Western discourses, the second one emphasizes the former's self-determination and power to produce hybrids of local and universal phenomena.

The second set of chapters deal with the development and growth of a globalized construction economy at the end of the twentieth century. Łukasz Stanek's article presents the case of a late-1970s export project by Polish architects and engineers – a power plant in Benghazi, Libya – that was realized in collaboration with international experts and construction firms from the East and West. Focusing on printed images of this project and their presence across different media and archives whilst paying close attention to these images' materiality, Stanek discusses not only their performance as indexes for the "network of architectural mobilities from socialist Poland," but also highlights their ambiguity as commentaries on the state of the construction sector within the country, particularly in the context of scarcity and the economic crisis of the early 1980s. Max Hirsh, in turn, demonstrates how such transnational exchanges of technical and managerial expertise could also lead to unintended consequences. His article deals with two 1980s construction projects for luxury hotels in the East German cities Dresden and Berlin by the Japanese Kajima corporation. Examining the processes of their commissioning, design, and construction, he shows that – rather than resulting in a one-directional transfer of knowledge (usually presumed from West to East) – the experience of collaboration between East German and Japanese architects led to multi-directional translation and cross-cultural exchange, for instance, as the latter acquired knowledge about neo-historical design. Moreover, Hirsh uncovers the hidden thick materiality of assemblages of international technologies, skills, finance, construction materials and labor that has so far remained concealed behind both the buildings' pervasive imagery of local and national identity as well as in commentaries in (East) German media from the time of their construction (and after).

The third set of texts in this first part of the volume address the ways in which history and meaning in architecture figure – both metaphorically and materially – in the construction of identities and ideologies in relation to the conditions produced by different social and political structures. Focusing on the well-known and influential Czech *émigré* architect, theorist, and educator Dalibor Vesely, Joseph Bedford discusses how the former's reflections about his experience of the "underground" city of Atlanta may serve as a conceptual device for understanding his theoretical outlook on architecture as well as his pedagogical practice in Great Britain. Bedford proposes a broader interpretation of "underground" as a notion that allows Vesely's personal experience of the conflict between historical meaning and technological progress in postwar socialist Czechoslovakia to be connected with both his conceptual understanding of this conflict through the lens of phenomenology and with the latter's extension into architectural education, whereby history and theory were viewed by Vesely as the means for resisting the instrumental character of design practice. In contrast, the story of the so-called Hungarian tulip dispute in the early 1970s – discussed in Daniel Kiss's chapter – rather than pointing to a resolution of the growing conflict between history and meaning on one side and modernism's insistence on technological and social progress on the other, highlights the historical continuity and eventual escalation of this conflict into the contemporary ideological standoff between a traditionalist, populist faction of the intelligentsia and a cosmopolitan, urbanist one. Triggered by the young Pécs group of architects' addition of folklore ornament to prefabricated mass housing, which led to sharp accusations of antimodernism from mainstream figures, this debate soon extended well beyond the architectural discipline into the realms of culture, society and politics – and from there continues to paralyze the former.

Part II: The Turn to History

The second part of this book has as its leading theme "The Turn to History" in architecture and urban design, focusing on the one hand on (critical) historiography of modern architecture and on the other hand on the mobilization of history by various European architects; including such canonical representatives of postmodern architecture as Aldo Rossi, Paolo Portoghesi and Hans Hollein, but also lesser-known figures such as the Croatian architect Boris Magaš.

Joan Ockman's contribution to this volume revisits the project of establishing a new methodological foundation for the historiography of architecture by Manfredo Tafuri and his colleagues at the so-called Venice School. The author reflects extensively on the broader "cultural" and intellectual as well as political and socio-economic context of late 1960s and early 1970s Italy, from which Tafuri's framework for studying the development of modern architecture in relation to three major historical systems – American capitalism, European social democracy, and Soviet communism – had emerged. By doing so, Ockman highlights the strong resonance between historical subject matter(s), interpretative frameworks and this wider context. She notes a certain correlation between the attested convergence of those three systems in the 1930s, as Tafuri had argued, and their actual convergence at the end of the last century. If Tafuri's approach for a revisionist and critical history is historicized in Ockman's article, the chapter by Alla Vronskaya adopts this approach in order to mount a critique of mainstream Western historiography of modern art and architecture, which continues to juxtapose the aesthetic program of the avant-garde – Soviet Constructivism in particular – and the notion of totalitarianism as developed in political theory. Focusing on the 1988 "Deconstructivist Architecture" exhibition at MoMA, New York and the primarily formalist interest in Constructivism shared by its curators as well as the architects on display, the author unpacks the history of the – chiefly North American – postwar realignment of Russian avant-garde art and architecture with a Western (neo)liberal political program, and points to Marxist French, Italian, and Russian historiographies as possible alternatives.

The remaining chapters in this section deal less with historiography than with how different architects have theorized and utilized history in their design practices. For instance, in her article Angelika Schnell detects the roots of Aldo Rossi's later theories of architecture and the city in his formulation of a new historiographical model in one of his earliest writings from 1956: "The Concept of Tradition in Neoclassical Milanese Architecture." This historiographical model, she argues, rather than viewing architectural history as the development of forms, established the Enlightenment as a major historical turning point. This not only defined the classical legacy as the only valid aesthetic and philosophical tradition, it also allowed this legacy to be followed – looking both backwards and forwards – by bringing it in line with progressive political (i.e., Marxist) and social forces. Thus, Rossi's turn to history is political rather than formal in character, and in this sense transcends the modern-postmodern divide. Focusing on one of Rossi's contemporaries, the Italian architect Paolo Portoghesi, Silvia Micheli and Lea-Catherine Szacka also emphasize the relationship between politics and a specific aesthetic interest derived from history; albeit towards very different – and in fact diametrically opposite – ends. While for Rossi, the eighteenth-century enlightenment and neoclassicism provided a horizon of reason against which architecture from the past and present could be measured, distinguishing a valid "rationalist" tradition from the small-mindedness of all other non-classical formalisms including what he called "naïve functionalism," Portoghesi's historical engagement with the architecture of Francesco Borromini led him to criticize the "inhibitions" of modern architecture. In the architecture of Portoghesi, an active member of the Italian Socialist Party, we thus find the somewhat simplistic identification of a particular informal aesthetic with the idea of political and social liberalism, and the converse association between formal restraint and repressive politics.

The last two articles in this second part shift the focus from politics back to geography again. Karin Šerman traces in the work of Boris Magaš a number of key themes of postmodernism: history and meaning as creative repositories, engagement with place and phenomenology, regional language and identity. Focusing on three projects from the late 1960s to the mid-1980s alongside the influential architect's written work, she discusses his hesitant alignment with the current of Western postmodern discourse and instead argues for a more long-term perspective, which reveals the presence of these themes in the Croatian modernist tradition. The link between modernism and postmodernism in Central Europe is further explored in Ruth Hanisch's article about Austrian *enfant terrible* Hans Hollein. Hanisch shows how Hollein and his contemporaries were educated in, and began to rebel against, the sober climate of postwar Austrian culture that sought to sever ties with its prewar imperial history by focusing on "simple" reconstruction, social and political equilibrium. A young group of radically minded artists and architects began to engage with the neglected heritage of *fin de siècle* architecture in Vienna, exploring – both historically and creatively – the work of now much-appreciated figures such as Otto Wagner and Adolf Loos within the context of emerging modern culture in Austro-Hungary. By doing so, Hanisch shows how Hollein, among others, helped to reestablish an image of Vienna as a Central European metropolis at the end of the twentieth century, just as the Cold War geopolitical order began to disintegrate and the map of Europe changed.

Part III: Public Criticism and the Rediscovery of the City

The articles assembled in the third part of this book all deal – in various ways – with the topic of the "Rediscovery of the City," the public sphere and public life, showing just how fundamental those concerns were to European postmodern discourse. Michela Rosso unpacks the long controversy over the Mansion House Square Scheme in the City of London, designed by Mies van der Rohe for the British developer Peter Palumbo shortly before the former's death. She traces how, within the space of fifteen years (from 1969 to 1984), public perception of the scheme – a simple modernist slab with an open plaza characteristic of the architect – changed from an atmosphere of support to one of open hostility, eventually leading to the scheme's abandonment after the site and its surroundings had become listed. Through a close reading and analysis of materials presented at a public inquiry in 1984, including debates in the British media, Rosso illuminates a broader cultural shift towards heritage and preservation, and against architectural modernism, with widespread popular support from bottom-up community groups taking sides with prominent opponents of the project. The article by Andrew Demshuk presents two exemplary cases of emerging municipal preservation practices from East and West Germany. Focusing on Leipzig and Frankfurt/Main, Demshuk emphasizes how in both cities – under significantly different political conditions, however – public critiques came to play an important role in bringing about a shift in attitudes toward heritage and building preservation, leading to changes in policies as well as in practices from postwar comprehensive reconstruction to the establishment of often understaffed and underfunded municipal preservation offices and, finally, the turn to neohistorical postmodern urban design.

The article by Sebastiaan Loosen returns to the question of leftist politics in postmodern discourse – a recurring theme throughout this volume. Introducing the ideologically informed and highly polemical debates among the circle of architects and intellectuals around Maurice Culot and Leon Krier in 1970s Brussels as to who should rightfully lay claim to historicism – the bourgeoisie or the Left – Loosen illuminates their engagement with topics such as the socialist city and aesthetic concepts like socialist realism in Soviet Russia. Johannes Warda in turn shifts our attention to the divided Berlin, where at that time attempts were being made to realize the socialist city on the other side of the Wall – if, nevertheless, (still) following the modernist paradigm of the city. In West Berlin, as in Brussels, critiques of the excesses of modernist urban development – the wholesale demolition of the historic fabric (*Mietskasernen*) of urban residential districts and its replacement with modernist mass housing – developed in the post-1968 highly politicized atmosphere.[16] Yet, those critiques and the proposed alternative strategies for a socially just, "careful," urban renewal based on the maintenance and repair of the existing building stock were cast not so much in ideological terms, but rather founded on "materialist" arguments – detailed ground rent and construction cost analyses – that drew attention to the socio-political dimension of urban reconstruction. Fundamentally pragmatic in their outlook, and valuing the city as a material and social resource, they were distinct from conventional approaches to historic preservation. Moreover, as Warda also discusses, these strategies had an ecological dimension as well.

While the chapters by Loosen and Warda highlight how, in Western Europe during the 1970s, the city became a politically charged and highly contested territory – either by attempting to bring historicist aesthetics and urban design in line with Marxist ideology or by exposing the link between modernist planning and capitalist development and asking for citizens' rights to the city – the final two contributions in the book, in contrast, point to the simultaneous exhaustion of politics (by emptying it of the political) in the urban realm in Eastern Europe. Tijana Stevanović offers a critical reading of the architect and town planner Miloš R. Perović's study for the reurbanization of New Belgrade, revealing the project's fundamentally contradictory character – insofar as it advocated spontaneous urban development while taking a universal large-scale planning perspective, or fostered citizen participation while reinstating the authority of the architect. She also exposes how his study was situated within the context of changing relations of production in late socialist Yugoslavia, in which modifications to the legislative framework increasingly undermined the scope of planning. Drawing on Michel Foucault's concept of biopolitics, Maroš Krivý examines late socialist critiques of *sídliště* (mass housing settlements) in Czechoslovakia. The author explains how both the Party leadership and dissidents focused on the issue of "life" in these settlements – quality of life and life-in-truth, respectively, marking opposite ends of their criticisms – and shows how the embrace of artistic design strategies went hand in hand with the abandonment of effective political (Marxist) critique. The revival of the pedestrian street thus ends up as mere travesty, as the politics of urban life become replaced with culture and consumption.

Coda

Taken as a whole, the contributions in this volume show the degree to which some of postmodernism's central concerns continue to exert an influence on contemporary architectural culture. Viewed in this light, the caesura of 1990 – which also provides the historical framing for this collection – might not quite mark such a clear historic boundary, in perhaps a similar fashion as the Iron Curtain turned out not to be the insurmountable barrier that it has often been depicted as. It has been noted how the term "postmodern," from its inception in the second half of the 1930s by British historian Arnold J. Toynbee, had been characterized by a degree of ambiguity: "[o]n the one hand it is seen as a historical period; on the other it is simply a desire, a mood which looks to the future to redeem the present."[17] It is in this sense that we might agree with Reinhold Martin that it is perhaps much too early to historicize postmodernism.[18] We nonetheless hope that this book might provide insights into the historic origins of some of the dynamics that haunt architectural discourse and continue to shape our cities to this day.

Endnotes

1 The most prominent example was perhaps the large show "Postmodernism – Style and Subversion 1970–1990" on display at the V&A, London, and the Landesmuseum Zurich (2012). See: Glenn Adamson et al. (eds.), *Postmodernism: style and subversion, 1970–1990* (London: V&A Publishing, 2011). In addition to new books, there have also been translations and (commented) reeditions of original publications, for instance Charles Jencks's *Post-Modern Reader*, first published in 1992. See Charles Jencks (ed.), *The Post-Modern Reader*, 2nd ed. (London: Wiley, 2010).

2 An example "close to home" from the perspective of the editors of this publication is a series of discussions on "Die Aktualität der Postmoderne," currently held at the Swiss Architecture Museum (SAM) in Basel and sparked, in part, by the publication of a special edition of the Swiss architecture journal *archithese*, no. 3 (2016), "Die Postmoderne – neu gelesen." In a similar vein, the University of Zurich in a recent lecture series also asked about the continued relevance of Postmodernism: "Postmoderne: Genealogie und globale Aktualität eines umstrittenen Konzepts," Ringvorlesung der Kommission UZH Interdisziplinär. http://www.uzh.ch/de/outreach/events/rv/archiv/2015fs/postmoderne.html, accessed on October 30, 2016.

3 See in this context Emmanuel Petit's review of Reinhold Martin's book *Utopia's Ghost*, in which he argues that "postmodern architecture is yet another arena for the expression of the differences between European and American understandings of social and political life. While the historic cities have mostly provided the context for European architects, American architects have tended to cater to a different type of context: the mass media." Emmanuel Petit, "Utopia's Ghost: Architecture and Postmodernism, Again," *Journal of Architectural Education* 66, no. 1 (2012), 23–24.

4 The question whether and to what extent the term and concept postmodernism can be usefully applied to the Eastern European context has been discussed in the humanities and social sciences in the 1990s. See Bo Stråth and Nina Witoszek (eds), *The Postmodern Challenge: Perspectives East and West* (Amsterdam: Rodopi, 1999).

5 Jorge Otero-Pailos, *Architecture's historical turn: phenomenology and the rise of the postmodern* (Minneapolis: University of Minnesota Press, 2010).
6 Reinhold Martin, *Utopia's ghost: architecture and postmodernism, again* (Minneapolis: University of Minnesota Press, 2010).
7 Anthony Vidler, *Histories of the Immediate Present: Inventing Architectural Modernism* (Cambridge/MA, London: The MIT Press, 2008).
8 Ákos Moravánszky and Judith Hopfengärtner (eds.), *Aldo Rossi und die Schweiz: Architektonische Wechselwirkungen* (Zurich: gta Verlag, 2011).
9 *Arch+* 216 "Die Klotz-Tapes/The Klotz-Tapes" (2014).
10 Examples are the symposium "Intersections: Late Socialism and Postmodernism" initiated by Ana Miljački at MIT (2012) or the recent panel "Socialist Postmodernism: Architecture and Society under Late Socialism," chaired by Vladimir Kulić, at the Third International European Architectural History Network (EAHN) Meeting in Turin (2014).
11 Paul Kaiser and Claudia Petzold (eds.), *Boheme und Diktatur in der DDR: Gruppen, Konflikte, Quartiere, 1970–1989* (Berlin: Fannei & Walz, 1997); Forschungsstelle Osteuropa (ed.), *Samizdat: alternative Kultur in Zentral- und Osteuropa: die 60er bis 80er Jahre* (Bremen: Ed. Temmen, 2000); Aleš Erjavec, *Postmodernism and the postsocialist condition: politicized art under late socialism* (Berkeley: University of California Press, 2003).
12 See for example the contributions by Ines Weizman and Andres Kurg in: Ines Weizman (ed.), *Architecture and the Paradox of Dissidence* (London: Routledge, 2013).
13 Florian Urban, *Neo-historical East Berlin: Architecture and Urban Design in the German Democratic Republic 1970–1990* (Farnham: Ashgate, 2009).
14 Łukasz Stanek, *Postmodernism is Almost All Right: Polish Architecture After Socialist Globalization* (Warsaw: Fundacja Bec Zmiana, 2013).
15 On this notion see Richard Sennett, "Quant: The Public Realm," http://www.richardsennett.com, accessed October 30, 2016.
16 The infamous "Aktion 507" by young Berlin architects in 1968 had a lasting legacy, since most of those who took part in it would later become important protagonists of urban renewal practice in 1970s and 1980s Berlin; e.g. the IBA Altbau. See for instance: Dieter Hoffmann Axthelm, "Übrig bleibt, voraus zu sein," in *Werk, Bauen + Wohnen* 75, no. 11 (1988), 46–48.
17 Thomas Docherty, "Postmodernism: An Introduction," in *Postmodernism: a reader*, ed. Thomas Docherty (New York: Columbia University Press, 1993), 2.
18 Martin, *Utopia's ghost*, xi.

I

Identity Construct(ion)s

Ákos Moravánszky

Piercing the Wall: East-West Encounters in Architecture, 1970–1990

In their article published in 1980 in *Le Carré bleu,* the journal founded by Team 10 members, Alexander Tzonis and Liane Lefaivre criticized what they called the narcissism in contemporary architecture. The critics declared that a new architecture must be based on "a new conception of Universality and Dignity of Man. A basic feature of the new humanistic approach is the introduction of a historical point of view. Such a research is alien to the historicism of the narcissistic phase, which uses history as a refuge."[1]

This new turn to history was seen by many as a symptom of crisis – not only, famously, by Manfredo Tafuri. The narcissism-essay by Tzonis and Lefaivre was the first in a sequence of articles on the same topic. The theme had already been announced in the editorial statement by André Schimmerling in issue 2/1980, dedicated to historicism: the "identity crisis" of architecture. In an introductory essay, Dominique Beaux and Michel Mangematin offered a survey on the goals of functionalist architecture, diagnosing on the one hand a dichotomy between the aesthetic of industrial techno-culture – the dream of Le Corbusier and the constructivists – and what they called nostalgic "*décors et de styles regionalists ou passéistes.*"[2] They proposed an alternative to both extremes, based on "*participation a grande échelle*" (participation on a large scale).[3]

Hungarian architect Charles Polónyi, member of the editorial team of *Le Carré bleu* and a frequent contributor, published an essay in the journal in 1985 with the title "*La crise – Une occasion de repenser l'architecture*" (in the English summary, the title is translated as "Architecture, Planning and Worldwide Depression").[4] Referring to Hungary and Egypt, Polónyi advocated small-scale, local solutions – the "reconstitution of urbanity" in the physically and socially eroded housing schemes of the postwar years.[5]

It was obvious that the Western experience of modernity and its crisis included the experience of state socialism on the other side of the Iron Curtain. It is equally obvious that the socialist experience of modernity included the images of capitalism. The question is whether the disintegration process of state socialism in the 1980s is reflected in the popularity of postmodern architecture, which has a much stronger presence in cities of East-Central Europe than, for instance, in Switzerland.

The Summer of 1972

In June 1972, I had just finished my third year as a student of architecture at the Technical University Budapest when I was asked by the school administration to guide students from the ETH Zurich who were visiting the Hungarian capital. It was a large group of seventy-two architectural students and professors who came to Budapest for a week-long study trip. The so-called *Seminar extra muros*, conceived by the *Lehrcanapé* of Lucius Burckhardt and Dieter Bleifuss, was an in-situ research lab with groups divided into smaller units to investigate the politics of planning in Budapest. They used the cutting-edge IBIS – Issue-based Information System – developed by the design theorist Horst Rittel at the College for Environmental Design in Berkeley, California, to support coordination and planning in decision-making processes. IBIS had to help the identification, structuring and solving of problems.

The previous year, the *Lehrcanapé* visited Bologna, a model case of the planning policies of a left-wing city administration. "*Sozialistische Planungspolitik in einem kapitalistischen Land*" ["Socialist politics of planning in a capitalist country"] was the subtitle of the *Canapénews* booklet compiled by the group in Italy.[6] In Budapest, the participation of the population in the planning process was one of the key questions investigated by the students. Despite the very low level of public participation in urban development projects in Hungary, the final conclusion sounded quite positive. As the *Canapénews* booklet, which the group published after returning to Switzerland, emphasized:

> [T]he goals of the Hungarian government are oriented toward the interests of the people and not toward greed for profit and particular interests. In Hungary, the inner contradictions of the social and economic systems are much less grave than in capitalist countries. There is no private

fig. 1 Issue 4/1980 of the journal of the journal *Le Carré bleu: Narcissism and Humanism in Contemporary Architecture*. Source: Archive of the author.

fig. 2 *Canapénews 16*, publication of the *Lehr-canapé* of the architectural students ETH Zurich on their Budapest seminar trip in June 1972. Source: Baubibliothek, ETH Zurich.

land ownership that would hinder an ordered development. There is no state-supported exploitation of tenants by wealthy house owners. These are things to be considered, even if they don't fully compensate for the lack of participation.[7]

A group of six students was assigned to evaluate the Swiss architecture exhibition that took place during the study trip (May 27 to June 25, 1972) in the *Műcsarnok* exhibition hall in Budapest. The exhibition was enthusiastically received by the Hungarian press and by visitors whom the Swiss students interviewed: "I wish we could live in similar environments," they quoted from visitors' comments. The ETH group assessed such positive comments with sarcastic criticism:

> We congratulate the organizers of the exhibition on their "success." The impact of this kind of propaganda on the visitors must have fulfilled their expectations. But we have to blame the participating Hungarian institutions for not criticizing the ideological content of the exhibition with the necessary sharpness, and for exposing the population unprepared for such subtle propaganda.[8]

The metaphoric wall in the title of the present essay is a reference to the many strategies of dealing with very real walls, such as the demolition of the Pruitt-Igoe housing estate in St. Louis with a controlled explosion on July 15, 1972. For architectural critic Charles Jencks, blowing up Pruitt-Igoe was the salute at the funeral of modern architecture and, at the same time, the starting gun for the postmodern movement.[9]

The same year, Rem Koolhaas and his friends Madelin Vriesendorp and Elia and Zoe Zenghelis made the Berlin Wall the central artifact of their Architectural Association thesis project "Exodus, or the Voluntary Prisoners of Architecture."[10] For them, the entire significance of a wall lay in its insurmountable materiality, its capacity to divide the good half from the bad half. The *Lehrcanapé* students saw Hungary obviously as the good or at least the better half: a functioning socialist welfare state with no exploitation, while for Hungarian visitors at the exhibition Switzerland was the good half, a country that promised the fulfillment of their consumerist dreams: "Unbelievable richness – happy citizens, I wish we could also live like them," to quote another entry from the visitors' book.

But the *Lehrcanapé* study trip is just one of the trajectories crossing the historical moment; 1972 was a decisive year for Swiss architecture. The objectives of the avant-garde, the "*Die gute Form*" as the norm of a well-kept middle-class lifestyle, was not accepted anymore by a critical young generation. Stanislaus von Moos had already detected in his *New Directions in Swiss Architecture* (written with Jul Bachmann) the "turn away from formal perfectionism" and the concentration of interest "on the fundamental socio-economic processes which underlie the building activity of a mobile, open society that no longer accepts the dictation of an official architectural 'style.'"[11]

The FSAI, the Union of Independent Swiss Architects, started the journal *Archithese* in the same year, 1972, with von Moos as editor-in-chief. The first issue of *Archithese* was dedicated to urbanism, with Superstudio's "Warning

fig. 3 The controversial publication by the authors' collective of the Department of Architecture of the ETH Zurich, *"Göhnerswil". Housing in Capitalism*, Zurich: Verlagsgenossenschaft, 1972. Source: Archive of the author.

of a Mystical Rebirth of Urbanism," John Habraken's radical *Bandstad* proposal for social housing and Martin Steinmann's reassessment of the Athens Charter.[12]

But the return turn to issues of type and form was already on the horizon. On the very day when Lucius Burckhardt's group arrived in Budapest, June 2, 1972, Aldo Rossi wrote an entry in one of his blue notebooks, the *Quaderni azzurri*. Rossi was on his way to Zurich to give a seminar and open an exhibition of his work. As this entry shows, he was concerned by the xenophobia of the popular right-wing movement of James Schwarzenbach in Switzerland, directed mainly against Italian immigrant workers: "*Anch'io sono Gastarbeiter*" (I am an immigrant worker, too), Rossi noted, and went on to sketch the plan of a course at ETH based on typological and morphological analysis of the city. He wrote about "architectural history as a huge depository of experience, explanation and reference as a source of logical construction" – and proposed to design a housing project for immigrant workers. This is the part of his plan that he never realized.

At this time, in Zurich, a media storm was raging because of the publication of the book *Göhnerswil: Housing in Capitalism*, published by a team led by Jörn Janssen at the ETH architecture department.[13] The book was a harsh criticism of housing in capitalism. The ETH leadership must have suspected the outcome of what was seen as a threatening development. They had already decided not to renew the contracts of student-elected German guest lecturers even before the book came out, causing an outcry in the daily

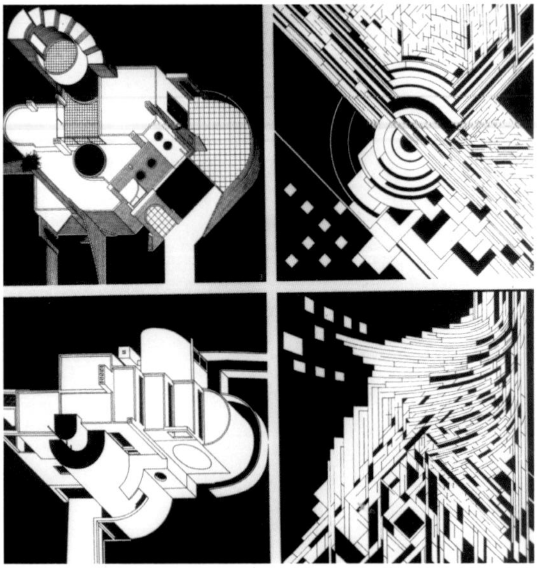

fig. 4 Leonhard Lapin, Isometrics for detached houses, Creation II and III, 1973. Source: Archive of the author.

press.[14] The journal *Werk*, in its 9/1971 issue, published statements about the crisis from the ETH president, who rejected any education in political ideology, from former and recent students, and from Lucius Burckhardt.[15] Was it a coincidence that in the same issue a longer essay by Urs and Rös Graf on the "open form" concept of Polish architect Oskar Hansen was published, quoting Hansen at length and calling for an architecture engaging the active participation of the user? A reader could certainly understand this as a possible response to the questions discussed above.[16]

It was in the midst of such turbulences that Bruno Reichlin and Fabio Reinhart, future assistants of Aldo Rossi, wrote a letter to Bernhard Hoesli in January 1971. They proposed an invitation to Aldo Rossi, whose professorship in Milan had been suspended because of his participation in student revolts. To hire a guest lecturer from Italy, a member of the Communist Party, must have appeared as a risky step – but in fact it turned out to be a brilliant move. Rossi's reputation as a person with a clear political message, who had visited Moscow and East Germany and was impressed by the Karl-Marx-Allee socialist-realist development in Berlin, made him acceptable to the rebellious student body. He shackled them to the drafting table: former revolutionary students spent hundreds of hours drafting cities street by street, as a former student reported.[17] He also made them aware of the significance of history, in the sense that Rossi described it in his notebooks.

I learned about these developments only later, however, when I visited Rainer Senn in Basel the next summer and we went to see Lucius Burckhardt.

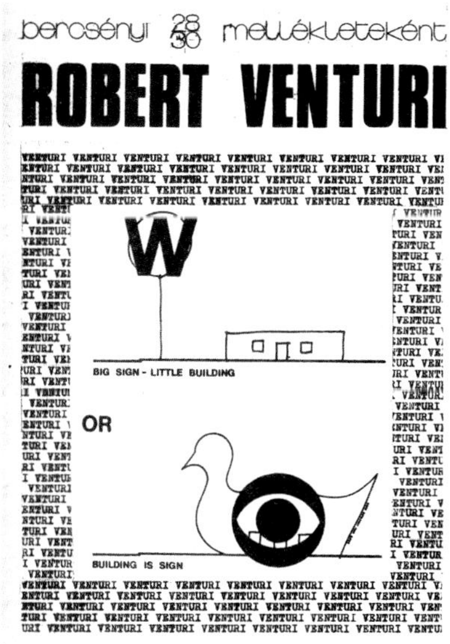

fig. 5 Cover of the journal *Bercsényi 28–30*, issue on Robert Venturi, 1976. Source: Archive of the author.

During the *Lehrcanapé* visit in Budapest, I had no idea about the goals and political underpinnings of the project. I invested my energy into the co-organization of another study trip to Budapest for architecture and engineering students from technical universities and art schools in France, Finland, Estonia, Switzerland and Poland. After a month in the Hungarian capital, a small part of that group took the train to Tallinn, capital of the Soviet Republic of Estonia. The camp and the Estonian trip had been initiated by the Technical University Budapest, so it not only had official blessing but was financed by our school as well.

The Tallinn month was exciting. We worked as bricklayers on the construction site of a sports stadium, and after work we visited young Estonian architects who were not only very knowledgeable about the Anglo-American discourse of postmodernism, but had already realized some buildings, which they called at that time Neo-Functionalist. Soviet constructivism, international modernism and Anglo-American postmodernism had a considerable influence on their work – although, remarkably, Estonian architectural historiography today treats this same group as the "Tallin school of the critique of modernism" ["*Tallinna kooli modernismi kriitika*"].[18]

As the composition of the summer camp suggests, "identity" was a major issue – this probably explains the emphasis on the Finno-Ugric: the Finnish-Estonian-Hungarian component. It was an experimental balloon, an experiment closely observed by the communist youth organization (KISZ) of the university.

fig. 6 György Csete, Jenő Dulánszky, Cave Research Station in Pécs-Orfű, 1971–8, as published in the 4th edition of Charles Jencks, *The Language of Post-Modern Architecture*, London: Academy Editions, 1984, p. 159. Source: Archive of the author.

309 GYORGY CSETE and JENO DULANSZKY, *Cave Research Station*, Pécs-Orfu Hungary, 1971-8. A geodesic dome is supported by a floral 'petal' in wood and a concrete base: the metaphorical equivalent of nature research is thus symbolised in the volume and stylised volutes and trefoils. A mixture of modern fabrication and hand-crafted ornament, nationalist and Celtic decorative motif. (Group Pécs).

ticality are too well known to need comment. Thus if one wishes to represent a flattering power and prestige for the client, the symbolic ornament will take on all these aspects which accentuate height.

This not very subtle argument and building show one of the undeniable characteristics of the New Representation: it has a tendency, like Pop Art, to be brash and obvious, hallmarks of a commercial society. At least one American architect, Stanley Tigerman, has developed this tendency as the subject-matter of his work. Many people, not surprisingly, find his explicit representation vulgar and exploitive. His Anti-Cruelty Society, for instance, represents a dog's face with part of a false pediment, the stray dogs involved either being adopted or unceremoniously extinguished. Some people find this black humour upsetting, although it has to be said the building *is* ambiguous and quite gay. Tigerman's Pensacola Place Apartments also use classicist elements – balconies which form the shaft of an Ionic column, a top cornice which hides mechanical equipment – because they lend themselves to this layout. There is no reason housing has to look like an Ionic Temple any more than a machine, and in that sense the imagery is arbitrary. But Tigerman, like Bofill, is arguing that classical references are less odious for mass-housing than Le Corbusier's *machine à habiter*.

Flat, brash, repetitive ornament – stylised and distorted – the formula that, as we've seen, Venturi proposes for an industrial society is perhaps one of the new rules, or canons of Free-Style Classicism. The Houston group called Taft have extended its use in all sorts of inexpensive buildings, and Terry Farrell in England has manipulated it with High-Tech details, again with ingeniously cheap methods of building. His television studios, TVAM, manages to 307,308
symbolise the exotic glamour of the medium – Japan, Mesopotamia and Hollywood – with thin, industrial materials. Perhaps the content of the symbolism is a bit trite – breakfast-egg-decorations are turned into gigantic finials, because this is a breakfast television station. But then the content of t.v. programmes is often like a runny egg. And if the detailing looks cheap and expedient that's because it is: realism in a fast-moving industrial society means a quick and deft reaction to immediate possibilities. Farrell, like Norman Foster, knows how to exploit available techniques on the site.

There are, however, other attitudes towards Free-Style Classicism and new technology which result in a different kind of ornament. A group in Hungary called Pécs (from this city) mixes materials and genres in a decorative way. They have produced several hybrids of concrete, wood and steel, mixing traditional domes and geodesic lanterns. 309
Their work is highly suggestive of regional craft and local symbolism, such as the trefoil taken from wooden Hungarian grave markers. But they combine this national expression with both metaphorical forms – the flowering blossom – and the latest technology. They have followed the development of Post-Modernism in the West, and perhaps been influenced by the metaphorical work of Tigerman and Goff. Indeed, in Hungary as in Yugoslavia, Rumania and Poland, Post-Modern developments are closely followed through the magazines and it wouldn't be surprising to see some more interesting developments coming from these countries in the near future.

Another approach to inventing a relevant ornament is to re-think the production methods and design elements that already have an order, or classical Order, in them. In this case the ornament can be constructive and three-dimensional, much like classical masonry of the past except usually at larger scale and in unmalleable material like reinforced concrete. Arata Isozaki has mixed flat metallic surfaces with heavy quoins turned on the diagonal – sculptural masses meant to recall Ledoux. Although 310,311
Michelangelo is recalled in floor patterns, no sculptor has spent his angst-ridden time chipping away at blocks of stone. An academic classicist, or an Italian, might be perturbed: how dare this motif be borrowed so brazenly? Looked at from Japan, however, the same theft can have a liberating effect because it is being absorbed into a new language of form, being combined with the syntax of rounded plastic forms and metallic sheets.

The most extraordinary invention of mass-produced ornament, or constructional ornament, is by Ricardo Bofill and his Taller de Arquitectura. Their scheme near Versailles called Les Arcades du Lac (because it borders an artificial lake) mass-produces arcades, window-walls, broken pediments at triple the usual scale, that is, about one storey high. New functions are poured into old forms – an end 312
column might be a stairway, or bathroom core. And a positive urban space is formed with this new constructional means – a pedestrian circus, or circular centre. The return to the notion of the 'heart of the city' is, as we've seen, a Post-Modern leitmotif. This new town area is well-scaled, successfully rented and as far as we can tell after a year's inhabitation, enjoyed by the user.

Much more controversial, and questionable because of its scale, is the Taller's Palace of Abraxas, also on the outskirts of Paris. Here again modern concrete is used to 313
do heavy Baroque tricks; again urban space is nicely

Two Schools of Architecture

Reflecting today on those parallel student trips in summer 1972, the title of this publication, *Re-framing Identities: Architecture's Turn to History*, takes on a specific meaning. Driven by an awareness of crisis (*Archithese*), ETH decided to redefine the identity of the architecture school, using the leftist reputation and charisma of Aldo Rossi's personality. At the same time, at the Technical University Budapest, where Marxist philosophy and political economy were part of the curriculum, the "turn to history," the interest of students in postmodernism, in Robert Venturi and Rossi, was understood as a sign of growing discontent. The dormitory for architecture students at 28–30 Bercsényi Street, in the 1970s, was the center of a vibrant alternative-culture scene. Art exhibitions that would have been impossible elsewhere, jazz-rock concerts, lectures and the samizdat architecture journal *Bercsényi 28–30*, edited by students, attracted a large audience.

The ETH architecture school must have been pleased with the sudden calm among students turning to typo-morphological studies under the supervision of Rossi. At the Technical University Budapest, however, strong voices of discontent were directed against the avant-garde. Máté Major, director of the Institute of History and Theory at TU Budapest, was the most influential

fig. 7 Hotel Hilton, Budapest (1969–1976) by Béla Pintér (KÖZTI). Photo: author.

of these voices, or at least he was the highest authority. Major was a member of the Party and of the CIAM group before the Second World War and was respected, because in the "big debate" in April 1951, he had defended the principles of modern architecture in the face of Stalinist criticism. Major must have felt that his students were betraying principles he had fought for in the early 1950s.

He published a series of articles. The most detailed criticism was the essay "On Postmodern Architecture, With Regard to a New Hungarian Publication," published in the widely read journal *Valóság* (*Reality*).[19] Major's irritation was obvious in the first sentences:

> We have Hungarian postmodernists who intend to concoct a new architecture out of Hungarian folk and art-nouveau architecture. They give lectures in the Bercsényi Street dormitory of architecture students, and publish the writings of such "famous" postmodernists as Venturi and the Krier brothers. Postmodernism has infected the University, the design office, even the Union of Hungarian Architects.[20]

According to Major, historicism had played a positive role in the nineteenth century: It had prepared the way for art-nouveau architecture and, in turn, for modern architecture – because it made the absurdity of eclecticism obvious. But the "radical eclecticism" of the twentieth century was nothing more than a "backward, antisocial and anti-architectural phenomenon, which, like all empty fashions, will sink in its own swamp. Reason, the source of creative thought, cannot be destroyed – not even in architecture," Major wrote, referring to György Lukács's famous Marxist critique of irrationalism as an international phenomenon of imperialism in *The Destruction of Reason*. This was not without some irony, since at the time when Lukács's book had been published in 1952, Major had defended functionalist architecture against precisely the criticism of Lukács, pointing out that Lukács's promotion of socialist realism was based on arguments of literary criticism, disregarding architecture's specificity.

The specificity of architecture – this was Major's most important point, meaning the production of a useful artifact on the basis of an individual concept but with collective labor.[21] If we, like Charles Jencks, disregard this primary usefulness, architecture will disappear in a quagmire of semantics, metaphors and analogies. "Young architects in Hungary," Major wrote, "are impressed by this nonsense, since postmodernism creates an illusion of the total freedom of design."[22]

Jencks, on his side, included in his book's fourth edition (1984) a postmodern building from Hungary, György Csete and Jenő Dulánszky's Cave Research Station in Pécs-Orfű (1971–1978) – a work of the organic school gathering around Imre Makovecz, the only one among these architects whose work was widely published in the West.[23] This building was a clear example of what Major called a "Hungarian postmodernism that intends to concoct a new architecture out of Hungarian folk and art-nouveau architecture."[24] Jencks, in his book, praised the same buildings for combining "national expression with both metaphorical form – the flowering blossom – and the latest technology. They follow the development of Post-Modernism in the West, and are influenced by the metaphorical work of Tigerman and Goff" – he wrote. "Indeed, in Hungary as in Yugoslavia, Rumania and Poland, Post-Modern developments are closely followed through the magazines and it wouldn't be surprising to see some more interesting developments coming from these countries in the near future."[25]

Major, however, was not alone in his critique. On the contrary, while his attack against postmodern architecture was seen in Hungary as a document of regressive, authoritarian academicism, in the West he was heard by many as an authentic voice from a figure of great integrity who had defended modernism when this was a dangerous move. Major had strong ties to the UIA – he wrote a monograph on the work of the Hungarian-born president of the organization, Pierre Vágó.

Le Carré bleu, in an issue on architectural education in 1982, published a letter from Major in which he decried not only the "borrowings of ready-made forms from the national past" to create a national architecture, but

fig. 8 International Trade Center, Budapest (1985–1990) by József Finta. Photo: author.

criticized other forms of postmodernism as well, like the Italian *Tendenza*. Major insisted on the "autonomy" of architecture, but for him, autonomy meant specificity, distinctness from painting or sculpture.[26] The editors of *Le Carré bleu* had responded earlier and angrily to criticism directed against the Athens Charter. This criticism was enunciated in the so-called Machu Picchu charter, written in 1977 in preparation for the UIA XIII Congress in Mexico, held in April 1978 with the theme "Architecture and National Development." In 1980, issue 3 of the journal published a press release issued by the Fondation Le Corbusier, "*Campagne de dénigrement de la Charte d'Athènes*" ["Denigration Campaign against the Athens Charter"], in which the authors of the statement accused critics of the Athens Charter of favoring a return to the "European classical tradition" and of an anti-industrial approach idealizing craftsmanship and turning to pastiche. This criticism was strongly endorsed by the editors: "The members of the editorial board of *Carré bleu* maintain that [...] the propositions by CIAM constituted the first progressive program to satisfy the aspirations of the 'plus grand nombre.'"[27] Architects who signed the declaration (among them Jaap Bakema, Anatole Kopp and Alexis Josic) stressed that the Athens Charter bore no responsibility for big housing schemes and accused opponents of an "esprit retrograde et impardonnable."[28] To prove these points, the editors included a discussion of new projects such as Ricardo Bofill's Antigoné housing in Montpellier, comparing them to CIAM principles.[29]

We should not forget that *Le Carré bleu* had been founded by CIAM rebels with the participation of structuralists including Bakema, organicists including Reima Pietilä, and protagonists of participation and the open form including Charles Polónyi and Oskar Hansen.[30] They were fighting therefore on two fronts: against CIAM functionalism and against the new narcissism whose main features were identified in issue 4 of *Le Carré bleu* in 1980 by Alexander Tzonis and Liane Lefaivre, in their article mentioned at the outset of this essay, as *formalism*, or a marked preoccupation with the purely visual features of architectural designs; *graphism*, a fascination with the evocative power of drawings and models; *hedonism*, a tendency to view the design as an object of gratification only; *elitism*, the conviction that the architect is supreme judge of the quality of the built environment; and finally, *anti-functionalism*, the rejection not only of the functionalist aesthetics, but often of the very idea of function.[31]

The task was to find an alternative to both functionalism and "narcissism" – and Tzonis and Lefaivre formulated a program for a "critical regionalism" in their essay "The Grid and the Pathway" in *Le Carré bleu* 2 (1982, also published in the journal *Architecture in Greece*). Evaluating the work of architects Dimitris and Susana Antonakakis, the authors contrasted the old "historicist regionalism" with Critical Regionalism, which with its emphasis on the singular and the local, on liberty and anti-authoritarianism, fits into a different social, economic, political and cultural context. This program resonated well in both East and West. Kenneth Frampton had developed Tzonis and Lefaivre's argument further in his *Towards a Critical Regionalism: Six Points for an Architecture of Resistance*, referring to Paul Ricoeur's question "how to become modern and to return to sources; how to revive an old, dormant civilization and take part in universal civilization".[32]

In Hungary, big state-owned design firms felt pressure to revise or abandon the functionalist dogma that was their official credo – despite the criticism of Major. These "plan factories" had already been working for Western clients in the early 1970s. The Hilton Budapest, by Béla Pintér (KÖZTI), opened in 1976 on the most prominent site possible, in the former royal castle of Buda, on the ruins of a medieval monastery. The architect József Finta (LAKÓTERV) was redefining Budapest's face with other new hotels on the Danube shore. Architecture firms that employed Pintér and Finta summoned their leading architects to discuss the future. KÖZTI, a large office specializing in public buildings, organized a retreat at its conference center in Csopak at Lake Balaton. Elemér Nagy, in charge of one design atelier and my predecessor as editor-in-chief of *Magyar Építőművészet*, the journal of the Union of Hungarian Architects, and member of CICA (*Comité International des Critiques d'Architecture)* was asked to present the keynote lecture, later published as the booklet *Mai építészeti irányzatok és a magyar realitások* [*Architectural Tendencies of Today, and the Hungarian Realities*].[33] In his lecture, Nagy briefly discussed and criticized both what he called

fig. 9 Publications of the international summer workshops organized by Charles Polónyi in Budapest in 1987 and 1990. Source: Archive of the author.

New Eclecticism and the national organic line as represented by Makovecz because it completely disregarded that Hungarian architecture always developed through amalgamations with other cultures. As with Tzonis, Nagy saw the task as defining a path between functionalism, organicism and historicism. The "purity" of a reinvented language could not communicate anymore, he maintained. Nagy's proposal was based on the analytical part of his lecture: Referring to the writings of Christian Norberg-Schulz and Martin Heidegger, he emphasized the notion of the *genius loci*, to develop it further not as a morphological study but as forms of everyday life: thinking, based not only on sociological and historical study, needs intuition and empathy as well. "To understand these messages and transform them into buildings requires the talent of the architect," he concluded.[34]

In the mid-1980s, the UIA was in the process of reinventing its own identity. Former editors of *Architectural Design* Haig Beck and Jackie Cooper left that journal in 1979 to launch a new postmodern review, *International Architect*. But *International Architect* soon widened its scope to present a fully global view of architecture, with issues on new architecture in Malaysia and Australia (1984), South Africa, Israel and Islamic Cairo (1985, with the latter issue published on the occasion of the UIA XV Congress in Cairo). I guest-edited an issue on Budapest architecture in 1985; the already laid-out number never came out, as the journal ceased to exist.

Charles Polónyi, associated with Team 10 and working in the 1960s and 1970s in Ghana, Nigeria and Ethiopia, started an international summer school in Budapest in 1983. In the summer of 1987, students and teachers – among them Peter and Alison Smithson – were living and working in a boat on the

fig. 10 Udo Kultermann, *Contemporary Architecture in East Europe*, Cologne: DuMont, 1985. Source: Archive of the author.

Danube. At that time, the planning for a world exhibition jointly organized for Vienna and Budapest in 1995 was in its initial stage, and using the Danube as the theme and exhibition site was an idea promoted by Polónyi.

Udo Kultermann, a German art historian living and teaching in the US since 1964, had written pioneering books in the 1960s on contemporary architecture in Africa and the Middle East.[35] In 1985, Kultermann published a book on contemporary architecture in Eastern Europe.[36] That same year, the Russian translation of Charles Jencks's *Language of Post-Modern Architecture* came out.[37] The publisher Stroyizdat stressed the actuality of the "bible of postmodernism" in Russia, where the struggle between tradition and innovation had pushed architecture into crisis. The Union of Architects in Moscow had organized a conference on architectural theory. There was a moment of excitement when, after the presentation by the young Polish architect Wojciech Kosiński, the head of the Department for Theory at the Institute for Urbanism and Architecture of the *Bauakademie* in the German Democratic Republic angrily accused him of spreading dangerous views on the Solidarity movement. But even this outbreak of ideology was not sufficient to trigger a debate; our Russian hosts were obviously not interested in an ideological controversy.

The Unbuilt Bridges

Piercing the Wall, to come back to the title of my essay, was not always an easy exercise – some concrete walls needed special drills. In 1985, a Hungarian

fig. 11 Catafalque and draping of the Műcsarnok exhibition hall façade in Budapest for the reburial of László Rajk in 1989, design by László Rajk jr. and Gábor Bachman. Source: Courtesy of 1956-os Intézet, Gábor Bachman, Budapest.

fig. 12 Interior of the Munka-Tett (Labour-Action) pub by Gábor Bachman and László Rajk, in Szigetszentmiklós, 1986. Source: Archive of the author, photograph: G. Bachman.

film, György Szomjas's *Falfúró* (*Wall Driller*), was released. It was about a young guy who discovers a business opportunity: with his power drill, he is able to drill holes in hard, precast concrete slabs of prefabricated houses. It is a strange comedy about young mothers on leave from work after the birth of their babies, yet they're immersed in the boredom of the new housing estates with thin walls, low ceilings and narrow corridors. Everything is open to gossip, everyone is observed by everyone, and what this gives rise to is repressed eroticism.

Was "piercing the Wall," those intensifying exchanges in the 1980s, a similarly voyeuristic endeavor after all? No real communication but a projection of personal desires onto the space of the other, as in the *Lehrcanapé* case? It certainly created curiosity and triggered desires, but resulted in an exchange of ideas, cooperation and a multitude of projects as well. Ironically, it is precisely the fall of communism, the opening of the borders and the extension of the EU that has lessened the significance of such encounters. The joint Budapest-Vienna Expo for 1995, with the theme "Bridges into the Future," was decided upon in 1987. But the Expo '95 idea was abandoned in 1991, two years after the collapse of state socialism.

In retrospect, piercing the Wall led to much more interaction than its full removal has. The fall of the Wall and full visibility did not result in more, but paradoxically in less, exchange. That crisis – or what was perceived as a crisis – had indeed been a catalyst for dreams, visions and models of cooperation.

Endnotes

1 Alexander Tzonis, Liane Lefaivre, "Narcissisme & humanisme dans l'architecture contemporaine," *Le Carré bleu*, 4 (1980), 1–17, 23–24 (p. 24).
2 Dominique Beaux, Michel Mangematin, "1920–1980 Rapprochements / Perspectives," *Le Carré bleu*, 2 (1980), 1–12 (p. 3).
3 Ibid.
4 Charles Polónyi, "La crise – Une occasion de repenser l'architecture," *Le Carré bleu*, 1 (1985), 7–12, 21. The essay was the translation of an article first published as "A válság – az újragondolás időszaka: Gondolatok az UIA XV. kongresszusa előtt," *Magyar* Építőművészet 6 (1984), 9–11.
5 Ibid.
6 *Bologna: Seminar extra muros, Canapé news* 9 (1971).
7 *Budapest: Seminar extra muros, Canapé news* 16 (1972), 15.
8 Ibid., 113–116. Author's translation.
9 Charles A. Jencks, *The Language of Post-Modern Architecture* (London: Academy, 1977), 9.
10 Rem Koolhaas and Elia Zenghelis with Madelon Vriesendorp and Zoe Zenghelis: "Exodus or The Voluntary Prisoners of Architecture," in *Exit Utopia: Architectural Provocations 1856–76*, ed. Martin van Schaik and Otakar Máčel (Munich, Berlin: Prestel 2005), 236–253.
11 Jul Bachmann and Stanislaus von Moos, *New Directions in Swiss Architecture* (London: Studio Vista; New York: George Braziller, 1969), 116.
12 Superstudio, "Drei Warnungen vor einer mystischen Wiedergeburt des Urbanismus," *Archithese*, 1 (1972), 3–6; N.J. Habraken, "Das Ende des Wohnbauprojektes," *Archithese*, 1 (1972), 7–14; M. Steinmann, "Neuer Blick auf die Charte d'Athènes," *Archithese*, 1 (1972), 37–46.
13 Autorenkollektiv an der Architekturabteilung der ETH Zurich, *"Göhnerswil": Wohnungsbau im Kapitalismus: Eine Untersuchung der Bedingungen und Auswirkungen der privatwirtschaftlichen Wohnungsproduktion am Beispiel der Vorstadtsiedlung "Sunnebüel" in Volketswil bei Zürich und der Generalunternehmung Ernst Göhner AG* (Zurich: Verlagsgenossenschaft, 1972).
14 Ernst Göhner AG, ed., *Dokumente "Göhnerswil" Wohnungsbau im Kapitalismus* (Zurich: Ernst Göhner AG, 1972).
15 Lucius Burckhardt, "Die Krise an der ETH-Architekturabteilung," *Werk*, 9 (1971), 578–581.
16 Urs und Rös Graf, "Die offene Form. Essay zum Problem nicht endgültig determinierter Planungen," *Werk*, 9 (1971), 614–624.
17 Hans-Peter Bärtschi, "Der Osten war rot," unpubl. manuscript quoted in Ákos Moravánszky and Judith Hopfengärtner, "Wie man wird, was man ist: Eine Einführung," in *Aldo Rossi und die Schweiz: Architektonische Wechselwirkungen*, ed. Ákos Moravánszky and Judith Hopfengärtner (Zurich: gta Verlag, 2011), 13.

18 Mart Kalm, *Eesti 20. sajandi arhitektuur – Estonian 20th century architecture* (Tallinn: Sild, 2002), 389.
19 Máté Major, "A 'posztmodern' építészetről egy új magyar kiadvány ürügyén," *Valóság*, 5 (1981), 24–34.
20 Ibid., 24.
21 Máté Major, *Az* építészet *sajátszerűsége* (Budapest: Akadémiai Kiadó, 1967).
22 Major, "A 'posztmodern' építészetről egy új magyar kiadvány ürügyén," 34.
23 Charles Jencks, *The Language of Post-Modern Architecture*, 4th rev. ed. (London: Academy, 1984).
24 Major, "A 'posztmodern' építészetről egy új magyar kiadvány ürügyén," 28.
25 Jencks, *The Language*, 159.
26 Máté Major, "Comments on Anatole Kopp's Lecture (1°)," in *Le Carré bleu*, 3 (1982), 22–23.
27 "Campagne de dénigrement de la Charte d'Athènes," *Le Carré bleu*, 3 (1980), 1–6.
28 Ibid., 15.
29 "Compte-rendu détaillé de la réunion du 8 mai à la Fondation Le Corbusier," *Le Carré bleu*, 3 (1980), 7–16.
30 Ákos Moravánszky, "Re-Humanizing Architecture: The Search for a Common Ground in the Postwar Years, 1950–1970," in *Re-Humanizing Architecture: New Forms of Community, 1950–1970*, ed. Ákos Moravánszky and Judith Hopfengärtner (Basel: Birkhäuser, 2016), 23–41.
31 Tzonis, Lefaivre, "Narcissisme & humanisme dans l'architecture contemporaine".
32 Kenneth Frampton, "Towards a Critical Regionalism: Six Points for an Architecture of Resistance," in *The Anti-Aesthetic: Essays on Postmodern Culture*, ed. Hal Foster (Seattle: Bay Press, 1983) 16–30.
33 Elemér Nagy, *Mai* építészeti *irányzatok* és *a magyar realitások*, Csopaki Füzetek 1 (Budapest: Középülettervező Vállalat Építészeti Tanácsa, 1983).
34 Ibid., 45.
35 Udo Kultermann, *Neues Bauen in Afrika* (Tübingen: Wasmuth, 1963); Udo Kultermann, *Architekten der Dritten Welt: Bauen zwischen Tradition und Neubeginn* (Köln: DuMont, 1980).
36 Udo Kultermann, *Zeitgenössische Architektur in Osteuropa* (Köln: DuMont, 1985).
37 Чарльз Дженкс, Язык архитектуры постмодернизма (Москва: Стройиздат, 1985).

Georgi Stanishev Sr, Sofia
Georgi Stanishev Jr, Paris

Notes on Centers and Peripheries in Eastern Bloc Architectures

Whoever scrutinizes the detail may lose perspective on the whole. Today, the excessive interest and curiosity about totalitarian regimes in postwar Eastern Europe has generated numerous books, exhibitions and films, and several conferences on architecture, arts and culture. This type of multicolor carnival, which can often seem closer to show business than to scientific analysis, deforms the terrain – the role and the significance of the communist period in this part of Europe – by marginalizing and ridiculing the specific intellectual and creative contexts in which architecture and artistic phenomena developed.

By now, sufficient time has passed to show the function of the communist period in a broader perspective, sketching it in larger strokes. In this context, it seems proper to replace the microscope with a telescope to enable a different contour of the whole to be observed and a more general conceptual framework of the cultural processes, models and correlations to be discovered. The coarsening of the picture by its distancing provides different information on the object, and the effect we intend to find by using these different optics is more like graffiti with general outlines, abstract configurations and rough statements, when compared to the nuances and overtones of a watercolor drawing. The purpose of such a large-scale depiction is to outline the political and cultural mechanisms that can be considered as premises for the process of architecture's development in the Eastern Bloc.

What we will observe at this macro level is how the process of the modernization of society, industry and politics was run simultaneously through two different but equally universalist ideological systems: communism and liberal capitalism. Both of these branches of modernity were challenged by local European nationalisms in a different manner: in some cases, they merged and modernized, in others, they radically confronted one another; in a few, they created monsters.

Observing confrontations between the universal and the particular throughout the history of the USSR and the Eastern Bloc, we will try to unveil the gradual merging of both programs: by encompassing the particular within the universal from one side, and from the other by neutralizing the particular in its generalized struggle towards universality. In other words, we could say that we are observing the ruination one into the other of two ideological agendas – the universalist project of communist modernism and the particularistic project of (bourgeois) nationalism.

This process of compromising, however, was in itself animated by singular creative energies and original cultural phenomena that need to be further scrutinized within this context. The center-periphery model[1] works as the most general layout for understanding this framework from the standpoint of a critical geography of culture and ideology. We will argue in this context that the center-periphery dialectic describes simultaneously two interdependent constructions. First, the political determination of a cultural area of influence; that is, the top-down determination of Central and East European cultures (CEE) as an internal periphery to both Western and Soviet universalizing discourses. And second, the bottom-up self-determination of these cultures as liberal particulars, that is, as peripheral forces remixing and hybridizing the universal and the local in order to edify their own identity.

Communist Modernization and Liberal Modernism

To understand these complex processes within the Eastern Bloc, we will first have to outline two distinct conceptions of modernism and modernization, and to sketch out differences between their forms, as they existed in capitalist and communist worlds simultaneously. The implementation of the processes of modernization within capitalist liberalism and as envisioned by communism – especially within the Soviet model – demonstrate two radically opposite models of universalism: on one hand, the self-organization of the free market, liberal and democratic organization of arts and culture; and on the other, the total rationalistic planning of economics, society and culture, following the rationalistic Enlightenment ideals of the scientific planning of society and its life.

The Western (capitalist) modernization was extremely successful but always seemed to be relatively ambiguous, as it had adopted and combined two contradictory organizational principles. It followed to some extent the modernist idea of planning: it had constructed an industry based on rationality and predictability; it had the logic of the machine as a rational model of organization, etc. But its economic system was organized on the natural and spontaneous principle of the market. The market, with all its unpredictability and ungovernability brings into the rationality of capitalist modernity the imagery of the primitive, spontaneous force of nonlinear randomness – an agent of natural wilderness inserted into the purely artificial and logical world of the rational. This wilderness and the presence of the irrationality of unknown nature periodically reasserts itself through economic imbalances and crises that have burst within the heart of modern capitalism since the beginning of the twentieth century.

Communism can be considered as a project that puts politics above economics or, as Boris Groys would say with respect to Stalinist communism, aesthetics above life. By replacing market spontaneity and its self-organizing capacities with planned goals governed by the political will, politics was liberated and became sovereign in the social domain. Comparing how modernism, with its positivism, determinism and philosophy of planning, fits both sociopolitical models, we will have to accept that it seems more organically apt for the communist one as opposed to the capitalist one.

Both systems have an eminently universalistic essence: they seek expansion and generalization, but through opposing means. The total planning of communist modernism was meant to fundamentally annihilate all particularities into a homogenous condition of society and culture, while liberalism uses the particular – personal taste, fashion, national sense, regionalism, all kind of differences – in order to implement a continuous state of average difference.

It was exactly this controversial complexity of cohabitation and symbiosis between the systems of the rational and the irrational within the liberal model – against the fragile isomorphic unity of the organization of economics, politics and life of the communist world – which led to the winning result in this contest at the end of the 1980s. As we will seek to discuss further on, the final implosion of Soviet communism could be seen as the result of a process of destructive particularization that the peripheries, such as the CEE countries engaged within the Eastern Bloc, inspired with the liberal dream of minor difference and specificity.

Two Types of Modernization: Revolution and Appropriation

In an interview in 1995, Japanese architect Kiyonori Kikutake differentiated between western and eastern models of cultural modernization, calling the western process "nostalgic" and "purist" while terming the eastern modernization "simultaneous" and "hybrid."[2] "Western civilizations develop through maturity but end in revolutions," Kikutake explained, "while we in Japan accept current influence from outside but convert and adapt it in accordance to our own culture." The uncertainty of the revolutions in European cultures inevitably awakens retrospective forces that look for footholds in the sacred past, which the Europeans call *revival.* Along with Kikutake's assessment, this paradoxical mechanism had been brilliantly outlined in the first section of Karl Marx's "The Eighteenth Brumaire of Louis Bonaparte," published in 1852. It is also confirmed by a smart statement in 1988 by Charles Jencks, who stated that "Revolutions are born out of our nostalgia [...] Because we trust that Golden Age, or Arcadia, or whatever myth of this kind has been realized long time ago, and what revolutions are trying to do is to reinstall it."[3] Thus, the essence of the Renaissance and all renaissances in European culture can be transcribed through this model, repeating the formula: to modernize means to bring back a certain past.

On the other hand, the eastern – the de-centered – cultures, as with the Japanese (per Kikutake's observation), do not return to the past, but rather "accept modernization to be imported from outside and then, well re-mix it with our own traditions, beliefs and culture."[4] This was indeed the case with the Chinese influence on Japan in the Edo period in the seventeenth century and in a similar way in the 20th century, but especially after the Second World War with American and European models of modernity being installed in Japanese culture and everyday life. Kikutake's own architectural discourse within the Japanese Metabolism of the 1960s was a product of the same type of appropriation – a hybrid, or symbiosis.

In the context of the typology mentioned above, the Russian modernization model shows a significant similarity to the one described by Kikutake. Basic historic shifts within the Russian kingdom, the Russian empire and the Soviet communist state trace a development that is not intrinsic, but is rather a history of periodic transformations based on imported ideologies. Although this acceptance of foreign models never happened as a result of military invasion, Russian history shows the clear tendency to behave through European models of development. This phenomenon was most insightfully described by Groys in his metaphor of self-colonization,[5] which was further developed by Bulgarian sociologist Alexander Kiossev,[6] demonstrating its paradoxical function in the context of the CEE countries.

Indeed, none of the large-scale shifts in the historic process in Russia have been made by ideas and programs produced and grown within Russian society. Whenever significant reforms were needed as certain social and economic processes reached maturity Russian elites selected voluntary self-imposed models predominantly from the West, appropriating and domesticating these new imported formal languages in society, culture, production, economics, even fashion.

A quick retrospective will show that none of the reformatory ideologies promoted in Russian history have been immanently born in Russia. In the seventeenth century, the reforms implemented by Peter the Great were based on the importing of Western management, technologies, war strategies fleet structure, army organization, and fashion (wigs). During the eighteenth century, the reforms of Catherine the Great were the imposition of elements from European political and parliamentary organization of power, state and property. She was a great admirer of Diderot and the other French luminaries, and even financed their initiatives. By the end of the nineteenth century, some progressive reforms were directly influenced by French revolutionary concepts of post-enlightenment, positivist and determinist philosophies, socialist ideas and the French language, which became an official cultural attribute of the upper class. At the beginning of the twentieth century, leftist revolutionary activities were importing modernism and rationalism from the West: the philosophies of Nietzsche, Marx, Engels, the belief in predictability and the possibility of planning history in the sequence of social formations and in the capacity of man to predetermine his own and society's destiny.[7]

Modernization through Communism

After the revolution, the new multinational state led by the Soviets began a project to modernize the country in all aspects of its life: from society, culture, industry, to the energy systems, the military and so on. The creation of Soviet Russia can be understood as a social-economic and cultural project for applying modernism through the communist program. Vladimir Paperny called Soviet Russia "the only country where modernism was fully integrated as official political doctrine."[8]

Communist ideology was accepted in Russia as a foreign model of scientific planning, which conceived the state as an artificial organism, planned *ex nihilo* and leaving no room for market spontaneity or for the forces of natural selection. Only this kind of plan was believed to be able to reconstruct the country's infrastructure, boost the industrialization process, solve Russia's backwardness in terms of political-management and radical social inequalities, and convert the country into a giant socioeconomic machine of a new order. The society as a machine of the Soviet state was brilliantly modeled by Evgeniy Zamyatin in his novel *We* (1921). Indeed, it seems that modernity had been fully accepted in the USSR not as a style, but as a state religion in the form of Marxism-Leninism, then Stalinism.

The political revolution in Russia coincided with the revolution in arts, and both political and artistic avant-gardes aimed at a demiurgic change of the world. But this put the arts into a competing position with political administration, sharing the same field and even the same projects, although having a totally different set of tools at their disposal. The avant-garde project of a total aesthetization of all fields of society proved less viable than the project of total politicization of life, as developed particularly under Stalin. This was one of the reasons why the Soviet artistic avant-garde lost the competition at the beginning of the 1930s and was dismissed as something which did not fit the bigger social project of the political elite. When the whole country with all its social, cultural and economic aspects is organized as a rational machine, its art and architecture no longer need the modernist-machine metaphor. Groys described this project: "together with the whole state machine of the country [...] as a giant artistic installation."[9]

Whatever aims were fixed by communist ideology, its force was used in CEE societies as a particular instrument for modernization that brought these countries into the twentieth-century industrialized world. The more stalled and backward the country was, the more effective was this process of implementing modernity as new organizational power. Stalin's total politics, merely ten years after the October revolution, engaged a complete metamorphosis of the universalist model within communism. One of the most important points in this process – often not given enough consideration – was the conceptualization of "socialism in one country," dismissing all competing versions of postrevolutionary communism, and especially Trotsky's concept of "permanent revolution," which supposed that the revolutionary process would only succeed as a nonstop developing and expanding process. The transformation of the revolutionary avant garde period into the Stalinist state was insightfully described from different points of view by Groys[10] and Paperny.[11]

This new state model had a fundamental repercussion on the development of the USSR. Within this conception is rooted the negation of modernism and its international and universal character, and the establishment of socialist realism as an unique philosophy of arts, justifying the revival of both classical and Arcadian, as well as national and regional, traditions and art forms.

fig. 1 Newsreel footage of a parade with a model of Vladimir Tatlin's *Monument to the Third International* (1919–1920) carried as a volumetric slogan on the streets of Moscow. Source: http://www.redwedgemagazine.com/

Hybrids of Communist Universality and National Particularism

Further along, the postwar formation of the Eastern Bloc was fundamentally characterized by this paradoxical equation between communist modernization and reinvented national continuity. The "socialism in one country" initially formulated as an internal alibi for Soviet state communism was exported throughout the CEE countries as a model for their sovietization. The national form of realist architecture within the Eastern Bloc was actually conceived as an essential element of the political-ideological front in the context of the Cold War. It was considered by the ideologists of Stalinist communism that the convergence with liberal capitalism was more dangerous than the merger between their own universal pattern and the local nationalisms. Therefore, national communism was implemented as a strategic instrument for the top-down permanent rooting of communism in the (previously) Western capitalist periphery. The melting down of communism with nationalism was supposed to enhance the systematic fight against modernism and Western formalism and against all acceptance of or inspiration by capitalist bourgeois arts.

This is the period in which the formula "National by form and socialist by content" appeared in the Marxist-Leninist philosophy of arts. For Stalin, the postwar expansion of the communist space set up the question of control by means of framed cultural specificity. The Soviet Union's ruling ideological apparatus was indeed particularly tolerant of any expressions of national character, traditional forms and local materials, not only in the satellites within the Eastern Bloc but also among Soviet republics and other countries under Soviet influence.[12] For example, when Soviet architects produced the first general plan for Beijing in 1950, commissioned personally by Stalin to convert the project into a significant gift to the young People's Republic of

China, he received a typical modernist plan with blocks and flat roofs. The reception of Stalin is characteristic of this ideological mindset. It is said that he approved the plan as a socialist city organization but regretted that the architects did not lend enough national identity to it. As an aftermath the typical Chinese family-house gable roofs have been installed atop of seven-to eight-story modernist buildings as specific national markers.

This enforced national-communist front was meant to counterbalance the expansion of the most powerful intellectual instrument of capitalist culture: the individual artist with unlimited freedom of expression. This front, however, could only be fulfilled if Moscow could assume the development and continuity of a culture totally original and detached from the rest of the world. Stalin's socialist realism was indeed a total model – a *Gesamkunstwerk* (Groys) – with its own conception of history, its own epistemology and its own mythology. This distinction, between modernist progress and the Soviet arrested time-space, permitted the definition for a short period after the war of a genuine if forcefully imposed system of values that radically opposed the Western ones.

We could say that the specificity of the Soviet experiment as a whole, CEE countries included, began to end during the mid-1950s when, after Stalin's death, the cultural processes were returned back to the natural development of culture – that is, the mainstream international (western) modernism. Groys incisively describes this loss of ideology:

The barricades against bourgeois progress, which were meant to delimit Soviet culture from the current of historical changes, decomposed – the country, however, wished to be part of history once again. A long time was needed in order to understand that there was no longer any place to return to: history itself had vanished in the meantime. The whole planet had already entered post-historical times, because – not without the influence of the Stalinist experiment – everyone had lost faith in the project of overcoming history, and when history does not strive for its accomplishment, it disappears; it ceases to be history and immobilizes within itself.[13]

Emergence of an Internal Periphery

This ambiguous situation was particularly felt by the young architects of that time, who actually went through the Khrushchev Thaw period with mixed emotions. Generally speaking, the return to sincere modernism was embraced with overwhelming enthusiasm, as this meant that architects would regain some lost creative liberty. However, as there was no constructive conceptualization of what Soviet or, more generally, socialist modernist could mean, architects and artists found themselves in the uncanny position of having to

fig. 2 Monument to the Soviet Army in Sofia (1951) repainted on June 29, 2011 as USA pop culture heroes, with the inscription "in pace with time."
Source: http://www.kultura.bg/media/article_pict/image/2642/24-4-w1.jpg

determine individually what architectural trends to work with. Paradoxically, the architecture scene started to become liberalized, thus Westernized, which was incisively presumed in the popular phrase "we were all socialists [in belief], yet we were all dissidents."[14]

CEE societies lived within a complex system of interactions and dependencies, indeed, which worked on different levels of public consciousness. Specific correlations and vectors of influences were formed within the culture of architecture itself. On a certain level, these societies definitely belonged to the communist bloc with the Soviet Union as the central power, which broadcast its influence on all levels of political, social and cultural life. But on another semiconscious level, the architecture scene wished to identify itself as a part of a larger – non-ideological, as it was imagined – European culture, and thus measured itself predominantly by modernist trends coming from the West. Both Western and Eastern modernisms were considered like two competing models, between which the space of CEE countries was a periphery subordinated to two centers – an internal periphery.

Whether or not centers generate rules and canons, the function of the periphery is to modify and adapt these canons as far as possible to the local structure, creating hybrids in this manner on all levels of social, economic and cultural life. In these specific conditions, and in the in-between space of the two controversial centers of influence, the periphery usually adopts elements of both, and inevitably bridges the centers, finding possibilities to manipulate and, in the final account, to paradoxically produce a space of convergence. The center-periphery model functions as a tandem, a system in which no part can exist without the others.

In 1986, to assess this double-oriented model, the journal *Architecture and Society* published a sophisticated issue debating the theme "Origins of Socialist Countries' Architecture: 1900–1940."[15] In this issue different modernist traditions in art and architecture, developing in countries of the CEE region in the early twentieth century – constructivism, suprematism and VKhUTEMAS in Russia, Czech cubism in Prague, the Bauhaus in Germany, various modernist national factions in Hungary, Romania and Bulgaria – were considered as historic predecessors and a foundation of the then-contemporary socialist architecture of the postwar period. On a political level, these countries were part of the communist bloc, while on cultural levels they at least semiconsciously considered themselves part of a larger European cultural space and tradition. One system was dominant in the predetermined political sphere, the other in the cultural and technological one. The common denominator between both – unwinding their radical ideological conflict – was considered to be the general modernist roots shared by both competing political systems.

What blurred the clarity of the communist framework further, as has been noted above, was the unleashed energy of ever-unresolved nationalisms. Unchained from the ideological constraints of the Stalinist period, the question of what national architecture was in each country first disappeared at the beginning of the 1960s, to return with full force in the 1970s and 1980s. Inspired as they were by the critique of the International Style, CEE architecture cultures turned to the looming specter of in-between positions: domestications, nationalizations, hybridizations, etc. These intermediate attitudes, as in every peripheral system, allowed CEE countries to experience significant flexibility and maneuvering: on a horizontal plane between dominant poles, but also vertically between contexts of politics and culture, by transmitting problems from one level to another.

The Curse of the Peripheral

Due to the geographic and cultural position of the region and its links to the European context, CEE societies had developed a set of tactics for benefiting from their inbetweenness regarding the two universalist centers. Thus, the artistic and architectural cultures of CEE countries were constructed on self-understanding as a peripheral and semi-liberal zone, bridging the opposing universal powers and constructing their identities upon this complex equilibrium. This debate was the most significant cultural and political task, orienting the development of the cultural situation of the region in the second half of the twentieth century. The result was the development of a variety of regional modernisms and national regionalisms especially strong in countries including Bulgaria, Romania, Hungary and Yugoslavia.

Typically for hybrid cultures and societies, these forms were functioning in several ways. They consolidated and constructed a platform for professional exchange between CEE countries and the Soviet Union on one hand, and between socialist countries as a whole and Western-world architecture on the other. In this way, they worked as a powerful source for the liberalization of the cultural horizon. Hence, by legitimizing the cultural image of the CEE, they formed an external point of view on the entire culture of the socialist bloc in the most positive light – in this aspect, it was definitively an instrument of propaganda.

The role of the CEE cultures, thus, was to some extent to mediate between competing worlds and to construct an acceptable common denominator between their cultures. This is why CEE architecture societies were far more liberal and active in professional exchanges during the period from 1960 to 1990, allowing the establishment of institutions and exchange formats such as the World Biennale of Architecture "INTERARCH" and the International Academy of Architecture in Sofia, Bulgaria, numerous international competitions and the international journal *Architecture and Society*.

Under the influence of communist ideology, CEE countries created a complex and multivalent culture in which the principal communist utopia born in Soviet Russia half a century before was adapted, softened and domesticated without being rejected. We may say that in the 1980s, when liberal ideas for convergence with market economies were flourishing, CEE communist societies were almost becoming a space where the positive qualities of each system were set to cohabit. It was a place for breeding dreams and intentions to reform the socialist model towards pluralism and towards elements of the open-market economic model, while still being part of utopia: a world of the best impossible future.

At this same time, the idyllic function – as it were – of the CEE as a liberalizing internal periphery was becoming the agent of its own annihilation. The fact that (leftist) intellectual elites in both the USSR and CEE countries not only tolerated but also incited peripheral national fronts is a clear sign that the socialist revolution did not sublimate bourgeois thinking in these societies. It is our conviction that, along with economic and social issues, it was the incapacity of communist powers and elites both in the USSR and within the broader communist space to generate a genuine collective identity and culture that was a major contributing factor in its failure. The fragmentation of cultural and aesthetic means that the periphery had so naturally implemented and appropriated was a constitutive part of this process.

The periphery is in fact a carrier of its own utopia – a delirious illusion – that itself might become a center at a certain point of development. The particular by its very essence dreams of the universal, and blinded as it is by its own geopolitical Oedipus, it is ready to commit all necessary compromises to obtain any kind of recognition as a real subject. For instance, the universalist discourse behind the "INTERARCH" World Biennale of Architecture in Sofia[16] and its International Academy of Architecture[17] demonstrate the most extreme manifestations of this program. Despite its peripheral position – and maybe even because of it – the driving force of these initiatives was the desire to re-establish a new geo-cultural project for reuniting the world of architecture in a center that is dislocated far from centrality, paradoxically exploiting the liberal capacity of the periphery.

Enthusiastic and prolific as it was from the point of view of creativity, cultural exchange, contacts and – at its most basic – human emotions, the action of this periphery could also be analyzed as the expression of the CEE bourgeoisie's aberrant attempt to become the center of planetary cultural attention. With its cross-cultural remixing and compromising actions, the CEE was developing in the direction of East-West convergence; it exerted from the outset a corroding action on the specificity of the Soviet communist experiment and thus on the society it envisioned. As mentioned at the beginning of this chapter, the desire for particularism (nationalism, regionalism, etc.), as critical as it might have been, could serve only one of the competing socio-political projects: liberal capitalism.

Having participated for half a century in the socialist experiment with all the consequences of this condition, the CEE countries were insistently invited to take a central role the historical drama of the twentieth century. From their condition of barely distinguishable provinces, most of them in rural state until the 1940s, they were thrown into the epicenter of geopolitical conflict. They became actors on the historical stage, a role the West had refused to acknowledge during the first half of the century and one that they have lost again today, in their post-communist present condition. To what extent this complex action is negative or positive is a historic judgment that lies beyond the remit of this essay. It will need – as with every historical observation – greater historical distance and a clear ideological framework.

Conclusions

The text above is a rough sketch of cultural and political models, reflecting the dialogical encounter of its authors – members of two consecutive generations of observers of the recent past. It defines polarities and facets of architectural ideologies in the postwar period in Europe, and correlates totalitarian and utopian *Gesamtkunstwerk* modernist models in Soviet society with the ambiguous democratic market-modernist model of Western European cultures. The Soviet cultural and political-dominance model played the role of a strong modernizing influence imposed onto CEE countries. It worked as the universalist pole irrespective of the style and lacking the elaboration of a genuine artistic language. The Western cultural model established far better elaborated and sophisticated architectural languages, and the influential broadcast of this pole was stronger on the sub-official level of cultural dominance.

If for Soviet society the whole state organization was the hyper-scale installation of a unique utopian-modernist project based on a seemingly rational and scientific understanding of life and history, for Western societies modernism was a reflection of the possibility for a rational organization of life and space in the irrational context of the market economy and of liberalism. In the final account, for CEE areas, modernism was both: a tool for modernization and a way to bring its own particular (national) identities to the modernist stage of universality, in an attempt at self-identification.

The experience shows how complex and demanding life in a utopian society directed towards an ideal future is, and how much more comfortable it is to live in a market-oriented world with unrestricted possibilities. But there are two dangers when living in this liberal de-ideologized world, imperfect and comfortable. First, there is always the possibility of creating a romantic nostalgia for unrealized utopias, for the ideal Arcadia and the lost perfection of the Golden Age, which has always been at the core of social revolts. And second, there is the danger of an alien ideological project "infecting," and eventually conquering, a well-fed and educated – yet individualist and fragmented – society that is easy to tempt with the pleasure of surrender, as Michel Houellebecq has ironically imagined in his latest novel *Soumission*.[18]

Endnotes

1 Georgi Stanishev Sr., "Der diskrete Charme des Grenzraums," *Der Architekt*, 11 (1998), 19-23; also in Adolf Stiller, *Bulgarien: Architektonische Fragmente* (Salzburg, Munich. Verlag Anton Pustet, 2007), 16–29.

2 Georgi Stanishev Sr., "Metabolism and Habitat," interview with Kiyonori Kikutake, in *World Architecture*, Nr 32 (London, 1994), 28-47; also in Архитектурни Теории в Монолози, (Sofia: Изток-Запад, 2016), 158–173.

3 Georgi Stanishev Sr. "Post Modern Strategy," interview with Charles Jencks, in Архитектурни Теории в Монолози, (Sofia, Изток-Запад, 2016), 26–37.

4 Georgi Stanishev Sr., "Metabolism and Habitat," 28–47.
5 Boris Groys, *Утопия и обмен*, (Moscow: Знак, 1993), 245.
6 Alexander Kiossev, "Notes on the Self-Colonizing Cultures," Monumenttotransformation, accessed August 16, 2016, http://monumenttotransformation.org/atlas-of-transformation/html/s/self-colonization/the-self-colonizing-metaphor-alexander-kiossev.html, first published in *Cultural Aspects of the Modernization Process* (Oslo: TMV-senteret, 1995).
7 For a more detailed reading on the question of self-colonization and its different political and cultural dimensions in Russian history, refer to Boris Groys's article „Россия как подсознание Запада" in *Утопия и обмен*, (Moscow: Знак, 1993), 245–259.
8 Vladimir Paperny, *Культура Два* (Moscow: Новое литературное обозрение, 1996), 5.
9 Groys, *Gesamtkunstwerk Сталин* [1987], (Moscow: Ад Маргинем Пресс, 2013), 2.
10 Ibid.
11 Vladimir Paperny, *Культура Два*
12 An extensive reference to the relation between communism and nationalism within Stalin's socialist realism could be found in Anders Åman's book *Architecture and ideology in Eastern Europe during the Stalin era* [1987], (Cambridge: The MIT Press, 1992).
13 Groys, *Gesamtkunstwerk Сталин*, 98.
14 In different forms, the position incarnated in this phrase was discovered by the authors of the text during their travels in CEE, mostly in the context of interviews with architects from Romania, Bulgaria and the countries of former Yugoslavia.
15 Georgi Stanishev Sr., ed., "Origins of Socialist Countries' Architecture: 1910–1940," special issue of *Architecture and Society*, 4–5 (1984).
16 The first edition of this world architecture gathering was initiated in 1981, and it is still being held in Sofia on a triennial base.
17 The International Academy of Architecture, based in Sofia, was founded as an NGO in 1987, under the auspices of the UN.
18 Michel Houellebecq, *Soumission* (Paris: Flammarion, 2015).

Łukasz Stanek

An Image and Its Performance: Techno-Export from Socialist Poland

In February 1981, the main Polish architecture journal *Architektura* dedicated an issue to "Polish Architects in the World"[1] (fig. 1). While the presentation of designs delivered abroad by Polish architects was not rare on the pages of *Architektura*, the dedication of an entire issue to this topic was unprecedented. The export of technical expertise, including architecture and planning, was the pride of socialist Poland. Capitalizing on postwar reconstruction, state-led urbanization, fast-track modernization and longer traditions of Central European architecture, Polish architects, planners, engineers and construction companies had been much in demand during the Cold War. They have been designing structures for Africa and Asia since the 1960s, including governmental buildings, social facilities and housing in Afghanistan, Iraq, Syria, Libya, Algeria, Nigeria and Ghana, as well as highly visible projects such as the master plan of Baghdad (1967, 1973), the General Housing Program for Iraq (1976–1980), and the master planning of the Tripolitania region in Libya (1979–1983).[2]

Strikingly, none of these high-profile projects is featured on the February 1981 cover of *Architektura*. Instead, the full-color image chosen by the editors was an enigmatic one: in the foreground one sees several palm trees; in the midground, something between a construction site and a beach – a lot of sand in any case; and in the background, where one would expect the blue sky to meet the sea, one discerns an object with three large white chimneys, which could be an ocean liner but a second glance confirms that it is, sadly, an industrial facility.

At first, this image appears as a mere curiosity; but it keeps popping up in various archives, including those of trade institutions, professional organizations and the government. These scattered images can be read as points on the networks of architectural mobilities from socialist Poland and, in this way, encounters with these images allow for a reconstruction of the networks in which they were circulated. The most striking feature of such encounters may be their serendipity, stemming from the compartmentalization of archives according to institutional categories, their fragmentation, insufficient cataloging and – often in post-socialist Poland – their incompleteness. This is why, in this article, passages between networks will be reconstructed on the basis of a previous identification of the image in question by means of a broad scanning of the archives. The archival metadata reveals how images were recruited to assume then consolidate networks of specific communities of practice (architects, engineers, administrators, managers of state-socialist companies) and to demonstrate the competence of those identified with these images. Sometimes they were planted to link various communities; at other times, these communities used specific images precisely in order to block such connections. In this sense, in what follows I will discuss networks of architectural mobilities not only in terms of associations but also in terms of gatekeeping protocols and entrance conditions.[3]

Images of Foreign Trade

The cover image from *Architektura* was not accompanied in the journal by any caption or credit, and employees at the journal recall neither the photographer nor the building shown. A visit to the archives of the International Trade Fair in Poznań proves to be more helpful. Founded in 1911 when Poznań was part of the German Empire, after the Second World War the Fair became an important hub for international trade in the socialist bloc: a meeting place for enterprises from socialist East and capitalist West but also from the post-independence South: Ghana, Nigeria, Egypt, Afghanistan, Libya, Iraq and Iran. Beginning in 1955, Polish industry was represented at the Fair by foreign trade organizations (FTO) – that is to say, institutions that processed all the foreign-trade contracts of Polish transactors during socialism. Created in the wake of the war, their first role had been to purchase technical equipment from abroad that was necessary for the state-led reconstruction of the country and for the program of rapid industrialization. But then, in order to generate convertible currency needed for import, the FTOs were given the task of exporting Polish products and services. These included the services of architects, engineers and planners, mediated since 1961 by the FTO Polservice. Polservice was present every year at the Trade Fair in Poznań: first hosted

fig. 1 Cover of *Architektura* 2, 1981, "Polscy architekci w świecie/ Polish Architects in the World".

En Libye...

Les exportations polonaises de travaux du bâtiment vers la Libye ont été inaugurées en 1966 par la construction de deux quartiers de la ville El Marj — situés près de la ville Barce détruite par un tremblement de terre (photo à gauche). Le contrat comprenait la construction des maisons, des immeubles d'utilité publique et des rues avec leur infrastructure complète.

A l'heure actuelle, les entreprises polonaises sont spécialisées dans la construction d'exploitations agricoles, de maisons d'habitation, de routes et de ponts, dans la construction d'unités énergétiques, que dans la livraison et le montage de réservoirs, services de consulting.

Les exportations polonaises de travaux du bâtiment vers la Libye sont réalisées par les entreprises de commerce extérieur BUDIMEX, DROMEX et POLIMEX-CEKOP — soit directement, soit dans le cadre de la sous-traitance pour le compte de firmes étrangères — ainsi que par POLSERVICE.

BUDIMEX

Entreprise de commerce extérieur du bâtiment

a été la première en Libye.

La construction intégrale des deux quartièrs de la ville El Marj sont l'oeuvre de BUDIMEX

BUDIMEX a réalisé, dans les années 1972–1977, la construction de 600 maisons, 1300 exploitations agricoles et 600 km de routes intérieures, de même que sur les travaux liés à la construction de la centrale électrique de Benghasi et de la station de captage d'eau l'accompagnant.

Actuellement BUDIMEX réalise les contrats relatifs à l'extension de la centrale électrique de Benghasi, et aux travaux de construction de la centrale électrique de Homs (édifiée en consortium avec des firmes occidentales) comprenant les travaux du bâtiment, le montage des installations électriques ainsi que le montage des appareillages de contrôle, et à la construction de 950 fermes agricoles.

Les specialistes polonais à l'étranger

fig. 2 *Magazine polonaise des foires* 3 (54), 1979, p. 18. Archiwum Międzynarodowych Targów Poznańskich (Poznań)

in a temporary, round pavilion,[4] it moved during the 1970s to the pavilion of Budimex, a construction firm authorized to work abroad, until it relocated to its own modest pavilion. The Polservice pavilion was often shown in the organization's advertisements in *Polish Fair Magazine,* the official journal of the Trade Fair, published in Polish, English, French and Russian.[5]

It is in an article about Budimex planted in *Polish Fair Magazine* that the building from the *Architektura* cover reappears.[6] A 1979 issue of the Trade

Fair journal reproduces the facility in black and white and the shot makes it clear that the building does not stand in a jungle but rather on dunes with scarce vegetation (fig. 2). The picture does not have a specific caption, but was included in an article presenting Polish export projects in Libya. The accompanying text in French lists several of them – neighborhoods in Barca (El Marj), agricultural farms, roads, a power plant in Benghazi with a water-treatment plant – and announces the construction of more farms, a power plant in Homs, and an extension to the plant in Benghazi.[7] It must be the latter that made it to the cover of *Architektura*; this is confirmed by a caption in another issue of *Polish Fair Magazine*, where the building pops up again, now in full color, trimmed to a square format.[8]

Socialist Poland had been present on the Libyan market since the country's independence (1951), and this included the participation of Polish architects and planners in numerous UN missions, such as the program of self-help housing in Tripolitania.[9] After the coup of 1969, followed by the proclamation of the Socialist People's Libyan Arab Jamahiriya in 1977, Libya became one of the most important trade partners for Poland and other European socialist countries.[10] The commercial involvement of Polish firms since the 1960s included the design and construction of roads, geological and cartographic surveys, fishing ports and irrigation infrastructure, but also preservation projects for historic urban centers.[11] The Warsaw Development Consortium (Wadeco) delivered the planning of the sewage system in Tripoli, geodesic surveys in Misratha and Sirte, and a factory for prefabricated housing elements in Tripoli.[12] By the late 1970s, Wadeco was commissioned to produce the regional plan and urban plans for the Tripolitania region, an area in which 60 percent of the population and two-thirds of the economic activity of Libya was concentrated. At the peak of fieldwork and planning activities, more than two hundred Polish planners and forty geodesists worked on site, sent by universities, research institutes and planning offices throughout Poland.[13] Architects were on board too, and their portfolios show various strategies for dealing with the cultural context of North Africa, from housing typologies that allowed outdoor sleeping – as at the Zanzour estate in Tripoli (1977) designed by Edward Wysocki at the service of Libya's National Housing Corporation – to Jan Wrana's opulent interpretation of an imagined Arab city in ornamental facades for department stores and tourist facilities in Misratha during the following decade.[14]

The collaborative character of these projects and the ability of Polish firms to collaborate with foreign contractors comes to the fore in another appearance of the Benghazi plant photograph in *Polish Trade Fair Magazine*, now in an advertisement for the state enterprise Energoexport, which as the

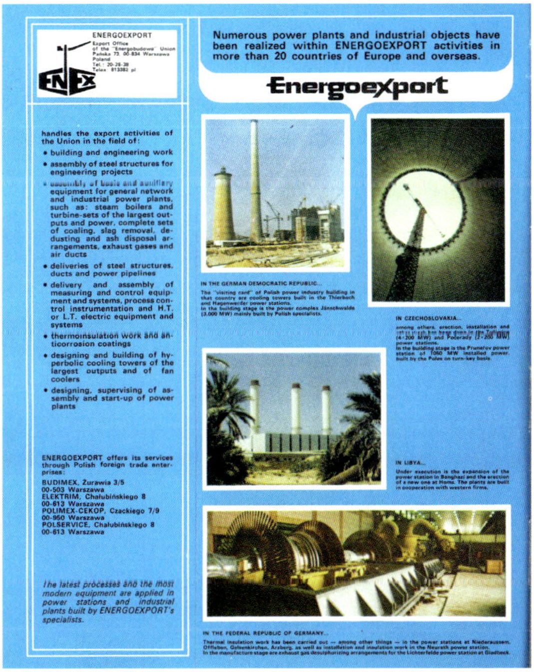

fig. 3 Polish Fair_Magazine 3 (62), 1981, p. 14, Archiwum Międzynarodowych Targów Poznańskich (Poznań)

advert stated specialized in power plants and industrial objects built in tandem with Western firms (fig. 3). The Benghazi plant's construction involved West German, French, Dutch and British enterprises providing materials and equipment, as well as a Belgian supervisor.[15] Cooperation was typical for Polish engagements in Libya, starting with the first large-scale contract for Budimex: the construction of Barca, planned as a new city by the American firm Lublin & McGaughy after the old town had been devastated by an earthquake in February 1963. The construction of five hundred thirty-four single-story houses and nineteen social facilities, including a mosque, schools, day cares, a market, a cinema and a post office resulted from an awarded tender. Advertisements like the ones from *Polish Trade Magazine*, by referring to such examples, reassured prospective foreign clients about the broad networks of Polish companies and about their pragmatism in cooperating with Western firms.

Such pragmatism reflected the shift in the Polish regime's motivation for exporting architecture and urban design over the course of the 1970s. In the previous decade, this export had been part of the political and economic support granted by the Eastern Bloc to independence movements in the colonies and to young postcolonial states. Inscribed into the general opening of Soviet policy under Khrushchev towards the "Third World," this support was presented to the Polish public as a means of stabilizing the international standing of the country, notably in the UN, in particular before West Germany's recognition of Polish borders in 1970 within Willy Brandt's Ostpolitik. Economic interests were a crucial motivation too, and they became more pressing with the necessity of repaying loans granted to the regime in Warsaw by Western financial institutions in the course of the 1970s.[16]

As a result, Libya, along with Iraq, became Poland's most important trading partners because neither country required the underwriting of contracts by the Polish government and both agreed to barter transactions. These transactions were accompanied by a discourse about a shared political commitment on the parts of both countries "to support national freedom movements and revolutionary forces in Africa," as the Libyan newspaper *Al-Fajr Al-Jadid* reported in 1978 on the occasion of Muammar Gaddafi's visit to Poland.[17] Along similar lines, an author writing in *As-Sadaka*, the journal of the Society of Polish-Libyan Friendship, after listing all Polish projects in Libya including the Benghazi power plant, concluded that "there is nothing odd about the fact that in Libya the Poles are called 'Libyans of the North.'"[18] The Polish regime, meanwhile, presented the engagements in Libya to the home public as "aid" granted to "a young country on the path toward socialism."[19] Yet such statements contrast with pressure put on Budimex by the government to improve its economic performance,[20] especially in view of the fact that its projects in Libya, including the power station in Benghazi, ended up in the red.[21]

Picturing Professionalism

Whether a commodity or a gift, the Benghazi power plant was for the Polish regime, first of all, a question of political economy. Yet it could also have been looked at with an aesthetic gaze, as proof of the architectural competence of its designers. In the archive of the Polish Architects Association (SARP) in Warsaw, among hundreds of dossiers of architects, there are two that contain photographs of the power plant. During the postwar period, SARP was a mediator in the international activities of Polish architects, which included the dissemination of briefs for international competitions, assistance in the submission of entries, and negotiations on behalf of its members with various authorities. In the SARP archive, the dossier of Wojciech Empacher – who claimed in the accompanying CV to have designed the power plant in Benghazi with a colleague, K. Goliński – contains photographs of the power plant and a set of schematic drawings of the technical facilities and administrative building.[22] A different photograph of the Benghazi plant is included in the dossier of the architect Maciej Siennicki, who listed in his CV the "architectural design and the collaboration on the draft design of a power plant in

Budowa elektrowni Benghazi II w Libii

Budowy elektrowni w Benghazi podjęło się, w drodze przetargu, międzynarodowe konsorcjum, w skład którego wszedł (z udziałem 48,6%) polski „Budimex". Polacy wykonali głównie roboty budowlane. Z uwagi na szczególne warunki budowy i nieczęsto spotykane rozwiązania techniczne, informacje o tych robotach zasługują chyba na opublikowanie.

Lokalizacja elektrowni i charakterystyka terenu

Elektrownia została zlokalizowana w odległości 15 km od miasta Benghazi nad brzegiem morza Śródziemnego, na wydmach porosłych gajami palmowymi i bagnach pokrytych wysuszoną przez słońce trawą. Teren płaski wzdłuż morza przekształca się w pagórkowaty o charakterze wydmowym. Różnice wysokości sięgają do 9 m. Działka przeznaczona pod budowę, o powierzchni 300 tys. m², graniczy z morzem na długości 800 m. Prace niwelacyjne wykonano na obszarze 170 tys. m². Przemieszczono 300 tys. m³ gruntu. Projektowane rzędne terenu wynoszą, ponad poziom morza, +4,50 m w części południowo-zachodniej, +4,00 m w północno-wschodniej oraz +3,80 m w północno-zachodniej.

Tam gdzie pozostał teren ukształtowany przez naturę, wydmy są porośnięte częściowo przez krzewy winorośli. Polski wykonawca zrobił wszystko, aby zachować możliwie jak najwięcej z istniejącego drzewostanu. Pozostawiono np. stare wysokie palmy.

Charakterystyka obiektu

Kompleks obiektów elektrowni wyposażonej w trzy turbiny kondensacyjne z generatorami o mocy 40 MW każdy oraz dwie turbiny przeciwprężne z generatorami o mocy 30 MW każdy, obejmuje również zakład odsalania wody morskiej zaopatrujący w wodę pitną miasto (rys. 1). Wzniesione obiekty można podzielić na budynki oraz na lądowe i morskie budowle inżynierskie.

• *Budynek główny* o kubaturze 130 000 m³ i długości 100 m składa się z: a) części środkowej — podpiwniczonej, pięciokondygnacyjnej o żelbetowej konstrukcji monolitycznej wykonanej z betonu B300÷350; b) turbinowni stanowiącej nawę boczną o szerokości 22,5 m i wysokości 23,5 m — zaprojektowanej w konstrukcji stalowej i wyposażonej w suwnicę o nośności 80/20 MG; c) kotłowni stanowiącej drugą nawę boczną o szerokości 24 m i wysokości 21 m, zaprojektowanej też w konstrukcji stalowej (rys. 2).

W przyszłości przewidziane jest powiększenie długości budynku.

Turbiny parowe są zasilane z kotłów opalanych olejem ziemnym. Obieg wody jest otwarty, tzn. jest ona pobierana z morza i zrzucana z powrotem do morza kanałem zamkniętym.

• *Stacje uzdatniania wody* wykonano z prefabrykatów żelbetowych.

• *Pompownia wody obiegowej* jest budynkiem składającym się z części nadziemnej o kubaturze 9000 m³ oraz części podziemnej o poziomie posadowienia od −6,60 do −5,27 m. Część podziemną zaprojektowano jako sztywną skrzynię żelbetową; część nadziemną zaś — jako konstrukcję prefabrykowaną, szkieletową o siatce słupów 5,5 × 16,0 m. Dźwigary żelbetowe o długości 15,5 m i ciężarze 19,5 MG wykonano jako prefabrykaty na specjalnie przygotowanym do tego celu placu, w pobliżu obiektu. Pozwoliło to na uniknięcie ich przewozu. Zastosowano beton B380. Obiekt jest wyposażony w suwnicę o nośności 8 MG.

• *Budynki: socjalny i warsztatowy* o kubaturze 11 000 m³ zaprojektowano jako żelbetową prefabrykowaną konstrukcję szkieletową. Część socjalna jest dwukondygnacyjna. Strop nad parterem jest żelbetowy, monolityczny. Warsztat jest parterowy. Prefabrykaty wykonano z betonu B380. Warsztat wyposażony jest w suwnicę o nośności 5 MG.

• *Magazyn*, o kubaturze 21 000 m³ i powierzchni 3100 m², ma również żelbetową szkieletową konstrukcję prefabrykowaną o siatce słupów 8 × 8 m.

Budowli inżynierskich jest kilka. Należą do nich:

• *Zbiorniki oleju* — cztery o pojemności 10 000 m³ każdy oraz jeden o pojemności 500 m³. Zbiorniki są odgrodzone

Rys. 1 Zakład odsalania wody morskiej dla miasta Benghazi

Rys. 2. Elewacja budynku głównego z płyt „Hunter Douglas"

INŻ. I BUD. nr 5 — 1977 169

fig. 4 Magdalena Łabęda, "Budowa elektrowni Bengazi II w Libii" [The construction of the power plant Benghazi II in Libya], *Inżynieria i budownictwo* 15, 1977, p. 169.

Benghazi," but did not mention the names of his collaborators, just as he had not been mentioned in the Empacher dossier.[23]

The determination of authorship in export projects is not an easy task, because of their specific labor conditions. Architects were working in large teams in which they were often assigned to highly specialized jobs, frequently shifting from one project to another. They had little control over the commissions and were often called back to Poland before the project was finished, or even before technical drawings were delivered. Empacher and Siennicki must have been members of such a big team, and their CVs in the SARP archive show that their paths crossed at the Warsaw state planning office Bistyp [Office for Studies and Type Projects of Industrial Constructions]. Since its creation in 1951, Bistyp belonged to the most innovative architectural and engineering offices in Poland, and besides type projects was responsible for many singular, highly visible buildings based on experimental engineering solutions such as the modernist "Supersam" supermarket (1962) and the central railway station (1975), both in Warsaw, the Spodek auditorium in Katowice (1971) and the Oliva sports hall in Gdańsk (1970). Since the 1950s, Bistyp had specialized in building export, including that of industrial facilities, and a publication celebrating thirty-five years of its existence lists, among numerous other projects, the power plant in Benghazi.[24]

Mapping references to Bistyp in journals specializing in building technology and construction permits a new set of images of the Benghazi plant to be added to the images gathered so far. One of these was included in an article published in the professional journal *Przegląd Budowlany* [*Building Review*], which featured numerous reports by Polish engineers sharing their experiences of building in Africa and Asia. The article was illustrated by a black-and-white snapshot of the power plant, centered on its large volumes and the three chimneys, surrounded by an array of technical equipment, vehicles, sheds and vegetation.[25] The most complete account of the plant for a professional audience interested in the nitty-gritty of export contracts, though, can be found in a paper from *Inżynieria i budownictwo* [*Engineering and Construction*], which included an account of the site, technological specification of all buildings and facilities, organization details of the building site and terms of contract between all firms involved.[26] This paper also accounted for technical solutions employed – the sun-protective finishing of roof and facades, for example – and reproduced their photographs (fig. 4).

The images from the SARP archive are very different. Probably taken by the architect, the photographs in the Empacher dossier emphasize the abstract quality of architectural details and rhythms of the facade (fig. 5). The images from Siennicki's dossier show the power plant under a dramatically cloudy sky, lit by sharp light emphasizing the volumes and lines of the facades, and are labeled in an elegant typeface ("Power plant in Benghazi [Libya]. Facade of the main building") (fig. 6). The shots are similar to those of other projects abroad included by Siennicki in his dossier, in particular the Polish Embassy in Islamabad, Pakistan. By means of these images, architects were aiming to persuade their SARP peers to see the depicted building as a piece of architecture and then to grant its designers the status of "architect-creator" that came with specific tax benefits in the era of socialism. In order to make the argument about the creative labor of architects and their authorship, their photographs omitted suggestions about other types of labor involved in the process, such as that of technicians and engineers, let alone that of Libyan and Polish workers employed at the construction sites.

Selective Visibility

When the editors of *Architektura* chose the cover image for their issue on export projects, no similar attempt was made to present the Benghazi plant as a piece of architecture. Browsing that issue of the journal might suggest that something else was at stake here. The issue was the last in a series offering an overview of Polish architectural culture in preparation for the International Union of Architects (UIA) congress in Warsaw in June 1981, just

fig. 5 "Elektrownia w Bengazi (Libia)" [Power plant in Benghazi (Libya)], in dossier no. 387 (Empacher Wojciech), Archiwum Stowarzyszenia Architektów Polskich (Warszawa).

fig. 6 "Elektrownia w Benghazi (Libia). Elewacja budynku głównego" [Power plant in Benghazi (Libya). The facade of the main building], in dossier no. 1254 (Siennicki Maciej), Archiwum Stowarzyszenia Architektów Polskich (Warszawa).

months before martial law was declared by the regime in December 1981.[27] In an atmosphere highly critical of modern architecture, the UIA congress proposed the "Warsaw Charter," which was a programmatic critique of the Athens Charter.[28]

In that climate of opinion, the cover of *Architektura* appears as a product of "double-coding," theorized by Charles Jencks – a prominent visitor to Warsaw in 1981 – as an essentially postmodern operation.[29] While for the general public the cover image presented an industrial facility in an exotic location, the architectural community may have read it as an ironic commentary about labor conditions on export contracts. Working in Africa and the Middle East was clearly a desired professional experience for Polish architects: it gave them an opportunity to realize ambitious projects beyond the precarious conditions at home of "real existing modernism" dominated by state bureaucracy and the building industry.[30] Export contracts offered them a rare opportunity for travel, which entailed trips to Libyan beaches but also to the origins of their discipline: the Roman cities of Leptis Magna and Sabratha, and Italian colonial architecture surveyed by several Warsawians during their stays in Tripolitania.[31] Yet for many architects, the most important reason to leave home for export contracts was financial, since these allowed earning much more than was possible in Poland. This atmosphere, combined with an often-unwarranted suspicion of political compromises allegedly being required from those applying for a passport, contributed to the fact the architects were not very eager to highlight such projects in their portfolios back in Poland. In light of this, what appears on the cover of *Architektura* to be an omission of architecture in favor of a piece of infrastructure reflected the highly ambiguous atmosphere around export projects.

This ambiguity was not restricted to the architectural community, but concerned the public at large. From the late 1960s, civic architecture and housing projects abroad designed by Polish architects and built by Polish firms became less and less visible both in the general mass media and in the professional press. Reasons for this omission might be found in a 1964 review published in a literary journal, "Export of Polish Architecture," in which the author contrasted the success of Polish architects in international competitions with the disappointing architecture "on the internal market."[32] The contrast stemmed, he argued, from "stingy building norms," "strict investment discipline," "general economic tendency towards lowering the standards and decreasing the quality of buildings," and "typization and standardization which […] result in a range of identical or very similar buildings, streets and whole neighborhoods."[33] Had *Architektura* chosen a more appealing cover, it might have provoked similarly uncomfortable questions about architectural production in Poland, even more pressing in the contexts of the economic crisis of the early 1980s than they had been two decades before.

While images found in an advertising brochure, a trade journal, an engineering journal, or a dossier in SARP seemed to have been put out there to perform a specific task in a circumscribed community of practice, the image from *Architektura* is ambiguous in its message, instrumentality and audience. Read in the context of late socialist Poland, *Architektura*'s cover could be a

fig. 7 The Bengazi power plant in the promotional folder of "Dona LLC," Zbigniew Kargol, Janusz Przychodzki, and Wiesław Rzepka, early 1990s.

celebration of export projects or their critique; an expression of complacency, a witty commentary or a conformist omission.

It was only after the end of socialism in Poland that the image of Benghazi's power plant was once again recruited to persuade and to connect. The photograph from Siennicki's SARP dossier was shown in the promotional leaflet of the architectural firm Dona, one of many bourgeoning private architectural offices in the early 1990s[34] (fig. 7). In this folder, the partners of the firm, who did not appear in any other context discussed before,[35] showcase the power plant in juxtaposition with their projects in Nigeria from the previous two decades, including embassies, university buildings, offices and industrial plants. In this way, the African experience was shown to prospective clients as a demonstration of the capacity of the partners to secure large-scale commissions in a competitive market, to collaborate with Western firms and to apply cutting-edge technology. The images were reproduced in full color, to make the most of the variety of materials, textures and forms employed in these projects – a variety that fed into the embracing of postmodernist sensitivities by investors and the broader public in post-socialist Poland. The assimilation of such sensitivities was yet another lesson that had been learned from the export contracts.[36]

Endnotes

This paper expands my text published in *ANZA*, 1 (Dar es Salaam, 2011), 22–23. I would like to thank Sławomir Gzell, Wacław Piziorski, Wiesław Rzepka and Bogdan Wyporek for granting me access to their private archives; Piotr Bujas, Alicja Gzowska and Aleksandra Kędziorek for assisting me with parts of the archival query for this research; and Razan Francis and Senna Al-Bachari for helping me with the translation of the Arabic materials.

1 *Architektura*, 2 (1981).

2 See Łukasz Stanek, "PRL™ Export Architecture and Urbanism from Socialist Poland," *Piktogram: Talking Pictures Magazine*, 15 (2011), 1–54; Łukasz Stanek, "Miastoprojekt Goes Abroad: Transfer of Architectural Labor from Socialist Poland to Iraq (1958–1989)," *The Journal of Architecture*, 17:3 (2012), 361–386; Łukasz Stanek, "Mobilities of Architecture in the Global Cold War: From Socialist Poland to Kuwait and Back," *International Journal of Islamic Architecture*, 4:2 (2015), 365–398; Łukasz Stanek, "Architects from Socialist Countries in Ghana (1957–1967): Modern Architecture and Mondialisation," *Journal of the Society of Architectural Historians*, 74:4 (2015), 416–442. For a bibliography of the architectural mobilities in the networks of socialist countries and of the Non-Aligned Movement, see Łukasz Stanek, "The 'Second World'"s Architecture and Planning in the 'Third World'," *The Journal of Architecture*, 17:3 (2012), 299–307; Łukasz Stanek, "Socialist Networks and the Internationalization of Building Culture after 1945," *ABE Journal*, 6 (2014), http://abe.revues.org/1266, accessed January 14, 2016.

3 Stanek, "Architects from Socialist Countries in Ghana."

4 The designers were the architect Andrzej Bołtuć and the artists M. Raducki and A. Strumiłło; SARP archive (Warsaw), dossier 154 (Andrzej Bołtuć).

5 *Poznan Fair Magazine*, 1 (1985), 16.

6 *Magazine polonaise des foires*, 54 (1979), 18. Archiwum Międzynarodowych Targów Poznańskich (Poznań).

7 Ibid.

8 *Polish Fair Magazine*, 60 (1981), 20. Archiwum Międzynarodowych Targów Poznańskich (Poznań).

9 *Fundamenty*, 132 (1959). Polish planners contributed also to the "Great Man-made River" project in Libya. See Bohdan Wyporek, *Daleko od Warszawy: architekta zapiski z trzech kontynentów* (Warsaw: Akapit, 2009).

10 For bibliography, see Aboulgasem Ahmed Gsuda, *Libia w piśmiennictwie polskim po II wojnie światowej* (Warsaw: Dialog, 2003).

11 *Rynki Zagraniczne*, 105 (1975), 24 (1979), 93 (1980), 138 (1989).

12 *Rynki Zagraniczne*, 138 (1989).

13 Polservice Consulting Office et al., "Tarabulus Agglomeration: An Outline of Physical Dvelopment–2000. Final Report" (Warsaw: Wadeco, 1982), Wacław Piziorski Archive, Warsaw.

14 SARP Archive (Warsaw), dossier 573 (Edward Wysocki); Jan Wrana Archive, Kraków.

15 Małgorzata Łabęda, "Budowa elektrowni Benghazi II w Libii," *Inżynieria i Budownictwo*, 5 (1977), 169–173.

16 See Odd Arne Westad, *The Global Cold War: Third World Interventions and the Making of Our Times* (Cambridge: Cambridge University Press, 2005); David Engerman, "The Second World's Third World," *Kritika: Explorations in Russian and Eurasian History*, 12:1 (2011), 183–211.
17 *Al-Fajr Al-Jadid,* July 2/1821 (1978).
18 Tadeusz Mrzygłód, "Gospodarka Libii i jej powiązania z Polską," *As-Sadaka: Miesięcznik kulturalno-społeczny. Organ Towarzystwa Przyjaźni Libijsko-Arabsko-Polskiej*, 1 (1981), 23.
19 Filmoteka Narodowa (Warsaw): "Polskie spotkania z Libią" (F. 2804), "Budimex w Libii" (F. 2912, 1977), "El Marj. Stara i nowa Barka" (F. 2941, 1977), "Budimex–export wewnętrzny" (F. 2899); see also newsreels from the same archive: KR6 b/69, KR 49 A/69, KR 45 A/76.
20 Archiwum Akt Nowych (Warsaw), "Centrala Handlu Zagranicznego Budownictwa BUDIMEX w Warszawie," zesp. 2350, 1967–1983.
21 Andrzej Warmiński, "Dolary wyrzucone… w piasek," *Fundamenty* 48 (1981), 1, 4.
22 SARP Archive (Warsaw), dossier 387 (Wojciech Empacher).
23 SARP Archive (Warsaw), dossier 1254 (Maciej Siennicki).
24 *BISTYP: 35 lat działalności, 1951–1986* (Warsaw: Bistyp, 1988).
25 Borys Zawadzki, "Eksport polskiej myśli technicznej," *Przegląd Budowlany* 10 (1976), 454–458.
26 Łabęda, "Budowa elektrowni Benghazi II w Libii."
27 *Architektura*, 35:3–4 (1981); "XIV kongres UIA Varšava 1981," *Arhitektura urbanizam*, 20 (1981), 8–30. See also *L'Union internationale des architectes, 1948–1998* (Paris: Epure, 1998).
28 Alexi Ferster Marmot, "Urbanism in Warsaw: Solidarity and Beyond," *Places*, 1:2 (1983), 78–81; Marmot, "The Warsaw Charter," *Places*, 1:2 (1983), 82–83.
29 Charles Jencks, *The Story of Post-Modernism: Five Decades of the Ironic, Iconic and Critical in Architecture* (London: Wiley, 2011).
30 Łukasz Stanek, ed., *Team 10 East: Revisionist Architecture in Real Existing Modernism* (Warsaw: Museum of Modern Art / Chicago: University of Chicago Press, 2014); Łukasz Stanek, *Postmodernism Is Almost All Right. Polish Architecture after Socialist Globalization* (Warsaw: Fundacja Bęc-Zmiana, 2012).
31 Sławomir Gzell Archive (Warsaw); Comp.: Giuliano Gresleri, Pier Giorgio Massaretti, Stefano Zagnoni, *Architettura italiana d'oltremare: 1870–1940* (Venezia: Marsilio, 1993).
32 Jan Paweł Gawlik, "Eksport polskiej architektury," Życie Literackie, November 22, (1964), 1.
33 Ibid.
34 "Przedsiębiorstwo Inwestycyjno-Handlowe Dona Sp. z o. o.," advertising leaflet. Wiesław Rzepka Archive (Warsaw).
35 The three partners were Zbigniew Kargol, Janusz Przychodzki and Wiesław Rzepka. Wiesław Rzepka Archive (Warsaw).
36 Stanek, *Postmodernism Is Almost All Right.*

Max Hirsh

Postmodern Architectural Exchanges Between East Germany and Japan

In the early 1980s, the East German government commissioned the Japanese construction firm Kajima to build two luxury hotels in Dresden and East Berlin.[1] The hotels were part of a broader urban renewal program that deployed postmodern design in order to counter widespread dissatisfaction with the dilapidated condition of East Germany's inner cities, and to convert them into attractive destinations for foreign tourists and businessmen. Against the backdrop of intensified economic relations between the Eastern Bloc and Japan – a largely overlooked facet of the late Cold War period – the GDR entered into trade agreements with Japanese corporations, who promised to upgrade the country's international business and hospitality infrastructure.

For the design practitioners involved, the hotels served as a crucial platform for the cross-cultural exchange of knowledge: introducing East German planners to more advanced Japanese construction and project management techniques, while exposing Japanese architects to postmodern design theories and architectural research methods that were being used in Europe. This chapter traces the encounter between these design professionals at the Hotel Bellevue in Dresden and the Grand Hotel in East Berlin. Drawing upon archival research and interviews conducted in both countries, it argues that these projects represented a back-door conduit for the transfer of architectural knowledge that circumvented conventional channels of transnational exchange. I begin by situating the interaction between these designers within the broader context of economic relations between Japan and the GDR, and against the backdrop of a renewed interest in history among East German architects and planners. I then investigate the use of historicist and contextual design approaches in Dresden and East Berlin, and finish by studying the unintended transfer of these architectural ideas back to Japan. I end by arguing that the interpenetration of East German and Japanese design techniques demands a reevaluation of the dominant history of postmodernism, and of the globalization of architectural practice: one that transcends reductive divisions into East and West, and into capitalist and socialist modes of production. By highlighting alternative pathways of architectural knowledge and practice that connected a socialist country in Central Europe to a capitalist one in East Asia, the essay points to the critical role played by architects and design firms from outside of North America and Western Europe in the globalization of architectural practice (fig. 1). Far from a simple transfer of services from Japan to the GDR, these projects abetted the multinational exchange of architectural knowledge, engineering technology, building materials, and labor between more than a dozen countries in Europe and Asia. East German cities like Dresden and East Berlin thus operated as loci of syncretic architectural experiments that recombined the aesthetic, technical, and managerial precepts emerging from very different cultural and ideological systems.

Learning from Japan

In 1975, Günter Mittag – the economic secretary of East Germany's politburo and chief architect of its planned economy – traveled to Japan in order to study the country's rapid postwar development. Impressed by what he saw, Mittag proposed a comprehensive trade agreement under which the East German government contracted Japanese conglomerates such as Mazda, Mitsubishi, and Nippon Steel to boost the GDR's output of high-value industrial products and consumer goods such as petrol, cars, and color TVs.[2] These projects were administered by a parastatal body known as the Japan-GDR Project Committee (JGPC), through which the East German government also contracted Kajima, one of Japan's largest construction firms, to build trade centers and luxury hotels in East Berlin, Dresden, and Leipzig. Though unusual within the larger geopolitical context of the Cold War, these contracts were part of the GDR regime's strategy to stimulate business with the so-called *nichtsozialistisches Ausland*, or "non-socialist foreign countries," in order to strengthen East Germany's hard currency reserves and reduce the crushing foreign debts that ultimately led to the regime's demise.[3] Moreover,

fig. 1 A documentary produced by Kajima-vision – Kajima's in-house film production company – narrates the cooperation between Japanese and East German design professionals during the construction of the Hotel Bellevue Dresden. In this still, the Japanese engineer Kusakabe Seiji conducts a site visit together with Heinz Michalk, Dresden's chief municipal architect; and Werner Bauer, director of VEB Gesellschaftsbau Dresden, a state-owned enterprise responsible for the construction of public buildings. Image courtesy of Kajima Corporation.

government planners were keen to learn about Japanese advancements in building technology and project management in order to upgrade the overall quality of the GDR's construction industry without abandoning its reliance on large-scale prefabrication.[4]

Founded in Edo in 1840, Kajima had made a name for itself in postwar Japan as an efficient builder of heavy infrastructure and high-rise modernist office buildings such as the Kasumigaseki Building (1968), the country's first "super-tall" skyscraper. By cooperating with Kajima, East Germany's economic planners hoped to sidestep three obstacles that hampered the growth of foreign trade: the absence of modern office facilities featuring basic amenities such as telex machines; the low standards of East German hotels, which were poorly designed and apathetically staffed; and the export restrictions of the West German government, which actively obstructed the transfer of engineering technology and building materials to the GDR.[5]

Cooperation with Kajima addressed all three of these challenges. The company's first project, the 25-storey International Trade Center (1978) in East Berlin, aimed to stimulate foreign investment by providing high-quality office and meeting facilities for international firms. The second project, a modernist skyscraper in Leipzig called the Hotel Merkur (1981), was intended to facilitate deal-making during the annual *Leipziger Messe*, East Germany's most important trade fair. To ensure the rapid completion of these projects, Kajima helped to establish a subsidiary office in Vienna, which functioned as a transshipment center for technical drawings and building materials that were sent from West Germany to Austria and then redirected to the GDR. Significantly, the Vienna office also supplied these projects with foreign construction workers, mainly from Greece and Yugoslavia, who could be deployed more cheaply and flexibly than their counterparts in East Germany's state-run construction combines.[6]

The Japanese architects encountered numerous hurdles, ranging from the intercultural to the logistical. Few of Kajima's employees had ever been outside Japan, and many were distressed by the prospect of working in a distant, isolated country. Moreover, they faced significant challenges to deeply held aesthetic and operational assumptions; and were perplexed by the vagaries of East Germany's planned economy, where systemic shortages often produced unexpected delays. As the GDR's economic crisis deepened, their East German clients increasingly resorted to high-end forms of barter, offering to exchange materials, technical services, and labor in the absence of a convertible currency.[7] Moreover, it was in East Germany where Kajima's architects were first exposed to the tenets of postmodernism: in particular historicism and contextualism which, under various socialist pseudonyms, became hallmarks of large-scale inner-city urban renewal plans throughout the country, including in Dresden and East Berlin.[8] These redevelopment projects aimed to bridge the gap between the "old" pre-war urban landscape and the "new" postwar city of socialist modernism by combining historicizing architectural elements with industrial construction methods.[9] Kajima's hotels for these cities – originally planned as modernist skyscrapers, the firm's area of specialization – were engulfed by this peculiar brand of socialist postmodernism, becoming show projects of both economic modernization and prefabricated neo-historicism.

Adventures in Contextualism

The lead architect for the two projects was Takeshi Inoue, a lifelong employee of Kajima who spent nearly a decade living and working in the GDR. When Inoue made his first visit to Dresden to survey the site of the future Hotel Bellevue, he was dismayed to find a windswept terrain that had been neglected for decades and was dotted with derelict pre-war structures. He soon learned that the hotel lay at the heart of an urban renewal scheme that focused on the reconstruction of the Saxon state opera house, or *Semperoper*. According to this larger plan, the hotel was to be sited on the northern banks of the Elbe, at a bend in the river whose sweeping vistas of Dresden's skyline had been captured in a painting by Canaletto. Working together with the chief architect of Dresden, the director of the city's department for historic preservation, and the lead architect of the state-run hospitality chain Interhotel, Inoue

fig. 2 Perspective drawing of the Hotel Bellevue Dresden. Image courtesy of Inoue Takeshi.

and his team – which included 15 Japanese architects, engineers, and interior designers – were charged with building a hotel that would pay tribute to the so-called *Canalettoblick* by providing a space in which well-to-do foreign visitors could enjoy the view of Dresden's reconstructed inner city (fig. 2).

The Bellevue's architectural brief foregrounded its role within that larger renewal scheme. It also pointed to a specific constraint – a Baroque townhouse sat at the center of the site – yet it did not provide any guidance on whether, or how, the townhouse should be preserved. The Kajima team prepared two design schemes: one incorporated the existing structure, which would lead to a longer and more expensive construction process; while the other projected the building's removal. Despite the protests of local preservationists, who had petitioned for the townhouse's restoration, Interhotel chose the cheaper scheme and instructed Inoue to plan for the building's demolition.[10]

None of this was out of the ordinary in the East German context, where the razing of pre-war structures was a routine phase of many new building endeavors. But what distinguished this particular project was its location within an area destroyed during the 1945 bombing of Dresden: which was recalled as an episode of severe national trauma by a large portion of the adult population in both German states. Dresden occupied a central position in national discourses on the history of WWII and more broadly on the savagery of war. In late 1981, the demolition plans were leaked to a journalist at the West German *Frankfurter Allgemeine Zeitung*.[11] In an editorial entitled "A piece of old Dresden is about to be torn down," the newspaper railed against the planned destruction of what it called "the last remaining example of what was once one of Dresden's most precious Baroque thoroughfares."[12] It noted that the destruction would come at the hands of "a Japanese company, from whom one can hardly expect any understanding for the significance of *la vieille Saxe*."

The article elicited a swift response on the other side of the border. Within days, Inoue was informed that his East German clients had changed their mind, and was told to incorporate the Baroque structure into the central facade of the building (fig. 3).[13] This proved to be difficult for the Japanese designers, none of whom had any experience working with traditional European construction techniques, and whose portfolio of postwar projects in Japan took a *tabula rasa* site as a given. Reared in a culture where it is common practice to demolish buildings after a few decades – and which assigns importance to the spiritual preservation of an historic site rather than to the literal continuity of its material composition – the Japanese architects were fascinated by the importance that their German clients placed on the physical preservation of historic building materials.

The attention that the hotel received in the West German press unleashed a hypersensitivity to history among Kajima's East German partners: who supplied Kajima's design staff with pre-war maps, photographs, and site plans; as well as scholarly articles on the architectural history of Dresden. The city's chief architect also asked Inoue to familiarize himself with the history of Saxon Baroque townhouses together with their constitutive spatial and structural elements, such as interior courtyards and barrel-vaulted ceilings. He also instructed the Kajima team to meet regularly with Wolfgang Hänsch – a prominent local architect who was leading the reconstruction of the Semper opera – in order to learn the basic principles of historic preservation and to coordinate with a team of craftsmen who had been trained in traditional construction and ornamentation techniques. Finally, Interhotel asked Inoue to conduct a study tour of exemplary instances of contextual and neo-historical design in both Eastern and Western Europe, including Budapest's Hilton Hotel (1977), designed by the Hungarian architect Pintér Béla.

In effect, Inoue and his colleagues were given a crash course in how to conduct historically informed design research. For the Japanese architects, trained in the strictly modernist ethos of postwar architectural pedagogy, this approach seemed both retrograde and ill-advised. Several of the architects whom I interviewed noted that they had learned – both at university and

fig. 3 The Hotel Bellevue in Dresden incorporated a Baroque townhouse into the building's central facade. Image courtesy of Inoue Takeshi.

afterwards in professional practice – that it was "forbidden" to use historical styles and motifs.[14] Yet Kajima's clients asked them to base their design process on a rigorous interrogation of archival materials that documented the historic urban fabric of Dresden. This entailed not just developing an appreciation for the aesthetic vocabulary of Baroque, Romantic, and *Gründerzeit* architecture, but also acquiring a working knowledge of its structural and technical underpinnings. The resulting hotel was invested with a heavy-handed dose of contextualism and labor-intensive restoration: efforts that were designed to demonstrate the ability of Dresden's architects and urban planners to adapt the historic inner city to contemporary technical demands and economic functions. The building's proportions acknowledged both the Baroque townhouse and the modernist apartment blocks across the street: juxtaposing 18th-century height restrictions and angled mansard roofs with the jagged allotment plan of postwar prefabricated housing blocks located across the street. The facade foregrounded the use of locally produced sandstone. In keeping with historic conventions, the roof was clad in copper, while the vertical window treatments were intended as a reference to the Japanese Palais, commissioned by the Saxon king August the Strong to house his porcelain collection (fig. 4).[15]

The Hotel Bellevue and the restored opera house were inaugurated simultaneously on February 13, 1985, which marked the 40th anniversary of the bombing of Dresden. Two hundred thousand people – nearly half of Dresden's population – flocked to the inner city to witness the premiere of Weber's *Der Freischütz*: the last piece that had been performed before the opera shut down at the end of WWII.[16] In the first media event of its kind, the premiere was broadcast simultaneously on both East and West German television. As the

fig. 4 The Hotel Bellevue's copper cladding and vertical window treatments reference the adjacent Japanese Palais. Photograph by Max Hirsh.

performance drew to a close, foreign dignitaries and tourists retired to the Bellevue, which afforded views of the opera house across the river Elbe.

Capital Commemorations

Kajima's successful contribution to what was not just a complex urban renewal project, but also an elaborate multimedia *mise en scène* of Dresden's belated rise from the postwar ashes, led to the company's participation in another one of the GDR's showcase urban renewal projects: the restoration of East Berlin's center, which was redeveloped in the run-up to the 750th anniversary of the city's founding in 1987. A key component of this urban renewal scheme was the reconstruction of Friedrichstrasse, downtown East Berlin's most important – and long-neglected – central avenue. Within a fifty-block zone, more than one hundred shops and high-end boutiques, fifty bars and restaurants, and a dozen luxury apartment buildings were to be erected.[17] The plan's ultimate goal was to turn Friedrichstrasse into an "attractive socialist world city boulevard": one that heralded the conversion of East Berlin's run-down inner city into an attractive destination for both East German citizens and foreign visitors.

The Grand Hotel, a luxury property designed for the needs of foreign tourists and businessmen, was one of the showpiece projects of the new and improved Friedrichstrasse (fig. 5). Under the tutelage of Erhard Gißke, the director of the construction ministry's influential Special Projects Division, Inoue designed an historically accurate amalgamation of two pre-war structures: the Kaisergalerie, a neo-Renaissance shopping arcade built on the site of the future hotel in 1873; and the Hotel Adlon, prewar Berlin's most famous luxury hotel, which was erected next to the Brandenburg Gate in 1907. To assist him, Gißke provided Inoue with a chronicle of the Adlon, published shortly before the outbreak of WWI.[18] He encouraged Inoue to use the chron-

fig. 5 The Grand Hotel Berlin. Image courtesy of Kajima Corporation.

icle, which featured photos of lavish interiors interspersed with portraits of the royal family, as a template for designing the new hotel as well as a street-level arcade filled with reproductions of historic restaurants, cafés, and nightclubs. In essence, Gißke requested a faithful reproduction of Wilhelmine architecture – with one large caveat. Instead of using traditional stonemasonry techniques, the Kajima team would need to rely on pre-cast concrete panels; the dominant building material deployed by the GDR's state-run construction combines, to which Gißke and his colleagues attached tremendous aesthetic and ideological importance. In order to grasp the formal potential of prefabricated historicism, Gißke invited Inoue to join him on a trip to the suburbs of Paris, where they toured several postmodern housing estates designed by Ricardo Bofill.[19]

The hotel consisted of a monolithic steel frame covered in pre-cast panels. Through the panels' clever deployment and the selective use of more expensive finishes such as sandstone cladding and granite plinths, the hotel appeared to be composed of six separate buildings, differentiated through the strategic use of fascia, setbacks, and jetties (fig. 6).[20] Considered one of the crowning achievements of neo-historical prefabrication in the GDR, the Grand Hotel's subdivided facade thus paid tribute to Friedrichstrasse's prewar allotment plan. Meanwhile, the hotel's interior, designed by the architect Yamane Kazuo, relied on the work of skilled East German craftsmen, who produced handmade reproductions of Biedermaier and "rococo-style" furniture, light fixtures, and finishes made of wood, brass, and stucco (fig. 7).[21]

fig. 6 The facade of the Grand Hotel. Photograph by Max Hirsh.

The Afterlife of Socialist Postmodernism

In both Berlin and Dresden, the Kajima team took an autodidactic approach to a postmodern design methodology that rested on the reproduction of individual reference cases and the careful study of local history and building traditions, coupled with an attempt to combine those traditions with modern construction techniques and building materials. This particularly conservative brand of postmodern design enjoyed an unacknowledged afterlife in Japan. As the GDR teetered on the brink of collapse, Kajima reassigned several architects who had worked in East Germany to produce a chain of "European" hotels in Japanese cities such as Kobe, Nagasaki, and Sapporo.[22] The choice of these locations was not accidental: due to a history of contact with European merchants and architects, they all contain an unusually large collection of both Western and "Western-style" (*giyofu*) architecture. From the late 1980s onwards, the "exotic" architectural legacy of these foreign encounters came to be viewed as a vehicle for stimulating domestic tourism. Working with the hotel operator Monterey, Kajima developed a series of European-themed leisure environments that drew extensively on the urban research skills and design techniques that the firm's architects had acquired in the GDR.

The parallels are perhaps most evident at the Hotel Monterey Sapporo (1994), whose facade represents an elaboration of Inoue's design for the Grand Hotel, adapted to the narrower plot sizes and high-rise proportions of Japanese cities (fig. 8). A close inspection reveals a high degree of continuity between the two hotels' vertical facade treatments, use of fake setbacks and ornamental balconies, and distinctive roof-level signage. Design features deployed by Yamane in the Grand Hotel's interior and landscaping,

fig. 7 The Grand Hotel's suites incorporated Biedermaier and Rococo design elements. Image courtesy of Inoue Takeshi.

such as a palm garden and pavilion, are likewise reproduced. Meanwhile, at the Hotel Monterey Kobe – opened in 1989, one month before the collapse of the GDR – the formal similarities to the Hotel Bellevue's Saxon courtyard are underscored by the use of pre-fabricated granite panels in the arches and pillars, echoing the emphasis on industrially assembled historicity applied in Dresden and East Berlin (fig. 9). The Baroque-era proportions of the Saxon merchant's house likewise extend to the barrel vaulted ceilings in the hotel's reception and lounge areas. Echoes of the Hotel Bellevue are also evident at the Hotel Monterey Kyoto, where Kajima's architects drew upon strategies devised to link the Hotel Bellevue to the adjacent *palais*, such as using horizontal strips and window treatments as a means of referencing a nearby bank building, designed in 1906 by the architect Tatsuno Kingo (fig. 10).

Conclusion

The accelerated circulation of images and styles, and their sometimes peculiar recombination, is a defining facet of both postmodern aesthetics and

fig. 8 Hotel Monterey Sapporo. Photograph by Max Hirsh.

the globalization of architectural practice. Berlin's Grand Hotel physicalizes their intersection: for while the facade represented a sanitized rendition of Wilhelminian architectural aesthetics, the hotel's massing, structural design, and perspectival orientation towards the street corner rehearsed the basic features of Kajima's standard perimeter-block office typology, which the firm developed in Japan from the 1950s onwards. Inoue had become familiar with that building type while designing a department store in Hiroshima in the early 1970s (fig. 11). In essence, then, the Grand Hotel combines the underlying structure of a Japanese commercial typology with a prefabricated historicist facade typical of East German postmodern urban renewal projects. The duplication of the Grand Hotel in Sapporo can thus be read as an act of typological re-import, enabled by the increasing global mobility of Japanese architects and the attendant exposure that working abroad gave them to postmodern design methods.

In the final years of the GDR, architects experimented with postmodern design techniques in order to instill a sense of patriotism – or what was called *Heimatgefühle* – in a population that was deeply critical of the regime's mismanagement of the economy, and was alienated by the practical and aesthetic shortcomings of the urban landscape. In response, architects and urban plan-

fig. 9 Detail of the inner courtyard of the Hotel Monterey Kobe. Photograph by Max Hirsh.

fig. 10 The Hotel Monterey Kyoto deploys contextual strategies, similar to those used by Kajima's architects in Dresden, in order to reference an adjacent building designed by Tatsuno Kingo, one of Japan's first Western-educated architects. Photograph by Max Hirsh.

ners deployed neo-historicism in order to promote civic pride and an appreciation for local traditions. They also deployed contextualism in order to enact a sense of continuity between these cities' disjointed pre- and postwar urban development. Yet while projects like the Bellevue in Dresden and the Grand

fig. 11 Study for the Mitsukoshi department store in Hiroshima. Image courtesy of Inoue Takeshi.

Hotel in Berlin were motivated by a desire to return to regional styles and local traditions, the means by which they were produced portended a fundamental shift away from national building cultures and towards the globalization of architectural practice. Beneath the neo Wilhelmine facade of the Grand Hotel and the Baroque fixtures of the Bellevue lay design, engineering, and construction processes that incorporated goods, people, and ideas from Japan, Sweden, Yugoslavia, Austria, Hungary, Switzerland, West Germany, France, the United Kingdom and Greece. In that sense, the two hotels can be read as the loci of a nascent European integration: coordinated, somewhat incongruously, by design professionals from Japan.

Contemporary publications about these hotels tended to elide the transnational dimensions of their production. One women's magazine, for example, published a full-color spread of the Grand Hotel, accompanied by a text that suggested that its superior design was the product of fruitful collaboration between workers hailing from all over the GDR – Berlin, Schwerin,

Cottbus, Karl-Marx-Stadt, Erfurt – who had come together to harness the collective strength of the entire republic in order to rebuild the national capital.[23] Grand Hotel certainly hosted an unusual confluence of architects, engineers and construction workers – but they weren't just from Cottbus and Karl-Marx-Stadt, but also from Tokyo and Thessaloniki. Indeed, the patriotic discourse that surrounded historicist renewal projects is rendered problematic when one considers the syncretic conditions surrounding the genesis of these hotels, which were designed by Japanese and East German architects, and which relied on construction workers from the Balkans to assemble West German technical equipment and prefabricated panels from Scandinavia. Moreover, the hotels catered primarily to foreign tourists and investors. After all, these were so-called *Devisenhotels*: where payment could only be made in hard currency, and which remained beyond the grasp of the average East German. In effect, the visual language of contextualism and the political discourse of national solidarity masked the incipient globalization of East Germany's construction industry. Both projects were built with the publicly averred commitment to the preservation of national culture and local identity – yet their ultimate effect was to accelerate the influx of global capital, migrant labor, and foreign visitors into East German cities.

Endnotes

1 This chapter is part of a larger research project on architectural exchanges between Japan and the GDR. The author would like to thank Kohei Kitayama, Setsuo Maruyama, Tadao Nodeki, Ken Tadashi Oshima, Hiroki Sugiyama, Takeshi Inoue and Osamu Ueno for their critical support during the fieldwork stage of this project. He also thanks Kirsten Angermann, Regina Bittner, Eve Blau, Bruno Flierl, Seng Kuan, Alexander Rehding, Tanja Scheffler, Thomas Topfstedt, Daniel Trambaiolo, Manfred Zache, and Jun Zhang for their helpful comments and suggestions; as well as Sayuri Kakiuchi and Anri Maruyama for their research assistance. The project was funded through the generous support of the Hang Seng Bank Golden Jubilee Education Fund for Research.

2 Hans Modrow et al., eds., *Die DDR und Japan* (East Berlin: Dietz Verlag, 1983), 101–102.

3 On the GDR's debt problem see Charles Maier, *Dissolution: The Crisis of Communism and the End of East Germany* (Princeton, NJ: Princeton UP, 1997).

4 Hans-Christian Herrmann, "Japan – ein kapitalistisches Vorbild für die DDR?," *Deutschland Archiv* 39:6 (2006), 1033, 1041.

5 Kazuo Sasagawa, "Vier große Bauprojekte in der ehemaligen DDR: Die schlüsselfertigen Bauprojekte durch [sic] Bauunternehmer Kajima, Tokio, Japan," Lecture at Brandenburg Technical University of Cottbus, June 1999. See also "Cocom: Ein 'Relikt des Kalten Krieges,'" *Der Spiegel* 34 (1988), 80–83.

6 *Fußspur: Kajima DDR Projects, 1985–1987* (Tokyo: Kajima, 2002), 38–39.
7 Ibid., 68–70.
8 On the reception of postmodernism in the GDR see Bruno Flierl and Heinz Hirdina, *Postmoderne und Funktionalismus: Sechs Vorträge* (East Berlin: Verband Bildender Künstler, 1985). See also Klaus Andrä and Wolfgang Weigel, "Tendenzen der städtebaulichen Entwicklung von Stadtzentren in sozialistischen Ländern," *Architektur der DDR* 37:8 (1988); Ule Lammert, ed., *Städtebau: Grundsätze, Methoden, Beispiele, Richtwerte* (East Berlin: VEB Verlag für Bauwesen, 1979); Torsten Lange, "Haus der heiteren Muse: Der Friedrichstadtpalast und die Kritik des 'Postmodernismus' in der DDR," *trans* 26 (March 2015), 128–137.
9 For more on postmodern urban renewal in East Germany see Max Hirsh, "Intelligentsia Design and the Postmodern *Plattenbau*," in *Use Matters: An Alternative History of Architecture*, ed. Kenny Cupers (London: Routledge, 2013), 169–182.
10 *Fußspur*, 17.
11 Takeshi Inoue, Interview with the author at Inoue's home in Higashimatsubara, Tokyo, February 28, 2015.
12 "Ein altes Stück Dresden vor dem Abriß," *Frankfurter Allgemeine Zeitung*, December 22, 1981, 7.
13 *Fußspur*, 59.
14 Tadao Nodeki, Interview with the author at Kajima KI Building, Akasaka, Tokyo, March 2, 2015.
15 *Fußspur*, 84–85.
16 "Der Freischütz mit der Wunderharfe," *Der Spiegel* 7 (1985), 176–180.
17 On the reconstruction of Friedrichstraße see Florian Urban, *Neo-Historical East Berlin: Architecture and Urban Design in the German Democratic Republic, 1970–1990* (Farnham: Ashgate, 2009), 181–214.
18 Inoue, Interview.
19 Ibid.
20 Roland Korn, "Schöpferische Beiträge der Architekten für die Beschleunigung des Wohnungsbaus und die weitere Ausgestaltung unserer Hauptstadt Berlin," *Architektur der DDR* 5 (1985), 263.
21 Inoue, Interview.
22 Ibid. See also Osamu Ueno, Interview with the author at Kajima KI Building, Akasaka, Tokyo, March 2, 2015.
23 Conrad Tenner, "Jungbrunnen für eine alte Straße," *Für Dich: Illustrierte Wochenzeitung für die Frau* 37 (1986), 12.

Joseph Bedford

Being Underground: Dalibor Vesely, Phenomenology and Architectural Education during the Cold War

In April 1974, Dalibor Vesely – the Czech *émigré* who played a fundamental role in the development of architectural education in the West in the 1970s and 1980s – encountered the American metropolis for the first time. On a road trip with his former student Daniel Libeskind, he arrived in Atlanta and visited John Portman's recently completed Hyatt Regency Hotel, riding its glass elevator to have a drink in its revolving rooftop restaurant (fig. 1). From the window of the restaurant Vesely glimpsed, for the first time, the fragmented asphalt landscape of parking lots and office blocks of Atlanta's new street level. He later recalled how, soon after emerging from the hotel at midnight, he and Libeskind had been delighted to discover the old city still lying beneath that new street level, "underneath [...] kept as it used to be; [with] cobbled streets [...] street lamps, and old bars."

> Suddenly we heard music, we discovered a staircase that took us down to the old Atlanta and everything was going on as if it was a normal evening. We found a bar where the sound of music was coming from and there was an old guy in his [...] nineties, playing on a very old piano and singing. We sat there, drinking gin and tonic until 2am.[1]

fig. 1 Advert for John Portman's Hyatt Regency Hotel placed in Newsweek, 1965.

This encounter between the Central European phenomenologist and the American metropolis captures the way that the theme of crisis was configured in Vesely's work, such that what lay below was considered "normal," while what lay above was considered abnormal. In Atlanta, Vesely saw the original ground of the city as buried beneath, covered-up by a historical process whereby modern life now spins, dizzy in its abstraction (fig. 2). As Vesely said to Libeskind's students, just before setting-off on their trip:

> We have fewer and fewer connections with the earth, fewer and fewer connections with the ground. Fewer and fewer links. Not only gravity but food, air; we are dizzy. […] From this, technology could advance to what it is for us. Again, what made this possible was the development of absolute analytical methods; the shifting from the visual to the imaginary. The creation of a perfectly controllable system – highway systems, new town centers or the systems of the private world, the regressive utopias. […] We are caught in a whole structure, a whole institution, a whole falseness.[2]

In Atlanta, therefore, the crisis of the human condition – in which instrumental reason had covered-over the human relation to being – was seen to be

fig. 2 Postcard, "Underground Atlanta," circa 1975.

manifest in the historical transformation of the city. That is, the encapsulation of Atlanta's old town by a layer of modern development presented Vesely with a spatial and urban image of phenomenology's diagnosis of the imprisonment of being in history.

Yet, crucial to this diagnosis was the fact that being could only ever be covered over. A vague conscience of being would always remain as a latent layer of existence. Underground Atlanta delighted Vesely that summer evening because its image was also one of resistance against oppression. Having spoken of the falseness of the present technological world to Libeskind's students, Vesely went on to tell them that all was not lost; that nonetheless, in spite of technology; "In front of you is a reality, […] not the created nor the constituted, but […] life itself."[3] That is, despite its oppression by instrumental reason, the life-world endured as a residual layer within the perception of reality; ever-present, underneath all the contemporary historical forms engendered by instrumental reason. It was still "in front of you," and still accessible just as the depth of the city was still accessible – one simply had to follow the staircase down that phenomenology had provided.

Phenomenology and Architecture in Underground Prague

Phenomenology had, from the beginning, diagnosed and sought to overcome the imagined autonomy of the subject dirempt from its objects. Its descriptions of "subjective" experience were always intended to reveal how the subject was related to transcendental layers of reality: first to the essences of things; then to being as such; to embodiment; language; and finally, to the world as a whole.[4] Yet, despite being a holistic discourse that aimed to bridge the divide between subject and object, relating beings to the world as a whole, phenomenology was also seen as a critical discourse that articulated a historical division between the instrumentality of modernity and the non-instrumentality of the premodern world. That is, in critically opposing modernity, phenomenology mirrored modernity's oppositional character.

Yet, while Vesely understood phenomenology in his own time as describing a Manichean opposition between instrumental reason and the life-world, this opposition is best understood today as a product of the particular historical time and place in which phenomenological ideas developed and in which Vesely encountered them, rather than as inherent to phenomenology itself. A recent body of literature by philosophers such as Leonard Lawlor, James Dodd, David Carr, and Dermot Moran, has begun to situate phenomenology in its historical context and argue that its motif of crisis and its method of bracketing were always dialectical and paradoxical and only became strict and dogmatic as a consequence of the political circumstances of the time.[5]

It is a peculiar fact that phenomenology flourished in the bifurcated reality of Eastern and Central Europe in the twentieth century, under conditions of political and cultural oppression in interwar Germany and neo-Stalinist Czechoslovakia.[6] Phenomenology's success in such a historical context was partly due to the socio-political implication of the holistic dimension of its discourse. Life in a totalitarian state was politically divided insofar as the "official culture" sponsored by the regime could be said to "cover-up" the older traditions of the Czech lands. Phenomenology's account of modernity in crisis seemed capable of diagnosing (and potentially curing) such a divided situation insofar as it promised to show how the surface of reality was inextricably related to its deeper transcendental and historical layers.

The socio-political implications of such phenomenological ideas had been evident from the beginning. As a Jew in Nazi Germany, Edmund Husserl expanded his own philosophical critique of modern science at the end of his life to account for the crisis of European civilization. And the Czech philosopher Jan Patočka, one of Husserl's last students in Freiburg who would become the principal intellectual influence on Vesely's theoretical orientation, was not only close to Husserl during this last period, but in his own

fig. 3 Photographs taken by the Czech Secret Police, Courtesy of the Czechoslovak Secret Police Archives. Author unknown.

experience in Prague continued to reflect on the theme of crisis under ongoing conditions of oppression (fig. 3).

Patočka escaped arrest when the Communists seized power in 1948, but was expelled from the university for his "bourgeois background," and because phenomenology was perceived as an idealist refutation of Marxist-Leninism.[7] He was fortunate to find work in the Comenius Archives and managed to publish occasionally, though only by concealing his own philosophy within factographic histories of science. After Patočka had written the introduction to the Czech translation of Husserl's *Crisis of the European Sciences*, for example, the book was only allowed to be sold once his text was literally cut out of the already-published book with a knife. And when he attempted to give a paper on Husserl in Bulgaria, the organizers interrupted his reading; his paper was removed from the proceedings of the conference; and his passport was seized permanently at the Prague airport when he returned. He only managed to continue his philosophy in underground seminars and it has survived only due to transcripts of those events having been reconstructed by his students and circulated as Samizdat texts.

Thus when Vesely studied phenomenology with Patočka in this underground context between 1960 and 1963, having cautiously approached the secret location of his seminars in an attempt to avoid the eye of the secret police, he was encountering phenomenology's conceptual tools at a time and place in which the polarization between tradition and technological progress had become deeply politicized by the ideology of neo-Stalinism.[8] And when he applied the phenomenological understanding that he had acquired in

Prague to the crisis that he saw facing architecture, he inverted the opposition between tradition and technological progress while maintaining its dogmatic character, defending tradition to the inverse degree that the neo-Stalinist regime in Czechoslovakia continued to suppress it.[9]

Writing in his first text on architecture in 1963, for example, at the end of his period attending Patočka's seminars, Vesely drew a sharp distinction between the spatiality of the life-world and "abstract space," and used this conceptual division to criticize what he called "quantitative," "abstract environments," "utterly devoid of a direct relation not only to the natural world but also to natural human existence."[10] In this first theoretical text, which reviewed the techno-utopian projects of the time as presented by Michael Ragon in his 1962 book *Where Shall We Live Tomorrow?,* Vesely deemed that the projects presented by Ragon had lost their relation to the historical depth of human perception and the historical depth of the city, because of their pre-occupation with the dominant idea of abstract space and thus their general submission to a culture of technological thinking.

Just as Vesely could not easily include the political reality of life and its dominant technological and calculative mode of thinking in an authoritarian state as an integral part of the whole of history, neither could he easily include an abstract understanding of modern architectural space as an integral part of the whole of architecture. In Vesely's discourse, the Heideggerian crisis of being and the Husserlian crisis of Europe came to be expressed as the civic crisis of the abstraction of space and of the forgetting of architecture's relationship to the deepest levels of cultural traditions. And given the politicized context in which he absorbed phenomenological ideas and Husserlian history, the crisis as he expressed it within architecture took on the non-dialectical form given to it by its development in the context of a life lived under an authoritarian regime.

Throughout his life, Vesely would continue to figure the relation between the depth of tradition and technological progress in similar oppositional terms. He would later remark, for example, in his seminar teaching at Cambridge several decades later that the "instrumental representation of reality" is nothing other than "reason motivated by the Will to Power,"[11] that it is a "domain of violence," and that "the phenomenological" by contrast struggles against such violence, and "struggles with the problem of overcoming the reified domain of thinking."[12]

Remaining Underground in the West

Vesely fled Prague for London in August 1968 as the Warsaw Pact tanks rolled in to the city and, once exiled in the West, began teaching his semi-

fig. 4 Essex University Campus, Photograph John McKean, 1972.

nars on phenomenology to architects in the first independent MA course in The History and Theory of Architecture anywhere in the world. Established by the architect-historian Joseph Rykwert, this new kind of course emerged as part of the expanding and subdividing institutional space of postwar higher education within the newly founded art history department of Essex University (fig. 4).[13] By employing Vesely as his teaching partner, Rykwert gave his approach to phenomenology a platform from which it would continue to flourish in the West as part of the postmodern critique of modern architecture.

This flourishing continued to be propelled by the twinned logic of holism and division because, yet again, phenomenology found itself in another kind of bifurcated reality, in a new space for "theory" initially separated institutionally from the space of design practice.[14] This separation signaled a context within architectural education of antagonism between on the one hand new interpretative research into deeper historical meaning and existing approaches to history; either reduced to a history of style or rejected by techno-scientific positivism.[15]

This antagonistic context that was perfectly captured by the wording of a petition that the students of Rykwert's new course put to the new chair of the department Michael Podro in 1972, when they discovered that he was attempting to close the course after only four years of its operation. They wrote to Podro stating that the value of the course was precisely in the way that it defended tradition against mere utility, writing that the course "serves as the basis for the task of re-founding an architecture of meaning and purpose beyond the narrow demands of utility."[16]

This opposition was also silently embodied within the contrast between the places of theory and practice themselves (fig. 5). Vesely's seminar teaching

fig. 5 Essex University Art History Department Corridor, Photograph John McKean, 1972.

took place in a small 10ft x 10ft room, of the long art-history corridor, in a remote campus an hour from London where he was at that moment supervising design students in the Diploma school at the Architectural Association. In his own words, "I remember sitting on a train between London and Colchester and doing the phenomenology over there and the studio here. I remember always being […] anxious to see […] how those two could possibly eventually connect. […] I was in a state of schizophrenia."[17] And with this additional form of spatial division exacerbating the institutional distance between theory and practice, the titular space around Vesely quickly assumed an atmosphere that paralleled that of underground Prague.

He adopted an ascetic lifestyle as an *émigré* resisting domestication in his new home. And like Vesely, the academic community that he fostered believed themselves to be standing apart from the fatefully instrumental nature of the contemporary present. While phenomenology was not forbidden by the state leadership in Britain, it nonetheless garnered little favor within the institutions in which Vesely taught, given over as they were to Kantian and Hegelian Idealism and British Analytical philosophy. When the course was forced to move into various private apartments and basement settings, after Podro did eventually cut the funds that previously paid for Vesely's teaching, this only further bolstered its underground atmosphere. From 1973 seminars began to be convened on the train, then in student apartments, and eventually in the basement kitchen of the Soane Museum and the disused darkroom at the back of the Royal Academy. The holistic impulse conveyed in the content of Vesely's seminars was thus implicitly reinforced by the division expressed by the unofficial settings in which they took place.[18]

The students in these tiny basement spaces would find themselves listening for three hours as the room gradually filled with cigarette smoke, hearing Vesely speak first about the fundamental continuity between perception and

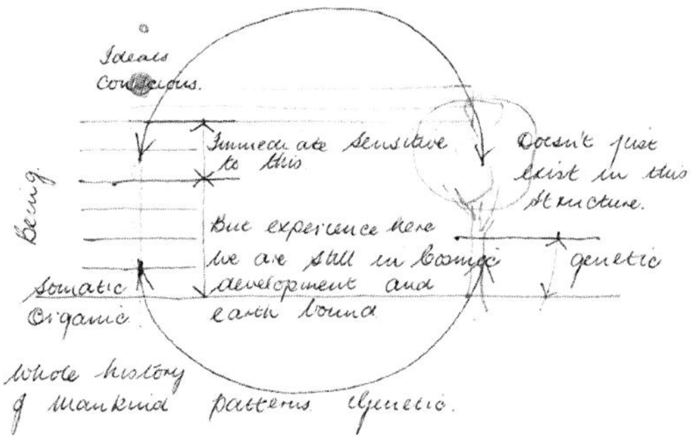

fig. 6 Dalibor Vesely, Diagram of Communication between the Concrete and the Articulate (copied down by Graham Frecknall, 1970).

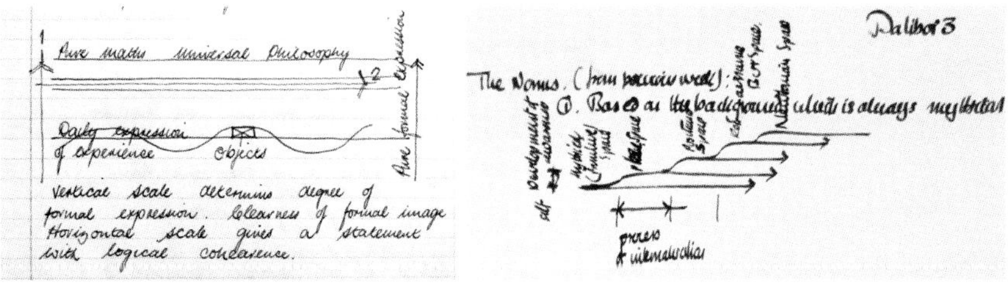

fig. 7 Diagrams of Crisis and Division between the communication of the lifeworld and the over-formalized abstraction of technical representation (copied down by Graham Frecknall and Michael Foster, 1970).

the whole of given reality – a continuity that Vesely would illustrate with circular diagrams showing a communication between concrete and articulate levels of reality (fig. 6) – and then about the crisis of history in which this fundamental continuity had been covered-over by highly formalized, abstract representation; a division that he would illustrate with a series of horizontally striated diagrams (fig. 7).

In these later diagrams, what Vesely considered to be the properly oscillating movement of representation kept within a zone of limited formalization, now existed beneath a surface coating of purely abstract representation, appearing in his diagrams in a delaminated region separated from the lifeworld by an unbridgeable gap. In one particular diagram with its temporal axis scaled to historical time, that oscillating movement of the life-world was also labeled as a "background" of "mythical space," and above it the increasing levels of formalization advancing towards "Newtonian Space" were shown piling-up one on top of the other. History was thus presented to the students as a process of increasing abstraction from the original ground of lived experience.

Vesely's diagrams capture succinctly in visual terms the overarching message that he was at that moment presenting to the student architects in his classroom after his arrival in the West. They depict the whole of reality as hav-

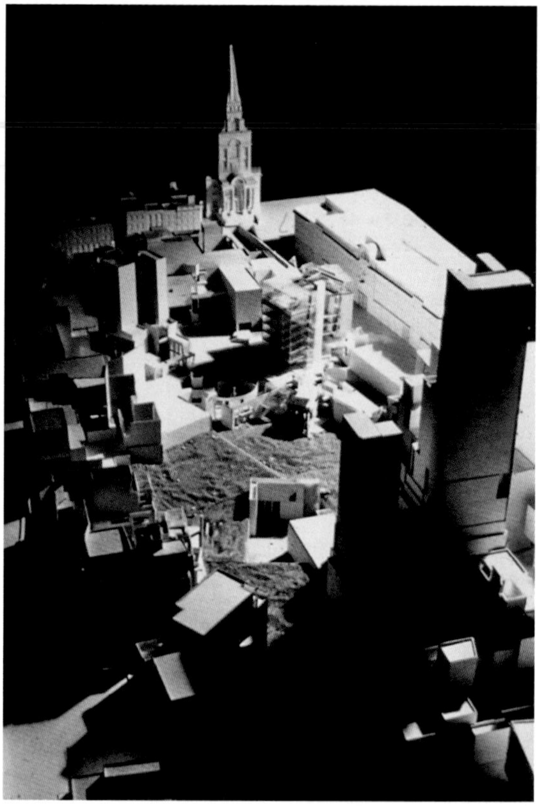

fig. 8 Cambridge Diploma Studio 1, Spitalfields Market, 1988–89. Photo courtesy Clare Gerrard.

ing been divided in two across historical time such that a truer layer of latent holistic reality had now become imprisoned in a partial reality of abstract representations – just as Czech culture had been imprisoned by the regime.[19]

Being Underground in the Design Studio

These ideas also informed Vesely's studio teaching, even though there was no direct link between his seminars and the drawing board. The idea of the whole and the idea of its division appeared within the studio in the way that Vesely framed the brief for each studio project. Projects were usually sited next to a significant church to provide a cultural context to the students that included a reference to the latent presence of a deeper European tradition based in Platonic philosophy and Christianity (fig. 8). And nearby would be a mark of urban crisis, whether a 19th century railway line dividing areas in the city or the urban gentrification of development either in the London Docklands or on the edge of the City of London.

Throughout his studio teaching, Vesely was continuously vigilant in policing any use of representation that seemed too instrumental in his view.

fig. 9 Example of Student Work that Vesely considered too rational. Drawing by Robert Wood, 1984.

fig. 10 Example of Student Work that Vesely considered more poetic. Collage by Matthew Barac, 1985.

He insisted that students recognize the primary nature of poetic representation and that they make all other forms of "calculative" or "reified" uses of representation secondary in their work. One student, in 1985, was told, for example, to sit to one side of the studio and not to participate further because he insisted on drawing in a hardline, rationalist style (fig. 9) that he had developed in his training at a previous school, and because he refused to adopt Vesely's favored technique of ambiguous metaphorical collage (fig. 10).[20]

Even though themes of the whole and its division dominated both Vesely's seminar and studio, and even though he spoke passionately about how to create a continuity between a building and deeper layers of historical reality, he was never able to overcome the institutional division between theory and practice and synthesize them in one unified project; nor would he in the end, despite his argument to the contrary, have wished to. His seminars always continued to be independent from the studio, taking place in the library after hours with the door locked, and his design students were not actively solicited to attend. He alluded to phenomenology in his studio, but he never wished to explicate it fully or translate it into anything as instrumental as a "method" for design.

In the way that he taught, therefore, as much as in what he taught, Vesely cultivated a degree of discontinuity, and thus crisis, in the separation that he maintained between the institutional spaces of theory and practice; a separation rooted in the first years of his teaching moving between Essex and London. In his teaching, Vesely implicitly recognized the dialectical or paradoxical understanding of crisis, by continuing to inhabit the distinctly separated roles of seminar theorist and studio professor; one moment tunneling down into the interpretative research activities within the seminar room, separated from the studio space – after hours, in dim light, in a locked room – and the next moment sketching with the students at the drawing board encouraging the practical task of design.

The practical form of Vesely's teaching in seminar and studio, therefore, carried the paradoxical nature of phenomenology that Lawlor, Dodd, Carr, and Moran, have begun to identify as a more accurate understanding of phenomenology's themes of crisis and bracketing. Vesely's explicit discourse of crisis, however, which manifested itself in his diagrams in seminars, through the narratives of his studio briefs and in his prejudices about drawing techniques, continued to convey the starker opposition between historical meaning and technological progress in the politicized form that it had been cast in by the context of neo-Stalinist Czechoslovakia. Yet this explicit level of his crisis discourse was just that; an imprint of the specific historical horizon in which he lived. It was neither inherent to phenomenology, nor – in the end – ever sustained in the practices of his own teaching.

That is to say: while Vesely might have expressed the politicized form in which the relationship between historical meaning and technological progress had been cast when he suggested that Atlanta's modern urban development was abnormal in contrast to the "normal" world that still existed underground, and while he might have expressed his delight in descending from the dizzy heights above the city into the smoke-filled speakeasies and Jazz bars below ground, in his teaching he remained half way between these two levels and continued to move between the crisis of reflection and immersion in the everyday habits and rituals of the practical world.

Endnotes

1 Dalibor Vesely, Interview #1, January 3, 2011, (Tape 45): 21:27 mins.

2 David Leatherbarrow, Student Notes, 1975.

3 Ibid.

4 This sequence designates the key historical stages of the development of phenomenological reflection that were synthesised in Vesely's thinking: from Edmund Husserl's transcendental phenomenology with its focus on quasi-Cartesian descriptions of the consciousness of essences as mental contents; to Martin Heidegger's existential phenomenology and its focus upon an underlying anxiety in the face of the question of being and non-being; to Maurice Merleau-Ponty's focus upon structures of embodiment; to Hans-Georg Gadamer's hermeneutic phenomenology with its focus upon culture and language; to Jan Patočka, who brought together these different accounts of transcendental reality and preconditions of conscious reflection under the Platonic notion of "the whole," and who, as Vesely's teacher, introduced him to this way of synthesising the diverse tradition of phenomenological thought. On Patočka's synthesis of phenomenology and his conception of "the whole" see in particular Jan Patočka, *Body, Community, Language, World*, (Chicago: Open Court, 1999) and Jan Patočka, *Plato and Europe* (Stanford, California: Stanford University press, 2002).

5 See in particular Leonard Lawlor, *Derrida and Husserl: The Basic Problem of Phenomenology* (Bloomington, IN: Indiana University Press, 2002), 13; James Dodd, *Crisis and Reflection: An Essay on Husserl's Crisis of the European Sciences* (Dordrecht: Springer Netherlands, 2006), 46–52; David Carr, *Phenomenology and the Problem of History: A Study of Husserl's Transcendental Philosophy* (Evanston, IL: Northwestern University Press, 2009), 241; and Dermot Moran, *Husserl's Crisis of the European Sciences and Transcendental Phenomenology: An Introduction* (Cambridge: Cambridge University Press, 2012), 186–196. Each of these authors converge in their own way on the observation that the concept of crisis in Husserl's writing was never capable of drawing a sharp dividing line between instrumentality and the life-world. And as Lawlor argues in regards to the paradoxical nature of its method of bracketing, drawing on Eugene Fink's early account of phenomenology "with the phenomenological reduction, one neither passes outside of the world nor remains within the world; one neither remains in the sense of being as an existent thing nor passes to non-being." (Lawlor, p. 13).

6 As the historian Michael Gubser has written; "phenomenology was widely seen by East European literati as [...] offering a vision of [...] freedom and transcendence that stood in stark contrast to the stultifying realities of [...] communism." Michael Gubser, *The Far Reaches: Phenomenology, Ethics, and Social Renewal in Central Europe* (Stanford, CA: Stanford University Press, 2014), 133.

7 "When the communists seized power in 1948 Patočka escaped arrest but [...] was [...] expelled from the university. The ideologists of Marxist Leninism tried to ensure his teaching was not allowed to reach disciples either by word of mouth or the written word" Barbara Day, *The Velvet Philosophers* (London: Continuum, 1999), 8–9.

8 The process of "de-Stalinization" initiated by Nikita Khrushchev after Stalin's death in 1953 was delayed in Czechoslovakia. As the historian Tony Judt writes, "The Czech experience of high Stalinist terror was so recent and so extreme that the Party leaders were reluctant to risk any admission of 'error' – lest the consequences of doing so dwarf the '56 upheavals in Poland or even Hungary. De-Stalinization in Czechoslovakia was thus deliberately delayed as long as possible..." Tony Judt, *Postwar: A History of Europe Since 1945* (London: Vintage, 2010), 436–437. It is for this reason that the regime in Czechoslovakia has been called neo-Stalinist by historians such as Judt (p. 428). The reform process began in 1962 when the 12th Communist Party Congress initiated an investigation of the show trials of the early 1950s, opening the door to the public acknowledgement that the Slánský trials had been staged. Yet as Judt puts it, "despite this *defacto* acknowledgement of past injustices, the Party and its Stalin-era leadership remained intact and in office." (p. 436). It was with the economic stagnation that became evident by 1963 and the call from economists that economic reform would require political reform that the process of liberalization properly began. Vesely's studies with Patočka thus preceded the years of liberalization in Czechoslovakia, which unfolded – after some delay – between 1963 and the crushing of the Prague Spring in August 1968.

9 The defense of tradition apparent in the short-lived phenomenon of Socialist Realism pushed upon Czech architects from Moscow in the early 1950s had little remaining credibility by 1960. Czech architects had largely mocked Socialist Realism in private, nicknaming it "Sorela" (a brand of popular shoe polish in the interwar years), as it meant covering their structures with superficial historicist molding. See Kimberly Elman Zarecor, *Manufacturing a Socialist Modernity: Housing in Czechoslovakia, 1945–1960* (Pittsburgh: University of Pittsburgh Press, 2011), 114. Czech architects including those Vesely named as formative influences upon him, such as Joseph Fragner, had reluctantly modified their designs in the early 1950s by adding such historicist elements, but then quickly stripped them off their projects before construction. If anything, Krushchev's intervention in 1954 to encourage the construction industry to adopt industrial methods led architecture in Czechoslovakia towards the increasingly centralized and industrialized methods of building construction, which Vesely later referred to as "the wasteland of the state run offices." Dalibor Vesely, "The Creativity of Time," *Zlatý řez*, no.13 (1996), 38–41 (p. 40). Vesely's defense of tradition is best understood as a defense of the Baroque legacy of Czechoslovakia affectionately written about by the art historians whom he admired and befriended – such as Vaclav Richter, Oldřicha Stefana, Vojtěch Volavka, and Václav Štec – against the industrialized building culture represented by *Stavoprojekt*; one of the largest State Offices in the world with 11,000 employees.

10 Dalibor Vesely, Afterward to Michel Ragon: *Kde Budeme Zit Zitra*, trans. Vera Smetanova, Jan Cejka (1963), 163. Trans. Tim West.

11 Dalibor Vesely, Mphil Seminars, 1988–89, Becket Recording Session #8.

12 Dalibor Vesely, Mphil Seminars, 1988–89, Becket Recording Session #7.

13 The Coldstream Report had mandated that all art schools in Britain include history teaching as fifteen percent of their curricular load spurring the growth in art history education under which new art history departments such as Essex and new MA courses such as Rykwert's were established. The Coldstream report, chaired by Sir William Coldstream and published as *First Report of the National Advisory Council on Art Education* (London, HMSO, 1960) stated that "about 15 % of the total course should be devoted to the history of art and complementary studies." (p. 8).

14 Dedicated seminar courses were not a common feature of higher education in the early 1960s; so much so that Ian Watt the former Dean of the University of East Anglia, one of the new "plate glass" universities like Essex, sought to advocate for the increasing use of seminars, in his 1964 paper "The Seminar," *Universities Quarterly*, 18, September, 1964. At many UK architectures schools in the early 1960s history teaching was still delivered exclusively in the form of lectures. Having experienced the German culture of the seminar directly studying informally with Rudolf Wittkower at the Warburg seminars in the early 1950s Rykwert sought to establish a form of study along the original lines of the German model. The most receptive conditions for the establishment of the dedicated seminar course as a new form for history and theory research lay not in the school of architecture where history and theory teaching was still seen as an adjunct to studio and was delivered still as an instruction in style. Rather it lay in the institutional space of expanding graduate level art history teaching in new plate glass universities looking to adopt the seminar form and looking to expand MA courses to supply a new demand for art history teaching, a space which emerged at some distance from the architectural studio.

15 Rykwert later recalled the resistance towards this new course writing that it "was seen as useless by some "academic" groups—but almost as a threat by others. Sometime after it was approved and announced the Vice-Chancellor asked to see me. He had been telephoned … by the Education Secretary of the RIBA and—to his shocked surprise—instructed that he was to suppress the proposed course" Joseph Rykwert, "Architecture and the Public Good," *Research and Practice in Architecture* (Helsinki: Building Information Ltd, 2001), 13. Similarly, the establishment modernist architect Maxwell Fry also expressed his suspicion about Rykwert's new endeavour in 1978 writing in a private correspondence with Jim Cadbury Brown assessing Rykwert's application to the Royal Academy to adopt his course, that "There is a case for architectural scholarship though a more doubtful one for theory or the study of theory," and that there is "a much more doubtful case for a study if architectural-historicism in schools of architecture where in my experience its introduction together with the fadish practice of young people writing supposedly learned dissertations has plagued the devil among them, and helped to give them the false impression of themselves and to divert them from their proper course …" Letter from Maxwell Fry to Jim Cadbury Brown, April 18, 1978. RA Uncatalogued file.

16 Student Petition, May 1972, Essex University Library, Special Collection.

17 Dalibor Vesely interviewed by Helen Thomas at the Architectural Association (January 22, 2002). Cited in Helen Thomas, "Invention in the

shadow of history: Joseph Rykwert at the University of Essex," *Journal of Architectural Education* 58:2 (2004), 39–45, (p. 41).

18 Even when Vesely's seminars eventually found their safer home at Cambridge University in 1978, Vesely was not allowed to be paid for his seminar teaching as University policy stipulated that there was no provision for taught courses for a research-level MPhil. Thus at Cambridge from 1985 onwards, as at Essex after 1974, Vesely's teaching efforts became a labor of love as his seminars became unofficial.

19 Vesely later argued that the world he had experienced in Prague was not different in kind, but only in degree, from the world which he found in the West: "Behind the official politics of the day are deeper issues and problems common to countries in both the East and West. The technical transformation of reality, politics and everyday life, the cult of efficiency and the determinism of technological and economic thinking tend to transcend political systems. It is not difficult to see retrospectively that in certain areas such as politics or everyday life, for instance, the process of technical transformation was probably more radical and advanced in the East, despite the general tendency of all industrial societies to develop a more effective form of an appropriation and monopolization of power, collecting and control of information and steady promotion of surveillance." Dalibor Vesely, "The Humanity of Architecture" in Neil Leach, ed., *Architecture and Revolution: Contemporary Perspectives on Central and Eastern Europe* (London: Routledge, 1999), 139.

20 As Robert Wood put it, "At one point he called me the death of culture. He didn't formally say leave my studio but the subtext was that he didn't want to talk to me anymore because I wasn't playing ball. […] It was just me that was singled out in this way. The questioning was what he had resisted. I just had lots of questions. Not even doubt, just lots of questions." Robert Wood, Interview, 14:22 – 17:34 mins. And as another of Vesely's students from Cambridge in 1979, Fred London, put it, speaking about Vesely and his co-teachers: "It was this very combative approach to teaching. […] They were definitely trying to people their studio with acolytes and not with awkward buggers who would ask questions. That is how it seemed." Fred London, Interview, 54:48–1:10:41 mins. And in the words of another student "You couldn't really question them. […] They just didn't broach dissenters at all. […] it was that you are either with us or against us. It was totally black and white. […] If you dissented, and you were deemed to be a non-believer, then you were out." Student from 1978, Interview, 17:50, 23:13 mins.

Daniel Kiss

From the Hungarian Tulip Dispute to a Post-Socialist Kulturkampf

It was not possible to openly discuss politically engaged issues under the socialist regime in Hungary. The critical architectural discourse of the 1970s over the possibility of humanizing socialist mass housing was one such rare occasion. It was first silenced, then absorbed after the regime change by a broader Kulturkampf between the traditionalist, populist faction of the intelligentsia and the cosmopolitan, urbanist one. This paper is based on the hypothesis that, while the so-called Tulip Dispute of 1975–1976 is often praised as a decisive moment in having facilitated a paradigm shift and progress in architecture, it has instead ended up decades later contributing to an ideological standoff.

Prelude: The Social and Architectural Dilemmas of Socialist Mass Housing

The first Hungarian public architectural debate on socialist mass housing and on attempts to humanize it rather symbolically marked the last year of the socialist regime's ambitious fifteen-year housing program that had targeted the construction of a million dwellings between 1960 and 1975. As part of that engagement, the first housing complex in Budapest using large prefabricated panels had been erected (fig. 1).[1] The implemented technology, imported from the Soviet Union, was based on a French construction system.[2]

A few years into this program, novelist György Konrád and sociologist Iván Szelényi published their critical research in The Sociological Problems of New Mass Housing Estates.[3] They argued that by studying new housing developments in socialist Eastern Europe, one can observe the most distinctive effects of socialist urban transformation. This, according to them, is due to the fact that new housing had been built almost exclusively in the form of mass housing estates (financed by the state), then administratively allocated. Consequently, Konrád and Szelényi had expected a rather strong working class presence in the estates they studied. In contrast, the authors found to their surprise that despite official propaganda on the rise of the proletariat, the bulk of the working class was nowhere to be seen among residents of the new mass-housing estates. It was rather the middle class – professionals, intellectuals and bureaucrats – who in large part inhabited these recent developments. Ultimately, their empirical study proved that new public housing was systematically allocated to higher income groups. According to Szelényi, this suggested two conclusions.[4] First, housing inequalities were created under socialist distribution of habitat, and second, they were created via administrative allocation, a distinctively socialist mechanism meant to replace "unfair" market methods of capitalism. According to Szelényi, the existence of urban social inequality in socialism also exemplifies how mechanisms of urban economy under different modes of production can result in similar urban phenomena.

Architects at the time had mixed emotions concerning prefabricated construction systems and the state's ambitious housing program. On the one hand, they perceived these as projects leading to the massive homogenization of the built environment and as tools of the Party-led state in marginalizing the architecture profession into engineering. On this account, topics of characterless milieus and routinized modernism appeared in the professional discourse by the 1970s.[5] The exaggerated centralization of building policies and the mass construction of housing were held responsible for hampering their possibility of self-expression.[6] On the other hand, most architects acknowledged the potential of prefabricated mass housing in responding to housing shortages. The latter was a central issue in the 1960s and 1970s, as the proletarianization of a formerly agricultural workforce had yet to be followed by a comparably rapid migration of this population from rural areas to urbanized centers, as Szelényi and Konrád pointed out in "Social Conflicts of Delayed Urbanization," their empirical study from 1971. They pointed out that in society's socialist transformation in the 1960s, urban population growth appeared to have fallen behind the expansion of the industrial population. According to the authors, this period of the "actually existing socialist societies" could be best described as a process of "underurbanization." This term referred to the regional system in which an increasing proportion of the newly proletarianized population maintained rural residences and commuted to urban work-

fig. 1 Budapest's first precast panel apartment blocks under construction in 1965. Source: Imre Perényi, "A korszerű város" [The up-to-date city], Népszabadság, October 13, 1965, accessed February 15, 2016, http://indafoto.hu/fovarosiblog/image/22071905-7fd5fc49.

places.[7] Furthermore, architects looked back at their brief 1950s misadventure with socialist realism as a detour imposed by a totalitarian regime and were all the more keen to embrace the modernist discourse, fully rehabilitated in Hungary by the 1960s.[8]

The Tulip Dispute and the Possibility of an Antimodernist Turn in Architecture

In this social, political and professional context in 1975, a heated architectural debate emerged apropos of a newly erected mass-housing complex in the provincial town of Paks. Young architects of the so-called Pécs Group – a studio within the state planning bureau Pécsiterv – engaged vernacular traditions and applied ornaments in the form of abstracted tulips in an attempt to humanize the facades of the prefabricated blocks (fig. 2). The group had become identifiable in 1973 when they exhibited and published their architectural manifest, "Csak tiszta forrásból" ["Only from Pure Sources"], making reference to architect Károly Kós and composer Béla Bartók as champions of folk art (fig. 3).[9] The Tulip Dispute commenced in the periodicals Élet és Irodalom and Magyar Építőművészet. It is seen as a decisive moment

fig. 2 The tulip-ornamented blocks in Paks after their completion in 1975. Source: Jeffrey Cook, Seeking Structure from Nature. The Organic Architecture of Hungary (Basel: Birkhäuser, 1995), 25.

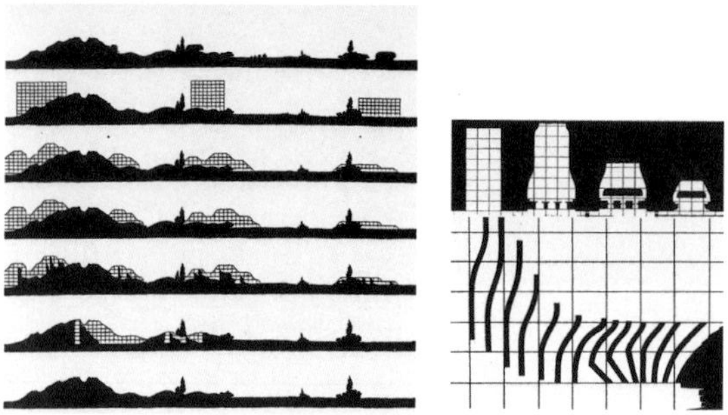

fig. 3 "Only From Pure Sources", plates six and nine from the Pécs Group's exhibit in 1973. Source: Jeffrey Cook, Seeking Structure from Nature. The Organic Architecture of Hungary (Basel: Birkhäuser, 1995), 24.

in Hungary's postwar architectural discourse, for having reinstated issues of regional and national identity in relation to mainstream modernism and European identity as central themes for the intellectual field in architecture.[10] The "Tulip houses" were designed within the framework of the socialist economic system's formal rationality that defined cost effectiveness and industrialized mass production of housing as the central criteria for socialist architecture. As such, the project was not meant as a fundamental critique of socialist mass housing, rather as an attempt to humanize its architecture. Key protagonists in the profession, however, criticized the experimental view of the project's young architects, claiming that it promoted antimodernism. Máté Major, head of the Chair for the History of Architecture at the Technical University of Budapest – himself a trusting communist and a dogmatic modernist – took the role of leading the opinions. While most Western accounts of the debate have had a hard time finding sufficient explanations for why the folk-art-inspired attempt at reform received such a harsh critique,[11] sociologist Virág Molnár offers one in her review of the dispute. Molnár interprets mainstream architects' vehement actions against the "Tulip houses" and their "regressive, authoritarian academicism"[12] as a consequence of their self-identification with modernism as a last link to international trends and European cultural identity.[13]

fig. 4 Between secession and modernism: the decorated facade of the Leitersdorfer House in Budapest, built between 1910 and 1912. Source: Pál Nádai, "Lajta Béla életműve" [Béla Lajta's Oeuvre], Ars Una, Vol. 8–9 (1924), 310, accessed March 10, 2016, http://lajtaarchiv.hu/wp-content/gallery/irasok-1921-1945-kozott/arsuna_1923_24_0003.jpg.

Their critique exhibited different arguments that attempted to reveal a flawed and reactionary nature in this tulip experiment. Making reference to the folk-art-inspired, antimodernist agenda of the semi-fascist interwar regime and to the socialist realism of the postwar Stalinist state, Major concluded that architecture movements in 20th-century Hungary that turned to folk culture had hidden political agendas, embraced authoritarian regimes and rejected progressive worldviews.[14] Others called attention to contradictions between the factory-produced buildings and their ornaments referencing handcraft motifs, claiming that decoration is mere camouflage that masks but does not settle problems of mass-housing blocks.[15] A third line of argument was also advanced, alleging that the young architects grasped the wrong issues, as the problem that needed to be resolved was not prefabricated construction technology itself but its poor application.[16]

Proponents of the Paks experiment, on the contrary, made reference to Hungarian Secession as an important milestone towards the definition of a modern architecture influenced both by international trends and regional heritage. Gábor Preisich pointed out that Secession heralded modernism insofar as it freed architecture from bondage to the classical order.[17] Preisich claimed that modernism's rage against Secession was a mere result of its aim of distinguishing itself. In contrast, referencing Béla Lajta's Rózsavölgyi House in Budapest, an early modernist building richly decorated with folk ornaments (fig. 4), he characterized the transition from Secession to modernism as smooth and gradual. Others used the secessionist reference to praise the Tulip Houses as generators for and intensifiers of local communities.[18] One of the most ardent proponents was, however, not an architect but the populist poet, László Nagy. He was first to confront Major's pivotal offensive and defend the ornamented concrete buildings.[19] He quoted Marcel Breuer, who had stated his disappointment with what had happened to the revolutionary Bauhaus conception in Hungary during his 1967 visit there, then proclaimed that Hungarian architecture faced an artistic crisis.

While the debate demonstrated expansive agreement concerning the need to humanize the production of habitat, competing opinions emerged regarding the possibility of an antimodernist turn. The dispute soon shifted from the question of ornaments to broader issues of socialist housing policies, which provoked the regime into action. The Paks experiment was stopped in an administrative way and the Pécs Group authoring the ornamented facades was dissolved.[20] This couldn't, however, prevent the strengthening of a populist circle of Hungarian architects who sought references from nature and native traditions.[21] György Csete, the Pécs Group's former head, and Imre Makovecz, leader of the studio Corvina Műterem, emerged to become this group's leading figures, influential both within and outside the profession of architecture.[22] The stormy Tulip Dispute pushed them and their intellectual supporters towards a more openly traditionalist and antimodernist position (fig. 5).[23] Nonetheless, being on the periphery by no means indicated the group's irrelevance. On the contrary, their marginalization at home was coupled with expanding publicity abroad: Makovecz came to be the most internationally renowned Hungarian architect of his time. This was most probably not only due to his architecture's oddity. With the propagation of postmodernism, images have become the primary ways of shaping the structure of the discourse, and the power of images of Makovecz's organic architecture was incontestable.

The Tulip Dispute Against the Backdrop of the Populist-Urbanist Polarization

This shift proceeded in parallel with the turn of the wider populist intellectual movement towards traditionalism. Roughly simultaneously with the Tulip Dispute, populist writers initiated a debate on "fridge socialism."[24] They argued that the poor consumerism of the Hungarian socialist regime of the 1960s, in which the "Hungarian dream" was symbolized by a household possessing a fridge, threatened to replace collectivist ideals through philistine

fig. 5 Its zooid shape and scaled skin characterize Makovecz's ski hut in Dobogókő, built in 1980. Source: Kós Károly Egyesülés, "Folytatni a Teremtést – Magyar élő építészet" [Continuing creation – Hungarian organic architecture], exhibit in the Museum of Applied Arts, Budapest (2009), accessed August 10, 2015, http://eloepiteszet.hu/hu/epuletek/epiteszek/kos-karoly-egyesules-tagok/makona-epitesz-tervezo-es-vallalkozo-kft/makovecz-imre/dobogoko-sihaz.

individual goals. Their urbanist opponents argued that the problem was not that there was too much market economy but that there was too little of it.[25] These oppositions reflect a long-standing intellectual polarization, rooted in Hungary's prewar history, between a more cosmopolitan, so-called urban faction of the intelligentsia and a nationalist leaning, so-called populist one.[26]

Whereas in the Tulip Dispute the populist position might appear more critical of the system, in the "fridge socialism" debate, by contrast, the populists seemingly defended the socialist ideal. This, and the omnipresence of the populist-urbanist polarization in both debates, leaves us with two conclusions. First, that the main fault line between populists and urbanists was not analogous to the division between supporters and opponents of the single-party state, thus one cannot state that populists were more critical and urbanists rather proponents of socialism. Second, despite the regime's efforts to monopolize the political discourse, the populist-urbanist disputes of the 1970s can be understood as the survival of the polarization from before the Second World War. Although political plurality was suppressed and competing opinions disallowed, this populist-urbanist opposition remained deeply engrained in the collective memory, to then resurge time and again.

The Tulip Dispute and the Post-Socialist Kulturkampf

This brings us to the hypothesis that the old polarization plays an important role now, decades later, and that the Tulip Dispute and its aftermath contributed to its renewal and intensification that has marked the architectural and wider intellectual communities in Hungary since 1989. This was analogous to the outbreak of a "war of ideologies" between the Christian-nationalist and leftist political blocks. In his account of the post-socialist Hungarian republic's failure, the philosopher János Kis coined the term "hundred years war" to describe the relationship between the political right and left in twentieth-century Hungary. According to Kis, two anachronisms – a political right yearning for the aristocratic interwar period and a left unable to separate from the socialist Kádár period – contested and denounced one another in the decades following the end of socialism.[27] The 1970s architectural debate has proved to be an important milestone en route to an all-out Kulturkampf that has divided architects into two warring camps in post-socialist Hungary, resulting in an ideological controversy over how the Hungarian nation-state should be represented by architecture. In the ensuing years, this bitter division has had its part – aside from financial shortages – in the frustration of many large-scale projects of cultural and symbolic significance.

I will illustrate this with the examples of the new National Theater and the Castle District in Budapest. In the first case, the change of governments in 1998 brought about the state's withdrawal from the theater project, already under construction then. Instead, the new Christian-nationalist government commissioned an alternative, historicizing design, reflecting their worldview.[28] The second case is related to controversy about the Castle District's symbolic role. A competition-winning project from 2004 aimed to convert the former national defense headquarters – ruined during the Second World War – into a cultural and tourist center, applying contemporary architectural vocabulary. This was canceled and then replaced by plans targeting the refurbishment of buildings to their original conditions, with the relocation of the executive branch to the Castle District. Important here is the fact that in both cases the ideological breach expanded to become a political one, with political decisions eliminating projects initiated by the opposing side.

The first casualty of this post-socialist Kulturkampf was, quite symbolically, István Janáky's competition-winning design for the Hungarian Pavilion at the 1992 Expo in Seville. Preparations for the world fair got underway parallel to the political change in Hungary, and the event in Spain presented a great opportunity for the young democracy to present itself to the international community. An open competition for the design of the Hungarian Pavilion was announced in December 1989 with entries due the following

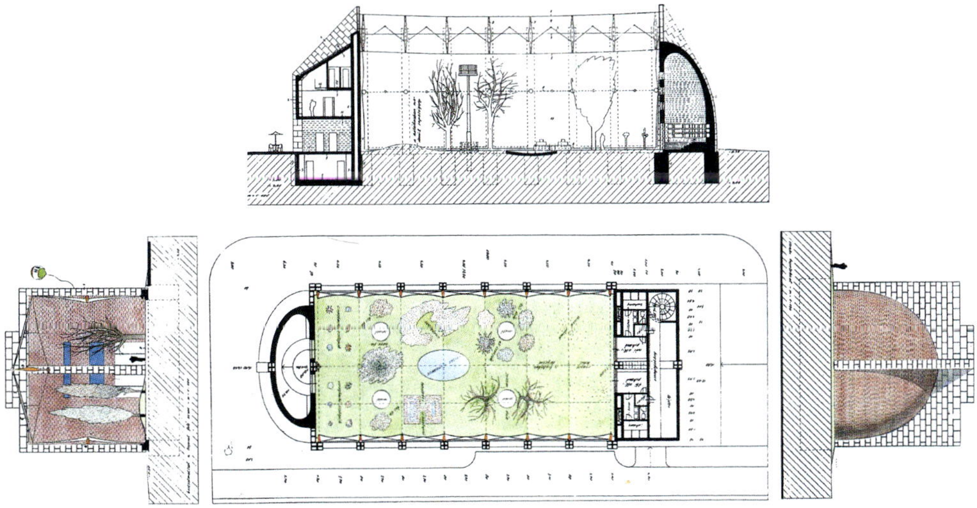

fig. 6 A metaphor of the political turnover: István Janáky's 1990 design of the Butterfly House. Source: Mihály Vargha, "Das Jahr der Schmetterlinge. Ungarische Architekturträume", Daidalos Architektur Kunst Kultur, Nr. 39 (1991), 43.

March. Janáky, who designed the winning proposal, grounded his concept in the Expo's meta-theme, "Times of Discovery". The Janáky design, a butterfly aviary exhibiting thousands of species, was meant on the one hand to be a symbol of Eastern European transformation, analogous to the caterpillar's metamorphosis into a butterfly (fig. 6). On the other hand, it was driven by the aim of exhibiting something "real" in the pavilion, rather than images or other abstract forms of content. The reception of the proposal was not undivided. Leaders of Hungexpo, the state-run firm responsible for the country's presence at fairs, openly criticized Janáky's project, as did populist intellectuals, for being too conceptual and for not properly representing Hungarian national identity.[29] According to these critical voices, the pavilion ought to have been conceptualized on emotional grounds and to have represented the history of Hungarians. Spiraling disputes and escalating confrontation resulted in the outgoing communist government withdrawing Janáky's commission in May 1990, after and probably influenced by the election victory of a right-wing coalition. The unfolding story of the pavilion's commission was not short of twists. The communist EXPO deputy, Tamás Beck, approached the organic architect Imre Makovecz – who had not himself submitted a proposal to the design competition – as early as in June 1990, straight after having withdrawn Janáky's commission. Makovecz then refused the direct commission. In the months to follow, Béla Kádár, the new EXPO deputy of the first freely elected government, resumed talks with Janáky but soon came to

fig. 7 Seven towers representing Magyar history: the Hungarian pavilion at the Seville world fair in 1992. Source: Imre Makovecz, "A magyartölgy mítoszai" [Myths of the Hungarian Oak], accessed February 10, 2016, http://www.hettoronyfesztival.hu/sevilla/.

the same conclusion as his predecessor. On August 17, 1990, Kádár proposed that Makovecz design the pavilion, who this time accepted the commission. (fig. 7).

Makovecz, as the leading figure of the traditionalist, populist group of architects, seemed a natural choice of the Christian-nationalist leadership. This interlude pushed Janáky, previously also known as an advocate of the banality of rural architecture, towards a deepening personal conflict with Makovecz. Although he maintained his position in propagating the beauty of the countryside's "architecture without architects"[30] (fig. 8) and criticized Makovecz for creating kitsch rather than architecture actually rooted in vernacular traditions,[31] Janáky came to be an emblematic protagonist of the cosmopolitan, urbanist faction of architects. At a roundtable discussion[32] in July 1990, he called Makovecz's circle a "peculiar architectural breed," then claimed in October[33] that Makovecz's decision in August to accept the commission was mere revenge for this vituperation. According to an alternative reading, however, Makovecz simply did not want to do business with the outgoing communists and his refusal in June and positive response in August is

fig. 8 Inspired by the vernacular: the Schaár Erzsébet Museum in Pécs by István Janáky and László Meditz, finished in 1990. Source: József Hajdú, "The Schaár Erzsébet Museum in Pécs", accessed February 10, 2016, http://www.artur.org.hu/#/pecs/schaar_erzsebet_museum.

a rational consequence of this attitude. Janáky continued giving voice to his resentment,[34] and his open confrontation with Makovecz only came to an end with their deaths in 2011 and 2012, respectively.

The controversies of the Hungarian Pavilion in Seville allow us to record three correlations. First, besides the conspicuous ideological affinity there was also continuity between the populist-urbanist debates of the 1970s and the clashes of the 1990s in terms of the protagonists. Besides Makovecz's central role in both periods, another example is the populist poet Sándor Csoóri. He had published in Új Írás at the time of the "fridge socialism" debate, and was later among the nine founders of Magyar Demokrata Fórum (Hungarian Democratic Forum), the leading party in the first freely elected government, which then commissioned Makovecz in 1990. Second, Janáky's case reveals that the populist-urbanist framework was so prominent that one could easily find oneself pigeonholed into either, while lacking real ideological conviction. Third, the personal character of Janáky's and Makovecz's wrangling exhibits the difficulty of rational and productive debate between the warring sides.

Coda: The Tulip Dispute, a Missed Opportunity

The ideological clash between the political right and left and between the populist and urbanist factions of the intelligentsia continued to mark Hungary's post-socialist development. Back in the 1970s, the Tulip Dispute's logic had also derived from this broader ideological controversy and it, therefore, contributed to the standoff's intensification. In that debate, mainstream architects had accused the Pécs Group of antimodernism, while they then stigmatized their critics as promoters of socialist nihilism. This did not allow for a rational debate on the production of habitat, which being a politically sensitive topic would not have been in the regime's interest either. Deep cultural and ideological rifts, mostly left over from the prewar period, were not allowed to be openly discussed in socialist Hungary and, ironically, the outbreak of a stormy Kulturkampf didn't leave room after the regime change for confronting past conflicts in a pragmatic discourse either.

This paper started by introducing the administrative allocation of housing as a policy that generated housing inequalities instead of its promise to eliminate them, and by discussing architects' ambivalent attitude towards prefabricated construction systems. The Tulip Dispute was an opportunity for the architectural community to confront sociological and design-related dilemmas in housing development. Although the Pécs Group's critics broadened the architectural debate into a conflict over social modernization,[35] by interpreting modernist architecture as the exclusive guarantee for societal progress, the dispute did not respond to the actual social controversies of socialist mass housing. Furthermore, instead of starting a process towards better understanding between rival positions in the field of architecture, it contributed to the ideological standoff that, in its turn, would be responsible for the frustration of large-scale projects of cultural and symbolic significance decades later.

Endnotes

1 The housing complex at Etele út 15–25 was constructed between 1965 and 1966.

2 In 1946, the French company Camus developed a panel-based construction system for postwar reconstruction, utilized widely in France from the 1950s and later exported to the Soviet Union. The Hungarian leadership acquired the Soviet adaptation in 1963 and commissioned a team of engineers lead by Jenő Gilyén to further develop it. Almost eight hundred thousand apartments were then built with prefabricated panel systems, including the Danish Larsen-Nielsen technology from the 1970s on. On mass housing in Budapest, see Gábor Preisich, *Budapest városépítésének története 1945–1990* (Budapest: Műszaki Könyvkiadó, 1998); on the typologies of Hungarian mass housing, see György Fátrai, "Funkcionalista és konstruktivista építészet," in Fátrai, Épített örökségünk (Budapest: Digitális Tankönyvtár, 2011).

3 György Konrád and Iván Szelényi, *Az új lakótelepek szociológiai problémái* (Budapest: Akadémiai Kiadó, 1969).

4 Iván Szelényi, *Urban Inequalities under State Socialism* (Oxford: Oxford University Press, 1983).

5 Mariann Simon, "Minták és módszerek. A hetvenes évek hazai építészete és a karakter," Építés – Építészettudomány, 3–4:29 (2001), 347–60.

6 István Janáky, "Magyarország két építészete," in *A hely: Janáky István épületei, rajzai és írásai*, ed. Judit Lévai-Kanyó (Budapest: Műszaki Könyvkiadó, 1999), 79–85 (p. 81).

7 György Konrád and Iván Szelényi, "A késleltetett városfejlődés társadalmi konfliktusai," *Valóság*, 12 (1971), 19–35; also György Berkovits, *Világváros határában* (Budapest: Szépirodalmi Könyvkiadó, 1976).

8 Virág Molnár, *Building the State: Architecture, Politics, and State Formation in Postwar Central Europe* (New York: Routledge, 2013), 115.

9 György Csete, Tibor Jankovics, and Péter Oltai, "Csak tiszta forrásból," Pécs Group exhibition and lectures, Fészek Galéria, Budapest, February 27–March 8, 1973; and György Csete, "Anyanyelvünkön beszélünk-e építészetünkben?," *Művészet*, 14:9 (1973), 12–13.

10 Molnár, *Building the State*, 23.

11 See Jeffrey Cook, *Seeking Structure from Nature: The Organic Architecture of Hungary* (Basel: Birkhäuser, 1995).

12 Ákos Moravánszky, "Piercing the Wall: East-West Encounters in Architecture, 1970–1990," in *Re-Framing Identities: Architecture's Turn to History, 1970–1990*, ed. Ákos Moravánszky, Torsten Lange (Basel: Birkhäuser, 2016), 27–43. The term is used by Moravánszky to describe Máté Major's character.

13 Molnár, *Building the State*, 120.

14 Máté Major, "Itt a tulipán!," Élet és Irodalom (October 11, 1975).

15 See Károly Weichinger, "A paksi lakóházakról," *Magyar Építőművészet*, 2 (1976), 60.

16 See Dezső Cserba, "Más nagypanelt – más tulipánt!," *Magyar Építőművészet*, 2 (1976), 61–62.

17 Gábor Preisich, "Modernség," Élet és Irodalom (November 8, 1975).

18 Katalin Berey, "Nemzeti ihletésű építészetet!," Élet és Irodalom (October 25, 1975).

19 László Nagy, "Hol a tulipán?," Élet és Irodalom (October 4, 1975).

20 Katalin Simon, "A tulipán-vita. Lakótelep – humánum – organikus építészet," *Iskolakultúra*, 6 (2006), 13–27 (p. 25).

21 Ibid., 25–26; see also András Ferkai, "Építészet a II. Világháború után," in *Magyarország építészetének története*, ed. József Sisa and Dora Wiebenson (Budapest: Vince Kiadó, 1998).

22 Krisztina Fehérváry, *Politics in Color and Concrete: Socialist Materialities and the Middle Class in Hungary* (Bloomington: Indiana University Press, 2013), 147; see also Jonathan Glancey, "Imre Makovecz and Corvina Muterem," *Architectural Review*, 3 (1981), 152–156.

23 Imre Makovecz, "In the Search of a Hungarian Architectural Identity," *The New Hungarian Quarterly*, 4 (1985), 225; Imre Makovecz, "Kérdések a szerves építészetről," *Országépítő*, 4 (1993), 10.

24 Tamás Turai, "Az Új Írás," *Beszélő*, 2:3 (1997).

25 The debate commenced with the poet Mihály Váci reflecting on the relationship between the boring Hungarian consumer society and the socialist movement's original goals in the periodical *Új Írás* in 1961, followed by nearly one hundred and thirty different contributors.

26 This polarization was most appreciable in the 1930s literary scene after the so-called second generation of the journal *Nyugat* split into two ideological camps. Progressive, cosmopolitan writers and poets such as Tibor Déry, Ferenc Fejtő, Attila József, Sándor Márai and Lőrinc Szabó contested a populist, traditionalist group led by Béla Hamvas, Gyula Illyés, László Németh and Áron Tamási. The two factions launched their own journals: *Szép Szó* was edited by the urbanists, and *A Válasz* by the populists.

27 János Kis, *Az összetorlódott idő* (Bratislava: Kalligram, 2013).

28 On the National Theater saga, see Mihály Varga, "Kudarc-sztori," Építészfórum (July 13, 2000).

29 Mihály Vargha, “Das Jahr der Schmetterlinge. Ungarische Architekturträume,” *Daidalos Architektur Kunst Kultur*, 39 (1991), 43.

30 István Janáky, *Az építészeti szépség rejtekei Magyarországon* (Budapest: TERC Szakkönyvkiadó, 2004).

31 Janáky wrote that “(m)aterial records of ancient historical times are rare and therefore enable the wizard drawers to utilize their fantasy in their illustrations to their […] financial advantage. Well, this is what Arcadia’s decorators fib as being the pure source!” István Janáky, “Levelek Arkádiából,” Építészfórum (November 16, 2011 [July 6, 2011]). Author’s translation.

32 Introduction of the new architecture magazine *A/3* at Tölgyfa Galéria, July 8, 1990. The host was Dezső Ekler, protagonist of Makovecz’s faction, while the magazine was recommended by architect Gábor Turányi and architecture historian András Ferkai, July 8, 1990.

33 István Janáky, “Prelúdium és fúga,” Élet és Irodalom (October 5, 1990).

34 It was probably his 2011 talk “Levelek Arkádiából” that had the biggest resonance as it was presented soon after Makovecz’s death, though written earlier, holding him responsible for Hungary’s visual pollution and labeling him and his followers as decoration designers (see note 34).

35 Molnár, *Building the State*, 121.

II
The Turn to History

Joan Ockman

Russia, Europe, America: The Venice School between the U.S.S.R. and the U.S.A.

An "Architectural Cross-Section"

Manfredo Tafuri's appointment in 1968 as director of the architectural history program at the Istituto Universitario di Architettura di Venezia (IUAV) coincided with the publication of his first major book, *Teorie e storia dell'architettura* [*Theories and History of Architecture*]. The play of plural and singular in the title reflected his "scientific" concept of history at this date. History was objective, factual, verifiable. Theories, on the other hand, were subjective, variable according to the interpreter's perspective. Twelve years later, in a searching introduction to another book, *La sfera e il labirinto: Avanguardie e architettura da Piranesi agli anni '70* [*The Sphere and the Labyrinth: Avant-gardes and Architecture from Piranesi to the 1970s*], Tafuri would take a very different position. Now characterizing history as a thicket of "tangled paths," he acknowledged that it could only be written "in the plural," even if that very plurality continually had to be questioned.[1] In the intervening dozen years, he launched a major new research project with a group of colleagues and students at his renovated history faculty in Venice.[2] The aim was to study twentieth-century architecture and cities in relation to the three "great systems" that had shaped them: Soviet communism, American capitalism, and European social democracy.

The reframing of the history of modern architecture in these terms, carried out between 1968 and 1980, was unprecedented and, indeed, subversive.

Tafuri also tested out his hypothesis in his book *Architettura contemporanea* [*Modern Architecture*], coauthored with Francesco Dal Co in 1976, which begins, unconventionally enough, with a chapter on nineteenth-century urbanism in the U.S.[3] The Venice school's historiography was a deliberate challenge to the "operative history" that writers on modern architecture had produced to date – to the accounts intended to establish and instrumentalize particular tendencies and validate their hero figures. Examples of the historiography that Tafuri denounced ranged from the canonical books by Nikolaus Pevsner and Sigfried Giedion to those by Bruno Zevi, Giulio Carlo Argan, and Leonardo Benevolo. By delving into history's complex structures and temporalities and laying bare the workings of ideology, he aimed with his own "critical history" to dispel the various myths these writers had constructed.[4] At the same time, his revisionism implicitly registered larger cultural and geopolitical currents that were surfacing in the wake of the 1960s and during the late Cold War era.

The title of this chapter is a nod to Erich Mendelsohn's 1929 book *Russland Europa Amerika: Ein architektonischer Querschnitt* [*Russia Europe America: An Architectural Cross-Section*] (fig. 1). The sequel to his better-known *Amerika: Bilderbuch eines Architekten* [*America: An Architect's Picture Book*], published in 1926 and based on his first trip to the United States two years before, Mendelsohn's second book is likewise a photographic album, its large-format heliogravure images presented one to a page and accompanied by brief, almost axiomatic caption-texts (fig. 2). Many of the photographs were taken by Mendelsohn himself. In *Amerika*, the architect-author had expressed deeply conflicted feelings about the dynamic new civilization he was witnessing – its mixture of progress and aesthetic chaos, its formidable dimensions and extremes of wealth and poverty, its bright lights, brash billboards, and soul-crushing technology. The pitched camera angles and the artful order in which the pages unfurl give the book a cinematic quality, as El Lissitzky, one of many admiring readers, wrote in a review in a Russian journal at the time.[5] Mendelsohn takes a similar approach in *Russland Europa Amerika*, but the montage strategy here is even more pronounced as the images of the three different locations rhythmically intermingle and contrast. The juxtaposition pits a pragmatic, individualistic, and mechanistic American civilization against Russian backwardness, irrationalism, and age-old spirituality. Between these two poles Europe emerges as a third term. Included among the Russian images are several unbuilt projects by avant-garde architects like Vladimir Tatlin and Ivan Leonidov, which Mendelsohn deemed utopian and impracticable. One of the last images in the book, presented like the others without specific identification, is a model photograph of Mendelsohn's

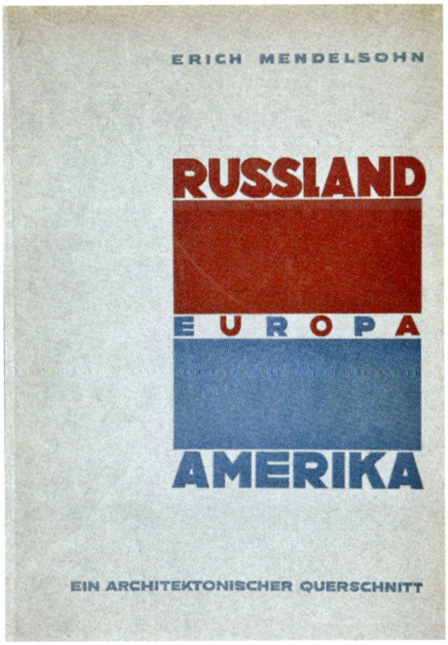

fig. 1 Cover of Erich Mendelsohn, *Russland Europa Amerika: Ein architektonischer Querschnitt*, Rudolf Mosse Buchverlag, 1929

own project for a textile factory in Leningrad. This commission, realized in 1926, was so poorly constructed under Russian building conditions that the German architect subsequently disavowed it, only allowing the model to be published. In the book's final plate, titled "Synthesis," Mendelsohn puts forward a hopeful vision of a humanistic European civilization capable of reconciling and transcending the contradictions of the other two political-economic systems and ushering in a harmonious future culture.

It is unlikely that Tafuri had Mendelsohn or his book in mind four decades later when he conceived the research program in Venice in terms of the same three world systems. Yet the superficial similarity is striking. While Mendelsohn's Hegelian synthesis and Tafuri's negative dialectics are an index of the philosophical gulf between their worldviews, and between two historical epochs, both saw the respective architectural productions of Russia, Europe, and the U.S. as alternate routes taken by twentieth-century building culture.[6]

A Lost Avant-Garde?

More specifically, the subjects on which Tafuri determined to focus the Venice school's energies and resources starting in 1968 were Soviet architecture and urbanism between the launch of Lenin's New Economic Policy (NEP) in 1921 and the end of Stalin's second Five-Year Plan in 1937; the American city from the 1920s through the New Deal; and the European city from its political experimentation with social democracy in the 1920s to the rise of fascism.

fig. 2 Two plates from Mendelsohn's *Russland Europa Amerika*: the Barclay-Vesey building in New York, designed by Ralph Walker in 1927; and Ivan Leonidov's 1927 project for the Lenin Institute in Moscow

These phenomena and their convergences, Tafuri asserted, constituted "the fundamental nodes of architectural and urbanistic experience of our century."[7] They would be the primary focus of his teaching and other activities at the school until 1980.[8]

Tafuri's objectives were not just pedagogical and interpretive but also documentary. For years, the Russian context had been flagrantly neglected by historians of modern architecture. Sigfried Giedion continued to remain silent on it through the fifth and last edition of *Space, Time and Architecture*, published in 1967. If one reason for the inattention of historians was the paucity and spottiness of research materials available in the West, even more significant was the chill induced by the Cold War. But with the thaw that followed Khrushchev's accession to power after Stalin's death, a stream of scholarship began trickling out from official Soviet sources, starting in the early 1960s with publications by Vigdaria E. Khazanova and Selim O. Khan-Magomedov.[9] At the same time, Western historians and curators slowly began rebuilding channels of communication and exchange with their counterparts in the East.

fig. 3 Cover of catalog for the exhibition *Art & Architecture USSR 1917–32*, Institute for Architecture and Urban Studies, New York, 1971. Graphic design by Robert Slutzky

In England, Camilla Gray's *The Great Experiment: Russian Art, 1863–1922* (1963) broke the ice. Five years later Kenneth Frampton followed with a pair of essays on Soviet architecture, "Notes on Soviet Urbanism, 1917–1932" and "The Work and Influence of El Lissitzky," and the following year with "Notes on a Lost Avant-Garde: Architecture, U.S.S.R., 1920–1930."[10] *A.D.* magazine put out a special issue with translations of writings by contemporary Soviet scholars in 1970, guest-edited by Oleg Shvidkovsky, and republished the following year as a book.[11] Anatole Kopp, whose *Ville et révolution* appeared in 1967, was the key figure in France.[12] In the Netherlands Gerrit Oorthuys was a go-between, traveling to the Soviet Union and Eastern Europe and bringing back primary material. On some of his trips he was accompanied by the young Rem Koolhaas. In 1969–70 Oorthuys's forays yielded an exhibition at the TU Delft that subsequently traveled to the recently established Institute for Architecture and Urban Studies in New York, where Frampton was now based and with whom he collaborated on the installation (fig. 3).[13] Also noteworthy in the U.S. in these years were Eric Dluhosch's translation (from German) of El Lissitzky's 1930 *Russland: Die Rekonstruktion der Architektur in der Sowjetunion*; Arthur Sprague's master's thesis and translation of Nikolai Miliutin's 1930 plan for a linear city; and S. Frederick Starr's research on Konstantin Melnikov, a project also inherited from Sprague.[14] In 1967 El Lissitzky's widow brought out a monumental monograph on her husband's work and career, initially published in Dresden.[15]

Probably the most prolific contributions to the burgeoning Western scholarship on Soviet architecture, however, came from Italy. The first significant publication was a special issue of *Casabella* in 1962 devoted to Soviet architecture, guest-edited by Guido Canella (fig. 4).[16] The Galleria del Levante in Milan staged the exhibition *Il contributo russo alle avanguardie plastiche* in 1964, and Italian translations of seminal architectural documents began appearing in *Rassegna sovietica* in 1965. Pioneering books came from Vittorio de Feo and Vieri Quilici, and an edited collection of texts on the Soviet city from Paolo Ceccarelli.[17]

This list is incomplete.[18] Yet it is evident that Tafuri's interest in the Soviet avant-garde was in line with other scholarship that was already underway in the 1960s in Europe and the U.S., not to mention Japan. At the same time, much more than new documentation – however valuable in itself – was at stake in Italy. In concluding his introduction to the 1962 issue of *Casabella*, Canella made the subtext fully explicit: "[P]aradoxically, the history of Soviet architecture up to the present, with its contradictions and internal struggles, is comforting to us, as it cannot but offer a further, if extreme, possibility for interpreting our own crisis."[19]

It was not an accident that the Russian avant-garde came to be embraced as a new subject in Italy precisely at a moment of "crisis" – of widespread social and political unrest. The 1950s had been a decade of extraordinary economic expansion and social transformation. The country had grown rich, yet the "miracle" of Italian modernization had done nothing to alleviate oppressive working conditions and low wages in the factories of the north, and had perpetuated a burgeoning state bureaucracy that had failed to carry out its promised reforms in sectors like housing and town planning. Rampant real estate speculation was gentrifying the urban centers and suburban sprawl was starting to encroach on the countryside. The ideology of the newly affluent class was "superconsumption." Italy's Communist Party (PCI) was now a major force in society, the largest Communist organization in the West. But it was no longer identified, as it had been formerly, with antifascist resistance and revolutionary class struggle. Under the leadership of Palmiro Togliatti for two decades from 1944 to 1964, the PCI sought to integrate itself into the political system, opting for what its founding father Antonio Gramsci had called a "war of position" – a long-haul road to socialism through the state institutions. Compounding the sense of dissatisfaction and alienation among a new generation of Italian youth in the early 1960s was the massification of the universities. Students found themselves reduced to passive recipients of knowledge in "education factories" that had inadequate funding, inaccessible and entrenched faculties, and few guarantees for future employment.

No surprise, then, that the decade of the 1960s saw the rise of left-wing militancy and student revolt. Some of the activists reserved their greatest con-

fig. 4 Cover of *Casabella–Continuità* 262 (1962). Special issue on the Soviet Union

tempt for the PCI and its ineffective brand of reformism. The intellectuals who founded the Operaist (workerist) journal *Quaderni Rossi* in 1961 engaged in heated debates over neocapitalist ideology and revolutionary praxis. Fueling the general climate of insurgency was widespread international turbulence: war in Vietnam, a missile crisis in Cuba, political struggles in Africa and Latin America, Cultural Revolution in China, the rise of the counterculture in the U.S. Whether inspired by Marx, Mao, or Marcuse, Italian students took up the banner of collective struggle, proclaiming their solidarity with their counterparts around the world and, at home, with the factory workers already on strike in the industrial centers. In 1968, a chain reaction of explosions was to occur in many countries. But the agitation began in Italy earlier than elsewhere and, as historian Paul Ginsborg has chronicled, its repercussions were "the most profound and long-lasting in Europe."[20]

Nor is it a surprise that in these circumstances the "great experiment" undertaken in the Soviet Union in the years after the October Revolution took on emblematic value as a historical precedent, offering at the very least a "principle of hope."[21] Yet if a certain buoyant and utopian spirit prevailed during the first half of the 1960s, the mood in the universities turned more disciplined and resolute by the summer of 1968 as students coordinated their actions with the labor strikes. To quote Ginsborg again:

> From the summer of 1968 onwards the student movement itself underwent a profound transformation. As students abandoned the universi-

> ties and began picketing outside the factory gates, the movement lost its libertarian and spontaneous character. The accent was now on organization and on the need to lay the bases for a new revolutionary party which would wrest workers' loyalties away from the PCI. […]
> From the autumn of 1968 onwards, the Italian new left was born, a left that was really not new at all, but as old as the Russian Revolution itself. Leninism, in one form or another, became the dominant model for nearly all the new groupings; the disagreements which had characterized fifty years of international Communism were now repeated on a miniature scale.[22]

The alliance between the students and workers came to a head in the "hot autumn" of 1969, and over the next few years the trade unions succeeded in wringing important concessions from the national government. Yet by 1972, when long-time conservative Christian Democrat Giulio Andreotti was appointed to his first term as prime minister, a rightward shift was at hand. Fears stirred the following year by a U.S.-backed overthrow of the leftist government in Chile, together with the severity of consecutive economic crises in 1974 and 1976, galvanized the PCI under its new secretary, Enrico Berlinguer, toward a "historic compromise" with the political center. In 1976, the Communists entered into a coalition government with the Christian Democrats and Socialists under the reappointed Andreotti. This accommodation, which undid the gains the leftists had made over the previous decade, provoked a backlash among the most militant elements, unleashing a reign of terror by the Red Brigades. By 1980 the *compromesso storico* was over, but so was the PCI as an effective force in Italian society.

In the end, the new left's "revolution from below" had proved no match for capitalism's counterrevolution from above. Ginsborg offers the following conclusory assessment:

> [T]he "cultural revolution" of 1968 emerges as an extraordinary but unsuccessful attempt to challenge the predominant values of a rapidly changing society. The movement gained force from the unique international conjuncture of that year; it was aided by the traditions of the Resistance and of working-class militancy; it attracted support because of the dramatic and disorderly way in which Italy was becoming urbanized; but, in the last analysis, it was in direct conflict with the underlying trajectory of Italian modernization.[23]

It is worth recalling this momentous history at some length here as it constituted the background of the first decade of Tafuri's tenure at the IUAV, and also helps to explain the evolution of his thinking about modern architecture. More immediately, Tafuri's intellectual trajectory was influenced by tensions within and outside the PCI, which were amplified by the atmosphere in Venice when he arrived. A core group of scholars and students – including Massimo Cacciari, Marco De Michelis, and Francesco Dal Co – was already radicalized, and the theoretical debates taking place within the school were exceptionally intense.[24] The precocious political-intellectual culture of Venice reinforced Tafuri's response to the trend of current events and confirmed his verdict on the fate of left-wing culture under advanced capitalism. He would express this anti-utopian and pessimistic verdict most polemically in an essay published in 1969 in the journal *Contropiano*, "Per una critica dell'ideologia architettonica" ["Toward a Critique of Architectural Ideology"].[25] The same post–'68 disillusionment and doubt about the path to socialism likewise infected his Soviet research project. Tafuri summarized his aims as follows in 1971: "to contribute to specifying, within a delimited disciplinary context, the political reasoning that led to the mystifications of realized socialism, to the identification of socialism with planning, to the birth and consolidation of the ideology of the proletariat as a new historical subject and a new totality capable of bringing about universal 'liberation' through the *liberation of work*."[26]

This was his critical gambit. Against the "lost avant-garde" that was being exhumed and celebrated by Russian specialists elsewhere, Tafuri adamantly refused to engage in nostalgic recuperations. His objective was a genealogical inquiry into the origins of "planning" as an instrument of technocratic domination and a global ideology. Notwithstanding his vociferous protestations against *critica operativa*, his project was motivated in no small measure by an immediate desire to "challenge everything that had been consolidated on the left."[27] As he told his interviewer in 1992: "The present was our task. Our dream was to demolish the Partito Comunista to its very foundations. It was crazy, but with this in mind, we developed a theme that brought everything together, a theme that no one had yet confronted historiographically – no one had ever even noticed it."[28]

With a certain perversity, Tafuri had rejoined the PCI in 1968, forming a cell at the IUAV with the party's sanction. To some degree it was a contrarian move, flying in the face of the students who were demonstrating in the streets. But Tafuri's decision to renew his party membership also aligned with a strategy that Mario Tronti was putting forward during these years. It would be more effective, the Operaist theorist argued, to criticize communism from inside the party, where the working class had its base of operations and organization, than from outside it.

Beyond Manicheanism

The Venetians' study of Soviet architecture and urbanism was ambitious, even if some projects did not come to fruition. Since no one in Tafuri's immediate circle had direct access to archives in the Soviet Union – or even read Russian, according to one close collaborator[29] – Tafuri and his colleagues seized on the idea of mining untapped materials scattered in private archives and collections in the West. The strategy of focusing on exchanges between the Russian protagonists and their European counterparts was more than just pragmatic, however.

Indeed, the thematic of East–West encounter became a structural feature of the Venice historiography, raised almost to the level of a methodology. Marco De Michelis and Bruno Cassetti undertook a compilation of the writings of André Lurçat, Ernst May, and Hans Schmidt, three European architects – French, German, and Swiss respectively – who had attempted to put their professional expertise in the service of the U.S.S.R. in the 1930s.[30] Dal Co did the same for Hannes Meyer.[31] Tafuri's first doctoral student in Venice, Dal Co also wrote his dissertation on Soviet architecture and published two chapters of it in *Contropiano*, the second in a special issue dedicated to the early Soviet debates on industrialization (fig. 5).[32]

In June 1970 the initial phase of Soviet studies at the IUAV culminated in a three-day international conference. Its proceedings were edited by Tafuri and published by Officina the following year as *Socialismo, città, architettura: URSS 1917–1937. Il contributo degli architetti europei* [*Socialism, City, Architecture: U.S.S.R. 1917–1937. The Contribution of the European Architects*] (fig. 6). Besides Tafuri, Dal Co, De Michelis, Cassetti, and Giorgio Ciucci – an architectural historian and colleague from Rome whom Tafuri had recruited to Venice soon after his arrival – the speakers included two leading left-wing intellectuals from outside the discipline. One was Alberto Asor Rosa, a literary historian and coeditor of *Contropiano*. In a seminal paper on Mayakovsky, "Lavoro intellettuale e utopia dell'avanguardia nel paese del socialismo realizato" ["Intellectual Work and Avant-Garde Utopia in the Land of Realized Socialism"], Asor Rosa argued that short of a fully achieved communist society, experimental art could only retain its bourgeois background and was consigned to operate on the margins of revolutionary praxis. "Engaged literature" did not exist in his view – this was Mayakovsky's tragedy. The other outside participant was Rita di Leo, an expert on Soviet political economy. Also a contributor to *Contropiano* and a founding editor of the earlier Operaist journal *Classe operaia*, di Leo had just published her first book, *Operai e sistema sovietico* [*Workers and the Soviet System*], 1970. Her radical interpretation of the implications of state capitalism under the NEP was sufficient to get her

fig. 5 Cover of *Contropiano* 4:1 (January–April 1971). Issue on the Soviet debate on industrialization

expelled from the PCI not long after the conference.[22] Also invited to participate were four speakers who hailed from the old-line left: the Swiss Hans Schmidt, now seventy-seven years old; the historians Kurt Junghanns from East Germany and Vítězslav Procházka from Czechoslovakia; and Oorthuys from Holland. While their presentations had "a strong emotional impact," according to Tafuri, he found them more hagiographic than critical, typifying the "faith and delusion" of a generation still clinging to an idealistic conception of Marxism.

After the conference, work on Soviet architecture and urbanism continued apace in Venice. In 1971–72 Tafuri gave the course "Avanguardie, città e pianificazione nell'Unione Sovietica" ["Avant-Gardes, Cities, and Planning in the Soviet Union"]. In 1976–77 he taught "Avanguardia e architettura: le avventure nel linguaggio nell'arte contemporanea" ["Avant-Garde and Architecture: The Adventures of Language in Modern Art"]. In 1972, a French journal under the direction of the gallerist Françoise Karshan-Esselier, *VH 101*, invited the

fig. 6 Cover of Manfredo Tafuri, ed., *Socialismo, città, architettura: URSS 1917–1937. Il contributo degli architetti europei*, Officina Edizioni, 2nd edition, 1972

Venice scholars to collaborate on an issue on Soviet architecture (fig. 7). The main impresario for the double number, titled "L'Architecture et l'avant-garde artistique en URSS de 1917 à 1934" ["Architecture and the Artistic Avant-Garde in the USSR from 1917 to 1934"], was Dal Co. Besides those from Venice (Dal Co, Tafuri, Ciucci, De Michelis, Cassetti, Françoise Very), it contained contributions by De Feo, Quilici, and Giorgio Kraiski. Translations of a selection of historical documents were also included. Tafuri's essay, "URSS/Berlin 1922: du populisme à 'l'internationale constructiviste'" ["U.S.S.R.–Berlin, 1922: From Populism to 'Constructivist International'"] would subsequently become a chapter of *The Sphere and the Labyrinth*. Centered on Berlin, the essay is framed once again around a series of encounters, in this case between members of the Russian and European avant-gardes in the early 1920s.

In 1976, a monograph on the Soviet city by De Michelis and Ernesto Pasini saw publication,[34] and three years later the second phase of work at the Venice *dipartimento* resulted in another major book, *URSS 1917–1978: La città, l'architettura* [*U.S.S.R. 1917–1978: City, Architecture*] (fig. 8). Edited by the young French scholar Jean-Louis Cohen in collaboration with Tafuri and De

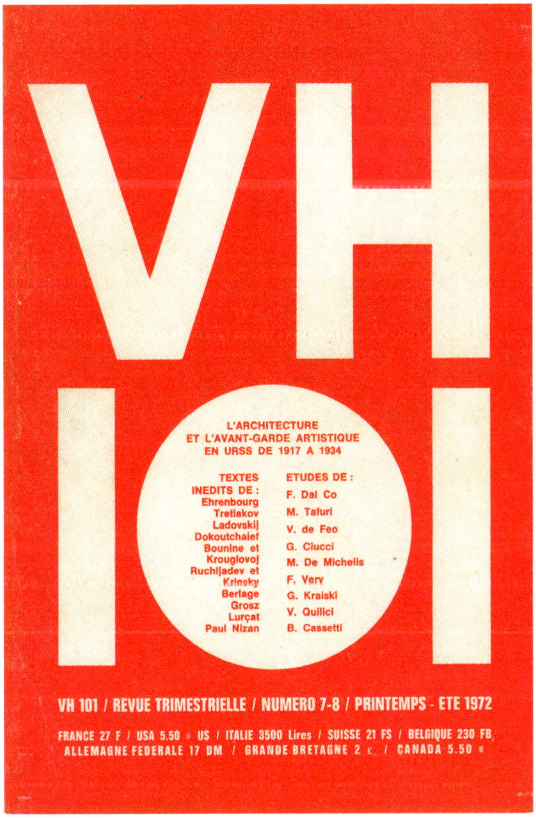

fig. 7 Cover of *VH101*, no. 7–8 (Spring–Summer 1972). Double issue on architecture and the avant-garde in the Soviet Union, guest-edited by Francesco Dal Co and Giorgio Ciucci

Michelis, and based on an exhibition that took place at the Centre de Création Industrielle–CNAC Georges Pompidou in Paris in 1978,[35] it was co-published by Officina and L'Équerre, with parallel texts in Italian and French. The Soviet Union of Architects was a nominal co-sponsor, and the project brought together an international roster of contributors, including Kopp and Quilici, Catherine Cooke from England, Christian Borngräber from West Berlin, the Soviet historians Khan-Magomedov, I. N. Khlebnikov, G. Gorvic (Grigori Horwitz), and the contemporary Soviet architect and urbanist Alexei Gutnov.[36] The volume represented a "moment of reflection," according to the introduction, affording an opportunity to move beyond older "Manichean" myths and to question uncritical recent interpretations.[37] The framing dates, 1917 to 1978, put the accent on continuity rather than rupture, implicitly making the case that it was possible to write a history running from the October Revolution through the Stalin era to the present. Taken together, the editors' substantial essays, which made up the first half of the book, directly challenged the conventional periodization. They also revealed their shared intent to deconstruct epiphenomenal battles of ideology and aesthetics; hence the attention paid not just to avant-garde hero figures of the mid–1920s but also to their subsequent careers and to conservative architects like Ivan Fomin and Alexsei Shchusev.

Tafuri's essay concludes rhetorically:

> The return of art to itself, its extinction of *the real*, which one finds in all the significant experiences of Soviet architecture at the beginning of the '30s, has absolutely nothing "heroic" about it. Stalinian kitsch is no more than a litmus paper revealing a historical destiny that the Soviet avant-gardes share in common with those in the West, and it should be reexamined as such.
>
> It is rather significant that the recent analyses so often avoid taking note of how much Russian Constructivism anticipates – ideologically, symbolically, and metaphorically – the moment of productivist organization [...] what remains obscured is the ultimate meaning of the organization and rationalization of labor *in itself*, as a means of control and power over class movement. [...]
>
> The Russian intelligentsia reveal how much, in their will to construct a "new world" for the new man, they remain invested in the old dream of the European intellectual: to become the *moral* guide of a political avant-garde. [...]
>
> And it is legitimate to ask whether one ought to see in this adventure a tragedy or rather a necessary "irony of history."[38]

Between Marx and Coca-Cola

Meanwhile, in tandem with their work on Soviet architecture and urbanism, the historians in Venice were carrying out a no less revisionist reading of the American city: "Immediately after [beginning to work on the Soviet Union], we turned our attention to the other big system: the United States. If the Soviet Union had served its destiny from the start by rigidly imposing the Five Year Plan, how had this other huge system been built?"[39] As Tafuri's question suggests – and this is our main hypothesis here – the structure of the Venice research project had a certain parallelism with subcurrents of thought that were percolating in the global arena in the waning decades of the Cold War.

American culture had begun making major inroads in Italy immediately after World War II, during the very same years the PCI was integrating itself into the political mainstream. The efforts of the U.S. government to counteract the influence of communism in Western Europe were at first directed through Marshall Plan aid and propaganda programs like those of the United States Information Service. But the American "way of life" also infiltrated Italy in the form of consumer goods and through images disseminated by

fig. 8 Cover of Jean-Louis Cohen, Marco De Michelis, and Manfredo Tafuri, eds., *URSS 1917–1978: La città, l'architettura*, Officina Edizioni, 1979

mass-media publications, Hollywood films (which commanded three quarters of the Italian box office in 1949, despite the prestige of Italy's own neorealist cinema), and eventually television.[40] As Vittorio Gregotti put it: "The American invasion of Italy brought not only peace and national liberation, the end of destroyed cities and prostitutes, but also chewing gum, powdered milk and Coca-Cola, and first and foremost the idea of 'comfort' and the mechanization of the home. The myth of the refrigerator was born."[41]

The reception of America was more than a matter of alluring commodities in a previously poor country, though. The experience of two decades of fascism and authoritarian rule gave American political values renewed appeal. Bruno Zevi, for one, found a model for a post–Fascist society in its founding ideals of freedom and democracy, which he saw embodied in the expressive individualism of Frank Lloyd Wright's "organic architecture." Meanwhile, captains of industry like Adriano Olivetti – an engineer, journalist, politician, and head of the company that would become a leading international manufacturer of business machines in the 1950s – had taken a strong interest in American management techniques ever since the 1920s. After the war, Olivetti launched his Comunità movement as a "third force" against both fascism and communism, adapting aspects of American industrialism and liberalism to the specific economic, social, and political context of Italy.

For those committed to forging a new Italian society along communist lines, Americanization naturally carried more negative implications. Nonetheless, as the Marxist intellectuals whose analyses would become central to the new architectural historiography in Venice grasped, the history of the U.S. labor movement contained crucial lessons. Mario Tronti and Antonio Negri insisted that the Taylorist–Fordist factory and, in particular, the reorganization of American labor during the Depression era demanded study. "The northern Italian workers' struggles of the early '60s were closer to those of New Deal America than to those of the southern Italian farm workers in the 1950s," Tronti explained.[42] In "Marx a Detroit" ["Marx in Detroit"], a postscript written in 1971 to his book *Operai e capitale* [*Workers and Capital*], he argued that Marxist thinkers had failed to credit the effectiveness of the tactics developed during the 1930s by American labor unions, which were responsible for bringing about structural changes in the capitalist system.[43] Negri made a slightly different argument in a contribution to the first issue of *Contropiano*. While the impact of American industrialism on Stalin's Five-Year Plans was evident, the October Revolution had had a reciprocal impact in the West during the 1920s, stirring up ardent Bolshevik sympathies not only among European workers but also among Americans. In order to tamp down the threat of militance, American factory owners devised more stringent techniques of worker control. These included, Negri elaborated, further dividing up the labor process and deskilling the work force. This "technological path of repression" served to neutralize the workers' bids for autonomy. After the crisis of 1929 and in the face of catastrophic unemployment and worker unrest, the U.S. government, too, turned to scientific planning for the first time (fig. 9). Under the Roosevelt administration, policy makers strove to mitigate the risk of factory shutdowns, treating labor reform as a safety valve against economic disruption. "Capital," as Negri put it, "learned to read *Das Kapital*."[44]

Clearly the seeds of the Cold War were sown well before World War II. In Venice, Negri's writings on American technocratic planning in the 1920s and '30s captivated Dal Co and De Michelis even prior to Tafuri's arrival, and they sought him out in Padua while still students. With Tafuri's reformulation of the problem of planning in specifically architectural terms, the history of the American city became a prime subject of investigation. In 1969–70, his second academic year at the IUAV, Tafuri taught "Architettura, città e 'piano' in America (1500–1970)" ["Architecture, City, and 'Plan' in America, 1500–1970"]. He followed this with "Storia dell'ideologia antiurbana" ["History of Anti-Urban Ideology"] in 1972–73. The bureaucratic environment of white-collar work came into focus in 1973–74 with "Struttura e architettura della città terziaria in America (1850–1973)" ["Structure and Architecture of the Tertiary City in America, 1850–1973"]. In 1974–75, he turned his attention to housing: "Lo sviluppo urbano negli Stati Uniti e il problema del housing

fig. 9 "The mania for planning." Cartoon from *Classe operaia* 2, no. 4–5 (October 1965)

(1780–1974)" ["Urban Development in the United States and the Problem of Housing, 1780–1974"]. Finally, in 1975–76, he taught "Il grattacielo e la struttura terziaria in America e in Europa (1850–1975)" ["The Skyscraper and the Structure of the Service Sector in America and in Europe, 1850–1975"].

Tafuri's close collaboration on these topics with his Venice colleagues bore fruit in the volume *La città americana dalla guerra civile al New Deal* [*The American City: From the Civil War to the New Deal*], published in 1973 (fig. 10).[45] Coauthored by Ciucci, Dal Co, Mario Manieri-Elia, and Tafuri, the book was based on work carried out in private and public archives in the United States. The four authors divided the territory as follows: Manieri-Elia wrote on Daniel Burnham and the City Beautiful movement,[46] Dal Co on regionalism and the reformist projects of the circle around Lewis Mumford, Ciucci on agrarian ideology and Frank Lloyd Wright's Broadacre City, and Tafuri on the American skyscraper. Written from a "class" point of view, as the authors put it in their joint preface, the book was more than an act of revisionism; as they correctly pointed out, "a history of the American city [had] still not been written" as of the early 1970s.[47] Once again the Venice historians warned against the respective dangers of Scylla and Charybdis: on the one hand, against studies that failed to go beyond mere collections of facts; on the other, against partisan accounts intended to push a particular agenda. It was Mumford in this context whom they deemed guilty of operative criticism. Even though his accounts were "lively and stimulating" (and even as the authors thanked him for generously facilitating their research), they faulted his interpretations for having "a 'progressive' stamp."[48]

Above all, the capitalist metropolis was revealed in each of the successive chapters of *The American City* to be "an enormous, form-defying product of technique."[49] And precisely in this respect it posed a question that proved difficult to resolve: was the American city an exceptional phenomenon, unique to the special historical circumstances that gave birth to it; or was it an unconscious anticipation of what was to come everywhere? Gertrude Stein's quip that the United States was the oldest country in the world because "it is she who is the mother of the twentieth century civilization" nicely captures the ambiguity that the Venice historians struggled to address.[50] In his own chapter, "La montagna disincantata: il grattacielo e la City" ["The Disenchanted Mountain: The Skyscraper and the City"], Tafuri resorted to his favored methodology, beginning with a section on the respective American and European entries to the 1922 *Chicago Tribune* tower competition. He then worked his way to the New York of Hugh Ferriss, Raymond Hood, and Rockefeller Center in the 1920s and '30s, concluding with a leap forward to the gigantic constructions of the Kennedy and post-Kennedy era. He characterized these edifices of the late 1960s and early '70s – the World Trade Center was just being completed in 1973 when the book appeared – as "antiurban paradoxes, artificial technological 'miracles'"[51] within the ever-expanding, laissez-faire megalopolis.

Much as Tronti and Negri had read New Deal policy and Keynesian economic theory as defensive strategies against the chaos of capitalism, Tafuri typecasts the skyscraper throughout his writings on the American city as a "typology of exception," an (ultimately futile) effort by technocratic architects and planners to resist urban formlessness by means of a singular, monumental building. He reprises this argument in a central chapter of *The Sphere and the Labyrinth*. Sandwiched between chapters on the Soviet city of 1917–28 and the Social Democratic city of Weimar Germany, the chapter on the American skyscraper – "The New Babylon: The 'Yellow Giants' and the Myth of Americanism" – once again pits European against American conceptions and mythic constructions against realities.

In the concluding chapter of *The Sphere and the Labyrinth*, "The Ashes of Jefferson," Tafuri offers his grand finale on the American city. Its title is likely an echo of Pier Paolo Pasolini's *Le ceneri di Gramsci* [*The Ashes of Gramsci*], 1957, a long autobiographical poem in which the left-wing poet had expressed despair over the direction taken by Italian society and politics after World War II. Among the events that triggered Tafuri's essay was a competition for a second stage of housing on Roosevelt Island in New York, announced by the New York State Urban Development Corporation in 1974.[52] By the following year, the city was on the verge of bankruptcy – experiencing in a particularly acute way the effects of the same economic recession and global oil crisis that were roiling Italy – and despite the participation of an impressive roster of architects, the competition had to be canceled. Tafuri describes the

fig. 10 Cover of Giorgio Ciucci, Francesco Dal Co, Mario Manieri-Elia, and Manfredo Tafuri, *La città americana dalla guerra civile al "New Deal"*, Editori Laterza, 1973

paper projects of the New York architects as cruel and empty formal exercises. Drawing on an essay from 1907 by Georg Simmel – one of a series of travel sketches that the German sociologist had written on Italian cities in which he depicts Venice as a tragic place where life is a rootless adventure and architecture little more than a rarefied game of artifice[53] – Tafuri's chapter turns on an allegory of present-day New York as a new Venice, a city where alienation has reached carnivalesque heights: "In the 'new Venice' – allegory of a general human condition – it is necessary to wear a mask to 'save one's soul.'"[54]

In 1976, the Swiss journal *Archithese* devoted a monographic issue to the European mythography of New York, including an essay by Manieri-Elia on the experiences of three European architects in the U.S. (Saarinen, Mendelsohn, and Neutra) and one by Giusi Rapisarda, Tafuri's wife, comparing Fritz Lang's film *Metropolis* to *King Kong*.[55] Two years later Manieri-Elia's book *Le città capitali nel XX secolo* (Capital Cities in the Twentieth Century) appeared, with cameos by Dal Co on Wright's Broadacre City, by Rapisarda on Hollywood as "capital of the imaginary," and by Ciucci on Disneyland as "capital of verisimilitude."[56] For all intents and purposes, however, the topic of the American city was now exhausted, as was the engagement in Venice with the "great systems" of twentieth-century modernity. Tafuri's writing of "The Ashes of Jefferson" not only coincided with his departure from the PCI, at this point under 's tenure, but also with the full-fledged arrival of postmodernism. After the publication of *The Sphere and the Labyrinth* in 1980, Tafuri would distance himself from the architecture of his own century, turning his full scholarly and pedagogical attention to the Renaissance, a subject he had pursued from his early career with equal intensity.

The end of convergence theories

"It always seemed to me that modernity violently asserted itself across all ideological borders. For this reason the Soviet Union and the United States merely substitute one kind of efficiency for another," Tafuri commented retrospectively. "In reality the problem was modernity."[57] If Tafuri's historiographic project chimed with that of other historians and critics who were likewise committed to dismantling the orthodoxy of modernist architecture in the 1970s, it also differed profoundly from them. The "turn to history" took many forms. While self-proclaimed postmodernists like Paolo Portoghesi and Charles Jencks sought to liberate contemporary architecture from modernism's "prohibitions," reveling in surface appliqués and historical pastiches, others, in an apparent contradiction, were engaged in a "search for roots," yearning for architectural substance as a means of counteracting late modernity's leveling effects. In the adjunct realm of architectural practice, the American architect Louis Kahn dreamed of new institutional forms that could renew a Jeffersonian sense of civicism and democratic community, while in Italy Aldo Rossi upheld Stalinallee in East Berlin as a model of collective urban order.

For Tafuri, however, answers to the present were to be found neither in eclectic and ironic *repêchages* (his word) nor in outdated utopias. Only a labor of the negative, a praxis of demythification, was possible: no synthesis, no overcoming of contradictions, just rigorous dissection of the different ideologies and bitter knowledge of the underlying logic they shared. The various architectures put forward under the regimes of the NEP, the New Deal, and the New Frankfurt – and for that matter during the postwar economic miracle in Italy – were differences that didn't make much difference from the perspective of modernity's *longue durée*. The question would remain the same one that Walter Benjamin had posed in 1934 in his essay "The Author as Producer": what was the role and agency of the architect and planner not just in relation to social and technological production but within it? "We were interested in the figures who had participated firsthand in the New Deal, in the first Soviet Five-Year Plan, in Weimar Germany," stated Tafuri, "figures who weren't merely form-makers who created beautiful objects, but rather those with positions like Ernst May or Ludwig Landmann, the mayor of Frankfurt [...] in which the author actually assumed responsibility for the new relations of production."[58]

Undoubtedly there is profound historical irony in Tafuri's "ongoing tragic reflection on modernity."[59] Was his stance not a kind of left-wing version of the convergence theory put forward, at the other end of the ideological spectrum, by triumphalist Cold Warriors? Orthodox modernization theorists in the West at the height of the Cold War optimistically predicted that the antagonism between capitalism and communism would fade away once the underdeveloped countries around the world became fully industrialized societies and entered the global marketplace. Yet at the very same time, from the other end of the telescope, some of the most radical observers of the Soviet system perceived the U.S.S.R. to be inching toward a profit-based economy and speculated that the imperatives of rationalization would ultimately cause Marxist–Leninist dogma to be jettisoned.[60] As already suggested, Tafuri's historiographic project partakes of a structure of thought that belongs to a moment when the binary logic of the two superpowers, though officially still in force, was breaking down. It would give way a decade later not to the vaunted "end of ideology," but rather to a more complex and paradoxically also more monolithic formation, one that tends to be labeled today – somewhat too loosely – "global capitalism."[61]

In his introduction to *The Sphere and the Labyrinth* – written after most of the book's other chapters and at a moment when the effects of French post-structuralism could no longer be ignored in Venice – Tafuri argues for the necessity of a plurality of historical interpretations, for the interminability of analysis, for the inevitability of narrative discontinuities. Yet his opening metaphor (borrowed from Carlo Ginzburg) of history as a jigsaw puzzle that admits of multiple solutions can only appear a contradiction of the *grand récit* that he narrates in the following chapters and that he had constructed with his fellow scholars over the previous dozen years. In a similar vein, Tafuri and Dal Co state on the last page of *Modern Architecture* that they feel "ill at ease" writing the word *finis*.[62] Yet the word is already inscribed on every page of the book. This unresolved contradiction is a symptom of the tensions of the period in which they were writing. As Tafuri could not help but sense, to embrace a plural history was to sacrifice the clarity of taking a position. In the end, the turn to history that he instigated with such polemical force in the late 1960s became a turn away from politics.

Epilogue

In 1975, Vittorio Gregotti, head of a new section of the Venice Biennale on the visual arts and architecture, began working with Carlo Ripa di Meana, the Biennale president, on two consecutive exhibitions on Soviet architecture. The Soviet Ministry of Culture took part in the planning, and on Gregotti's invitation Tafuri agreed to join the project. The first exhibition, focusing on the years 1917 to 1930, was supposed to take place in 1977, the sixtieth anniversary of the Revolution. Early that year, however, Ripa di Meana decided the overall theme of the exhibition would be "cultural and political dissent in the Soviet Union and the Eastern European countries." This decision proved highly provocative with respect to Soviet–Italian diplomatic relations, eliciting strong protests from the Soviet ambassador. It also stirred up a hornet's nest of controversy inside Italy, exposing rifts between leading political and cultural figures. Giulio Carlo Argan, a Communist and mayor of Rome at the time, attacked the exhibition in advance as a "Solzhenitzyn parade." The "Biennale of Dissent" finally opened in November, but the two exhibitions on architecture never materialized. Tafuri's reaction to this course of events is unknown. However, Dal Co gave an interview in which he denounced the Biennale as an institution.[63]

Meanwhile, the year before, Gregotti had staged another exhibition, "Europa/America: Architetture urbane, alternative suburbane" ["Europe/America: Urban Architectures, Suburban Alternatives"]. Yet another cross-sectional encounter – between fourteen architects from Europe and eleven from the U.S. – it concluded with a public debate in which Aldo van Eyck, one of the exhibitors, launched an *ad hominem* attack on Tafuri, repudiating his antihumanistic stance. Tafuri, who was in the audience, replied that the sole discourse he was capable of understanding was that of institutions and power and their role in the relations of production. He scornfully dismissed the "piccole angosce" [little anguishes] of European architects still clinging to a sentimental belief in "technological humanism."[64]

Exactly fifty years earlier, El Lissitzky appropriated an image of Times Square that Erich Mendelsohn had published in his book *Amerika*. The photograph of New York's dazzling nocturnal illumination (shot by Fritz Lang, who accompanied Mendelsohn on his American journey), became the backdrop for Lissitzky's apparitional photocollage-portrait of an athlete bounding over a hurdle, a "new man" fleet and fit for life in a technologically enhanced modernity (fig. 11). For those in Venice, this exhilarating leap across space would remain suspended in historical time. In the 1970s Italy was plunging into its "years of lead," and while the fall of the Berlin Wall would soon blur the boundaries between East and West, a different system of global relations

fig. 11 El Lissitzky, *Record (Runner in the City)*, 1926. Photocollage. Collection of the Museum of Modern Art, New York

was coming into being. It would engender a new culture of architecture, and require a new historiography.

Endnotes

I wish to express my gratitude to Jean-Louis Cohen for his comments on this essay and to Torsten Lange and Ákos Moravánszky for their editorial suggestions and encouragement.

1 Manfredo Tafuri, "The Historical 'Project,'" *The Sphere and the Labyrinth*, trans. Pellegrino D'Acierno and Robert Connolly (Cambridge, Mass.: MIT Press, 1987), 21, 5.

2 The program in architectural history at the IUAV, established by Bruno Zevi in 1960, was initially known as the Istituto di Storia dell'Architettura. It became a full-fledged department in 1976 under Tafuri, the Dipartimento di analisi critica e storia dell'Architettura. The name was shortened to the Dipartimento di Storia dell'Architettura in 1981.

3 "Most books, when it comes to accounting for the birth of modern city planning, concentrate on the role of utopian thought and of the great European capitals in the early nineteenth century. [...] Yet it was in the United States that progressive impulses, unique phenomena of interrelationship between income and profit, an economic development based on an indiscriminate laissez-faire, and cultural movements of opposition [...] created a true and proper tradition." Manfredo Tafuri and Francesco Dal

Co, *Modern Architecture*, trans. Robert Erich Wolff (New York: Harry N. Abrams, 1979), 17.

4 Among recent commentaries on Tafuri's historiography that intersect with some of the concerns in the present essay, see Marco Biraghi, *Project of Crisis: Manfredo Tafuri and Contemporary Architecture* (Cambridge, Mass: MIT Press, 2013; Italian ed., 2005); Tyrus Miller, "The Historical Project of 'Modernism': Manfredo Tafuri's Metahistory of the Avant-Garde," *Filosofskivestnik* XXXV, no. 2 (2014), 83–101; Gail Day, "Looking the Negative in the Face: Manfredo Tafuri and the Venice School of Architecture," in *Dialectical Passions: Negation in Postwar Art Theory* (New York: Columbia University Press, 2011), 70–131; and Pier Vittorio Aureli, "Recontextualizing Tafuri's Critique of Ideology," *Log* 18 (Winter 2010), 89–100.

5 El Lissitzky, "Glaz arkhitektora: izlozhenie knigi E. Mendel'sona," *Stroitel'naia promyschlennost'* 4:2 (1926); trans. "The Architect's Eye: A Review of Erich Mendelsohn's *America*," in *Photography in the Modern Era: European Documents and Critical Writings, 1913–1940*, ed. Christopher Phillips (New York: Metropolitan Museum of Art/Aperture, 1989), 221.

6 Tafuri's theoretical framework bears some resemblance to the "world-systems analysis" developed by Immanuel Wallerstein in the early 1970s, but it should also be differentiated from it. Both are indebted to the work of the Annales School, but Tafuri's theory of modernity remains rooted in Marxian thinking and Frankfurt School negative dialectics. For a concise summary of Wallerstein's theory, see Immanuel Wallerstein, *World-Systems Analysis: An Introduction* (Durham, N.C.: Duke University Press, 2004).

7 "Premessa," in Manfredo Tafuri, ed., *Socialismo, città, architettura: URSS 1917–1937* (Rome: Officina, 2nd ed., 1972), 7.

8 For reasons of space but also importance we shall concentrate here only on the Venice school's research on the Soviet Union and the United States. The most significant product of the work on the European city was the book *Vienna rossa: la politica residenziale nella Vienna socialista, 1919–1933* (Milan: Electa, 1980), edited by Tafuri with Alfredo Passeri and Paolo Piva. A comparative study of the politics of housing in Italy, France, and Germany in the 1920s and '30s was projected but went unrealized, although it inspired a related French-German-Italian effort led by Jean-Louis Cohen, Hartmut Frank, and Marco De Michelis; see a triple issue of the French journal *Les Cahiers de la Recherche Architecturale*, nos. 15–17 (1985): *Architecture et politiques sociales: les principes architecturaux à l'âge du réformisme*.

9 For early bibliographies on Soviet architecture and urbanism, including writings by both Russian and Western scholars, see S. Frederick Starr, "Writings from the 1960s on the Modern Movement in Russia," *Journal of the Society of Architectural Historians* 30:2 (1971), 170–78; and Anatole Senkevitch, Jr., *Soviet Architecture 1917–1962: A Bibliographical Guide to Source Material* (Charlottesville: University Press of Virginia, 1974). Specifically on Russian constructivism (but not including Russian sources), see Bernard Karpel, "Selected Bibliography," in *The Tradition of Constructivism*, ed. Stephen Bann (New York: Viking, 1974), 303–33.

10 The first two initially appeared in *Architects' Yearbook* 12 (1968); the third in *Art News Annual* 34 (1969).

11 *Architectural Design*, February 1970; O. A. Shvidkovsky, ed., *Building in the USSR, 1917–1932* (New York: Praeger; London: Studio Vista, 1971).

12 English translation: *Town and Revolution: Soviet Architecture and City Planning, 1917–1935* (New York: Braziller, 1970).

13 The exhibition at the architecture school in Delft was curated by Oorthuys with Otto Das and Max Risselada. The catalog of the show at the IAUS in New York, *Art & Architecture USSR 1917–32* (New York: George Wittenborn, 1971), was edited by Risselada and Frampton. In 1977 Oorthuys and Koolhaas would collaborate on another exhibition at the IAUS, on Ivan Leonidov; this publication appeared belatedly in 1981 as IAUS Catalogue 8, also edited by Frampton. Koolhaas, who made his first trip to Russia in 1965 as a young journalist, developed a lasting fascination with Soviet architecture. Like Tafuri – but with completely different politics – his interest in modern architecture would continue to oscillate between the polar experiences of the Soviet Union and the United States.

14 El Lissitzky, *Russia: An Architecture for World Revolution*, trans. and ed. Eric Dluhosch (Cambridge, Mass.: MIT Press 1970); N. A. Miliutin, *Sotsgorod: The Problem of Building Soviet Cities*, trans. Arthur Sprague, ed. George Collins (Cambridge, Mass.: MIT Press, 1974); S. Frederick Starr, "Konstantin Melnikov," *Architectural Design*, July 1969, 367–73; S. Frederick Starr, *Melnikov: Solo Architect in a Mass Society* (Princeton: Princeton University Press, 1978).

15 English edition: Sophie Lissitzy-Küppers, *El Lissitzky: Life, Letters, Texts* (London: Thames and Hudson; Greenwich, Conn.: New York Graphic Society, 1968).

16 *Casabella-Continuità* 262 (April 1962). On Canella's contributions to the Soviet discourse, see Jean-Louis Cohen, "Milano–Mosca: le attese di Guido Canella," in Enrico Bordogna, Gentucca Canella, and Elvio Manganaro, eds., *Guido Canella 1931–2009* (Milan: Franco Angeli, 2004), 420–28.

17 Vittorio de Feo, *URSS: Architettura 1917–1936* (Rome: Editori Riuniti, 1963); Vieri Quilici, *L'architettura sovietica contemporanea* (Rocca San Casciano: Cappelli, 1965), and *L'architettura del costruttivismo* (Bari: Laterza, 1969); Paolo Ceccarelli, ed., *La costruzione della città sovietica* (Padua: Marsilio, 1970).

18 Among other early contributions to Soviet scholarship were a series of exhibitions mounted by the Moderna Museet in Stockholm.

19 Guido Canella, "Attesa per l'architettura sovietica," *Casabella-Continuità* 262, 16.

20 Paul Ginsborg, *A History of Contemporary Italy: Society and Politics 1943–1988* (New York: Palgrave Macmillan, 2003), 298.

21 Mario Tronti, "Our Operaismo," *New Left Review* 73 (January–February 2012), 132. For Tronti, a founder of the Operaist movement, Bolshevism remained "the most advanced revolutionary experiment ever launched."

22 Ginsborg, *History of Contemporary Italy*, 312.

23 Ibid., 343.

24 For Tafuri's impressions of the political atmosphere at the IUAV, see his remarks in two interviews: Luisa Passerini, "History as Project: An Interview with Manfredo Tafuri, Rome: February–March 1992," trans. Denise L. Bratton, in *ANY* 25–26 (2000), 54 and passim (hereafter Passerini interview); and "Entrevistas por Mercedes Daguerre and Giulio Lupo: Manfredo Tafuri," in *Materiales* 5 (March 1985), 17. I am grateful

to Giulio Lupo for supplying me with the original transcript of the latter interview.

25 *Contropiano* 2:1 (January–April 1969), 31–79; English translation in K. Michael Hays, ed., *Architecture Theory since 1968* (Cambridge, Mass.: The MIT Press, 1998), 6–35. This essay would be expanded into book form as *Progetto e utopia: Architettura e sviluppo capitalistico* (Rome–Bari: Laterza, 1973); English ed., *Architecture and Utopia: Design and Capitalist Development*, trans. Barbara Luigia La Penta (Cambridge, Mass.: MIT Press, 1976). It should be emphasized that the program of the Venice school strongly reflected the political and intellectual preoccupations of *Contropiano* during the period of the journal's existence. A self-described journal of "Marxist materials" and a de facto successor to the Operaist journals *Quaderni rossi* and *Classe operaia*, *Contropiano* was founded in 1968 by Massimo Cacciari, Alberto Asor Rosa, and Antonio Negri. Negri departed after the first issue following a dispute over a contribution by Mario Tronti. The final issue dates to the last third of 1971. In addition to the essay that became the first draft of *Architecture and Utopia*, Tafuri contributed three more essays to *Contropiano*, two on the early twentieth-century European city: "Socialdemocrazia e città nella Republica di Weimar" (4:1, January–April 1971) and "Austromarxismo e città: Das rote Wien" (4:2, May–August 1971).

26 "Premessa," in *Socialismo, città, architettura*, 7. Author's translation.

27 Passerini interview, 30.

28 Ibid., 44.

29 Conversation with Jean-Louis Cohen, June 2016. Cohen entered the orbit of the Venice school in the mid–1970s. See two essays by him and a book: "Ceci n'est pas une histoire," *Casabella* 619–20 (January–February, 1995), 48–53; "'Experimental' Architecture and Radical History," *ANY* 25–26 (2000), 42–46; *La coupure entre architectes et intellectuels, ou les enseignements de l'italophilie* (Paris: Ecole d'architecture Paris-Villemin, 1984).

30 The project never saw publication.

31 Hannes Meyer, *Architettura o rivoluzione: Scritti 1921–1942*, ed. Francesco Dal Co (Padua: Marsilio, 1969).

32 Francesco Dal Co, "Architettura e piano in Unione Sovietica: stalinismo e 'destino dell'avanguardia,'" *Contropiano* 2:3 (September–December 1969), 527–75; "Sviluppo e localizzazione industriale," *Contropiano* 4:1 (January–April 1971), 81–123. The journal also published Dal Co's essays on the architecture of the Weimar Republic and on American "plans without cities, cities without plans."

33 Passerini interview, 55.

34 Marco De Michelis and Ernesto Pasini, *La città sovietica, 1925–1937* (Padua: Marsilio, 1976).

35 Titled *L'Espace urbain en URSS, 1917–1978*, this show, curated by Cohen and Alexei Gutnov, should not be confused with another one at the Centre Pompidou the following year, *Paris–Moscou, 1900–1930* (1979). The latter was one of three monumental cross-cultural exhibitions held in 1977–81 at the Pompidou, conceived by the museum's first director, Pontus Hulten; somewhat like Tafuri's project, each staged a confrontation between two cities.

36 Gutnov was a founding member of the NER (New Element of Settlement) Group, a collective formed in the late 1950s at the Moscow Institute of

Architecture. The megastructures designed by the group have a rare neo-avant-gardist flavor at this time and also reveal a currency with developments in the West. On Gutnov, NER, and their connections with Italy, see Elke Beyer, "From 'New Units of Settlement' to the Old Arbat: The Soviet NĖR Group's Search for Spaces of Community," in *Re-Humanizing Architecture: New Forms of Community, 1950–1970*, ed. Ákos Moravánszky and Judith Hopfengärtner (Basel: Birkhäuser, 2016), 211–228.

37 Jean-Louis Cohen, Marco De Michelis, and Manfredo Tafuri, eds., *URSS 1917–1978: La ville, l'architecture / URSS 1917–1978: La città, l'architettura* (Paris: L'Équerre, and Rome: Officina, 1979), 7.

38 Manfredo Tafuri, "Avanguardia e formalismo tra la NEP e il primo piano quinquennale," in *URSS 1917–1978*, 51, 53, 55. Author's translation.

39 Passerini interview, 56.

40 See Stephen Gundle, *Between Hollywood and Moscow: The Italian Communists and the Challenge of Mass Culture, 1943–1991* (Durham, NC: Duke University Press, 2000).

41 Vittorio Gregotti, "Italian Design 1945–1971," in *Italy: The New Domestic Landscape*, ed. Emilio Ambasz (New York: Museum of Modern Art, 1972), 322. Translation slightly modified.

42 Tronti, "Our Operaismo," 130.

43 Mario Tronti, "Marx a Detroit," *Operai e capitale* (Rome: DeriveApprodi srl, 2006), 293–307; Eng. trans.: http://libcom.org/library/postscript-problems.

44 Antonio Negri, "La teoria capitalistica dello stato nel '29: John M. Keynes," *Contropiano* 1:1 (January–April 1968), 7; Eng. trans.: http://libcom.org/files/negri_keynes.pdf.

45 Giorgio Ciucci, Francesco Dal Co, Mario Manieri-Elia, and Manfredo Tafuri, *The American City: From the Civil War to the New Deal*, trans. Barbara Luigia La Penta (Cambridge, MA: The MIT Press, 1979).

46 Like Ciucci, Manieri-Elia came to Venice from Rome on Tafuri's invitation. He had previously authored *L'architettura del dopoguerra in U.S.A.* (Rocca San Casciano: Cappelli, 1966).

47 Preface, *American City*, ix.

48 Ibid., x.

49 Ibid., xi.

50 Gertrude Stein, "Why I Do Not Live in America," *transition* 14 (Fall 1928), p. 19.

51 Manfredo Tafuri, "The Disenchanted Mountain: The Skyscraper and the City," *American City*, 503.

52 Tafuri briefly visited New York in 1974 on his second trip to the United States; his membership in the Communist Party did not permit him to obtain a longer visa. The initial version of the essay, "Les cendres de Jefferson," appeared in *L'Architecture d'Aujourd'hui* 186 (August–September 1976), 53–72.

53 Georg Simmel, "Venice," *Theory, Culture & Society* 24:7 (December 2007), 42–46.

54 Tafuri, *The Sphere and the Labyrinth*, 299. On the rapprochement between the architectural cultures of Venice and New York in the 1970s, and more generally on the thematics of "distance" in Tafuri's writings, see my essay "Venice and New York," *Casabella* 619–20 (January–February 1995), 56–71.

55 "New York: ein europäischer Mythos," *Archithese* 17 (1976). This was the first of three issues from 1976 devoted to the theme of the American metropolis; the first version of Tafuri's essay on New York as New Babylon would appear in the third issue. Under the editorial direction of Stanislaus von Moos, *Archithese* in the mid-1970s often reflected Venice school themes, if not its politics. Tafuri also contributed an essay to *Archithese* 7 (1973), an issue addressing the question of a "socialist architecture": "Les premières hypothèses de planification urbaine dans la Russie Soviétique, 1918–1925."

56 Mario Manieri-Elia, ed., *Le città capitali nel XX secolo* (Milan: Fratelli Fabbri, 1978). The volume also contains contributions by (among others) Alessandro Fonti on New York as "capital of the world" and by Tafuri on Vienna as capital of the *finis Austriae*.

57 Passerini interview, 62.

58 Passerini interview, 45. Translation slightly modified.

59 Ibid., 57.

60 One such observer was Rita di Leo, whose contribution to the Venice school's volume *Socialismo, città, architettura* has been mentioned above. See an important later essay by her, "The Former USSR in Search of New Rules," in Stephen White, Rita di Leo, and Ottorino Cappelli, eds., *The Soviet Transition: From Gorbachev to Yeltsin*, special issue of the *Journal of Communist Studies* (London: Routledge, 1993). In this essay di Leo essentially retracts her earlier analysis of the rise of Soviet state capitalism, calling it a "real mistake" (p. 3). She forecasts that in the future, rather than moving toward a convergence with the West, rival factions within the republics of the former Soviet Union – from oligarchs, nationalists, and government bureaucrats to Western-style stockbrokers and black marketeers – would continue to vie for power.

61 A more sophisticated formulation that has been put forward by Fredric Jameson is that of a "singular modernity." See his book of that title: *A Singular Modernity: Essay on the Ontology of the Present* (London and New York: Verso, 2002).

62 Tafuri and Dal Co, *Modern Architecture*, 410.

63 For an informative history of this event, see Luca Guido, "La Biennale del Dissenso del '77," www.archphoto.it/archives/1712. See also Furio Colombo, "Italy: The Politics of Culture," *New York Review of Books*, July 14, 1977.

64 "Quale Movimento Moderno," in Franco Raggi, ed., *Europa/America: Architetture urbane, alternative suburbane* (Venice: Edizioni La Biennale di Venezia, 1978), 179–80. For background on this exhibition and debate, see Léa-Catherine Szacka, "Debate on Display at the Venice Biennale," in *Exhibiting Architecture: Place and Displacement*, ed. Thordis Arhennius et al. (Zurich: Lars Müller, 2014), 97–112.

Alla Vronskaya

Deconstructing Constructivism[1]

The Red Nailer

When Zaha Hadid was awarded Pritzker Architecture Prize in 2004, the ceremony took place at the State Hermitage in St. Petersburg. Wishing to please Hadid, city officials offered her a visit to any architectural monument in St. Petersburg and its surroundings, expecting a request to see the famous imperial palaces and gardens. "Take me to the Red Nailer," the architect said instead. "Excuse us?" "To the Red Nailer." The officials still did not understand. "The Red Nailer." To their complete embarrassment none of the organizers knew what Hadid meant. The situation was finally smoothed over by the St. Petersburg historian of art and architecture Alexei Leporc, who happened to be in the audience. Leporc, a specialist in contemporary Western architecture who personally knew its major protagonists, realized that Hadid wanted to see the water tower of a rope-making workshop at the Krasnyi Gvozdil'schik [Red Nailer] factory, constructed in 1931 from a project by Soviet architect Yakov Chernikhov (fig. 1).[2] Forgotten today and not part of the tourist trail, the water tower was (and still is) in a state of shameful disrepair.

Who was Yakov Chernikhov and why did Hadid want to see his factory water tower above all the architectural splendors of St. Petersburg? And most importantly, why has a figure so significant for the London-based architect remained completely unknown to prominent cultural bureaucrats in Russia? Rather than testifying to the former's eccentricity or the latter's ignorance, this anecdote points to a dramatic difference in how the canon of Russian architectural history has been compiled in Russia and abroad. As this article will argue, the borderline between these two approaches followed the Cold War political divide, as both were informed by dominant ideological narratives. This article will focus on the Western and predominantly the American historiographic paradigm, suggesting a questioning of some of its foundational notions and analytical tools that remain instrumental today.

fig. 1 Yakov Chernikhov, the water tower of the Red Nailer factory, 1931. Photograph by the author.

Trained as both artist and architect, Chernikhov was a passionate designer of architectural ornament. At the heyday of functionalism in the 1920s, he embarked on an unusual task, developing a novel art form – "aristography" (from the Greek *aristo*, the most beautiful), which suggested a way of intensifying spatial compositions through color. Published as a series of colorfully illustrated books, Chernikhov's drawings merged Expressionist, Cubist, and Suprematist painterly techniques of representation with axonometry and the conventions of architectural plan to create fanciful images of utopian cities, factories, machines and abstract geometric forms and their combinations. Never a member of the architectural elite and never associated with a radical theoretical platform, Chernikhov led a prolific yet quite unremarkable pedagogical and practical career throughout the 1930s and 1940s. His work remained outside the accounts of the Soviet avant-garde until the 1980s, when it was rediscovered by the British historian of Soviet architecture Catherine Cooke. Published by Cooke in *Architectural Design* as an important example of Russian Constructivism, Chernikhov's fantasies became a source of inspiration for Hadid and other architects who had developed an interest in early Soviet architecture during the 1970s, when due to the economic crisis architectural work had become largely theoretical.[3]

That Chernikhov was to become an icon of Constructivist architecture remains an irony of architectural historiography, explained perhaps by the fact that one of his albums was titled *Construction of Architectural and Machine Forms*.[4] Unlike Chernikhov, the Constructivists – a formally organized group of Soviet architects who aspired to develop communist architecture by relying on recent technological solutions and a strict adherence to function – were often accused of dullness and inexpressiveness. The Constructivists' functionalist architecture, in fact, was very different from that of Chernikhov, which playfully merged architecture with art, graphics and ornament and remained far from political ambition. But it was precisely the latter's apolitical quality, as I will suggest below, that made it – contrary to the definitions of its own time – an exemplification of Constructivism. In what follows, I will trace the roots of this depoliticization of the notion of Constructivism, demonstrating how it circulated in Cold War historiography in the West largely on the basis of the preexisting – and ideologically charged – concept of the avant-garde.

The Avant-Garde

Russian Constructivism has often been cited as a canonical example of "the avant-garde."[5] Initially used in a military sense, this term was borrowed in the 1910s for artistic context, but only in the 1930s did it come to represent all radical modernist art, which had previously been named after a predominant local movement or style (such as Futurism in Russia or Neue Sachlichkeit in Germany). In the parlance of critics, "the avant-garde" was opposed to "the rear-garde," which authors, depending on their political platform and historic context, associated either with petty-bourgeois tastelessness or with "kitsch" produced for the poor. On the one hand, radical Soviet critics of the 1920s, such as Aleksandr Bogdanov, the founder of the famous Proletarian Culture movement, saw the proletarian masses as the source of the true avant-garde. On the other hand, liberal critics such as Clement Greenberg in the US espoused a fear of the masses ("the mob," as they were dismissed at the time), recalling the right-wing mass psychology of Gabriel Tarde and Gustave Le Bon at the turn of the century while anticipating the writings of Hannah Arendt and other liberal American postwar social theory. In his seminal essay "Avant-Garde and Kitsch" (1939), Greenberg illustrated kitsch with the work of the Russian academic painter Il'ia Repin, which belonged to the tradition of nineteenth-century theatrical historicism (as initiated by Paul Delaroche), but which was attributed by Greenberg to a proto-socialist realism.[6] Greenberg, nevertheless, tied kitsch not to the Soviet political regime but to a lack of education and taste among presumed admirers of Repin's painting, and maintained that kitsch was a typical product of Western urbanization.

During the 1940s in the US, as Serge Guilbaut has demonstrated, the idea of an artistic avant-garde was appropriated by the ideology of "new liberalism" embodied in Arthur Schlesinger's *The Vital Center* (1949), "an ideology that, unlike the ideologies of the conservative right and the Communist left, not only made room for avant-garde dissidence but accorded to such dissidence a position of paramount importance."[7] Arguably, the presumed connection between abstract art and liberal ideology that Guilbaut detected continued to inform art criticism through the Cold War and beyond, determining the understanding of art and its social role. Autonomy – from consumer culture, demanded already by Greenberg; from politics, declared by the 1940s generation of American artists; from the market and its institutions, elaborated by postwar theoreticians of the avant-garde – became a key characteristic of this notion.

Whereas Renato Poggioli (*Teoria dell'arte d'avanguardia,* 1962) defined the avant-garde as an aesthetic rebellion against bourgeois lifestyle and the culture of consumption, Peter Bürger (*Theorie der Avantgarde,* 1974) characterized it as an attack on the autonomy of art and as its sublation into the praxis of life.[8] However, while attacking autonomy, Bürger at the same time identified it as the avant-garde's prerequisite. He was particularly indebted to the *Ästhetische Theorie* of Theodor Adorno (written during the 1960s, published in 1970), which claimed that autonomy did not exclude the political significance of art but on the contrary enabled it.[9] Adorno emphasized that it was precisely autonomy that gave art an agency to resist existing social relationships, a task that it accomplished indirectly through an impact on the human consciousness and even the subconscious – thus authors like Samuel Beckett expressed the contradictions of the bourgeois society formally, without a need to resort to explicit political statements. In spite of differences in their approaches, Greenberg, the New York modernists, Poggioli, Adorno and Bürger alike juxtaposed the avant-garde with readily consumable bourgeois art, reading it as a Nietzschean, quasi-aristocratic gesture of resistance of high culture to the forces of mass culture or capitalism. Not always explicit, this connection between the avant-garde and capitalism (via the operation of negation) has become the dominant theme of subsequent discussions of the avant-garde.

Writing in the wake of the failed protests of 1968, Bürger expressed a more pessimistic position than his predecessors, asserting the avant-garde's ultimate appropriation by the institution and its subsequent degradation into the neo-avant-gardes, which employed the avant-garde's forms without retaining its political content. The English translation of Bürger's book (1984) provoked a polemical response from those who, like Rosalind Krauss and Benjamin Buchloh, believed in the possibility of the neo-avant-garde. In *Originality of the Avant-Garde and Other Modernist Myths*, a collection of essays written in the 1970s and published as one volume in 1986, Krauss questioned some of Greenberg's categories but preserved intact and indeed perpetuated the notion of the avant-garde itself, which she associated with aesthetic rather than political radicalism.[10]

Due to the weight of this formalist tradition, the notion of "the avant-garde" was applied to architecture later than to art, and has always preserved an intuitive connection with the latter. This even allowed Giorgio Grassi to claim that an architectural avant-garde is a contradiction in terms because it relied on forms that it received second-hand from modernist art.[11] Nevertheless, Krauss took an interest in some contemporary architecture discussions, supporting most notably the self-proclaimed neo-avant-gardist and champion of architecture's autonomy Peter Eisenman.[12] Through Eisenman's efforts, the term has persisted and an "avant-garde" architecture remains viewed first and foremost as formally innovative.[13]

Russian Constructivism

While the notion of the avant-garde had circulated in art theory since the 1930s, Russian art (and by extension Soviet modernist art) had been concealed behind the iron curtain until the late 1950s, when for the first time it became a matter of concern for English-language scholarship in the wake of thefirst attempts at easing relations between the US and the USSR, such as Khrushchev's official visit to the US in 1959. Behind this scholarly interest and sympathy, however, one could find a reductive and ideologically biased position. For instance, the groundbreaking 1962 book *The Great Experiment: Russian Art, 1863–1922*, written by Camilla Gray, the daughter-in-law of Sergei Prokofiev, cautiously assessed only the early development of modernism in Russia and stopped at the very dawn of politicized artistic approaches.[14] Although deeply sympathetic, Gray's book approached the Russian avant-garde as a failed utopian experiment, interesting primarily for its formal innovation – the very title suggesting that Russian modernist art was a one-time endeavor, unique and essentially different from the development of art elsewhere.[15]

Gray's vision informed British architectural utopianism of the 1960s, which itself took a delight in formal experiments and futuristic technological fantasies but refrained from social criticism. One of the movement's major protagonists during the 1960s, the Archigram, was based at the Architectural Association in London, where it translated that image to Rem Koolhaas (graduated in 1972) and Hadid (who studied under Koolhaas and graduated to join OMA in 1977). Thus in his "Story of the Pool" (1977), Koolhaas evoked utopian student projects produced at VKhUTEMAS, while Hadid's master thesis from the same year adapted Suprematist forms to a design for a fourteen-story hotel across a Thames bridge.

During the same decade, the term "Constructivism" became widespread in English language academic discourse. Initially coined by artists around 1920, the word pointed to construction as a modern aesthetic and organizational principle. Because this principle was more literally expressed in three- rather than in two-dimensional art, early Constructivist art often took sculptural form; such was the case, for instance, with Rodchenko's "spatial constructions" or the work of OBMOKhU [Society of Young Artists][16] (fig. 2). However, Russian Constructivism soon abandoned this initial sculpturalism and moved to the design of utilitarian objects, intending thus to follow the spirit rather than the letter of engineering.

This early connection between Constructivism and sculpture was never seen as definitive by Russian scholars, well aware of the group's prolific and diverse legacy. Meanwhile, in the West, where this early period, as opposed to subsequent ones happened to become most well-known, sculpturalism was recognized as the major attribute of Constructivism. On the one hand, exported to Germany by El Lissitzky (himself, however, not formally associated with the movement) in the early-1920s, Constructivism was a term used by artists like László Moholy-Nagy to describe their technological, modern approach to art and, particularly, sculpture. On the other hand, sculptor Naum Gabo, who had belonged to the early Constructivist movement, left Russia in 1922, residing first in Germany (where he taught at the Bauhaus in 1928), then in Britain, and finally in the US between 1946 and his death in 1977. Through his activity, most notably the 1937 book *Circle: International Survey of Constructivist Art,* Gabo attempted to present Constructivism as an international art movement with his own persona at its roots.[17]

Both the "German" and "Anglo-American" afterlives of the term reflected its early sculptural understanding and could thus comfortably fit into the formalist narrative of the Russian avant-garde as autonomous from social institutions. So comfortably, in fact, that from the 1970s on, "Russian Constructivism" in common academic parlance became a synonym of "the Russian avant-garde," referring to all modernist artistic production in the country.[18] As a consequence of this substitution, the early, pre-Constructivist period of Russian modernism – which had been the focus of Gray's book – was no longer seen as pertaining to the avant-garde and thus as being worthy of scholarly interest. Similarly, other, non-Constructivist approaches to art were either ignored (such as prolific efforts at modernizing painterly realism) or mislabeled as Constructivist (such as Suprematism).

fig. 2 Aleksandr Rodchenko, *Spatial Construction. Kino-fot*, No. 4 (1922), 1.

fig. 3 Vesnin brothers, ARKOS company building Competition entry, 1924. Public domain.

Constructivism in Soviet architecture emerged later than in art. It was promoted by the Union of Contemporary Architects (OSA), which operated between 1924 and 1932[19] (fig. 3). In spite of the sculptural interpretation of the "Constructivist style" in Western Europe and the US late in the Cold War, Soviet Constructivists never treated architectural form as sculpture – this approach was associated, in fact, with their opponents, the so-called Rationalists, and with independent architects like Konstantin Mel'nikov, whose formalism the Constructivists fiercely criticized.

Deconstructivist Architecture

As expressed by Koolhaas and Hadid, the fascination with the Russian avant-garde as a sculptural approach to form and its artistic representation received international attention in 1988 when the two architects, along with Eisenman, Coop Himmelblau, Frank Gehry, Daniel Libeskind and Bernard Tschumi were featured at the *Deconstructivist Architecture* exhibition at the Museum of Modern Art in New York. Curated by Philip Johnson and Mark Wigley, the exhibition was not devoted to the Soviet avant-garde but contributed to the development of the narrative by juxtaposing Russian modernist paintings and sculptures from the museum's collection to the works of contemporary "neo-avantgardists" (fig. 4). Most of this work was visionary or simply unrealized, while its authors, who came of professional age during the 1970s, were known as theoreticians rather than as practitioners. Although they did not comprise a group or a movement, their work – according to the curators – demonstrated a similar approach and similarly formal results. All of them, they claimed, drew upon the formal experimentation of Russian Constructivism. In Wigley's words:

> Russian Constructivism constituted a critical turning point where the architectural tradition was bent so radically that a fissure opened up through which certain disturbing architectural possibilities first became visible. Traditional thinking about the nature of the architectural object was placed in doubt. But the radical possibility was not taken up. The wound in the tradition soon closed, leaving but a faint scar. These projects reopen the wound.[20]

Despite Wigley's dramatic tone, the fissure he saw in the development of modernism was merely formal: the threat to tradition lay in breaking the stability, balance and hierarchy of classicist composition, which was replaced with dynamics, restlessness and instability. These new values of architecture, however, were soon thought to be lost in a return to classicist sensibility in postwar modernism.

Wigley's program reflected the agenda of another exhibition, in dialog with which *Deconstructivist Architecture* had been conceived. Curated by Johnson together with Henry Russell Hitchcock more than half a century earlier, the iconic *Modern Architecture – International Exhibition* (commonly known as *The International Style*) opened at MoMA in 1932. If *The International Style* claimed to have initiated the development of modernist architecture in the US, promoting the work of Le Corbusier, Mies van der Rohe, Gropius and Oud, *Deconstructivist Architecture* proclaimed a war on the presumed corruption of their legacy during the postwar period – a cor-

fig. 4 *Deconstructivist Architecture* exhibition at MoMA, 1988. Photograph by Mali Olatunji courtesy of Museum of Modern Art, NY.

ruption that consisted not in expelling the social program, which lay at the core of early European modernism, but in compositional flaws.

In spite of the curators' claims, the connection between the seven exhibited architects and Russian Constructivism was problematic. Although Koolhaas, Hadid and Tschumi demonstrated a formal interest in Russian art and architecture of the 1920s, strictly speaking none of the projects engaged the legacy of architectural Constructivism. Instead, the curators relied on the expanded definition of Constructivism as a sculptural approach to architectural form, which they updated to refer to dynamism and instability. Johnson stretched Constructivism to the 1930s, when Soviet architecture assumed an American ideal of modernization and explored the forms of Art Deco (a trend that Chernikhov's fantasies represent). On the other hand, Wigley, who evoked Malevich, Lissitzky and Tatlin, was interested in the period that preceded Constructivism, a transitional phase from the dynamism of Futurism and Expressionism to more static forms of later modernism. Wigley singled out this period as a moment of the self-critique of modernism, which he qualified as "unease," "disintegration," "decentering" and "dislocation."

If such a critique took place, however, it would have to have been targeted at what was to come only a decade later – including Constructivism proper. Singling out Russian Constructivism, Wigley and Johnson concealed another source of deconstructivist architecture: its indebtedness to the philosophy of Jacques Derrida, which was in fact the original source of the term.[21] This de-intellectualization of the notion of deconstructivist architecture allowed a shift in its meaning, transforming it from a theoretical program into a *style* – a transformation that *The International Style* exhibition had earlier performed with modernism and that Western art criticism had performed with early-Soviet modernist art.

The (Utopian) Avant-garde versus Totalitarianism

The "expanded" Western concept of Constructivism smuggles a hidden formalist agenda into a discussion of Soviet postrevolutionary art and architecture, through the very depoliticization of the original program betraying the Cold War atmosphere. Meanwhile, another set of notions results from the shifting political context of the 1980s. With the arrival of Gorbachev's liberal *perestroika*, Western political powers assumed a flattering tone in negotiations with Russia, sweetening requests of dismantling its imperial legacy and destroying its military complex by symbolic recognitions of Russia's future place among the world's elite. Consequently, Western propaganda elaborated an image of Russia as an *enfant terrible* of the European family: imprudent, incautious, maximalist, naive and idealistic, making grave mistakes because of an adolescent desire for perfection but ready to make up for them – an image matching perfectly the clichés about artistic personality. Western audiences were especially fascinated with the revolution of 1917, which was seen as a sublime eruption of unconscious, quasi-libidinal forces through the dull surface of the bourgeois everyday – an eruption both fearful and seductive. Already encountered in Gray's book, such terms as "experiment," "fantasy," "utopia," "dream," "the visionary" and "the impossible" now flooded accounts of early-Soviet art and architecture: take, for instance, Richard Stites's *Revolutionary Dreams: Utopian Vision and Experimental Life in the Russian Revolution* (1989) or the Guggenheim Museum's seminal exhibition *The Great Utopia: The Russian and Soviet Avant-Garde, 1915–1932* (1992), for which Hadid designed the architectural setting.[22] If the "paper" architects of the 1970s saw utopianism in a positive light, during the pragmatic 1980s it became a condescending label that pointed to early-Soviet art's inadequacy – utopia was, after all, essentially unrealizable, and any attempts at its realization inevitably led to its degradation into a dystopia.

A vague and essentially mystifying notion, "utopia" was avoided by critical art historians. Instead, they applied to Soviet art analytical paradigms developed for the Western context – substituting state power in the USSR for the power of capital in the West. According to this logic, in state-capitalist Soviet Russia the state (rather than capital) was the threat to art's autonomy, the source of deception and of the instrumentalization of the subject. Most notably represented by Buchloh, this approach asked how the transition from the avant-garde to totalitarianism could have been possible. "Constructivism," which for these historians as well as for their contemporaries stood for all Soviet modernism, seemed to embody an aesthetic program appreciated by progressive Western intellectuals: materialism, respect for labor, collectivity as well as a modernist visual language that resembled postwar American abstraction. State totalitarianism, on the other hand, was viewed as a return to representational art and classicist architecture, and as philosophical dogmatism. While the avant-garde and totalitarianism were presented as two ethical rather than aesthetic opposites, the fact that the same artists sometimes contributed to both became the key riddle that these historians tried to solve.[23]

Since its emergence, totalitarianism – a notion used in the late 1930s and early 1940s by Friedrich Hayek and other theoreticians of economic liberalism in the US – has functioned as a tool of political propaganda. Unlike the universally applicable kitsch of Greenberg, totalitarianism targeted only selected countries. During the 1940s in the US, Moscow was constantly evoked as the scarecrow that shooed artists away from leftist ideologies – there is little wonder, therefore, that the Soviet Union (now made a synonym of totalitarianism) and "the avant-garde" came to be seen as irreconcilable opposites.[24]

In the mid-1990s, when Russia's absolute defeat in the Cold War became clear and irreversible and when political negotiations acquired a harsh and imperative tone, historians (particularly historians of politics and culture) shifted their attention from the aspirations of the avant-garde to the crimes of totalitarianism. They explicitly re-politicized the notion of the avant-garde by identifying it with artistic pluralism (and consequently, with political liberalism). This new generation of architectural historians rejected formalist analysis for the sake of archival "truth." Hugh Hudson's ominously titled *Blueprints and Blood: The Stalinization of Soviet Architecture, 1917–1937* (1994) serves as an example.[25] The gravest of totalitarianism's crimes was, according to this narrative, the assassination of the avant-garde. The chronological scope of Hudson's book was defined by political events (the revolution and the so-called Great Purges – another term invented by American historiography) rather than by the events of cultural life. Politics, not the art and architectural production that resulted from it, was at the focus of these scholars' investigations: the architecture that followed was considered a criminal betrayal of the ideals enforced by omnipotent state power and thus not worthy of attention.

Alternatives

Although predominant, the interpretation of the Russian avant-garde (including early-Soviet modernist architecture) as an autonomous, formally innovative artistic movement antithetic to totalitarianism was not the only possible approach to the problem. Among those discontented were authors both in Russia and abroad, both on the left and right of the political spectrum. The optimists among them believed that early-Soviet architecture should be dissociated from totalitarianism, while skeptics accused the avant-garde of complacency with the latter.

A generation of postwar left-wing architectural historians emerged in European countries, first in France and Italy; some embarked on sympathetic studies of Russian postrevolutionary architecture. Adhering to Marxist humanism, they likewise accepted the values and principles of Jean-Paul Sartre's aesthetics of engagement, trying to bring into harmony their political beliefs, practical work and historical research. Such architects-turned-scholars as Anatole Kopp and Vieri Quilici saw in Soviet revolutionary architecture a repository of ideas for the architecture of the future.[26] Unlike their American colleagues, they devoted significant attention to urban planning – a field of architecture that avoids formal interpretations. However, their approach found little following among the next generation, brought up in the frigid political climate of the 1970s and 1980s.

Meanwhile, another Italian Marxist historian, Manfredo Tafuri in his *Architecture and Utopia: Design and Capitalist Development* (1973) accused the Soviet avant-garde (among its other variants) of bearing the seeds of its own demise: by trying to heal (which, for Tafuri, meant masking) the contradictions of capitalism with first urban then ultimately economic planning, "architecture as an ideology of the plan [was] swept away by the reality of the plan when, the level of utopia having been superseded, the plan [became] an operative mechanism."[27] Somewhat similarly, Soviet historians emphasized either political or aesthetic connections between "the avant-garde" and "totalitarian" periods. On the one hand, Selim Khan-Magomedov introduced the notion of post-Constructivism as a formal category that described the architecture of the late 1920s and early 1930s as the missing link in the evolutionary development of architecture from Constructivism to Socialist Realism.[28] On the other hand, émigré cultural historian Boris Groys claimed that totalitarianism was nothing other than one of the avant-garde's avatars.[29] Groys pointed to the militant radicalism characteristic of all modernists, who were intolerant of pluralism and often demanded political persecution of their opponents. According to him, Stalin's transformation of the USSR could be interpreted as an aesthetic project, the medium of which was the entirety of life in the country.

These French, Italian and Soviet historians attempted to move beyond the problematic juxtaposition of "the avant-garde" (a term of art criticism) and "totalitarianism" (that of political theory). Their work questioned the often-implied link between the formalistically interpreted avant-garde and the ideology of new liberalism. But even these sympathetic or skeptical attempts, made at a time when the Cold War battles were still being fought, were not free of carving out a strategic positions and searching for military alliances. And whereas the universal notion of the avant-garde as an opposite of bourgeois culture has retained its validity due to the continuing preeminence of (neo)liberalism, today, long after the Soviet bloc has ceased to exist, the notion of the Russian avant-garde as an opposite of totalitarianism has lost the ground beneath its feet. The time has come to reevaluate this notion, looking for new explanatory paradigms that assess Soviet modernist art from a broader perspective than its subordination to the state politics of control. It is the time to analyze it as a part of international social-democratic movements, within its social and economic contexts, and amidst aesthetic and philosophical debates of the period – time to stop focusing on suppressing agency and instead search for neglected voices in forgotten corners of early-Soviet culture.

Endnotes

1 I am thankful to Daniar Yusupov for giving me a tour of Chernikhov's tower in St. Petersburg in the fall of 2014 and for sharing the story of Zaha Hadid's Pritzker Prize ceremony, and to Torsten Lange for organizing the "East West Central" conference and commenting on various parts of this paper.

2 This story is given after Daniar Yusupov's account.

3 "Chernikhov: Fantasy and Construction; Iakov Chernikhov's Approach to Architectural Design," special issue AD Profile 55 guest-edited by Catherine Cooke, *Architectural Design* 54, no. 9/10 (1984); "Russian Constructivism and Iakov Chernikhov," special issue guest-edited by Catherine Cooke, *Architectural Design* 59, no. 7/8 (1989).

4 Iakov Chernikhov, *Konstruktsiia arkhitekturnykh i mashinnykh form* (Leningrad: Izdanie Leningradskogo obshchestva arkhitektorov, 1931).

5 For a historical account and a critical discussion of this notion during the twentieth century, see Ann Gibson, "Avant-Garde," *Critical Terms for Art History: Second Edition*, ed. Robert S. Nelson and Richard Shiff (Chicago and London: The University of Chicago Press, 2003), 202–216.

6 Clement Greenberg, "Avant-garde and Kitsch," in *Clement Greenberg: The Collected Essays and Criticism*, ed. John O'Brian (Chicago: University of Chicago Press, 1986), 1, 5–37.

7 Serge Guilbaut, *How New York Stole the Idea of Modern Art: Abstract Expressionism, Freedom, and the Cold War* (Chicago: University of Chicago Press, 1983), 3.

8 Renato Poggioli, *Teoria Dell'arte D'avanguardia* (Bologna: Il Mulino, 1962). The book was written in 1949–1951 and translated into English in 1968. See also Peter Bürger, *Theorie Der Avantgarde* (Frankfurt am Main: Suhrkamp, 1974).

9 Theodor W. Adorno, *Ästhetische Theorie* (Frankfurt am Main: Suhrkamp, 1970).

10 Rosalind Krauss, *The Originality of the Avant-Garde and Other Modernist Myths* (Cambridge, MA: The MIT Press, 1985).

11 Giorgio Grassi, "Avant-Garde and Continuity," [1980], *Oppositions Reader: Selected Readings from a Journal for Ideas and Criticism in Architecture 1973–1984*, ed. K. Michael Hays (New York: Princeton Architectural Press, 1998), 391–401.

12 Rosalind Krauss, "Death of a Hermeneutic Phantom: Materialization of the Sign in the Work of Peter Eisenman," in *House of Cards,* ed. Peter Eisenman (New York: Oxford University Press, 1987), 166–184.

13 Around 2000, when a renewed interest in the avant-garde emerged in the US, architecture became the subject of much of its focus. The discussion, however, demonstrated a historiographical rather than a critical character, and the discourse continued to be defined by notions of autonomy and formal experimentation. See Robert E. Somol, ed., *Autonomy and Ideology: Positioning an Avant-Garde in America* (New York: Monacceli Press, 1997); Benjamin Buchloh, *Neo-avantgarde and Culture Industry: Essays on European and American Art from 1955 to 1975* (Cambridge, Mass: MIT Press, 2000); Hilde Heynen, "'What Belongs to Architecture?' Avantgarde Ideas in the Modern Movement," *The Journal of Architecture*, 4 (1999), 129–147; "Return of the Avant-Garde: The Post-War Movements," special issue of *The Journal of Architecture*, 6 (Summer 2001); Esra Akcan, "Manfredo Tafuri's Theory of the Architectural Avant-garde," *The Journal of Architecture*, 7:2 (Summer 2002), 135–170.

14 The revised posthumous 1986 edition was renamed by Thames and Hudson *The Russian Experiment in Art 1863–1922* for the World of Art series.

15 Camilla Gray, *The Great Experiment: Russian Art, 1863–1922* (London: Thames and Hudson, 1962).

16 See Maria Gough, *The Artist As Producer: Russian Constructivism in Revolution* (Berkeley: University of California Press, 2005).

17 John Leslie Martin, Ben Nicholson, and Naum Gabo, eds., *Circle: International Survey of Constructive Art* (London: Faber & Faber, 1937). The layout of the book was developed by British artist Barbara Hepworth. Gabo's vision was reflected in *The Tradition of Constructivism*, ed. by Stephen Bann (New York: Viking Press, 1974).

18 See, for instance: Jaroslav Anďel, *Art into Life: Russian Constructivism, 1914–1932* (Seattle: Henry Art Gallery, University of Washington, 1990).

19 Selim Khan-Magomedov's book *Aleksandr Vesnin and Constructivism* uses the term in this narrow definition.

20 Mark Wigley, "Deconstructivist Architecture," in *Deconstructivist Architecture: The Museum of Modern Art, New York*, ed. Philip Johnson and Mark Wigley (Boston: Little, Brown, 1988), 10–20.

21 Both Tschumi and Eisenman collaborated with Derrida in the early 1980s, and just a few months before the opening of the MoMA exhibition, Tate Gallery in London hosted the symposium "Deconstruction in Art and Architecture," which discussed the potential opened by Derrida's philosophy. Wigley devoted his doctoral dissertation, defended in 1986, to the philosophy of Derrida. Interestingly, the dissertation and the book that came out of it, *TheArchitecture of Deconstruction: Derrida's Haunt* focus on philosophy alone, without evoking the architects represented at *Deconstructivist Architecture*, while the exhibition catalog claims that Derrida's philosophy was irrelevant for the group.

22 Richard Stites, *Revolutionary Dreams: Utopian Vision and Experimental*

Life in the Russian Revolution (New York: Oxford University Press, 1989); *The Great Utopia: The Russian and Soviet Avant-Garde, 1915–1932* (New York: Guggenheim Museum, 1992); Susan Buck-Morss, *Dreamworld and Catastrophe: The Passing of Mass Utopia in East and West* (Cambridge, Mass.: MIT Press, 2000). With its roots in the 1980s, this tradition persists today: a recent publication, *Utopian Reality: Reconstructing Culture in Revolutionary Russia and Beyond*, ed. Christina Lodder, Maria Kokkori, and Maria Mileeva (Brill: Leiden and Boston, 2013) serves as an example.

23 For instance, in Buchloh's seminal essay "From Faktura to Factography" (1984), he examined the presumed transformation of El Lissitzky from a carrier of emancipatory aesthetics to an agent of totalitarian propaganda. See Benjamin H.D. Buchloh, "From Faktura to Factography," *October*, 30 (1984), 83–119.

24 Plentiful examples can be found in Guilbaut, *How New York Stole the Idea of Modern Art.*

25 Hugh D. Hudson, *Blueprints and Blood: The Stalinization of Soviet Architecture, 1917–1937* (Princeton: Princeton University Press, 1994); Dmitrij Chmelnizki, *Architektur Stalins: Ideologie und Stil, 1929–1960* (Stuttgart: Ibidem-Verlag, 2007).

26 Anatole Kopp, *Ville Et Révolution* (Paris: Éditions Anthropos, 1967); Manfredo Tafuri, et al., *Socialismo, Città, Architettura Urss 1917–1937: Il Contributo Degli Architetti Europei* (Roma: Officina Edizioni, 1971).

27 Manfredo Tafuri, *Architecture and Utopia: Design and Capitalist Development* (Cambridge, Mass.: The MIT Press, 1976) 135. The book, published in Italian as *Progetto e utopia: architettura e sviluppo capitalistico* in 1973 and translated into English in 1976, was based on Tafuri's 1969 essay "Per una critica dell'ideologia architettonica" ["Toward a Critique of Architectural Ideology"]. For more on Tafuri's notion of the plan, see Tilo Amhoff, "Architecture as the Ideology of the Plan: Revisiting Manfredo Tafuri's Critique of Ideology," the International Conference Architecture and Ideology, Ilija Milosavljević Kolarac Foundation, Belgrade, September 28–29, 2012. I am thankful to Torsten Lange for alerting me to this text.

28 See Selim Khan-Magomedov, *Arkhitektura Sovetskogo Avangarda* (Moskva: Stroiizdat, 1996).

29 Boris Groys, *The Total Art of Stalinism: Avant-garde, Aesthetic Dictatorship, and Beyond* (Princeton: Princeton University Press, 1992).

Angelika Schnell

The (New) Concept of Tradition: Aldo Rossi's First Theoretical Essay

In 1956, Aldo Rossi, whose impact on architecture's "turn to history" is among the most influential, published his first notable essay on architecture and urbanism: "Il concetto di tradizione nell'architettura neoclassica milanese."[1] The author was still an architecture student, and it might be concluded from the title that he sought to deliver a solid historical examination.[2] Indeed, in this quite long essay, Rossi seemed to rehabilitate the late eighteenth-century architecture of his hometown; in particular the works of Giuseppe Piermarini, Luigi Cagnola, Luigi Canonica and Giovanni Antonio Antolini, which are not counted among the masterpieces of neoclassical architecture by certain architecture historians.[3]

However, "Il concetto di tradizione nell'architettura neoclassica milanese" ["The Concept of Tradition in Neoclassical Milanese Architecture"] is neither a historical essay nor an early postmodern example of a neo-historicist approach. In the essay, Rossi pursued a renewal of architecture and architecture theory as such, which he thought should be derived from an important but rather misunderstood concept of tradition invented in the late eighteenth century. According to Rossi, this concept of tradition was at the same time a progressive concept of renewal. It was thus not based on the conventional notion of tradition based on submission – becoming servile – to the architectural past, but rather entailed a fundamental revision of modernism that, according to the author, had lost its philosophical basis. It turns out that Rossi imagined a singular historiographical model that already contained most of his fundamental theoretical ideas on architecture and urbanism and differed significantly from those of his contemporaries.

A New Historiographical Model

The first sentences leave no doubt about the young author's self-confident position:

> When one explores the historical development of some motifs that had the highest impact on the discontinuous and often contradictory development of architecture from the nineteenth century until today, then one will encounter neoclassical architecture. Those motifs branch out from here and show increasing complexity along the way. The most original and valuable outcomes of neoclassical architecture – as the depository of the great humanistic arts – refer to the origins of their complex formal experience and review them on the basis of the new social, political and economic conditions.[4]

Obviously the main topic of this abstract, dense, even compressed overture is neoclassical architecture and not modernism or the modern movement. However, reading on, we quickly learn that Rossi does not discuss terms such as "modern" or "neoclassical" in the way art historians would use them, as distinct categories of style. Referring to the writer Carlo Muscetta – then editor of the journal *Società*, where Rossi's essay appeared – he instead introduces two different theoretical types of classicism: an "archaeological and platonic" classicism that, according to Rossi, was introduced by historians such as Francesco Milizia, Johann Joachim Winckelmann and others, and a classicism that was "visionary and materialistic" and belonged to the modern culture of the Enlightenment.[5] To Rossi, the former type of classicism is to be considered as mere formalism; it is "abstract," "academic," a "dead" formula, and Rossi even terms it *contra classicismo*. (This is the classicism that would later become the basis for its postmodern renewal.) The latter type, on the other hand, as "the depository of the great humanistic arts," has to be conceived as a philosophical category with progressive ambitions. It almost goes without saying that this latter classicism is where Rossi discovered the significant "concept of tradition." It is in fact the first type of art and architecture that legitimizes its classical legacy (presumably the architecture of Greek and Roman antiquity, and the architecture of the Renaissance) by reviewing and evaluating it "on the basis of the new social, political and economic conditions." Precisely this autonomous critical evaluation was the beginning of modernism, since from then on architecture became an inseparable "part of the general history of society."[6]

To Rossi, modern architecture and neoclassical architecture are not necessarily different or even contradictory, since they are both rooted in the philosophy of the Enlightenment. In order to understand modern architecture as such, we have to study its legitimate precursor: neoclassical architecture. By analogy with the different types of classicism, it follows that there must also be two types of modernism. In particular from the 1960s onward, Rossi distinguished between valuable modernism (to which "rationalist" architects such as Ludwig Hilberseimer, Le Corbusier, Ludwig Mies van der Rohe and Hannes Meyer belong) and a modern architecture that he criticized as "naive functionalism."[7] Since the modern architecture of the postwar period seemed to be driven purely by technological methods, Rossi aimed to liberate modernism from such "small-minded" ideology, and it was mainly in this first essay that he sought to bring to mind the philosophical and political context in which modernism was born.

From his earliest published words, we can conclude that Rossi tried to introduce nothing less than a new historiographical model. To him, architecture's history was no longer the description of linear evolutions of form. Instead, we have to consider a turning point: the age of the Enlightenment can be seen as a hinge from which we look back and understand the classical – that is, valuable – parts of architecture's past much better than before, and from which we also look forward to where we may observe the temporal development of this classical legacy in its modern fashion, as driven by progressive political and social forces. From here, we might also understand the comprehensive character and importance of the name *Architettura Razionale,* which later became the label for Rossi's architecture and architectural thought: it functions as a theoretical and philosophical nucleus for a completely new architecture (philosophical modernism born in the age of the Enlightenment) and as an umbrella for the iterations of classical architecture (including modern architecture).[8] Naturally, *Architettura Razionale* excludes or at least neglects almost all nonclassical architectural forms and periods such as medieval architecture, many baroque and eclectic examples, art nouveau, etc. Rossi's theory of a new "concept of tradition" is not only a call for a new contemporary architecture, but also a plea for a new interpretation of the past. Obviously, it differs fundamentally from other historical turns of the postwar era, be they historicist or formalistic.

Dialectic between Realism and Rationalism

What are the origins of this historiographical model? We know that Rossi was a member of the Italian Communist Party; his historical thinking was very likely derived from Marxist theory, and we may assume that he strove for a politically progressive theory of architecture. Indeed, parts of the answer can be found in the essay, since it is the consequence of two very specific influences: Rossi's first trip to Moscow and his reading of Italian neo-Marxist authors.

In 1955, Rossi was invited to Moscow as a member of an Italian communist student group. There he encountered Stalinist architecture – an architecture he admired throughout his life, but oddly enough did not mention in his essay, written the year after the trip.[9] However, it is not very speculative to assume that the architecture of the Lomonosov University – of the famous metro stations and works by the neo-Palladian architect Ivan Zholtovsky – were immediate models for his specific interpretation of a nonacademic classicism that is at the same time non-elitist and monumental, progressive and traditional, easy to understand and that lends itself – precisely for the aforementioned reasons – to political and social change.

These same characteristics might be discovered in neoclassical Milanese architecture. Similar to the architecture of socialist realism, it referred on one hand to the formal tradition of classical architecture and on the other exploited it for a political and social renewal driven by apparently progressive or even revolutionary forces. Naturally, those progressive forces were the ideas of the Enlightenment and the French Revolution, which subsequently became powerful in Lombardy (during the reign of the Habsburg monarchy then at the latest with Napoleon's invasion in 1796).

Rossi wrote:

> Precisely from here, from this upswing, the concept of tradition arose. The architects did not follow the realm of forms of ancient culture in a disciplined and unassertive way. Instead – encouraged by the prevailing circumstances – it was their free will. They accepted an order, and from its core it was possible to advance to something more comprehensive and new, by rationally criticizing the existing order. Outside the continuity of these elements, no progress was recognizable, only inexactitude and disorder. The modern town was built in the name of these principles.[10]

The obvious question is: how we can recognize this critical process of architectural and political renewal (from an inner rational core) – how did it happen?

Although Rossi does not explain it expressly, it becomes successively clearer that he tried to discuss a dialectical model, while the neoclassical architects of Milan used a dual design strategy of "realistic" and "rational" (or "idealistic") approaches at the same time. His first example is the architect Giuseppe Piermarini (1734–1808) and Piermarini's renovation design for Palazzo Reale (adjacent to the famous Cathedral; fig. 1).[11] Rossi complains

fig. 1 Giuseppe Piermarini, Palazzo Reale (1773–1778), seen from the Cathedral. Photograph: Angelika Schnell.

that his architecture, which includes the La Scala opera house in Milan, has been characterized as "servile" and "modest" by biographers.[12] Rossi instead honors Piermarini's utilitarian "professionalism," which does not obsessively seek a "*tema optimum*." According to Rossi, Piermarini and many other Milanese neoclassical architects had a concrete and realistic "understanding of the town and its needs,"[13] which should not be considered mere opportunism, but a completely new "*spirito cittadino*."[14]

In contrast to interpretations that see Piermarini's neoclassical renovation of the Palazzo Reale as the eradication of "any architectural trace of Lombard art,"[15] Rossi insists that the architect's approach was careful. According to him, Piermarini respected the yellow stucco, eaves and typical courtyard layouts of traditional buildings in Milan (fig. 2). At the same time, however, the building is structured according to rational principles of classical order: its floor plan is symmetrically organized; its main facade is "ordered by an extraordinarily simple rhythm of Ionic pilasters."[16] According to Rossi, it was impossible for Piermarini to reflect the medieval architecture of the adjacent Milan Cathedral or the medieval architecture of the city as such. Instead, Palazzo Reale (1773–1778) is a prime example of the specific dialectic between idealism and realism: its architect foresaw the necessity of extending and restructuring the city of Milan in order to create a truly modern city.

fig. 2 Giuseppe Piermarini, Palazzo Reale (1773–1778), part of the main facade. Photograph: Angelika Schnell.

The basis for this renewal of the city and its society was only made possible by a re-establishment of the formal order and rational logic of the classical language of architecture. Yet referring to local traditions at the same time and holding them in tension with classical rigidity prevents the building from becoming an example of academic, elitist classicism.

However, it is still not easy to understand why simply referring back to classical architectural language might be equated with a new "concept of tradition" and above all might lead to a political renewal of the entire city and its people. We might also find the example of Piermarini less than fitting, since he was a loyal architect of the Habsburg era in Lombardy. He was given the title Architetto Ufficiale dello Stato by Austrian Empress Maria Theresa in 1770,[17] and had to flee after the invasion by Napoleon's troops.

Another example discussed by Rossi might serve to explain his ideas even better. Giovanni Antonio Antolini (1756–1841) was an admirer of Napoleon, and his design for a gigantic *Foro Bonaparte* (1801) as a modernization and extension of Milan may certainly count as an idealistic approach influenced by Claude-Nicholas Ledoux (fig. 3): it is based on a monumental interpretation of the classical language of architecture and, at the same time, it is a political and progressive proposal for a new civic society, since the buildings that form the vast circle (with a diameter of around 535 meters) are public buildings (museum, theater, thermal bath, university, courthouse, etc.). Antolini proposed an alternative city center to replace major parts of Castello Sforzesco, which had previously been the residence of the dukes of Milan, its fortifica-

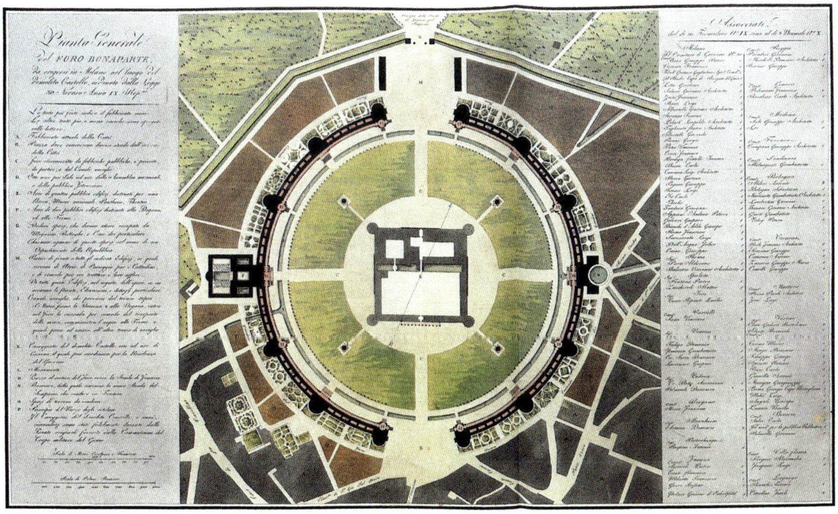

fig. 3 Giovanni Antonio Antolini, *Foro Bonaparte*, diameter c. 530 m. Source: Bibliothèque nationale de France, Paris.

tions demolished by French troops. This new city center was dedicated to the people and to Napoleon Bonaparte. It was called *Foro* since it referred to the ancient Roman Republic; the architecture of its many public buildings was to be based on the heroic, simple Doric order (fig. 4).

The enormous dimensions of Antolini's plan prompted one writer to call it the "Jacobin equivalent of Red Square or Tiananmen Square."[18] Rossi, on the contrary, honored its monumentality, since to him a monumental and grave architecture was necessary for a fundamental renewal of society. This was the lesson he had learned in Moscow.[19] At the same time, he called Antolini's proposal "realistic," and in this instance not because Antolini left the core of the Castello untouched – Antolini only proposed remodeling it in the neoclassical style. Even though the plan was never realized, it had an effect on the further development of the city due to its realistic anticipation of a compelling infrastructural and symbolic linkage (fig. 5). According to Rossi, the plan anticipated the connection between the religious center, the area around the cathedral, and the secular center of the city, Castello Sforzesco. This connection had not existed before; in medieval Milan, the Castello was encircled by its fortifications and had no morphological connection to the urban fabric. It was only in the nineteenth century that the city constructed this connection with Via Dante, which became an important commercial street in the city center. Thus to Rossi, the plan for *Foro Bonaparte* was not just an issue of architectural style: it was both a consequence and an anticipation of progressive social and urban development.

fig. 4 Giovanni Antonio Antolini, *Foro Bonaparte*, perspective
Source: Bibliothèque nationale de France, Paris.

The Concept of History

One might still wonder why Rossi insisted on classical architectural language for any progressive renewal. Why did he ignore vernacular, regional and popular architecture, which had become a theme among Italian leftist architects at the time?[20] As a Communist, he may have been looking for a revolutionary architecture; it is worth noting that the essay "The Concept of Tradition in Neoclassical Milanese Architecture" appeared in *Società*, which was not an architecture journal but a leftist social and political periodical. In the essay, he ultimately concluded that neoclassical Milanese architecture was "*realista e popolare*."[21]

However, Rossi refused any servile ingratiation to the "people." His notion of *realismo* had nothing to do with the neorealism of postwar Italian filmmakers such as Roberto Rossellini, Vittorio de Sica and Luchino Visconti (although Rossi admired the latter's work). Their films celebrated everyday life and included nonprofessional actors speaking in dialect. Yet Rossi deliberately did not pursue an analogous vernacular or popular architecture. In his essay, he clearly explains that the "history of architecture as cultural history is the history of the upper and literate classes." According to him, the "search for spontaneous or autonomous characteristics in vernacular solutions makes no sense at all."[22]

With this historiographical model of a self-critical rebirth of classical architecture of the upper classes, Rossi was referring less to the popular, somewhat lavish architecture of socialist realism that he had encountered

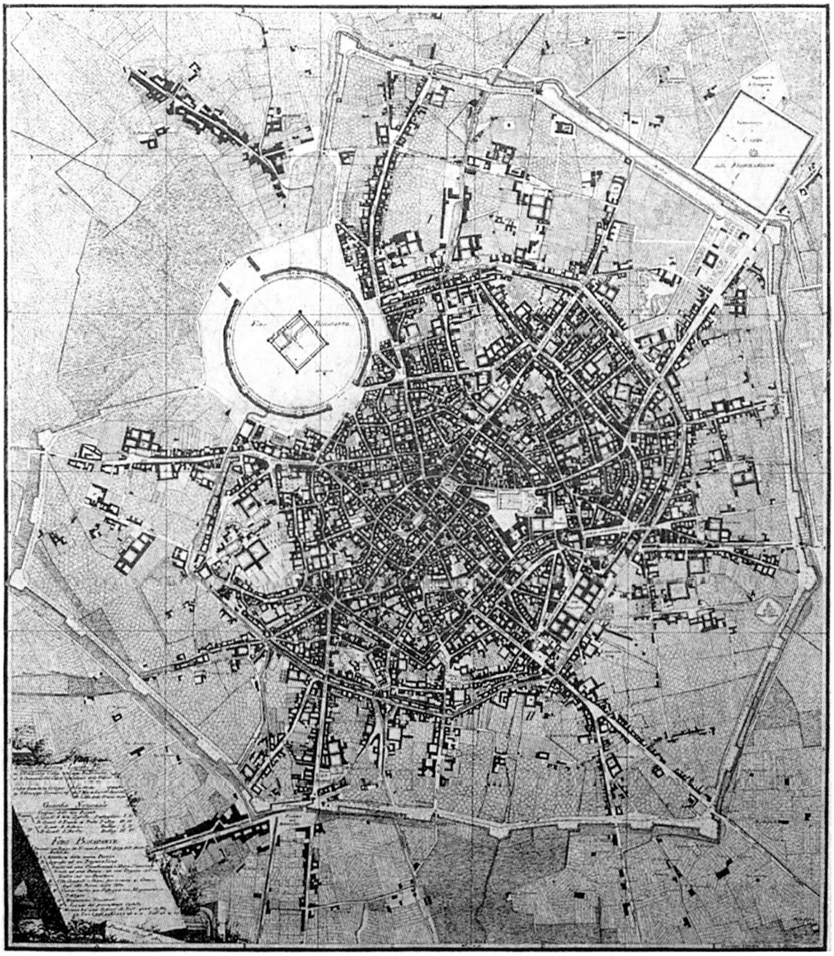

fig. 5 Giacomo Pinchetti, map of Milan, 1801, including Giovanni Antonio Antolini's design for the unrealized *Foro Bonaparte*.

in Moscow than to Italian neo-Marxist architects of the time. He quoted Antonio Gramsci and, implicitly, Gramsci's materialistic theory of "cultural hegemony," according to which new ideas are born as "renewed expression of the historical development of reality,"[23] – that is, of the existing cultural products. Among these can undoubtedly be counted the classical architectural language that stands for order, logic and outstanding quality of execution. In particular, Rossi referred to Cesare Luporini, a contemporary Italian philosopher who – like Louis Althusser – was one of those intellectuals who tried to link Marxism with structuralism, and was also one of the editors of *Società*. Just two years before Rossi's essay appeared, Luporini had published an essay, "Il concetto della storia e l'illuminismo ["The Concept of History and the Enlightenment"],[24] which evidently inspired the title of Rossi's essay. In his essay, Luporini discussed the era of the Enlightenment from a Marxist perspective. He aimed to exonerate the era from the accusation of being completely ahistorical. Instead, Luporini tried to prove that particular French philosophers such as Voltaire had invented "history as the science of the birth of the present,"[25] that is to say modern historiography, where history is considered as man-made history based on social, political, economic, scientific and cultural decisions. He used the dialectical method in order to detect both "idealistic" and "realistic" positions within the different philosophical positions of the Enlightenment, which, according to Luporini, created a fruitful tension.

It seems only a small step from there to Rossi's dialectic between "realistic" and "classical" (later termed "rational") design approaches, for which the Enlightenment era was the beginning of the history of architecture and therefore of modern architecture. Rossi does not distinguish between political history or history in general and the history of art and architecture, since to him, architecture had become "part of general history" as such. Therefore the architecture of that specific era – neoclassical architecture – is not only an aesthetic legacy, it is also a political and philosophical legacy to the present day. Hence, in his first essay, we find Rossi's real ambition in his "turn to history": it is a political turn and not a formalistic one, it is not postmodern (in the sense of postmodern historicism) and it is quite singular, since it wants to theorize the history of architecture in a new way. Above all, it wants to hail back to modernism's noble philosophical roots. Those who saw and still see Rossi's theory of architecture as an antimodern manifesto, a return to elementary geometrical forms and archaic types, overlook this fundamental ambition.

Conolucion

However, many questions remain unanswered. It is still not really clear why classical architectural heritage should be an appropriate basis for social and cultural renewal in the twentieth century, since antiquity or knowledge of the classical orders does not play an important role for architects of the modern age. Every non-European, or more precisely every non-Italian reader and architect in particular, might wonder why. Also, Rossi does not explain the classical legacy very well. Which architecture of the past and of the present definitely belongs to that legacy? Why should we continue to refer to it? What is its specific, inherent political power compared to other architectural styles such as Gothic, which was also exploited in the nineteenth century for moral, social and aesthetic renewal?

Yet to be left with several open questions is a typical effect in all of Rossi's written works: though he very often pretended to explore and discuss certain issues in a stringent manner, he never wrote precisely and systematically enough to establish his theory of architecture on a firm foundation.[26] This also holds true for "The Concept of Tradition in Neoclassical Milanese Architecture." The text is not structured by topics or with any logical continuity of the main arguments. One encounters different architects, projects, concepts, historians and philosophers in an irregular sequence. Sometimes crucial topics are mentioned only implicitly or are hidden in footnotes (such as philosophical links to Gramsci and Luporini). Very often, Rossi's explanations remain abstract – despite the many examples reviewed. Though he mentions several projects by Piermarini (besides the Palazzo Reale, La Scala and the Palazzo Belgioioso), he does not really discuss them in detail, let alone compare them with the architecture of contemporaries or predecessors. Piermarini's "professionalism," which, according to Rossi, stood out as a prime example of the dialectical design approach between idealism and realism, might also be understood as mere pragmatism or even compromise.

But Rossi does not argue like a scientist. To him, the purpose of writing was to consistently confirm his ideas, which were basically established very early, as "The Concept of Tradition in Neoclassical Milanese Architecture" makes clear. Finally, reading only one essay by Rossi generally does not lead to a well-founded understanding of his complex, even complicated theoretical world.[27] Rossi was always inclined to jump between persons, projects, time and space without expanding on certain topics. For example, he never clarified the Marxist basis of his architectural thought well enough, so it is not very surprising that both admirers and critics of his work tended to misunderstand this. He also referred to other movements and theories such as surrealist art or Maurice Halbwachs's concept of "collective memory," which led to inner contradictions that he never resolved or even critically discussed. Instead, Rossi used only those parts of these authors' thoughts that were useful to him. Such is also the way, then, that we have to read "The Concept of Tradition in Neoclassical Milanese Architecture," the high ambitions of which aimed at a renewal of architecture and architecture theory as such.

Endnotes

1 Aldo Rossi, "Il concetto di tradizione nell'architettura neoclassica milanese," in Società XII, 3 (1956), 474–493; republished in Aldo Rossi and Rosaldo Bonicalzi, eds., Scritti scelti sull' architettura e la città. 1956–1972 (Milan: clup, cooperativa libraria universitaria del politecnico, 1975), 1–24.

2 Gianni Braghieri, Aldo Rossi (Zurich, Munich: Verlag für Architektur Artemis, 1983), 210. Rossi was born in 1931 and died in 1997; according to Braghieri, his biographer and former collaborator, Rossi took his diploma in 1959 at Politecnico di Milano.

3 See Robin Middleton and David Watkin, Neoclassical and 19th Century Architecture: History of World Architecture (New York: Harry Abrams, 1980).

4 *"Se si risale nel tempo seguendo la storia di alcuni motivi che più hanno influenzato lo svolgersi dell'architettura dall'Ottocento ad oggi nella sua discontinuia linea di soluzioni, spesso contraddittorie, si giunge all'architettura neoclassica da cui questi motivi sembrano ramificarsi e via via svolgersi con sempre maggiore complessità. Depositaria della grande arte umanistica, l'architettura neoclassica, nella sua più originale e valida formulazione, riassume e rimanda la complessa esperienza formale da cui ha origine, verificandola sulle nuove condizioni sociali, politiche, economiche."* Rossi, "Il concetto di tradizione," 474.

5 *"Il Muscetta vi propone [...] tra un neoclassicismo illuministico e materialista e un neoclassicismo, o 'controclassicismo,' archeologico e platonizzante [...]."* Ibid., 475.

6 *"La linea principale dell'arte neoclassica si trova così legata al razionalismo illuministico, mentre il problema della forma in architettura si vede intimamente legato al problema stesso della storia dell'architettura, la quale, per la prima volta, si presenta non come una lenta e naturale evoluzione, svolgimento quasi organico di certe forme, ma come storia partecipe della più generale storia della società."* Ibid., 474.

7 Rossi's rejection of modernist functionalism can be found in almost all of his writings of the 1960s and 1970s.

8 Rossi did not use the term Architettura Razionale before the late 1960s and 1970s.

9 Aldo Rossi, A Scientific Autobiography (Cambridge, Mass.: MIT Press, 1981), 40.

10 *"Da questo stesso slancio sorgeva il concetto di tradizione, che andava definendosi non come disciplinata e timida soggezione al mondo formale che le antiche civiltà avevano espresso, ma come libera scelta di quanto la storia andava porgendo, come accettazione di un ordine dal cui interno era possibile risalire ad altro più ampio e nuovo mediante la critica razionale di quanto si era fatto. Al di fuori della continuità di questi elementi, appunto, non era possibile riconoscere progresso, ma solo imprecisione e disordine."* Rossi, "Il concetto di tradizione," 482.

11 Palazzo Reale [Royal Palace] in Milan dates back to the Middle Ages. It was used by the Sforza family as a residence closer to the center and less fortress-like than Castello Sforzesco. At the time, it was called Palazzo Ducale. When the Austrian Habsburg family took over the city government in 1714, the palace became a center of court life; as Palazzo Reale it was thoroughly refurbished by Piermarini. After Napoleon's government, the palace had several names (including Palazzo Nazionale della Cisalpina). Today it is called Palazzo Reale again and hosts a museum of art.

12 *"Invece, nella decisione del Piermarini di accettare l'incario sembra di poter vedere qualcosa di piú di quella sottomissione e di quella modestia che i biografi hanno attribuito all'architetto."* Rossi, "Il concetto di tradizione," 476.

13 *"[...] dalle reali necessità cittadine, sia pratiche che ideali."* Ibid., 489.
14 Ibid., 477.
15 Official Palazzo Reale website: http://www.palazzorealemilano.it/wps/portal/luogo/palazzorealeEN/palace/history/, accessed on February 4, 2016.
16 *"E ancora lo scarso risalto delle grosse bozze di granito che sulla fronte formano lo stilobate della pilastrata jonica che, con grande simplicità, si alterna lungo tutto l'edificio."* Rossi, "Il concetto di tradizione," 477.
17 Rossi refers to this only in his third footnote.
18 Franco Maria Ricci, "The Publisher to the Reader (L'editore al lettore)," in Aurora Scotti, Il Foro Bonaparte: un'utopia giacobina a Milano (Milan: Franco Maria Ricci, 1989), 12.
19 In the 1960s Rossi met Hans Schmidt in East Berlin (the Swiss architect and communist moved to Moscow in the 1930s and to the GDR in the 1950s). Schmidt's positive writings on Stalinist architecture confirmed Rossi's preference for monumentality. See Angelika Schnell, "The Socialist Perspective of the XV Triennale di Milano," in Candide, 2 (2010), 33–71.
20 Manfredo Tafuri, Storia dell'architettura italiana (Turin: Giulio Einaudi, 1982).
21 Rossi, "Il concetto di tradizione," 493.
22 *"La storia della architettura, in quanto storia della cultura, è la storia delle classi colte. Il cercare quindi nelle soluzioni populari caratteristiche spontanee o autonome, non ha alcun senso."* Ibid., 488.
23 *"[...] la limpida formulazione di Gramsci, 'le idee non nascono da altre idee, ma sono espressione sempre rinnovata dello sviluppo storico del reale.'"* Ibid., 485.
24 Cesare Luporini, Voltaire e le 'Lettres philosophiques' – Il concetto della storia e l'Illuminismo (Florence: Sansoni, 1955).
25 Ibid., 225.
26 Most architects of the "turn to history" failed to "establish a theory of history that would provide a firm foundation for their newfound historical awareness." Alan Colquhoun, "Three Kinds of Historicism (1983)," in Collected Essays in Architectural Criticism (London: Black Dog Publishers, 2009), 160.
27 For a critical reading of Rossi's complete writings, see Schnell, *Die Konstruktion des Wirklichen. Eine systematische Untersuchung der geschichtstheoretischen Position in der Architekturtheorie Aldo Rossis* (PhD thesis, Staatliche Akademie der Bildenden Künste Stuttgart, 2009).

Silvia Micheli, Léa-Catherine Szacka

Paolo Portoghesi and the Postmodern Project

> —At the crossroads of the four fountains long ago, during a dark evening [...], we met the Chevalier Francesco Castelli, the said Borromini. Close to the church of St. Carlo, the first major work of the suicide architect. The facade, taut and amazing, as a perfect stone, is the very face of memory.[1]

These lines are part of a handmade book, *Paolo Portoghesi di Francesco Borromini*, written in 1947 by the Italian architect and historian Paolo Portoghesi, then just a teenager in high school.[2] Typewritten, produced in only five copies and sold to classmates and friends, this precocious publication materializes Portoghesi's first encounter with the great Francesco Borromini, an architectural and spiritual event that was to change the course of his life and career. The black and white drawings are abstract while the text is in prose, with a clear influence – as much as it is naive – from Italian Hermetic poetry. This book embodies Portoghesi's dedication to history, yet it was not only at the service of history that Portoghesi used Borromini and his work. Portoghesi's attention was caught by Borromini's skills in breaking the theoretical and projective rules seemingly fixed by Renaissance architecture. Setting itself free of conventions, Borromini's work became a symbol of liberation and innovation not only in Portoghesi's architectural approach but also in his political convictions.

In the wake of this formative fascination for freedom in reinterpreting the rules, Portoghesi acted as a great cultural force in post-1968 Italy, shaping what one could describe as his "postmodern project": an architectural, cultural, intellectual and political endeavor, as it appears today in the light of historical distance. Portoghesi operated in the distinctive cultural scenario of the rise and fall of postwar social-democratic politics in Italy and the post-1968 cultural crisis – playing a central role in the development of architectural discourse in the postmodern cultural context. He did so particularly in relation to the diffusion and acceptance of the "historic turn" in architecture and urban design during the 1970s and 1980s – one facet of international postmodernism that took on a particular color in the case of Italy. While European modern architecture was generally associated with the socialist agenda and implementation of the welfare state, postmodernism in most European countries and the US is related to the rise of the free-market economy and the liberal right. However, Italy offered an alternative scenario. There, the Italian Socialist Party (PSI), after undergoing a drastic transformation, ruled the country throughout most of the 1980s, fostering a new socio-political program.

The Italian Context: Portoghesi and the Notion of "Project"

Proposing an approach to design based on the recovery of historical methodologies and on freedom from orthodox rules of the International style, Portoghesi formulated a personal response to modern architecture well before the expression "postmodern" came into use in architectural discourse at the end of the 1970s.[3] Indeed, Portoghesi arguably conceived his "turn to history" as a "project" based on the interweaving of architectural history, design, pop culture and political values in the wake of the socialist political stream (fig. 1). In so doing, he differentiated himself from other contemporary international critics and historians who contributed to the international success of post-modern architecture, such as Charles Jencks, Christian Norberg-Schulz and Heinrich Klotz. However, he aligned himself with his Italian colleagues in the understanding of history as part of a wider "project."

In 1960s and 1970s Italy, the word *progetto* (project), often translated into English as "design," meant much more than a simple set of architectural drawings. It was usually understood in its broader sense[4]: *progetto*, that is to say, a projection into the future, a long-lasting plan motivated by an intention or a construction of a scenario to be carried out on ideological and political assumptions. And yet, despite the common assumption of history as part of a *progetto*, the program of this *progetto* was carried out in personal and original ways. For Bruno Zevi, the architectural project had to support democratic ideals through operative criticism.[5] For Manfredo Tafuri, as was observed by Marco Biraghi, history itself was a project. Tafuri believed that the historian's task is not limited to a mere reconstruction of facts, but rather is the result of a construction, in the wake of the thought of Walter Benjamin and ultimately Friedrich Nietzsche.[6] In 1973, Tafuri published his *Progetto e utopia* (*Project*

fig. 1 Paolo Portoghesi, Dean of the Faculty of Architecture, Milan Polytechnic 1970 (© Giovanna Massobrio, Paolo Portoghesi Archive).

and Utopia), which in turn explicitly referred to art historian Giulio Carlo Argan's *Progetto e destino* (1965, Project and Destiny).

Portoghesi's approach was, however, substantially different from that of his friend and colleague Tafuri. For Portoghesi, the history of architecture is a survey through all possible methods, including analytical knowledge and the study of architects' ideas through all kinds of documents. Tafuri, who had strictly applied Benedetto Croce's vision of the art as intuition early in his career, eventually became an "orthodox Marxist."[7] He tried to see the phenomena of architectural history through that kind of lens, with the greatest rigor and dedication, producing an innovative methodology. All in all, Marxist theory had created a historiography with a general character, but its resonance was not as strong in architecture as in other fields. Tafuri offered himself as a guide at the international level, especially in the English-speaking world. For the American architect and theorist Peter Eisenman, for example, Tafuri was a prophet of an international Marxism – not a political Marxism, but an intellectual and quite abstract one. Portoghesi's historical attitude aimed to understand the self-criticism of the creative architect: that is, the path through which one gets to a certain form, not so much the ideal reasons, rather the methods used to build the form. In other words, Tafuri was a pure historian, while Portoghesi understood his role as a historian in function of his interest in design.[8]

Another figure who made personal use of the word *progetto* was architect Aldo Rossi, who had aimed to "write projects, story, film, painting [...] a projection of reality."[9] Differently from both Portoghesi and Tafuri, for Rossi the project includes something that is unexpected and unpredictable. More recently, according to this sensibility, Pier Vittorio Aureli referred to Italian architectural theories of the 1960s and 1970s,[10] expanding on the idea of the city "as a project" in that it is the result of the relationships among urban history, architecture and politics.[11] In the wake of these interpretations, the design, theory and history of architecture cannot be understood autonomously from political ideologies; instead, they are strictly intertwined with the broader cultural and political dynamics – that is, "the reality."

Portoghesi had initially participated in the architectural debate in his capacity as an architectural historian in collaboration with Zevi and in dialogue with Tafuri. Yet unlike Zevi and Tafuri, Portoghesi was constantly engaged in the architecture profession even prior to his graduation in 1957. His greater ambition was to create a bridge between "writing" history indirectly by designing, and "writing" history directly by investigating the legacy of the past, as he wrote in his first theoretical book, *Le inibizioni dell'architettura moderna* [1974, *The Inhibitions of Modern Architecture*]. Casa Baldi (1959–1961) and the design for the Opera House in Cagliari (1965) served as experimental laboratories for his historical explorations of baroque architecture. In this sense, Casa Baldi and his book on baroque architect Guarino Guarini (1956) were two sides of the same coin (fig. 2). Although Portoghesi's studies of the baroque reached further – developing within a broader circle of intellectuals including Rudolf Wittkower, Sigfried Giedion, Bruno Zevi and Gillo Dorfles – Portoghesi primarily chose to be an architect and carry out his own design projects, in which the history of architecture was instrumentalized as a means of liberating form and exposing design to new opportunities of spatial and linguistic expression.

Portoghesi's postmodern project becomes clearer if framed in the broader context of Italian architectural culture of the 1950s and 1960s, when an increasingly critical attitude toward modernism led to a growing concern for history. This generational reaction occurred in Italy much earlier than in other cultural contexts. After the Second World War, the support of Ernesto Nathan Rogers for greater dialogue with the history of architecture in order to achieve compositional "freedom" exerted significant influence on the architecture community. "History" and "design" were considered synergic factors and architects accordingly undertook rigorous historical studies during their training.[12] This educational approach was typical in the working group at the Milan office of the journal *Casabella-continuità*, directed by Rogers between 1953 and 1964. At the same time, in Rome, Zevi, first in the pages of the journal *Metron* then in *L'Architettura cronache e storia*, was also insisting on the need for the critical-operative recovery of the organic dimensions of modern architecture and a direct confrontation with its architectural problems. These

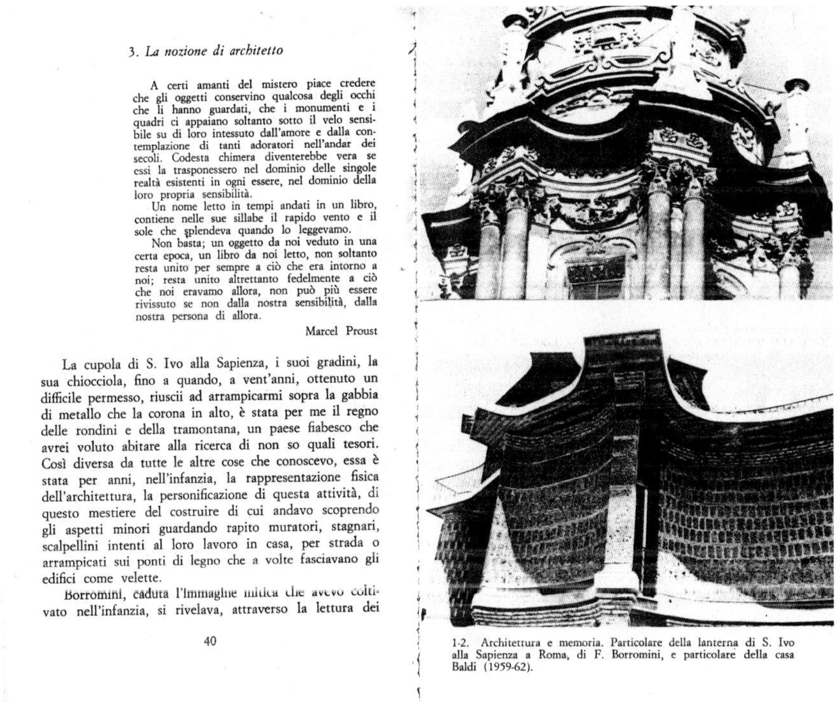

3. *La nozione di architetto*

A certi amanti del mistero piace credere che gli oggetti conservino qualcosa degli occhi che li hanno guardati, che i monumenti e i quadri ci appaiano soltanto sotto il velo sensibile su di loro intessuto dall'amore e dalla contemplazione di tanti adoratori nell'andar dei secoli. Codesta chimera diventerebbe vera se essi la trasponessero nel dominio delle singole realtà esistenti in ogni essere, nel dominio della loro propria sensibilità.

Un nome letto in tempi andati in un libro, contiene nelle sue sillabe il rapido vento e il sole che splendeva quando lo leggevamo.

Non basta; un oggetto da noi veduto in una certa epoca, un libro da noi letto, non soltanto resta unito per sempre a ciò che era intorno a noi; resta unito altrettanto fedelmente a ciò che noi eravamo allora, non può più essere rivissuto se non dalla nostra sensibilità, dalla nostra persona di allora.

Marcel Proust

La cupola di S. Ivo alla Sapienza, i suoi gradini, la sua chiocciola, fino a quando, a vent'anni, ottenuto un difficile permesso, riuscii ad arrampicarmi sopra la gabbia di metallo che la corona in alto, è stata per me il regno delle rondini e della tramontana, un paese fiabesco che avrei voluto abitare alla ricerca di non so quali tesori. Così diversa da tutte le altre cose che conoscevo, essa è stata per anni, nell'infanzia, la rappresentazione fisica dell'architettura, la personificazione di questa attività, di questo mestiere del costruire di cui andavo scoprendo gli aspetti minori guardando rapito muratori, stagnari, scalpellini intenti al loro lavoro in casa, per strada o arrampicati sui ponti di legno che a volte fasciavano gli edifici come velette.

Borromini, caduta l'immagine mitica che avevo coltivato nell'infanzia, si rivelava, attraverso la lettura dei

40

1-2. Architettura e memoria. Particolare della lanterna di S. Ivo alla Sapienza a Roma, di F. Borromini, e particolare della casa Baldi (1959-62).

fig. 2 Pages from Paolo Portoghesi, *Le inibizioni dell'architettura moderna*, Roma-Bari: Laterza, 1974.

experiences in turn informed the editorial line of the architecture journal *Controspazio*, founded in 1969 and directed by Portoghesi.[13]

In a moment of intense debate concerning the role that the history of architecture should take in relation to design, it was therefore of primary importance to find a way for orientating oneself, a valid method to refer to. Aldo Rossi, who at the end of the 1970s was recognized as the theoretical leader of *La Tendenza*,[14] undertook a poetic recovery of historical forms that, like fragments, gained new meaning through a process of abstraction and juxtaposition. Alessandro Mendini, director of *Casabella* between 1970 and 1976 and of *Domus* between 1979 and 1985 and one of the souls of Studio Alchimia, used to "borrow" forms from the history of architecture that he reconsidered in a playful and ironic way. As for Portoghesi, he took an autonomous path, based on the concept of "contamination" of historical sources, convinced that each form of architecture is generated by other architectures "by a not-so-fortuitous convergence among precedents combined together by the imagination."[15]

Political context: the Rise of a "Midway" Socialism

On July 16, 1976, Benedetto (Bettino) Craxi was elected leader of the PSI, marking a watershed moment in the history of the socialist movement in Italy and of the Italian Left in general. Following Craxi's election and during the second half of the 1970s, the socialist party was redefined to become completely autonomous toward dogmas of Marxist-Leninist ideology. In other words, the PSI kept a distance from most economical theories of communism and focused instead on the liberal reform of the party – a reform of the Left mainly oriented towards the middle class and trading the needs of social justice for a poignant desire for individuality. What Craxi and the "new" PSI were first to understand was the changing status of Italian society and its evolution in a direction opposed to communist theory.

In Italy, following the postwar economic boom – the so-called *miracolo economico* – a de-proletarianization and expansion of the tertiary sector fueled the rise of laic, liberal and modernist forces as well as a general consumerism and strong individualism. What Craxi defended was liberal socialism rather than the "common sense" of almost all the Italian Left that, at the time, was governing with the typical weapon of Bolshevik tradition; that is to say, "ideological terrorism." In a way, by the start of the 1980s Craxi embodied an enemy for Italian communists, who saw him as a subaltern of the United States and associated him, his party and ideology with neoliberalism and with the right wing of Ronald Reagan and Margaret Thatcher. In this neoliberal economical context, postmodern architecture could flourish, intertwined in different ways with political ideology, events and affairs.

Although Portoghesi's history of architecture was not soaked in politics, as was the case with Zevi, Tafuri and other Italian architecture historians, but was fundamentally dedicated to the investigation of form and its meanings,[16] it is hard to read Portoghesi's postmodern project without taking into account his ideological convictions and political orientation (fig. 3). Indeed, it could be argued that it was precisely the political implications of Portoghesi's project – or its relating architecture to politics and vice versa – that triggered a high level of resistance in Italy among the abovementioned politicized historians and critics of architecture, while making its intended "historical turn" particularly appealing for Eastern European countries.

Portoghesi joined the PSI in 1961.[17] From a highly politicized and mainly Catholic family, Portoghesi – unlike many of his fellow architects including, most famously, Vittorio Gregotti, Aldo Rossi and Carlo Aymonino, who all adhered to the Communist Party (PCI) – decided to follow the ideals of the more moderate Left. In fact, the PSI had, after the Soviet repression in Hungary in 1956, distanced itself somewhat from the PCI, a party which remained

fig. 4 Paolo Portoghesi talking at the 45th PSI Congress, Milan 1989 (Paolo Portoghesi Archive).

ideologically aligned with the Soviet Union until the late 1960s and received financial support from Moscow. For Portoghesi, socialist ideology also constituted a reaction to the dominant bourgeois culture. He was interested in the celebration of individual freedom, the pursuit of an antidogmatic vision and research into the complexity of reality. After getting his PSI membership, and just before 1968 as students were preparing their "cultural upheaval," Portoghesi was appointed dean of Milan Polytechnic's faculty of architecture. There, in an extremely politicized context, Portoghesi's militancy in the PSI was well-regarded by students.

Soon after joining the party, Portoghesi met Bettino Craxi, with whom he "developed a friendship, which then also coincided with a time of political solidarity."[18] Their ideological and personal closeness was facilitated by the fact that both Portoghesi and Craxi lived in Milan, a city that during the 1970s was experiencing an intense moment of creativity and successful tertiary business in the wake of the postwar industrial boom. When becoming PSI leader in 1976, Craxi exploited what he had understood as a desire for change shared by the vast majority of the Italian population. The motto was "liberation." Craxi operated a full reform of the party ushering in a new attitude that came to be called "*craxismo*," a political and journalistic term used to refer to Craxi's actions or, more broadly, a way of doing politics. In 1976, Craxi announced that he aimed for revisionism of communist ideology and toward a socialism that was neither that of "misery" nor that of "bureaucracy," but one that would promote social justice, political freedom and productive efficiency.[19]

Significantly, it was during Craxi's PSI leadership that a more explicit marriage of politics and architecture was consummated. Exuberant post-modern aesthetics and forms became an expression of the liberal ideology of the 1980s (fig. 4). While the party was looking for ways of reinventing itself – somewhere between the burden of Christian Democrats and the austerity of communists – Portoghesi fomented a reinvention of architecture. "However, I found fascinating his [Craxi's] program for a country like Italy that had always been repressed, first by the Christian Democrats and then by a strict policy" imposed by the communists, Portoghesi recalled, adding that "Craxi showed a desire for redemption from this difficult situation. His approach was libertarian and in this sense, his discourse fascinated me."[20]

From 1980 onwards and in the wake of success garnered at the Venice Architecture Biennale, Portoghesi started publishing his ideas on postmodern architecture. His communication strategy included a precise use of political vocabulary, generating strategic analogies – namely, those of political totalitarianism and of prohibition, the legal prohibiting of manufacture, transport and sales of alcoholic beverages. With "The End of Prohibitionism," first published in the catalog of the 1980 Venice Biennale, Portoghesi promoted architecture's "return of the repressed": "without preconceived discrimination, to involve memory and imagination with the maximum effectiveness, the projection into the future and the desire for the environmental quality of citizens."[21]

It was mainly the First International Architecture Exhibition at the Venice Biennale in 1980 that set the preconditions for Portoghesi and his work to be discovered by architects and students from Eastern Europe. No East European nations were on the list of countries represented in the "Strada Novissima" and the associated mezzanine exhibition.[22] Yet, as Portoghesi recalls, many young architects coming from unexpected countries – particularly Poland – wrote or visited after seeing the Venice exhibition or as a result of flipping through the pages of the Biennale catalog. "I was also visited by architects from Latvia and Albania, who thought that the postmodern had caught on in Italy, and there was a kind of structure that supported this effort," he states, although interest in postmodernism in Italy fell away pretty quickly. Their interest was motivated by a desire to make a counterpoint to the Soviet architecture of prefabricated barracks – a return to the logic of the "traditional village."[23]

Portoghesi and Eastern Europe

Following this interest and the beginning of an affinity on the Eastern European side toward his work, Portoghesi started to consciously connect his "postmodern project" to liberatory movements appearing in communist countries, in order to force a political point. "I was interested in the fact that postmodern ideas had found fertile ground in the communist countries," he said in a recent interview, "which were in the process of liberating themselves from the obsession of prefabrication – one of the last vestiges of modernism and a very deleterious one at that."[24] In 1982, in *Postmodern: l'architettura nella società post-industriale* – a book almost immediately translated into English – Portoghesi mentioned Solidarity, the Polish independent self-governing trade union that ushered in the beginning of the end of the Soviet regime:

> That Postmodern theses have deep roots in the present human condition is confirmed today in the document on architecture issued by the Polish union Solidarity. This text accuses the modern city of being the product of an alliance between bureaucracy and totalitarianism and singles out the great error of modern architecture in the break of historical continuity. Solidarity's words should be mediated upon, especially by those who have confused a great movement of collective consciousness with a passing fashion.[25]

Whether this connection between postmodernism and the fall of the Soviet-backed regimes in Poland is true or not, is open to discussion. Relevant, however, is how Portoghesi had consciously subsumed Solidarity into his "postmodern project."

For him, the postmodern signifies "getting away from the center in all possible directions."[26] While Charles Jencks was an observer and a gatherer and Heinrich Klotz was an historian and a collector, Portoghesi's approach to postmodern culture was that of an architect, concretely thinking about how to realize buildings. But was Portoghesi's modus operandi truly dedicated to the social relevance of architecture? In retrospect, the process that he had set up in order to carry out his "postmodern project" appears mostly personal, to such an extent that it became increasingly difficult to organize a school of thought around Portoghesi – in a way that Tafuri, who eventually became a fervent communist militant, did in Venice but on a completely different ideological premise. In this respect, Portoghesi's call for freedom and his battle against dogmatism and totalitarianism turned him into a singular voice in the national architecture debate.

Rather than being interested in the social relevance of architecture – its embeddedness in and reproduction of social relations – Portoghesi was constructing associations between a particular formal interest: On one hand, along with a program that sought to go beyond the rulebook of so-called dogmatic modernism and of stylistic convention, and on the other hand a neoliberal ideological program that defied "repression" and totalitarianism (conservatism as well as the alleged austerity of communism). Yet the political reality of the Eastern Bloc just before the fall of the wall was much more complex than this binary vision. Portoghesi's "postmodern project" was partly based on a conscious yet far from objective link between formal poverty and repressive politics. He might therefore have lacked a rigorous critical eye, being rather unaware of the constructedness of his own position.

Endnotes

1 Original Italian: "Al crocicchio delle Quattro fontane molto tempo fa nello stesso luogo dove avevamo accompagnato Arturo Bimbaud, in una sera oscura incontrammo il cavalier Francesco Castelli detto Borromini. Li vicino è la chiesa di S. Carlino la prima grande opera dell'architetto suicide. La facciata tesa e incredibile come un sasso perfetto è il volto stesso della memoria."

2 The book is in Paolo Portoghesi's personal archive, Calcata, Italy.

3 The term "postmodern" was first used in relation to architecture by Charles Jencks in 1975 in "The Rise of Post-Modern Architecture," *Architectural Association Quarterly* 7, 4 (October–December 1975) which also contains many of the constitutive characteristics that will appear in the first edition of *The Language of Post-Modern Architecture*'s first edition in 1977.

4 Marco Biraghi, *Project of Crisis: Manfredo Tafuri and Contemporary Crisis* (Cambridge, Mass.: The MIT Press, 2013), ix.

5 See *La critica operativa e l'architettura,* ed. by Luca Monica (Milan: UNICOPLI, 2002).

6 Marco Biraghi, *Project of Crisis*, 12.

7 The label "orthodox Marxist" comes from Portoghesi. Paolo Portoghesi, interview with the authors, Piazza della Piscinula, Rome, February 25, 2015.

8 Paolo Portoghesi, interview with the authors, Piazza della Piscinula, Rome, February 25, 2015. Translated by the authors.

9 Aldo Rossi, *Autobiografia scientifica* (Parma: Pratiche, 1990), 55.

10 Pier Vittorio Aureli, *The Project of Autonomy: Politics and Architecture within and against Capitalism* (Princeton Architectural Press, 2008).

11 http://thecityasaproject.org/about/. See Pier Vittorio Aureli, ed., *The City as a Project* (Berlin: Ruby Press, 2014)

12 In Italy, unlike in the Bauhaus tradition, there was no break with history, a subject that has always been taught in architecture schools. Between the mid-1950s and 1960s, while teaching at the Milan Polytechnic and directing the journal *Casabella-Continuità*, Rogers cited a great contribution to the role of history as instrumental to design. This approach was welcomed in other schools of architecture, in Rome and Venice, for example.

13 For a deeper analysis of the period, see Silvia Micheli, "La cultura architettonica italiana degli anni '60 e '70," in Marco Biraghi, Gabriella Lo Ricco,

Silvia Micheli, Mario Viganò (eds.), *Italia 60/70. Una stagione dell'architettura (*Padua: Il Poligrafo, 2010), 15–30.

14 Frédéric Migayrou, ed., *La Tendenza: Architectures Italiennes 1965–1985* (Paris, France: Centre Pompidou, 2012).

15 Giancarlo Priori, *Paolo Portoghesi* (Bologna: Zanichelli, 1985), 15.

16 Giulio Carlo Argan, "Nella crisi del mondo moderno," in Argan, et al., *Paolo Portoghesi* (Rome: Gangemi, 1993) 13.

17 Portoghesi interview, Rome.

18 Ibid.

19 Bettino Craxi, "Per l'avvio del governo della 'non sfiducia,'" Camera dei Deputati, August 10, 1976, in *Discorsi parlamentari*, ed. by G. Acquaviva (Rome-Bari : Laterza, 2007). From Marco Gervasoni, "L'impossibile intesa: Craxi, e il PCI," in *Bettino Craxi, il riformismo e la sinistra italiana*, ed. by Andra Spiri (Venice : Marsilio, 2014), 122.

20 Portoghesi interview, Rome.

21 Portoghesi, "The End of Prohibitionism," in Portoghesi, et al., *The Presence of the Past - First Internaitonal Architecture Exhibition of the Venice Biennale* (Milan: Electa/La Biennale, 1980), 10.

22 The US, France, Switzerland, Italy, Spain, the United Kingdom, Germany, Belgium, Norway, Japan, Holland and Austria were represented. For details on "Strada Novissima," see Léa-Catherine Szacka, *Exhibiting the Postmodern - 1980 Venice Architecture Biennale* (Venice: Marsilio, 2016).

23 Portoghesi, Rome interview.

24 Ibid.

25 Portoghesi, *Postmodern: The Architecture of the Postindustrial Society,* transl. By E. Shapiro (New York: Rizzoli, 1983), 8.

26 Portoghesi, in Eva Branscome and Léa-Catherine Szacka, "Architectural Postmodernism and Its Midwives in Conversation with Charles Jencks and Paolo Portoghesi," *Arch+ Klotz Tapes*, 2014, 23.

Karin Šerman

Boris Magaš and the Emergence of Postmodernist Themes in the Croatian Modernist Tradition

The following chapter is a survey of the flexibility of conceptual systems. It explores the capacity of a set of values and ideas to endure global paradigm shifts – to uphold consistent cultural production regardless of radical changes of ideological, political, social and intellectual frames. It focuses primarily on the resilience of architectural modernism, while also registering a certain preconsciousness of postmodernism, which is to say the early appearance of postmodernist themes even within the modernist discourse. The chapter also addresses the issue of identity, in particular the fact of its constant and recurrent reframing. The category of identity is thereby taken to connote both cultural and national identity, as well as the identity of the discipline of architecture proper.

In addressing these topics, the article relies on a particularly illustrative case: that of the eminent Croatian architect Boris Magaš (1930–2013), as an admirable representative of local architectural modernism. Magaš is chosen for several reasons. First, for the high quality of his architectural work: he was an exceptional architect and practitioner, with works that strongly marked the Croatian architectural scene of the period from the 1960s to the 1990s. Second, Magaš was among the first who operated with postmodernist ideas and introduced postmodern topics into Croatian architectural practice and discourse. And third, he was a theorist himself, a longtime professor of architectural theory at the Zagreb Faculty of Architecture, and as such was required to thoroughly rationalize and explain his own design decisions, in the context of theorizing the ongoing conceptual transition and intense reformulations of the inherited architectural apparatus.

When reflecting on the famed Haludovo hotel complex (1968–1970) on the island of Krk, his successful early work, Magaš remarked: "At the time when Venturi was writing about complexities and contradictions in architecture, I was already building them. I lived postmodernism before it actually arrived."[1] Indeed, many key postmodernist topics can be easily detected in Magaš's works. In the Haludovo project, for instance, Magaš focused primarily on the issue of meaning in architecture, inviting the audience to read and decode the messages of his architectural elements and forms (fig. 1). Later, in his celebrated Split City Stadium (1976–1979), he relied instead on the corpus of phenomenology, pointing to the issues of genius loci, spirit of place and natural ambience, as well as psychological responses to it as guiding forces in designing that masterpiece. Then followed the sequence of Magaš's church projects, primarily his St. Nicholas Church in Rijeka (1981–1988), in which he emphatically relied on history as a source, using inherited forms and researching the potentials of their creative manipulation, evoking issues of national and regional language and identity.

These projects clearly manifest an entire spectrum of central postmodernist themes: meaning, history, issues of place and phenomenology, regional language and identity. The intriguing aspect here is that these very projects were considered by the architect and by the overall local architectural historiography to be leading modernist accomplishments. Also indicative in this regard is the fact that Magaš had realized from 1958 to 1963 – just before the three projects mentioned above – the notable Museum of the Revolution in Sarajevo, as the most abstract modernist crystal, an impeccable abstract cube; the purest symbol of local architectural modernism.

Things would not be so perplexing if the architect did not insist on his unswerving conceptual consistency – on the uninterrupted constancy of his conceptual apparatus – and if he did not firmly believe in precisely that apparatus to be the permanent, unfailing bearer of local cultural and architectural identity. In other words, instead of some conscious and deliberate change in his disciplinary apparatus – the transition from modernism to postmodernism, following the ongoing overall paradigm shift – his testimony would point to quite a different instance: to a peculiar case of surprising, paradoxical, conceptual permanence.

fig. 1 Boris Magaš (right) in front of the Haludovo Hotel Complex, Malinska, Island of Krk, Croatia, 1968–1970. Source: Boris Magaš's Personal Archive, The Croatian Museum of Architecture Zagreb.

The Role of Architectural Modernism in the Croatian Cultural Sphere

In order to understand this conceptual puzzle, we should briefly devote attention to the subject of architectural modernism in Croatia in general, as an indispensable context for this particular case.

Perhaps somewhat unexpectedly for Croatia's rather peripheral cultural space, architectural modernism there had quite an early appearance and soon assumed a central cultural role and eminence. By the late 1920s and '30s, modernism had reached practically every region of Croatia and permeated various social spheres, defining almost all levels of interwar urban reality. Soon it had assumed the proportions and rank of a category of cultural identity. This, however, has a solid historical explanation and grounding.

Croatia's small yet varied territory has always spanned diverse geographies and comprised distinct cultural spheres. Throughout history, this dense social, cultural and political quilt persisted without a unified architectural expression. It nevertheless shared a pronounced common proclivity towards abstraction, formal reduction, pragmatism and rationality, and developed a specific design dexterity deriving from an enduring scarcity of means. Difficult historical circumstances had stimulated a tendency towards simplicity, functionality and the rule of objective, sober reality. Yet this permanent lack in the material realm was regularly compensated for by a heightened attention to conceptual spatial thinking. Instead of turning into a limiting factor, the condition of restricted means thus resulted in heightened creativity, filtered through sharp conceptual rigor and discipline. Such were historical circumstances over the centuries, in terms of both fragmented cultural and political entities and of shared, formal reductionist responses.

Modernism, therefore, when it arrived, entered a fairly prepared ground. With its abstract forms and autonomous procedural apparatus, modernism overlapped with inherited local reductive tendencies and thus served as a genuine common platform for the alignment of disparate architectural vernaculars. The close overlap of their formal and procedural features in fact explains an apparent paradox: the continuity of local architectural culture was preserved not by defying modernism, but by embracing it. Modernism's universalist essence coincided precisely with particular local affinities. Modernism was thus suitably co-opted to form a cohesive cultural identity.

And it immediately acquired distinctive historical relevance. Due to the country's precarious position at a crossroads of cultures and geographies, Croatia throughout history underwent frequent and radical shifts of political, ideological and socioeconomic frames. Yet where the political field suffered radical changes and instability, architecture demonstrated a surprising resilience and constancy; where political conversions were abrupt and rapid, building was persistent and slow. The fundaments for effective identity formation thus resided, to a great degree, in the realm of architecture. Modernism, as a common denominator of various local architectural vernaculars, thus assumed the vital role of a bearer of national identity.

There is yet another productive trait deriving from the condition of periphery. This relates to the nature of creative procedure. As a peculiar "center of the edge," always on the margins of great European empires – Roman and Byzantine, Habsburg and Ottoman – Croatia was historically destined to learn to juggle conflicting influences. Benefiting from the position of distance from major political centers, its art and architecture enjoyed the favorable "freedom of the periphery" and developed a method of creative and critical play with incoming cultural paradigms. This in turn resulted in outbursts of spatial innovation and experiment.

A good example of such creative play is the corpus of medieval Croatian churches, the so-called free-plan churches, of small scale but with remarkably strong and innovative spatial effects. Through intense play with diverse incoming models – primarily Roman and Byzantine – they developed a wide-ranging selection of types, forms, structures and plans, all invariably reduced to clear spatial concepts and restrained elementary volumes.[2]

Precisely because of the nature of this perennial play, the concept of identity was understood early to be an open, dynamic, permanently unfinished category. And instead of depending on petrified, fixed forms, it relied for its construction rather on relations, on procedure, and on the logic of creative process. The kernel of identity thus lay in the operation of critical alterations of the adopted model, in the act of its transcending and its specific, targeted adjustment.

Such adjustments might be regarded as some sort of attributes – qualities that modify the adopted model in a certain desired way. The model itself thus profitably survives, but gets transformed in such a way as to corroborate and uphold local intentions and interests. With time, the set of such consistent attributes solidified into a stable value system, a distinct system of architectural qualities, which in itself, regardless of the model embraced, guaranteed a degree of cultural subsistence and identity. And even if this was not always visible in direct, overt forms, it was nevertheless continuously present in the architecture's effects, experiences and performances.

Among the most vital of those historically formed attributes were: sublimation of distinct regional characteristics, interaction with natural settings and landscapes, attention to valuable historical urban contexts, respect for local building tradition and effort in generating social space, and constructing a sense of community.

This set of values was handed down as a precious legacy to the busy modern century. Modernism, as a newly embraced cultural model, was thus not only highly congruent with local conceptual and architectural procedures but was also calibrated with specific historically distilled attributes to best fit the frame of local, identity-laden value system. Largely recognized by its abstract forms and pure elementary volumes, modernism's universal essence was nevertheless fine-tuned by the subtle presence of sublimated regional features, by interactive relations with nature, by careful interpolations in valuable historical urban substance, and by overall social ambition and commitment.

Fitted in that way, modernism in Croatia successfully defined the interwar world of a burgeoning young capitalist society, developing within the political frame of the Kingdom of Yugoslavia, as a multinational construct to which Croatia belonged after the demise of the multinational Austria-Hungary.[3]

The Second World War brought on yet a new phase in the chain of recurrent geopolitical transitions, launching Croatia into the realm of socialism, this time as part of the newly formed Federal Yugoslavia. This radically altered political and social context demanded a radically different expression. Sanctioned from the highest Communist Party circles was the dictate of socialist realism, as the normative poetics of the new socialist system. Although Croatian architects deemed modernism a more than suitable apparatus for answering pressing new social needs along with the new vein of social engagement and a new wave of restricted material means, the functionalist tradition was censured officially and resolutely, accused of being empty and purely mechanical, devoid of real, full, inner human substance and, as such, a clear signifier of the decadent bourgeois West.

In answering these accusations in 1947, and in an effort to save the revered, identity-laden functionalist tradition, the Croatian architectural theorist Andre Mohorovičić constructed the breakthrough term of "comprehensive functionalism."[4] The term was introduced as a unique, broad theoretical concept that embraced – besides the necessary layers of function, construction and economy – so many other levels as well, such as aesthetics, history, regional morphology, meaning, culture, psychology and phenomenological dimensions and qualities. In a word, "comprehensive functionalism" effectively embraced all those layers that we encountered while briefly reviewing the interwar period of Croatian functionalist architecture. So, although Croatian postwar modernism did indeed rely on international, Western modernist models, they transcended in that way – as Mohorovičić claimed – their mere mechanical, technical dimensions and became a sort of "humane functionalism," "functionalism with a human face," fully in line with the broad humanistic aspirations of the new socialist system.[5]

Eventually, this "comprehensive functionalism" became a formula that worked well, with more or less contention and debate, and Croatian architects were allowed to build the socialist world in the inherited syntax of functionalist modernism (without a single socialist-realist project ever being realized). In that way they maintained, albeit tacitly, the implied memory of national identity.

To be sure, this recuperated legitimacy of the modernist tradition coincided with a favorable moment in the political sphere – Tito's famed break with Stalin in 1948 and Yugoslavia's subsequent expulsion from the Soviet ambit. Croatia, along with the whole of Yugoslavia, thereby regained a familiar and productive position in the center. The center of the edge, again, to be sure: wedged between two opposing blocs, two opposing systems, two competing ideologies, East and West, yet with a possibility to mediate between them and with the freedom to define its own political grounding. And indeed, exploiting this new favorable freedom of periphery, Yugoslavia developed its own experimental socioeconomic system (of undisputed socialist character, of course) known as "workers' self-management," just as it introduced a new political course, the so-called Third Way, between East and West: the famed Non-Aligned Movement. In any case, for Croatia specifically, such a position of peripheral freedom meant returning to a quite familiar terrain – the possibility of once again creatively using and exploring beneficial external influences. In the sphere of architecture, the door was thus open again to critically import the newest Western models or, for that matter, to continue profiting from a broadly set concept of "comprehensive functionalism."

fig. 2 B. Magaš, E. Šmidihen, R. Horvat: Museum of the Revolution in Sarajevo, Bosnia and Herzegovina, 1958–1963. Source: Boris Magaš's Personal Archive, The Croatian Museum of Architecture Zagreb.

Boris Magaš and the Modernist Tradition

As a young architect entering such dynamic and complex cultural and political terrain, Boris Magaš launched an instructive creative trajectory. His early step was to manifestly declare his own personal alignment with the modernist cultural footing. With two of his co-authors, he mounted the floating abstract cube of the Museum of the Revolution in Sarajevo as an explicit sign of the functionalist tradition[6] (fig. 2). This is all the more interesting knowing that this purest of modernist crystals housed the artifacts and the institute of the socialist revolution. Socialism, obviously, had begun to feel comfortable wearing elegant modernist garments.

Once such an unequivocal statement was declared, Magaš could proceed with pursuing more refined local modernist attributes. In his next major work, the Solaris hotel complex (1967–1968) near Šibenik, he decomposed the initial pristine cube into an elaborated open spatial system to house intricate tourist urbanity and to form, as he would call it, "Mondrian in the coastal landscape" (fig. 3). A balanced network of closed volumes and various outdoor spaces evoked the complexity and experience of a traditional Mediterranean city, while resting on an intricate modular grid as a prime abstract tool from the modernist inventory. Using atriums and terraces as reminiscences of local urban forms, the space was set to promote intense social interaction and gathering. On the level of the detail, another regional element gained prominence: traditional window shutters sublimated in a way so as to form the complete modern sliding facade membranes. And as a particularly intriguing segment, Magaš started experimenting with the decomposition of the corner, once so resolutely closed and compact and now signaling a clear structuralist impact (fig. 4). While remaining firmly within a modernist inventory, he started considerably extending and transcending modernism's limits.

fig. 3 B. Magaš: The Solaris Hotel Complex near Šibenik, Croatia, 1967–1968. Source: Boris Magaš's Personal Archive, The Croatian Museum of Architecture Zagreb.

Such research was continued in his Haludovo hotel project (fig. 5). It was an even more elaborate network of an extensive complex, where he addressed the issue of history by referring to vernacular and classical architectural forms, highlighting their messages and meanings. In an overall modernist framework, Magaš introduced the expressive element of the vault as a regional building form par excellence, in order to intensify the spirit and experience of Mediterranean ambience (fig. 6). Particularly interesting was his original, quite unorthodox treatment of the column, in which he communicated its structural logic by flaunting an unusually exuberant capital as a reference to a classical architectural syntax. The invitation was clearly conveyed to begin reading architectural language and deciphering its meaning.

In the memorable case of the Split City Stadium, Magaš turned to another set of fitting attributes (fig. 7). Intervening in an exciting urban setting and the impressive broader natural scenery – deep in a sea bay and between two prominent mountains – he focused on the topic of place, its spirit and potentiality, by striving to capture and enhance its extraordinary latent quality. Thinking of the experience of a classical Greek theater, which was always carefully set in fascinating landscapes and where the audience was invited to simultaneously enjoy the drama on the stage and the vistas of the natural setting, Magaš decided to recreate that historical sensation and offer both audience and competitors a similarly intense experience. He therefore designed the stadium as two connected Greek theaters, which together form a perfect shell that effortlessly floats in the scenic coastal landscape. The stadium was partially covered with a transparent roof to leave the multiple views unobstructed and to enable its users full appreciation of the broader context. Neatly nested in a striking topography, this detached, floating shell thus becomes an elabo-

fig. 4 B. Magaš: The Solaris Hotel Complex near Šibenik, Croatia, 1967–1968, detail of the corner. Source: Boris Magaš's Personal Archive, The Croatian Museum of Architecture Zagreb.

fig. 5 B. Magaš: The Haludovo Hotel Complex, Malinska, Island of Krk, Croatia, 1968–1970. Source: Boris Magaš's Personal Archive, The Croatian Museum of Architecture Zagreb.

fig. 6 B. Magaš: The Haludovo Hotel Complex, Malinska, Island of Krk, Croatia, 1968–1970, detail of the vaults. Source: Boris Magaš's Personal Archive, The Croatian Museum of Architecture Zagreb.

fig. 7 B. Magaš: Split City Stadium Poljud, Split, Croatia, 1976–1979. Source: Boris Magaš's Personal Archive, The Croatian Museum of Architecture Zagreb.

fig. 8 B. Magaš: Split City Stadium Poljud, Split, Croatia, 1976–1979, detail of the roof structure and view of the neighboring mountain. Source: Boris Magaš's Personal Archive, The Croatian Museum of Architecture Zagreb.

rate viewing machine, interacting intensely with its distinct surroundings as it remains an atemporal abstract object, self-sufficient in its elegant curved form. Architecture, mediating in its broader setting and capturing the extant spirit and quality, managed here to (re)create a tangible, fully charged place out of a promisingly potent location (fig. 8).

Dialogues with nature turned into ardent dialogues with the past in the next corpus of Magaš's projects: a series of churches, starting with his St. Nicholas Church in Rijeka (fig. 9). Searching for the true spirit of Croatian sacral architecture, Magaš focused on Croatian "free-plan" churches from the medieval tradition. For him, the essence of Croatian sacral space was attained precisely there: in their strong spatial effects and striking formal and volumetric variety, which resulted from the experimental and innovative play with various incoming external models.[7] It is in the analogous creative operation that Magaš would then seek to recreate this particular spiritual quality – in the free combination of inherited spatial and formal elements. St. Nicholas

fig. 9 B. Magaš: St. Nicholas Church, Rijeka, Croatia, 1981–1988. Source: Boris Magaš's Personal Archive, The Croatian Museum of Architecture Zagreb.

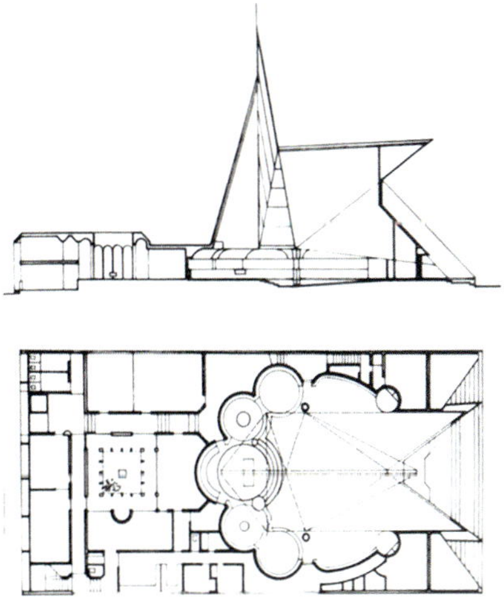

fig. 10 B. Magaš: St. Nicholas Church, Rijeka, Croatia, 1981–1988, section and plan. Source: Boris Magaš's Personal Archive, The Croatian Museum of Architecture Zagreb.

Church is thus a central round space with five apses in plan, reminiscent of the schemes of those pre-Romanesque buildings, which he then unites with expressive sharp vertical elements of evident Gothic character that structure the church volume (fig. 10). No matter how innovative and ultimately modern in its overall effect, this church confirmed the definite opening of the historical architectural inventory, in an effort both to capture the transcendental mystical spirit and to revive the feeling of national cultural identity.

With all of his works – as is demonstrated here – Magaš obviously mapped the field of modernism's local attributes systematically as fitting adjustments of modernism's generally universal essence, which made it suit the particular, identity-laden value system. In some of these cases, he extended modernism's apparatus to its utter limits. Yet in this way he thoroughly investigated the very scope and range of the theoretical concept of "comprehensive functionalism" – registering what specific qualities this broad term can ultimately comprehend and embrace.

There is no doubt that Magaš ventured into precisely such a search as a close collaborator of the theorist Andre Mohorovičić, author of this groundbreaking concept. He was Mohorovičić's longtime assistant at the Zagreb Faculty of Architecture and later his successor in the chair of architectural theory. Their intellectual affinity and shared conceptual and historical understanding explain the intentions of Magaš's own research and the purpose of his architectural operations.[8]

Postmodernist Themes Within the Extended Modernist Field

Issues of meaning, history, spirit of place and phenomenology, regional language and morphology, culture and identity – all these qualities that we encountered while analyzing Magaš's works – fell comfortably within this extended modernist field. The challenge here is that this same set of topics may just as well be listed on the roster of central postmodernist preoccupations and themes. What does all this say about the local architectural condition?

It is implied that the major later themes of postmodernist discourse were already incorporated in immediate postwar debates on Croatian architectural modernism. What is more – quite paradoxically so – it is precisely those specific postmodernist themes that then served as arguments for legitimizing the Croatian modernist tradition (within the context of socialist-realist dictates), as those postmodernist issues were likewise deeply ingrained in the local modernist architectural production.

The new postmodernist discourse of the 1970s and 1980s, then, would fall on fruitful ground and reawaken extant architectural values and qualities. All this would point to a certain specific local postmodernism *avant la lettre*: postmodern topics rehearsed in the midst of modernist practices. This unusual conceptual encounter raises, however, a list of further questions. How did all of this ground and direct local postmodernist reactions? How did postmodernism manifest itself at all within such a strong modernist context? And what then was the destiny of local modernism, along with that of postmodernism?

Shortly before his death in 2013, Magaš declared that at the end of the 1960s, when he had been completing designs for his Haludovo hotel project, he was not yet familiar with Venturi's postmodernist theories. When he then became acquainted with those, he was quite glad of the intriguing overlap of ideas – that he, like Venturi, elaborated topics of history and meaning in his architectural thinking, and that he had been building this new architectural complexity and not just theorizing on and writing about it. Magaš was pleased, in a way, that his applied ideas preceded the latest international architectural discourse. Yet soon after, Magaš retracted and distanced himself from this standpoint, classifying his own venture into this pool of strategies – as with those of his Croatian contemporaries – as pseudo-postmodernism, claiming that his was, after all, a clear modernist course.[9]

So what then was the key difference? I would propose that the answer might lie in the very direction or prefix of the similar set of ideas and strategies. At what goal were they directed? Targeted to what purpose? If modernism's central underlying feature is that it still presupposes the existence of one core question, one correct answer, one truth, one exact interpretation, one major historical narrative, and by extension the existence of a fixed standpoint and solid ground, then postmodernism's general shift would raise the awareness of precisely the opposite: of the existence of multiple truths, multiple histories, multiple interpretations and the impossibility of reaching any final and fixed universal meanings. On the contrary, with postmodernism the awareness was reached of belonging to a different historical age, with prevailing pluralism, heterogeneity, multiplicity and overall relativity and instability.[10]

In postmodernism, therefore, cultural disciplines were expected to convey precisely this new condition: to communicate the impossibility of stabilizing meanings, to model this newly understood heterogeneity, to express this all-pervasive relativity. This was expected also of architecture, when perceived as a relevant cultural subject. If earlier coherent cultural and architectural production reflected the underlying stable and coherent intellectual condition, then new cultural material should express just such general, global loss. Venturi's complexity and contradiction, Eisenman's appropriation and repetition, Rossi's permutation of emptied historical forms as emblems reduced to ghosts – they all perform exactly that loss: communicating this new relativity, this impossibility of stabilizing meanings, the predominance of Barthesian empty signs.

In a Croatian cultural context, however, things were to a great extent different. The historical condition of this permanently unstable territory had always been that of multiple histories, multiple truths, multiple visions, ever-present relativity and all-pervasive transient political and social circumstances. The only permanent element was, in fact, change itself. In which case it was cultural and architectural production – with the goal of securing elementary cultural subsistence – that was forced to assume the task of constructing at least some sort of provisional permanence. Architecture was summoned to construct a sense of constancy in the face of ever-fleeting social and political reality, and thus was engaged as a suitable bearer of national and cultural identity.

In order to complete this task, architecture needed to develop an enormously complex system of dynamic, flexible, even paradoxical creative procedures, malleable and supple enough to endure instability, relativity, heterogeneity and unpredictability. But its goal was always to run counter to the overall transiency and instability, to endure the relativity and to construct within it some tenable moment of permanence and identity. This became inscribed in the local architecture's operative code as its deeply ingrained intuition and intelligence. So when confronted after the latest global paradigm shift with a new, postmodern cultural period, it soon realized that it was in fact faced with a fairly familiar condition. And instead of starting to simulate this new all-pervasive relativity, architecture realized that its task remained, as before, quite the opposite – that of constructing a provisionally reliable and stable position within this new instability. The idea was not to further aggravate or simply communicate the extant unstable and heterogeneous ground, but to actively construct within it a moment of precarious constancy.

Thus the quest for "truth" – for the correct answer, the precise solution, the exact function, the full meaning, for economy, rationality, logic and construction, along with other modernist tropes – largely survived here, in spite of the heightened awareness of belonging to a radically different cultural moment. The modernist apparatus profitably survived, in fact, even if heavily extended, adjusted and modified.

This is the reason that Magaš's way of using history and the historical formal inventory, unlike that of Venturi or Rossi, always manifested complexity but never contradiction; that his elements sought to maintain their legibility and unequivocal messages and not to disrupt and compromise one another's meanings; and that his forms still remained full signs as opposed to empty signifiers drained of real content and meaning. Even when using productive structuralist strategies, Magaš, unlike Eisenman, never surrendered to empty syntactical exercises or formal permutations of emptied historical forms; the point was never the structuralist game itself, but how its precision may contribute to grasping and saving still-prevailing content.

Even if conscious of belonging to a new, postmodern age – or maybe precisely because of it – Magaš nevertheless believed that his inherited modernist apparatus, if flexibly fitted and adjusted, might still remain operative. Thus it came to that unusual encounter of postmodernist themes and modernist strategies, and how the modernist apparatus was retained in the face of the new postmodern condition. That is also why I have registered a welter of postmodernist themes (all implicitly present throughout Croatian modernist history) treated in a way far from postmodernist, which also, in fact, explains Magaš's assessment of local postmodernist practices to be outright pseudo-postmodernist. Indeed, if we inspect the broader Croatian scene from the 1970s on, full-fledged examples of postmodernist experiments are quite rare; most are somehow tamed, as if ashamed, feeling uncomfortable in their postmodernist formalistic abandon. The underlying collective, functionalist unconscious stood in the way. Before it even seriously began, excessive postmodernist playfulness was already over.

Conclusion

To come back to the initial questions of the flexibility of conceptual systems and their capacity to endure global paradigm shifts while sustaining consistent cultural production, and issues of identity and the necessity of its recurrent reframing – with this analysis, I propose that we have located one such interesting case where, confronted with radically changed and reframed overall context, one vein of cultural practices refused to follow such substantial reframing and decided instead to maintain its character, apparatus and strategies unchanged. This is what I propose happened with Croatian modernist architecture. The radically reframed overall environment did not entail the reframing of the discipline of architecture proper.

As this entire case sought to demonstrate: if instability was a destiny; if, as a consequence, the concept of national identity was understood to be a dynamic, open, relational and permanently unfinished category; if architecture, in such a state, managed to produce a flexible apparatus by which to create a sense of continuity and permanence; and if that apparatus was persuasive enough to make the category of national identity rely for its construction precisely on that cultural discipline, then it was exactly architecture, along with its complex conceptual system, that was to be kept stable and unchanged in order to maintain the overall precarious balance – to guarantee the essential cultural subsistence in the face of profound relativity and transience.

"Comprehensive functionalism," as the conceptual crux of such a flexible creative principle, a product of local architectural intuition and intelligence, was precisely that resilient and robust apparatus. Regardless of how drastically the external social, political and economic conditions were changed, this "comprehensive functionalism" consistently proved its unconditioned operative and functional performance. Thus architecture was not being significantly reframed even within this last instance of a radically reframed global social and intellectual context and remained, as a matter of fact, profoundly modernist in its goal and character. Only with this character unchanged could it construct ever-anew a tenable identity within the recurrently reframed environment.

Regardless of whether the concept of "comprehensive functionalism" was broad enough to embrace the array of postmodernist themes while maintaining its own modernist course and itinerary, or whether postmodernism was perceived as yet another external model to be critically revised and adjusted to suit local goals and interests, this elaborate mechanism proved functional either way. It steadily directed local architectural production of the 1980s and 1990s toward reinforcing Croatian cultural and national identity even within the most recent phase of violent geopolitical shifts and socioeconomic reversals. With its complex logic, it in fact enabled modernism to reinforce an existing design culture extending historical trajectories right up to the present date. A good deal of credit for this should undoubtedly be attributed to Magaš's theoretical and architectural legacy. It remains to be seen, however, whether this repeatedly tested theoretical concept will prove resilient and potent enough to afford a tenable operative platform even in today's multiply exacerbated rhizomatic and unpredictable reality.

Endnotes

1 Boris Magaš in a television interview, "Portraits: Boris Magaš," with Renata Margaretić Urlić for Croatian Radiotelevision, 2011. I am greatly indebted to Renata Margaretić Urlić for her substantial and generous help in preparing this essay.

2 In using the concept of "freedom of the periphery" and the case of Croatian "free-plan" churches, I refer to the theory of Croatian archeologist and art historian Ljubo Karaman (1886–1971), who theorized the relation between artistic production and its geopolitical context, and recognized three distinct cases: center, province and periphery, distinguishing provincial from peripheral art production. Provincial art production, Karaman proposed, is directly influenced by one distinct strong center, whereas the peripheral is influenced by multiple cultural and political centers, offering local artists the possibility to combine and synthesize influences and thus generate independent and original artistic approaches. Karaman called this specific instance "freedom of the periphery." See Ljubo Karaman, *Iz kolijevke hrvatske prošlosti* (Zagreb: Matica Hrvatska, 1930); Ljubo Karaman, *O djelovanju domaće sredine u umjetnosti hrvatskih krajeva* (Zagreb: Društvo historičara umjetnosti NRH, 1963).

3 The newly formed state was initially named the Kingdom of Serbs, Croats and Slovenes (1918–1929), after which it changed its name to the Kingdom of Yugoslavia (1929–1941).

4 Andre Mohorovičić, "Teoretska analiza arhitektonskog oblikovanja," *Arhitektura*, 1–2 (1947), 6–8.

5 These are paraphrases of standing terms, "humane socialism" or "socialism with a human face," as ideas of a mild and more liberal variant of socialism. This is precisely how Yugoslavia, after political changes in 1948, saw its own variant of socialism, the so-called socialist self-management, as opposed to the more rigid and state-controlled Soviet version.

6 Boris Magaš, Edo Šmidihen, and Radovan Horvat were the architects of the Museum of the Revolution in Sarajevo, Bosnia and Herzegovina, then in socialist Yugoslavia.

7 Boris Magaš, "Suvremena arhitektura pred zadatkom projektiranja sakralnih prostora," in *Bogoslužni prostor: Crkva u svjetlu teologije, arhitekture i umjetnosti*, conference proceedings (Zadar: Hrvatski institut za liturgijski pastoral, 1996), 85–96.

8 Boris Magaš, "Saznanja i mogućnosti teorijske misli," *Arhitektura*, XXXIX, 196–199, also in *Arhitektura u Hrvatskoj 1945–1985*, (Zagreb, 1986), 27–30; Boris Magaš, "Land Culture and Architecture," in *The Cultural Dimension of Scientific and Technological Development*, conference proceedings (Zagreb: HAZU, AGM, 1993), 49–54; Boris Magaš, "Andre Mohorovičić i teorija arhitekture u Hrvatskoj," in *Stota obljetnica rođenja akademika Andre Mohorovičića*, conference proceedings (Križevci: HAZU, 2013).

9 Magaš in a television interview, "Portraits: Boris Magaš," with R. Margaretić Urlić, Croatian Radiotelevision, 2011.

10 "If modernism distinguishes itself by striving for absolute domination, then postmodernism might be the realization or the experience of its end, the end of the plan of domination," as Jacques Derrida defined the postmodern condition. Surely postmodernism, just like modernism, defies any easy definition, yet some of its central features might be recognized as the loss of full meaning, of consensus and firm ground. As Jean Baudrillard would note, since culture becomes dominated by simulation, by images and communication, objects and discourses no longer have any firm referent or grounding. Instead, the real has been bypassed, the image has supplanted reality. For Jean-François Lyotard, the postmodern period witnesses the collapse *of grand narratives*, or *metanarratives*, which marks the end of the modern era and of consensus, and only *petit recits* along with the multiplicity of meanings remain operative. Postmodernism thus generally might be perceived as a sensibility of inclusion in a period of pluralism, defined by a multiplicity of points of view rather than any unified vision, resulting in intensely heterogeneous and complex cultural material. See Jacques Derrida, "Architecture Where the Desire May Live," *Domus*, 671 (1986), 17–24; Jean Baudrillard, *Simulacra and Simulation*, trans. Sheila Faria Glaser (Ann Arbour: The University of Michigan Press, 1994); Jean-Francois Lyotard, *The Postmodern Condition: A Report on Knowledge* (Minneapolis: University of Minnesota Press, 1984).

Ruth Hanisch

"Keep Your Hands Off Modern Architecture": Hans Hollein and History as Critique in Cold War Vienna

Vienna's situation in the geopolitical framework of Cold War Europe was ambiguous in more than one way: Austria was neutral, though firmly based in the West politically; spatial proximity to the Iron Curtain secured its capital an important role in international affairs. Nevertheless, due to its now marginalized location at the border between East and West, Vienna could not develop into an attractive international business location and the population rapidly declined. As the destruction of the Second World War had not been as comprehensive as in many German cities, there was not the same spirit of *Wiederaufbau* (reconstruction) and *Wirtschaftswunder* (economic miracle) as in both West Germany and the GDR.

A certain feeling of stagnation that increasingly overcame many Austrian cultural protagonists after the *Staatsvertrag* (State Treaty) in 1955 had of course several sources. The Austrian philosopher Robert Menasse very convincingly established one main reason in the specific Austrian version of the welfare state, the so-called *Sozialpartnerschaft* (social partnership) – an informal permanent exchange between trade unions, chamber of labor, chamber of commerce, and chamber of agriculture – that was established as a joint commission in 1957 to prevent social uprisings. Due to Austria's geographical location between the geopolitical blocs, any kind of social upheaval – especially any communist activity – was suspected of triggering shifts toward the sweep of the Soviet Union and was to be avoided at any cost. According to Menasse this social stability was seen as a grant for economic growth:

> "Avoidance or rather a channeling of social conflicts: consolidation of the existing distribution of power within society and avoidance of all attempts at change in this regard; strengthening and concentration of political power to keep social processes under control at any time" (Dieter Bichelbauer). One can see therefore that this is basically achieving what any form of social organization intends; all the others, however, with less efficiency.[1]

Thus the *Sozialpartnerschaft* produced and aimed to maintain a sort of super-capitalism, while at the same time conflicts over social redistribution were suppressed. This kind of shadow regime worked on an informal level, bypassing legitimate democratic procedures and institutions only a decade and a half after the end of the Nazi regime – so for many critics it felt like a form of state capitalism that prohibited any real participation in the democratic process. Menasse examined the effects of that situation on Austrian literature, where in his view it led to a disproportionate dominance of Austrian writers in the German-speaking part of Europe, such as Ingeborg Bachmann, Thomas Bernhard and Peter Handke, to name just a few. But of course the impact of the *Sozialpartnerschaft* was perceptible in architecture as well – if not even more so, due to the close relationship between architecture and the economy.

To young architects who had studied directly after the war, the architectural scene seemed equally catatonic. The major rebuilding work was dominated by architects who had studied before the war, representing a "moderate" modernism continuing the production of the 1930s: Carl Appel, Georg Lippert, Oswald Haerdtl, Erich Boltenstern, Max Fellerer and Eugen Wörle. In parallel, Roland Rainer, Karl Schwanzer and Ernst Hiesmayr aimed at a reanimation of modernism and an orientation towards international developments.[2] Many of the emigrants had not come back to Vienna – like Josef Frank, Walter Sobotka and Felix Augenfeld – and some who did come back, like Ernst A. Plischke and Margarete Schütte-Lihotzky, would not get any building commissions due to their left-wing political convictions. Until 1961, when Friedrich Achleitner took up his column in the newspaper *Die Presse*, there was no architectural critique to speak of.[3] Many young architects became increasingly frustrated with the predominating moderate modern architectural language and the functionalist dogma. In the following years, groups like Coop Himmelblau, Zünd Up and Haus-Rucker & Co. set out to

fig. 1 Hans Hollein, Hoarding, Candle Shop Retti, Vienna, 1965 (© Archiv Hollein, Wien)

create a "Visionary Architecture"[4]. Others like Hans Hollein and Hermann Czech would look for a different way to escape established practices by turning towards history – particularly to the neglected and almost forgotten buildings of Otto Wagner, Adolf Loos and Josef Hoffmann.

Flirting With the Historic City

In 1965, on the Kohlmarkt – one of the main shopping streets of the inner city next to the Loos House on Michaelerplatz and the Royal Castle – a strange, colorful hoarding appeared showing a beautiful young woman (probably the model and fashion icon Kati Sarnitz, later Katarina Noever) looking out from a space helmet (fig. 1). A speech bubble read "*Hier baut Retti Wachwarenwerk ein Kerzengeschäft*" ["Retti Waxworks is building a candle shop here"]. This later gave way to a very unusual shop that vaguely resembled that helmet, consisting of an aluminum front with a narrow keyhole opening, which led into a tiny interior made from smooth plastic prefabricated elements (fig. 2). The space age had finally arrived in Vienna and had put it on the map of visionary international architecture, earning the young Hans Hollein the prestigious Reynolds Award. But despite its undeniable relation with spaceships and with Hollein's own avant-garde art projects, this futuristic facade was densely woven into the architectural history of the city and was closely

fig. 2 Hans Hollein, Candle Shop Retti, 1965 (© Franz Hubmann/ Brandstätter)

connected formally to its immediate setting. It replaced a moderate, modern shop front with a large glass window that denied every connection with the historicist facade. Hollein instead blended his futuristic shop front with great care into the disposition of the town house, accepting and emphasizing the window axis. The new intervention and its old immediate surroundings can be read together as one form that resembles a mask.

This was in fact a feature that can be associated with houses built by Adolf Loos in the 1920s – most prominently, the Moller House (1928) in Vienna (fig. 3). But earlier shop displays by Loos also played into Hollein's design, especially the Knize Shop (1913) – literally around the corner – especially in the similar small display openings that merge into the cladding. Even the allegedly new material – aluminum – was not new at all in the context of modern Viennese shop fronts: Otto Wagner had ventured into a very famous experiment with this material with his dispatch office for *Die Zeit*, which had been situated around another two corners at Kärntnerstrasse 39, though only from 1902 to 1908 (fig. 4). Nevertheless, it had been well- enough publicized to be known to Hollein. In fact, in 1985 when Hollein designed the exhibition "Traum und Wirklichkeit" (Dream and Reality) in the Künstlerhaus,

fig. 3 Adolf Loos, Moller House, Vienna, 1928 (© Photograph Martin Gerlach 1930, Heinrich Kulka, Adolf Loos, Wien: Schroll 1931).

he exhibited a full-scale reconstruction of that shop front by Wagner.[5] What Hollein did with his tiny shop on the Kohlmarkt was not only use aluminum – "in a fresh invigorating way," as was noted in the Reynolds prize address[6] – but to fit his design into the existing nineteenth-century facade scheme as well as referencing the modern architecture which had developed in Vienna from 1900 onwards.

The reactions among upcoming architecture critics were mixed. Friedrich Achleitner praised the compact interior and compared Hollein's achievement with Loos's ability to create a maximum of possibilities within a minimum of space with the help of mirrors and mastery of details.[7] Hermann Czech attacked Achleitner for being uncritical, rejected the comparison with Loos, and associated Hollein instead with Joseph Maria Olbrich, which he clearly meant pejoratively:

> Olbrich as well is – rightly – questioned, but for example Achleitner avoids applying his insights [...] onto Hollein, who he compared to Loos because of the use of two mirrors. These parallels reach into the biographies, the vociferous underestimation at home, the shouting of a new time, the shadowboxing with cheap architectural problems – rural building then,

fig. 4 Adolf Krischanitz and Otto Kapfinger, 1:1 Model of Otto Wagner's Depeschendepot "Die Zeit" for the exhibition "Traum und Wirklichkeit," 1985 (© Wien Museum)

> urban planning today. A design that remains attached to […] motives, that never penetrates to the core of the architectonic thought […].[8]

What made these discussions unique was the fact that historic architecture was scrutinized just as critically as contemporary building production. Czech "responded" with his Kleines Café on the Franziskanerplatz, where in several steps from 1970 to 1984 he created a completely unspectacular interior, which only a very careful observer would recognize as the work of an architect. Czech's aim was to show that you could indeed reproduce qualities of historic architecture with modern means, simply because the essential needs had not changed.

Hollein instead used historic architecture to prove modernism wrong. He looked for a new architecture that was an antithesis of the kind of modernism that was practiced in Vienna in the 1950s and 1960s. Where the modern shop window was wide and transparent, he closed it; where the modern shop front neglected the historic setting, he referred to it. He used the historical references to set his architecture off from existing modern architecture. This became even more evident where he inserted his interventions in one of these postwar buildings, as was done with his *Verkehrsbüro* into the so-called

fig. 5 Carl Appel, Georg Lippert, Opernringhof, Vienna 1955. (© Carl Appel, Architekt zwischen Gestern und Morgen, Vienna, Cologne, Graz: Böhlau 1988)

Opernringhof. To fully appreciate Hollein's contentious design, we must consider the history of that building site: until World War II, this was the location of the Heinrichshof, erected from 1861 to 1863 by Theophil Hansen for Baron Heinrich von Drasche-Wartinberg, owner of the Wienerberger brick-and-tile works. The Heinrichshof was one of the biggest blocks on the Ringstrasse, unifying three separate apartment buildings with one coherent facade. Like the nearby opera house, the block was hit by bombing raids toward the end of the war. The damage was substantial but repairable. Many of the inhabitants returned and started to rebuild their apartments and a complete reconstruction did not seem unlikely. However, economic pressure led to the destruction of the building in 1954. Remains of its very elaborate terracotta decoration are still found in art-dealing. The following year, its successor – the Opernringhof – was erected by Georg Lippert and Carl Appel in a moderate if not plain modernism quite typical for the area in Vienna (fig. 5). The Opernringhof was praised in the 1950s, but in the 1960s this kind of unpretentious postwar modernism was seen as a sort of self-abandonment of architecture.

In 1976, Hollein was commissioned to design the new sales office of the *Österreichisches Verkehrsbüro* on the north side of the Opernringhof, facing the Ring and the opera. The *Verkehrsbüro* was a state-run travel agency founded

fig. 6 Hans Hollein, "Österreichisches Verkehrsbüro" in the Opernringhof, Interior, 1976 (© Archiv Hollein)

in the interwar years to promote tourism in Austria and help Austrians venture abroad.[9] Hollein inserted into the existing 1950s building a stage-like setting that was everything the structure was not: colorful, flamboyant, full of references (fig. 6). The main room recalls the service hall of the Postsparkasse by Otto Wagner, with its higher and lower aisles and translucent white ceiling. Pavilions – like the gold-domed seating area – had been a constant motif in Wagner's work. Prominently, in 1881 Wagner had designed the pavilion for the welcome ceremony for Crown Princess Stephanie on the opposite side of the former Heinrichshof (fig. 7). Wagner's pavilion had featured textile elements similar to the pelmet Hollein draped over the information desk in the Verkehrsbüro. But Hollein did not stop with local references – the palm trees were most certainly an educated nod to the kitchens of the Royal Pavilion in Brighton by John Nash, an early nineteenth-century folly evoking Indian architecture. The dome of the pavilion very much recalls the Indian Gate in New Delhi by Edwin Lutyens from the 1920s. This would in fact make some sense, as the Verkehrsbüro was the first travel agency in Austria to offer intercontinental flights to India. The Verkehrsbüro was destroyed in 1987, so I cannot judge the quality of execution, but if it was on the same level as the Juwelier Schullin store (1972–1974), it must have been exquisite.

In no way did Hollein connect his intervention with the existing Opernhof. The interior betrayed the very principles the exterior stood for:

fig. 7 Otto Wagner, Pavilion for the reception of crown princess Stephanie in Vienna, 1881 (© Wien Museum Inv. Nr. 46.915/2)

repetition was countered with variety, austerity with richness, industrial production with meticulous craftsmanship. Whether deliberate or not, for every Viennese passerby this was a look to the bright and colorful future of architecture as well as a reminder of the destroyed past of this particular site. With his second *Verkehrsbüro* office in the Ringturm, Hollein made his dissatisfaction with postwar modernism even more visible by virtually blasting the rhythm of the structural grid designed by Erich Boltenstern in 1953–1955 with his facade.

In his texts, Hollein left no doubt what he was opposing. Most important for our topic was a lecture he gave in 1962 in the Galerie nächst St. Stephan, the meeting place of a group of young artists. Already the title "Back to Architecture" was a contradiction of Le Corbusier's "Vers une architecture" (1923). The entire text is an antithesis to key sentences of the modern movement: "Architecture is without purpose," then further down, "Keep your hands off modern architecture. Simply engage with architecture. In fact, many ideas of today's so-called modern architecture are not ideas born out of the spirit of the twentieth century. They are rather ideas of the nineteenth century."[10]

The newly developed format for big historic exhibitions by the Museum der Stadt Wien (today called the Wien Museum) at the Künstlerhaus provided Hollein with a genuine field for further investigations into the history of Vienna's architecture. As Kenneth Frampton noticed about the exterior

fig. 8 Hans Hollein, exhibition design "Die Türken vor Wien," Künstlerhaus Vienna, 1983 (© Archiv Hollein)

decoration of the Künstlerhaus for the exhibition "Die Türken vor Wien"[11] in 1983 (fig. 8):

A single stroke of felicitous intervention proclaimed Hollein's characteristic brilliance. He had the idea of covering the classical portico of the Künstlerhaus in a Turkish campaign tent, which appeared with great effect in two parts and at two different scales; the first being the full tent with attendant figures on top of the portico, the second being the wall panels of a much larger tent arranged symmetrically on either side of the classical entrance. One is astonished by the proliferation of metaphors and metonyms which this juxtaposition engendered. On the one hand, the Turks are represented as having returned mysteriously to conquer classical Vienna and in so doing they seem to reverse history and challenge once again the supposed preeminence of occidental over oriental values; on the other hand, an internal play is set up between the tent panels and the light enameled steel cladding of Otto Wagner's nearby Karlsplatz station, so that the mind is bounced back and forth between the tent and the building, between the canvas and the stone, between the light and the heavy, between stressed skin and classical stereotomy. The priority given to stone as material of classical architecture is severely challenged by the ricocheting of these metonymic references.[12]

Apart from the fact that the covering of the iron frame of Wagner's Karlsplatz station was made from marble (originally from Carrara, later from Laas) and not from enameled steel, Frampton's observation of the close relation between tent and station is very convincing. It took into account the

fig. 9 Celebration of the Declaration of the independency of Austria in the Obere Belvedere May 15, 1955 (© cand. med. Wolfgang Jilek)

Viennese discussion on cladding and dressing that derived from Semper and was so productive, especially in the years before the First World War. Moreover, there is a popular saying in Vienna that the roof of the Upper Belvedere palace (1717–1723) by Lukas von Hildebrandt was modeled after a Turkish campaign tent, to celebrate the role of its owner – Prince Eugen of Savoy – in defeating the Ottomans. And if you compare the tent on the roof of the Künstlerhaus with Hildebrandt's roof, there is a striking similarity (fig. 9).

So with this rather circus-like showpiece, Hollein managed to connect not only with the architectural discourse of around 1900 but also with the praised Austrian baroque architectural tradition. Yet Hollein was certainly not a traditionalist – especially not in his early career. As an outspoken neo-avant-gardist, he was always trying to challenge architectural certainties. Joseph Rykwert observed: "There is a formal problem which has interested Hollein since the early sixties, and which is an interesting inversion of one of the 'modern architecture' clichés, the one about the unification of interior and exterior. He has wanted to unify above and below, make a building whose roof is also a floor or pavement or lawn."[13] This is a recurring set up one finds in Hollein's work, from the early design for a bank in Vienna to the museum in Mönchengladbach. The spectacle of Ottoman archers aiming at visitors from the top of the Künstlerhaus is not just a hoax, but refers to this fundamental question of how a building is conceived as empty space and volume.

Re-Framing Fin de Siècle Vienna

Fin de siècle architecture was pretty much forgotten in the 1950s and early 1960s. Hollein stated in an interview that when he studied at the Academy of Fine Arts in the late 1950s, only about twenty people knew the names of Adolf Loos and Otto Wagner, and that he bought Loos's writings in the first edition for the original price from a Viennese secondhand bookshop.[14] Even if this was an exaggeration, the historian Heidemarie Uhl notes on the genesis of the myth of "Vienna 1900":

> In Vienna, the time "around 1900" was still controversial for decades after 1945. Especially from the perspective of the socialists, the turn of the century counted in no way as point of reference for a splendid cultural heritage, but on the contrary as a negative backdrop for the "New Vienna," the model of the "modern" metropolis in the 1950s and 1960s and its architectural and planning representations.[15]

It was to the credit of postwar students of architecture that they discovered and saved some of the most important structures of worldwide early modern architecture in Vienna. Hollein, Czech, Johannes Spalt, Friedrich Kurrent, Achleitner, Otto Kapfinger and Adolf Krischanitz took on the study, conservation and adaptation of the architecture of the first half of the century. Major discussions and public protests were triggered by the plan to destroy or alter parts of Wagner's *Stadtbahn* (city railway). Czech demonstrated in several articles and design projects that the city railway as infrastructure as well as architectural superstructure was as important for the city in the 1960s as it had been in the late nineteenth century.[16] In 1969 Ottokar Uhl organized a student demonstration against the destruction and relocation of Wagner's Karlsplatz stations. Kapfinger, Krischanitz and Angela Hareiter (forming the Missing Link group) studied the situation and potential of the decaying stations and presented their results as an exhibition in the Museum des 20. Jahrhunderts in 1973.[17]

Some important buildings had to be reattributed: Gustav Peichl recalls how he and Hollein searched the archives to find evidence that the threatened Wittgenstein House really was codesigned by Ludwig Wittgenstein[18] – the house was saved due to the efforts of Bernhard Leitner. This interest in the past was not mere sentimentality but was the protest of angry young men (all but Hareiter were men) against the dominating architecture of the 1950s and 1960s and an establishment within the city administration that too willingly sacrificed historic buildings to commerce and investment. We must not forget that Achleitner, who agitated for Wagner's Stadtbahn, also produced avant-garde dialect poems with the Wiener Gruppe and had publicly smashed a piano as part of a performance with writer Gerhard Rühm in 1959.

These politically motivated efforts were paralleled by an increase in historical research on eminent figures of the period from 1900 by the same activists, starting in the 1960s and reaching a peak around 1980: Max Geretsegger and Heinz Peintner published their book on Wagner in 1979, Eduard Sekler's biography of Josef Hoffmann appeared in 1982, followed in 1984 by Czech and Wolfgang Mistelbauer's book on the Michaelerhaus by Loos.[19] That same

fig. 10 Hans Hollein, exhibition design "Traum und Wirklichkeit," Künstlerhaus Vienna, 1985 (© Archiv Hollein)

year, Gustav Peichl edited the exhibition catalog *Die Kunst des Otto Wagners* with essays by Achleitner, Vittorio Magnago Lampugnani, Ákos Moravánszky and Manfredo Tafuri. Along with Otto Antonia Graf's volumes on Wagner and Achleitner's architectural guides, these still form the backbone of any research on the architecture of that epoch. The rediscovery of Josef Plecnik, Max Fabiani and the School of Otto Wagner in general put Viennese development back into a central European perspective that had been neglected from the 1950s to the 1970s.[20] The historian Siegfried Mattl analyzed the mid-1980s change of cultural politics in Vienna under mayor Helmut Zilk: "Roll back of the Vienna clichés and the Habsburg Myth, highlighting of Viennese Modernism with heroes Freud, Wittgenstein, Schönberg, presentation of contemporary art in correspondence with the revitalized themes of classical modernism. Vienna should appear as the unbroken, vital, spiritual center of Central Europe, across the political blocs of East and West."[21] In 1985, the rediscovery of fin de siècle Vienna went from being the project of a young, critical left-wing elite to official city branding with the exhibition "Traum und Wirklichkeit," for which Hollein again produced the exhibition design (fig. 10). This marked a change in his work toward a more explicit referencing of historic buildings with the portion of the Karl-Marx-Hof on top of the Künstlerhaus and a loss of critical undertone. The political and cultural climate was about to change, the Cold War would finally end and Vienna was to move toward the center of Europe again.

Endnotes

1 *"'Vermeidung bzw. Kanalisierung sozialer Konflikte; -Festigung der bestehenden Machtverteilung in der Gesellschaft und Vermeidung sämtlicher Veränderungsbestreben in dieser Hinsicht; -Verstärkung und Konzentration*

politischer Macht, um die sozialen Prozesse jederzeit unter Kontrolle halten zu können' (Dieter Bichelbauer). Man sieht also, daß sie im Grunde das leistet, was jedwede gesellschaftliche Organisationsform intendiert, jede andere allerdings noch mit geringerer Effektivität." Robert Menasse, *Die sozialpartnerschaftliche Ästhetik: Essays zum österreichischen Geist* (Vienna: Sonderzahl, 1990), 23–24.

2 The activities in Vienna during the Third Reich of Lippert, Haerdtl, Fellerer, Wörle and Rainer have recently been documented in "*Wien. Perle des Reiches*": *Planen für Hitler*, ed. Architekturzentrum Wien (Vienna: Park Books, 2015).

3 Interview with Friedrich Achleitner, in *Die Architektur und ich: Eine Bilanz der österreichischen Architektur seit 1945 vermittelt durch ihre Protagonisten*, ed. Maria Welzig, Gerhard Steixner (Vienna, Cologne, Weimar: Böhlau, 2003), 141–156; Friedrich Achleitner, *Nieder mit Fischer von Erlach* (Salzburg, Vienna: Residenz Verlag, 1986).

4 This phrase was coined by Günther Feuerstein.

5 The research for that reconstruction was done by Otto Kapfinger and Adolf Krischanitz, see Hans Hollein, "Rekonstruktionen und Modelle in der Ausstellung," in *Traum und Wirklichkeit: Wien 1870–1930*, exhibition catalog (Vienna: Museum der Stadt Wien, 1985), 719–722.

6 Jury report, B.S. Reynolds Award 1966, quoted from: http://www.hollein.com/ger/Schriften/Zeitschrift-Bau/Retti.

7 Friedrich Achleitner, "Architektur und Werbung," in *Die Presse*, October 27/28, 1965; reprinted in Achleitner, *Nieder mit Fischer von Erlach* (Salzburg,Vienna: Residenz, 1986), 136–138.

8 "*Auch Olbrich wird – mit Recht – angezweifelt, aber Achleitner beispielsweise hütet sich, seine Erkenntnisse* [...] *auf Hollein anzuwenden, den er wegen zweier Spiegel mit Loos verglichen hat. Bis ins Biographische gehen diese Parallelen, die lautstarke Verkanntheit im Inland, das Geschrei von der neuen Zeit, das Schattenboxen mit publikumswirksamen Architekturproblemen – damals das ländliche Bauen, heute der Städtebau. Ein Entwerfen, das immer an den* [...] *Motiven bleibt, nie zum Wesentlichen, zum architektonischen Gedanken vordringt* [...]." Hermann Czech, "Eine Welt, erfrischend jung. Konvulsionen der Architekturtheorie," in *Manuskripte* 25, Graz 1969; reprinted in Czech, *Zur Abwechslung* (Vienna: Löcker & Wögenstein, 1977), 61–65 (p. 64).

9 The original building opposite the Secession building was erected by Wagner's former pupils Kastner and Waage in the 1920s.

10 "*Architektur ist ohne Zweck*"; "*Laßt die Hände von der modernen Architektur. Beschäftigt euch dafür einfach mit Architektur. In Wahrheit sind viele der Ideen der heutigen, der sogenannten modernen Architektur gar keine Ideen geboren aus dem Geist des 20. Jahrhunderts. Sie sind vielmehr Ideen des 19. Jahrhunderts.*" Hans Hollein, "Zurück zur Architektur," quoted in *Hans Hollein: Schriften und Manifeste. Eine Auswahl, herausgegeben von François Burkhardt und Paulus Manker* (Vienna: die angewandte, 2002), 29–34 (pp. 30, 33).

11 Marking the three-hundredth anniversary of the Turkish siege of Vienna.

12 Kenneth Frampton, "Meditations on an Aircraft Carrier: Hollein's Mönchengladbach," in *a + u, architecture & urbanism*, 2 (1985), 142.

13 Joseph Rykwert, "Irony: Hollein's General Approach," in *a + u, architecture & urbanism*, 2 (1985), 194–196 (p. 196).

14 Interview with Hans Hollein, in *Profil*, 26:3, 2009.

15 *"In Wien selbst war die Zeit 'um 1900' allerdings auch nach 1945 noch jahrzehntelang umstritten. Vor allem aus sozialistischer Perspektive galt die Jahrhundertwende keineswegs als Bezugspunkt eines glanzvollen kulturellen Erbens, sondern ganz im Gegenteil als Negativfolie für das 'Neue Wien', das Leitbild der 'modernen' Großstadt in den 50er und 60er Jahren und seine architektonischen und stadtplanerischen Repräsentationen."* Heidemarie Uhl, "'Wien um 1900'– Das Making Of eines Gedächtnisortes," in *Imaging Vienna: Innensichten, Außensichten, Stadterzählungen*, ed. Monika Sommer, Marcus Gräser, Ursula Prutsch (Vienna: Verlag Turia + Kant, 2006), 47–70, (pp. 49–50).

16 Czech, "Otto Wagners Verkehrsbauwerk," in Czech, *Zur Abwechslung*, 24–31.

17 Otto Kapfinger, *Architektur im Sprachraum: Essays, Reden, Kritiken zum Planen und Bauen in Österreich* (Graz: Park Books / diachron, 2014), 14.

18 Interview with Gustav Peichl, in Welzig, Steixner, *Die Architektur und ich*, 127.

19 Very important were the rediscoveries of Oskar Strnad and even more so Josef Frank. Immediately after its founding in 1965, the Österreichische Gesellschaft für Architektur organized the first exhibition on Frank.

20 Boris Podrecca, *Josef Plecnik 1872–1957*. Exhibition catalogue Österreichische Gesellschaft für Architektur (Vienna: Österreichische Gesellschaft für Architektur, 1967); Marco Pozzetto, *Joze Plecnik e la scuola di Otto Wagner* (Turin: Albra 1968); Damjan Prelovsek, *Josef Plecnik: Wiener Arbeiten von 1896 bis 1914* (Vienna: Edition Tusch, 1979); Marco Pozetto, *Die Schule Otto Wagners* (Vienna, Munich: Schroll 1980). Relations between Austria and its neighboring Eastern Bloc countries never ceased, with some exchange between single architects and organizations. But for architects, Germany and the US had always been the stronger attraction. See: Iris Meder et al., eds., *Lifting the Curtain: Architekturnetzwerke in Mitteleuropa. Central European Architectural Networks* (Salzburg: Müry Salzmann, 2015).

21 "*Zurückdrängung der Wien-Klischees und des Habsburger-Mythos, Herausstellung der Wiener Moderne mit den Heroen Freud, Wittgenstein, Schönberg, Präsentationen der zeitgenössischen Kunst in Korrespondenz zu den revitalisierten Themen der historischen Moderne. Wien sollte als ungebrochenes vitales geistiges Zentrum Mitteleuropas, über die politischen Blöcke von Ost und Weg hinweg, erscheinen.*" Siegfried Mattl, "Die lauen Jahre – Wien 1978–1985," in ed. Martin W. Drexler, Markus Eiblmayr, Franziska Maderthaner, *Idealzone Wien: Die schnellen Jahre (1978–1985)* (Vienna: Falter Verlag, 1998), 85–95 (pp. 93–94).

III
Public Criticism and the Rediscovery of the City

Michela Rosso

Heritage, Populism and Anti-Modernism in the Controversy of the Mansion House Square Scheme

In June 1962 the Anglo-Italian developer Peter Palumbo asked Ludwig Mies van der Rohe for the design of a two hundred ninety foot tower overlooking a square at “Bank Junction,” in the heart of the City of London. In May 1969 the Corporation gave its provisional consent for a scheme that would have resulted in the demolition of four blocks of Victorian architecture.

In 1982, after securing the ownership of the complete site, Palumbo submitted a second application, but this time the Corporation refused to grant him planning permission.

What had happened during this time? Although the 1982 proposal had not changed from that applauded by the Corporation in the late 1960s, since 1969, the whole of the site had been designated as a Conservation Area and nine of the twenty buildings threatened with demolition had been listed.

While a strong conservation movement had arisen, different sectors of society were also accusing architectural modernism of producing an environment marked by uniformity and mediocrity.

Through the selection of a group of evidences, articles and graphic materials produced before, during and after the public inquiry held in 1984, the chapter highlights the main issues at stake in the discussion over the Mansion House square scheme.

A Tower of Trouble

Determined to bring to London a true masterpiece of modern architecture, in 1962 Peter Palumbo approached Mies van der Rohe, then 76, to ask him for the design of a new public square to be built at the intersection of Poultry and Queen Victoria Street, in the City of London (figs. 1, 2). The heir to a large fortune, Palumbo had persuaded Mies to design a complex including a steel-and-glass office tower, severe and rectilinear in the manner of the Seagram Building, along with a plaza and an underground shopping mall[1] (figs. 3–6).

"Mies had not yet built in Britain, and was enthusiastic about this opportunity. By the time of his death, a full set of design working drawings and material specifications had been prepared, all under his direction."[2] These words, pronounced at the 1984 public inquiry by architect Peter Carter, Mies's appointed consultant and major partner in the scheme, immediately direct attention to an issue that was to become crucial within the debate surrounding this controversial project. The questionable paternity of the Mansion House Square project was in fact to be one of the preferred arguments of its detractors.[3] While Mies had died soon after the Corporation had given the scheme its conditional consent, too many years had passed between the commission and the moment when the client had finally acquired all the necessary control of the area: the legitimacy of a project that would have entailed the demolition of four blocks of Victorian architecture had thus become open to question.

The story had begun as early as June 1968, when the scheme had been submitted to the City Corporation for planning permission. Mies passed away in August 1969 and, as Carter would further highlight, "he had been working on detailed refinements up to a few weeks before."[4] Moreover, a project that would have involved the construction of a two hundred ninety foot tower only a third of a mile from St. Paul's Cathedral was soon recognized as a matter of national significance, and one for which it was desirable to ensure public participation in the decision-making process. Thus, four months after Palumbo's application, a twelve-day exhibition of the scheme's models, drawings and samples of materials was mounted inside the building of the Royal Exchange. An opinion poll was arranged on that occasion showing that 78 percent of the 3,329 respondents were in favor of the scheme, while 46 percent generally approved the building and only 17 percent expressed minimal reservations about the Mies's tower.[5]

On May 22, 1969, the City Corporation agreed in principle to the scheme and encouraged Palumbo to acquire the necessary property in order to be able to carry out his proposal in its entirety. Some concern at the height of Mies's tower had already been expressed by the Greater London Council

fig. 1 Aerial view of the existing site conditions at the time of the project's commission. Source: Peter Carter, *Mies van der Rohe at Work* (London: Phaidon, 1999) 147.

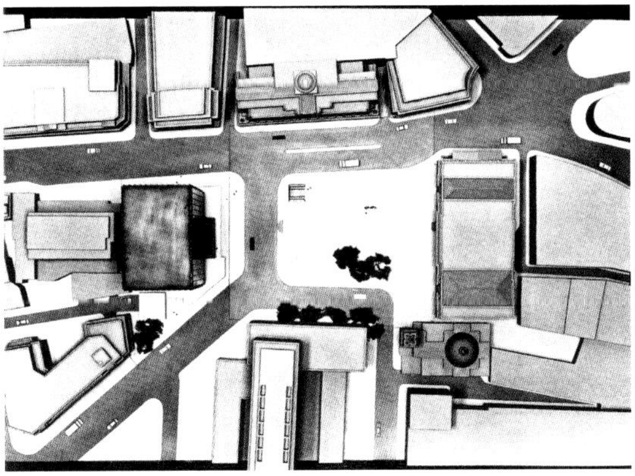

fig. 2 Aerial view of the model. Source: Peter Carter, *Mies van der Rohe at Work* (London: Phaidon, 1999) 147.

supported by the Royal Fine Art Commission, saying that the office building should not have exceeded two hundred feet.[6] Apart from this, although it cannot be stated with absolute certainty, there does not appear to have been public objection to the project in the late 1960s, it is worth noticing that no reference whatsoever was made at that time to the demolition of four triangular blocks of Victorian architecture implied by the realization of the project for Mansion House Square.

In the 1960s and early 1970s, redevelopment as a means of urban re-

fig. 3 "A New City Square and Office Tower." Photograph of the model (1967). Source: Peter Carter, *Mies van der Rohe at Work* (London: Phaidon, 1999) 146.

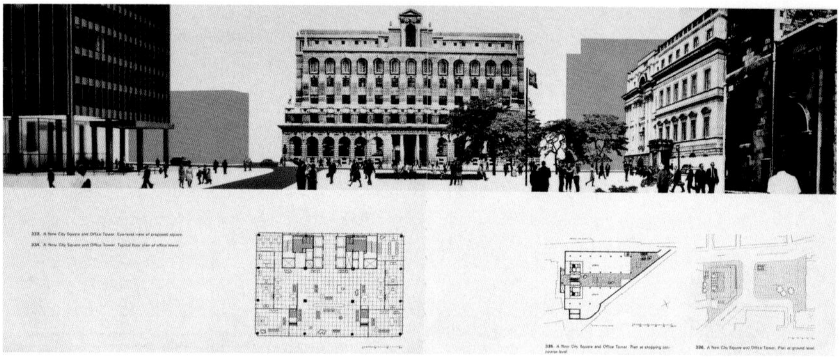

fig. 4 "A New City Square and Office Tower." Eye-level view of the square. Typical floor plan of the office tower. Source: Peter Carter, *Mies van der Rohe at Work* (London: Phaidon, 1999) 148–9.

enhancement was still the first priority of the Corporation. Emblematically, while planning permission was finally allowed to the six hundred foot NatWest Tower designed by Richard Seifert's team at 25 Old Broad Street, the Corporation designated eight Conservation Areas, the largest being Bank. On that occasion, it referred to it as a "national set piece," with the buildings of Mansion House, Bank of England and Royal Exchange not only all statutorily listed as Grade I, but also as representing the three principal elements of the City's historic functions: economic power, civic authority and world trade.[7] The Mappin & Webb building (John Belcher, 1870) which was to become the symbol of the preservation case in the 1984 public inquiry, would only become incorporated in the area in 1981 (fig. 5).

It took thirteen years for Palumbo to ensure complete ownership of the site, and when in January 1982 he finally resubmitted his application, the Court of Common Council unanimously rejected it.[8] Still resolute to have his ambitious project built, the developer then appealed to the Secretary of State,

fig. 5 View towards the Mappin and Webb corner. Source: John Harris, "London's square Peg?" *Country Life*, vol. CLXXII, 4429, July 8, 1982, 99.

fig. 6 Photomontage showing the proposed Mies van der Rohe tower. Source: John Harris, "London's square Peg?" *Country Life*, vol. CLXXII, 4429, July 8, 1982, 99.

citing in his defense the 1969 obligation, and warning of the possible damage to the City's future as a financial center if this new office accommodation was not to be allowed. What would have been a simple case of redevelopment in the late 1960s would now see the developer against the municipality and a number of conservation groups engaged in a three-month public inquiry in which many of the most prominent British and American architects, architectural historians and journalists swelled the ranks of both sides.

"The Wrong Building in the Wrong Place at the Wrong Time"

Just weeks after Palumbo had submitted his application to the City of London Corporation in February 1982, Save Britain's Heritage (SAVE), the pressure group founded in 1975 by *Country Life* journalist Marcus Binney, John Harris and a group of journalists, architects, historians and planners, published *The Mansion House Square Scheme: Stop It*, a twenty-three-page collective statement regarding the undesirability of the scheme.[9]

Strong opposition to the Mansion House Square project had begun to gather in the meantime. Besides SAVE, pressure groups and amenities associations strenuously opposing Palumbo's proposal included the Victorian, City Heritage, London and Middlesex Archaeological Societies, the Georgian Group and the City of London Retail Traders Association, worried that "their shops were to be relegated to an underground precinct that would have been cut off from the busy and thriving activity of the surrounding street level shopping area."[10]

The turbulent story of Palumbo's Mansion House Square scheme appears as an exemplary case study of the architectural polemics among an emerging conservation movement, the new postmodernist creed and what Martin Pawley, one of Palumbo's partisans and then editor of *Building Design*, had recognized as "the regrouped forces of modernism,"[11] reflecting the changes occurring in architectural culture and in the reception of a project that a decade earlier had obtained a favorable reaction at a public exhibition and conditional consent, and that was intended for a site that had since become a Conservation Area.

It has already been argued how discourses generated by this public debate did not simply encompass the formal and functional nature of this part of the City; neither were they merely the expression of a battle between old and new. In the span of half a century, the City had moved from the confidence afforded by the empire to a more competitive status: the former global prestige of Britain was hard to reconcile with postwar loss of empire and declining prominence in international economics. In this respect, the role played by this part of London was of paramount importance. Symbolically, this was the site where the memory – and nostalgia – of empire and of its former economic leadership found their most powerful expression. Thus, as urban geographer Jane M. Jacobs has argued, the long debate over the Mansion House Square scheme would soon become "a nodal point in the imaginative reaffirmation of the identity and status of the City in relation to the nation and the rest of the world."[12]

Behind the Scenes: Anticipating the Debate

What historical events had prepared the ground for such a profound change of attitude in the decision of the London Corporation over thirteen years? The period 1973 to 1975 had been years of deep economic recession, rising inflation and unemployment: the decline of Fordism as the dominant mode of production and the dismantling of its system of regulation had been paralleled by a new economic policy of *laissez-faire*. In 1979, elections that brought in Margaret Thatcher as prime minister would sanction the affirmation of the ideology of the New Right. The mode of operation of this ideology was to attack orthodoxies of the previous forty years – in economics, the Keynesian precepts of full employment and moderate inflation, in the cultural field, state support for the arts, and in architecture, the dominance of modernism. This conservationist turn was to pave the way to a new wave of revisionism in the fields of art and architecture, taking on several forms, from a deep disaffection with modernism to the emergence of neo-traditionalism and a call for the return to a classicizing aesthetic.

As has been argued, in the late 1970s the repudiation of modernism in Great Britain had seemed more feasible compared to what was happening in the United States. In Britain, the Modern Movement had arrived late, the heritage industry had been flourishing like no other, and there remained a large architectural legacy of an aristocratic culture and society readily available for reoccupation and rehabilitation. All these factors provided fertile ground for the flourishing of traditionalism, while modernism was accused of producing an environment weighed down by uniformity and mediocrity.[13]

1977 was crucial in the critical reassessment of the modernist legacy by means of architectural criticism. Two influential books were published in London: David Watkin's *Morality and Architecture* and Charles Jencks's *The Language of Post-Modern Architecture*. By acknowledging the autonomy of architectural form from any technological, economic, social or political factor or function, David Watkin, the architectural historian and champion of an architectural classicist revival, went so far as to declare the failure of modernism that Jencks then dated precisely to the 1972 demolition of one of Minoru Yamasaki's Pruitt Igoe housing estates in St. Louis.

In parallel, since 1969 the government had issued important legislative measures regarding architectural conservation and a widespread new concern for the disappearing fabric of historic London had emerged. In 1975, to celebrate the European Architectural Heritage Year, the Corporation had instituted two Heritage Walks in the City. Both walks had their starting points adjoining the Mansion House site. The following year, the Society for the Protection of Ancient Buildings, the Georgian Group, the Victorian Society and the Civic Trust launched *Save the City*, a detailed analysis of the City's architecture and townscape aimed at defining "the visual qualities" of this part of the British capital.[14] Among the study's recommendations was a substantial extension to the Bank Conservation Area, embracing all the existing buildings on the site. In 1977, following Circular 23/77 "Historic Buildings and Conservation Areas," nine of the Victorian buildings threatened with demolition by the Mansion House Square project were listed for their special architectural and historic interest, all Grade II and of group value. In 1980, the Common Council approved the report "City Development Plan, Aims and Objectives." The aim under the heading of "Townscape, Urban Design and the Environment" was "to improve the quality of the physical environment and townscape in the City." Finally, in 1981, the Bank Conservation Area was extended to include all the buildings on the Mansion House Square site.[15]

But what were the terms of the debate over the Mansion House Square scheme? What were its key words and main themes? The analytical reading of the hundreds of newspapers and journals' press clippings and proofs of evidence at the 1984 public inquiry highlights a number of recurring arguments articulated by detractors as well as supporters of the scheme. Some of these entailed the categories of "City's character" and "townscape" as reflected in the existing buildings and spaces of a site, the images of which – appearing in famous paintings and in countless prints – had come to identify the very essence of the City and its civic functions.

"A Tower That Would Rival Bomb Ruins"

Whereas the quasi-legal format of the public inquiry in 1984 was to have an inevitable impact on the language used by witnesses, resulting in tight presentations carefully constructed in order to persuade the audience, the mediatization of the discussion entailed a more accessible vocabulary in which metaphors, historical analogies and graphic humor were profusely and more freely employed.

Thus, on May 30 of that year, a new, powerful voice joined the discussion: at Hampton Court, Prince Charles labeled the design of the Mansion House Square tower "another giant glass stump better suited to downtown Chicago than the City of London," adding that "it is hard to imagine that London before the last war must have had one of the most beautiful skylines of any great city […]. What are we doing to our capital city now? What have we done to it since the bombing during the war?"[16] The analogy between modern architecture and wartime destruction was not an isolated jest. The critique of a "tower that would rival bomb ruins," as journalist Charles Knevitt would put it, that was almost the perfect though anachronistic incarnation of modernist dogmas of standardization and anonymous design, rested on the persuasion that architectural modernism had failed disastrously.[17]

"A Monument to the Dead"

A gloomy version of Mies's steel and glass tower painted in black and bearing the heading "Modern Movement R.I.P." had appeared at the center of a cartoon to illustrate the English architectural historian Gavin Stamp's vehement tirade against the project, signed under the *nom de plume* "Piloti" and appearing in the weekly satirical magazine *Private Eye*.[18] The conviction that the project was old hat and should be quietly put in a museum was shared by many commentators. Among them was "Astragal," the series of weekly editorials published in *Architects' Journal*, which acknowledged that the "pulling power of Mies's name is no longer as great as it was."[19] A similar position was voiced by the *Financial Times'* architecture correspondent Colin Amery, who argued: "No longer do we believe in Mies's maxims or in the imposition of grids of convenience on our activities," [20] echoed in its turn by the *Guardian's* architecture correspondent Martin Walker, who labeled Mies's tower "as old fashioned as Beatles' haircut."[21] The appropriateness of a building designed in the 1960s to the changed historical circumstances of the 1980s was then seriously challenged.[22]

"A Cuckoo in Wren's Nest"

Analogies with the planning history of London were frequent throughout the debate: lines of historical continuity were drawn that stretched from Mansion House Square back to particular episodes in the City's urban history. Thus, Palumbo had justified the idea of a public space in this area as the culmination of plans prepared over the previous three hundred years by Christopher Wren following the Great Fire in 1666, then subsequently by Sir John Evelyn and Robert Hooke. Later, the developer argued, following the devastation of London by bombing in the Second World War, the idea had received further support from the team of C.H. Holden and Lord Holford in their City of London Development Plan.[23]

A typical legitimization strategy of big-scale building operations such as this – the tendency to resurrect some purposefully selected episodes of the City's history in order to gather consensus around a project whose feasibility had seemed at least questionable – was lambasted by journalist Michael Cassell in the pages of the *Financial Times*, who ironically noted how "the magic name of Wren [could] always bring a tear to the eye of hard-headed businessmen who [were] quite happy to sweep away acres of the City's ancient street patterns for their new office developments."[24]

"A Threat to the City's Townscape"

Regarded by many as a gigantic intrusion from Manhattan wrecking the entire face of the area, Mies's tower and plaza (and their architect) had become the perfect scapegoat for all the major faults of the International Style: uniformity, indifference to the site and anonymous design. Those who accused the project of being alien and insensitive to the character of the City's fabric also

fig. 7 Title page of Peter Palumbo's promotional brochure *Mansion House Square Scheme. A Place for People* (London: Number 1 Poultry Limited, 1982). Source: Peter Carter fonds. Collection Centre Canadien d'Architecture/ Canadian Centre for Architecture. Gift of Peter Carter.

insisted on the fact that the architect had only visited the site twice and hardly knew London.[25] Mies's foreignness was touted by the scheme's opponents as among the clearest evidence for the project's lack of responsiveness to the City's context. Reacting to this accusation, Peter Carter had quoted from the architect's several visits to the British capital and Mies's ascertained knowledge of famous London architectural landmarks, such as Charles Burton's Palm House at Kew or Hendrik P. Berlage's 32 Bury Street office building.[26]

A repeated criticism of the scheme was that it would have been "ruinous for one of the best visual lessons in the financial district of Victorian architecture."[27] A City described as "the result of the delightful and unreasoned development of centuries of commerce" was confronted with an unimaginative design, depicted as one of the "latest manifestations of the vista-mania," gloomily evocative of Mussolini's tearing up of the unplanned streets around St. Peter's to build Via della Conciliazione.[28]

Ideologically tainted analogies such as this one were a constant feature of the debate: along with the reference to public-building programs of the fascist regime, allusions were often made to Nazi bombing in the sad days of 1940 and 1941, during the London Blitz.[29] Similarly, in his proof of evidence against the scheme, Watkin equated the project to the modernist vision of "a new world of gleaming glass towers" the origins of which he traced back to Le Corbusier's Plan Voisin, which he did not hesitate to define as "vandalistic."[30]

Suggesting the idea that architecture can be nationally determined, detractors of the scheme, emphatically insisted on the binary opposition of the "indigenous" and the "imported": an alien architectural aesthetic, authoritarian and undemocratic in style, "assertive," "dominant" and "unsympa-

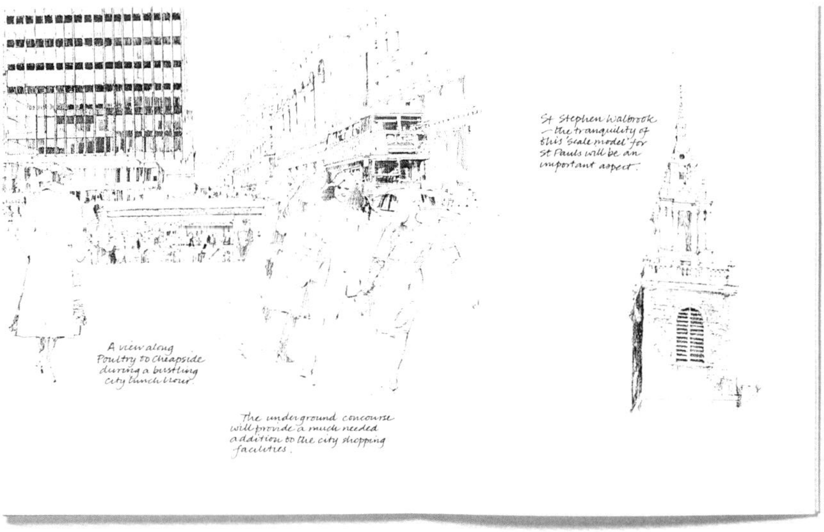

figs. 8, 9 Neil MacDonald's pictorial renderings of the Mansion Square Scheme as published in *Mansion House Square Scheme. A Place for People* (London: 1 Poultry Limited, 1982). Source: Peter Carter fonds. Collection Centre Canadien d'Architecture/Canadian Centre for Architecture. Gift of Peter Carter.

thetic," brought in from abroad – be it American downtowns, monumental formal spaces so typical of totalitarian regimes, or repetitive square grids of the Corbusian plans for Paris – was then set in contrast to a more layered and ineffable language of supposedly genuinely native origins. The analogies with Second World War German air raids then employed by some of the most vehement objectors to the scheme pushed this narrative even further, evoking the perils of an imminent foreign invasion as a serious threat to the integrity of national culture.

What exactly did this indigenous idiom consist of? How did it apply to this specific section of the City of London?

"The Familiar and Cherished Local Scene"

When asked to give his evidence before the inspector at the Guildhall, the architect Roy Worskett, principal architectural witness for the City of London, would speculate at length on this crucial point. For Worskett, the Mansion House Square project suffered from all the defects of the times in which it had been conceived, when "the same architectural expression [had been] repeated worldwide."[31] In the view of the former City Architect of Bath, the Mansion House Square project was to be a test case "of local and national importance," proving "the effectiveness and intentions of conservation legislation."[32] Its subject matter was "not ultimately, nor simply about architecture but [...] about the character and significance of the City as a place in which to live and work."[33] In this light, it could only be seen as the largely outdated product of a bygone age, which urgently needed to be reassessed against the backdrop of a radically changed cultural scenario. This one had been significantly marked by the emergence of a new public awareness towards matters of conservation.[34] By quoting Circular 23/77, that "public opinion is now overwhelmingly in favor of conserving and enhancing the familiar and cherished local scene,"[35] Worskett made it clear enough what that changed cultural scenario was about. The City's townscape, a unique urban and architectural quality made up of subtle hierarchies, visual variety and informal spaces, constituted, in Worskett's terms, the quintessence of the City's character.

But was this character a culturally or even nationally determined feature, as David Watkin had seemed to suggest when he claimed that "buildings with monumental porticos like the Mansion House, the Ashmolean [Museum], the British Museum [...] if built in the Continent would all have been fronted with monumental *piazzas* approached along axial avenues," further arguing that "rightly or wrongly the English tradition had been different"?[36] Or rather, was this insistence on an alleged genetic code of architecture and urbanism no more than the rhetoric of a polemic that had gone well beyond academic and professional circles, reaching the public at large in widely read magazines and newspapers as well as on TV screens?

"Townscape," a term so frequently used during the Mansion House Square scheme debate, had entered the *New Oxford Dictionary* in 1880. Its possible pseudonym, the expression "urban landscape," was introduced by *The Architectural Review* in an article on "the art of making urban landscape"

fig. 10 "Mansion House Square – Trial of the Century." The 1984 public inquiry seen by *Architects' Journal's* architectural cartoonist Louis Hellman, showing on the left: the City's defense represented by Marcus Binney (SAVE), a caricatural personification of the "City Character" pictured as a stereotyped London tycoon smoking a cigar, the Lord Mayor of London and the head of the Greater London Council, Ken Livingstone; on the plaintiffs' side, Palumbo, the architectural historian John Summerson, and Richard Rogers; in the middle: the Secretary of the Environment Patrick Jenkin, and Mies's coffin pictured in the shape of a steel and glass tower and displaying the headings "Less Is Mort" (a parody of Mies's renowned aphorism "Less is More") and "Rest in Peace Modern Movement." Source: "Hellman and Diary," *The Architects' Journal*, May 29, 1985, 27. Gift of Louis Hellman ©.

published in January 1944.[37] The term had also been widely employed by members of the *Review's* editorial board, J.M. Richards, Hubert de Cronin Hastings, Nikolaus Pevsner and Gordon Cullen, and adopted in the 1950s in plans promoted by the Civic Trust. During the 1940s, "townscape," a planning practice founded on the application of the eighteenth-century landscape principles of visual surprise, accident and variety, had been the focus of the *Review's* agenda.[38] As has been argued, "townscape was set in direct contrast to continental European ideas of planning and architecture [...] it was politically compatible with the English spirit and an English aesthetic based around an appreciation of 'age and quaintness.'"[39] Through the re-elaboration of a viable national tradition, at a crucial time for Britain's postwar reconstruction, a group of architects, planners, historians and critics had attempted to define a theory of vision and design deeply rooted in the English architectural and planning tradition, and capable of providing a peculiarly English alternative to international modernism.

Thanks to Conservation Area designation, what had been theorized in the pages of the *Review* was to become an important part of British planning practice. By the early 1980s, "townscape" was so intrinsically part of the current approach to planning that even the developers of the Mansion House Square scheme could not escape it. To make their proposal more attractive to the eyes of a public grown increasingly skeptical of wholesale functionalist high-rise developments, Palumbo and his team of consultants had appointed artist Neil MacDonald to draw a series of picturesque street views, in the manner of Gordon Cullen's sketches, of the planned Mansion House Square tower and plaza.[40] What resulted was a promotional brochure, *Mansion House Square Scheme: A Place for People* (figs. 7–9), the adaptation of a quintessential modernist design to the more familiar and reassuring aesthetics cherished by the average "man in the street" and at the same time a surreal document that could well have made the late Mies van der Rohe roll over in his grave (fig. 10).

Conclusion

The Mansion House square scheme debate is an extraordinary case study of how a narrative of a specifically English aesthetic was adopted by the scheme's opponents in order to counterbalance the shock provoked by the arrival of cultural influences from abroad.

The terms of the debate clearly show how the heritage was to become a crucial domain of contestation between groups and individuals. Thus, the discussion was accompanied by a range of specific terminologies: words like "tradition," "character" and "townscape" were continuously reiterated, and a number of historical precedents were put into use by Palumbo's partisans as well as by his detractors.

If in architectural circles the story of this never-built scheme is a good illustration of how an architectural project would be read as a text, manipulated and employed as a medium of legitimization of particular professional identities, this highly publicized controversy was to become the object of symbolic re-appropriations by single individuals, pressure groups, and institutions, each one interested in purporting a spatial arrangement of the urban form that would prove instrumental to the assertion of particular professional and economic interests.

Endnotes

1 The present chapter is a partial and provisional version of a broader ongoing study on the history of the Mansion House Square scheme (1962–1985), based on the scrutiny of graphic and textual documents held at the Peter Carter fonds of the Canadian Centre for Architecture (Montreal) and at Save Britain's Heritage's headquarters (London). The documents consulted include texts of witnesses' proofs of evidence presented at the public inquiry in 1984 at the Guildhall, the ceremonial and administrative center of the City of London Corporation, between May 1 and July 6, as well as correspondence files and the collection of newspaper and journal clippings related to the scheme and its public reception. Archival note: the notation of documents in the Mansion House Square Scheme Revised Scheme and Public Inquiry (MHSS) papers within Peter Carter fonds follows David Rose, *Guide to the Peter Carter Archive* (Montreal: Canadian Centre for Architecture, 1997), and is articulated into sections (s.) and boxes (b.). In the present text sections have been indicated with capital alphabetical letters and boxes with Roman numbers. As the pages of the proofs of evidence are not numbered, but are subdivided into numbered paragraphs, when quoting from these texts references to paragraphs instead of pages have been reported in the abbreviated form "par.," followed by the paragraph number.

2 Peter Carter, "Proof of Evidence at Mansion House Square Scheme Public Inquiry" (London: City Corporation, May–July 1984), par. 5, MHSS papers, s. O, b. VII.

3 John Harris, "Was the Design by Mies?", letter to *Financial Times* (April 30, 1982); Carter "The Design Was by Mies," letter to *Financial Times* (May 5, 1982), "Did Mies Really Design It?", *The Economist* (June 30, 1984); "Mansion House 'Authentically Mies,'" *Building*, 6 (July 6, 1984); "Authenticity of Mies Scheme Challenged," *Architects' Journal* (July 14, 1984), 32–33.

4 "Mansion House Square Debate: Expert Witness," *Architects' Journal* (August 22, 1984), 24–25 (p. 24).

5 *City Square and Tower Public Comment Analysis* (London: The British Market Research Bureau, 1968), MHSS papers: s. N, b. VI.

6 "Report of the Planning and Communication Committee Relative to Mansion House Square Scheme," (London: City of London Corporation, May 22, 1969), 9, MHSS papers: s. N, b. VI; "Mansion House Square Redevelopment: Joint Report by the Architect and Director of Planning" (London: Greater London Council, January 20, 1969), 3, ibid.; Godfrey Samuel, Letter of Godfrey Samuel to the Architect of the Greater London Council, February 26, 1968, ibid.

7 "Conservation Areas: Report Planning and Communications Committee" (London: City of London Corporation, 1970), in MHSS papers: s. N, b. VI; "Conservation Areas in the City of London: A General Introduction to Their Character," (London: City of London Corporation, 1994).

8 "Refusal of Permission to Develop" (London: City of London, Department of Architecture and Planning, September 23, 1982), SAVE.

9 *The Mansion House Square Scheme: Stop It* (London: Save Britain's Heritage, 1982), MHSS papers, s. G, Project and Public Inquiry Visual and Textual Documents. The pamphlet contains five statements: John

Harris, "The Wrong Building in the Wrong Place at the Wrong Time," 2–4; Marcus Binney, "Timeless Masterpiece or Old Fashioned Glass Box?", 6–13; Timothy Cantell, "Mansion House Square: Townscape – Planning," 14–15; John Maddison, "Mansion House Square Scheme: Buildings Threatened with Demolition," 16–20; Matthew Saunders, "The Mansion House Square Development," 21–23.

10 John Goldsmith, "Retail Traders Association Fights for Small Shopkeepers," *City Recorder* 1 (August 19, 1982).

11 Martin Pawley, "Palumbo Is Right," *Building Design*, 582 (February 19, 1982), 7.

12 Jane M. Jacobs, "Negotiating the Heart: Place and Identity in the Post Imperial City," in *City Worlds*, ed. Doreen B. Massey, et al. (London: Routledge, 1999), 137–156 (p. 137).

13 Michael Rustin, "Postmodernism and Antimodernism in Contemporary British Architecture," *Assemblage*, 8 (1989), 88–104.

14 David Lloyd, Jennifer Freeman and Jane Fawcett, eds., *Save the City: A Conservation Study of the City of London* (London: Society for the Protection of Ancient Buildings, Georgian Group, Victorian Society, Civic Trust, 1976), 12.

15 A thorough description of the statutory policies and conservation legislation related to the site is contained in the proof of evidence read at the 1984 public inquiry by Stuart J. Murphy, the City Architect. Stuart J. Murphy, "Proof of Evidence at Mansion House Square Scheme Public Inquiry" (London: City Corporation, May–July 1984), pars. 5–8, MHSS papers, s. L, b. IV.

16 Prince of Wales, "A speech by HRH the Prince of Wales at the 150th anniversary of the Royal Institute of British Architects," (London: Hampton Court Palace, May 30, 1984), http://www.princeofwales.gov.uk/media/speeches/speech-hrh-the-prince-of-wales-the-150th-anniversary-of-the-royal-institute-of, accessed February 9, 2016.

17 Charles Knevitt, "Mies Tower Will Rival Bomb Ruins," *The Times* (June 29, 1984), 12.

18 Piloti (Gavin Stamp), "Nooks and Corners," *Private Eye* (June 15, 1984), 9.

19 Astragal, "All Square," *Architects' Journal* (February 10, 1982), 3.

20 Colin Amery, "No Longer with Us," *Financial Times* (February 8, 1982), 23.

21 Martin Walker, "City's Old Mies Trap," *Guardian* (February 27, 1982), 13.

22 Louis Wilkins, "Is Mies Design Appropriate for Mansion House Square?", *London Architect*, 2, (1982), 17.

23 Peter Palumbo, *The Mansion House Square Scheme* (London: 1 Poultry Limited, 1981), 15–16, in MHSS papers: s. Q, b. IX; see also Palumbo, "What London Missed," letter to the *Daily Telegraph* (January 1, 1982); Deyan Sudijc, "The Cuckoo in Wren's Nest," *Sunday Times* (February 14, 1982).

24 Michael Cassell, "Mansion House Square under Fire," *Financial Times* (February 12, 1982).

25 Piloti, "Nooks and Corners," *Private Eye* (January 29, 1982), 4.

26 Peter Carter, "Proof of Evidence at Mansion House Square Scheme Public Inquiry" (London: City Corporation, May–July 1984), par. 5, in MHSS papers, s. O, b. VII.

27 "Plan to Demolish London District Draws Outrage," *Chicago Sunday Times* (January 13, 1982).

28 Gavin Stamp, "Non Momentum," *Daily Telegraph* (January 25, 1982), 3; Piloti, "Nooks and Corners," *Private Eye* (January 29, 1982), 4.
29 Knevitt, 'Mies Tower Will Rival Bomb Ruins."
30 David Watkin, "Proof of Evidence at Mansion House Square Scheme Public Inquiry," (London: City Corporation, May–July 1984), par. 4, in MHSS papers, s. L, b. IV
31 Roy Worskett, "Proof of Evidence at Mansion House Square Scheme Public Inquiry" (London: City Corporation, May–July 1984), par. 1.5, in MHSS papers, s. P, b. VIII.
32 Ibid., par. 1.1
33 Ibid., par. 1.2
34 Ibid., par. 1.3
35 Ibid., par. 1.4
36 Watkin, "Proof of Evidence," par. 10.
37 The Editor, "Exterior Furnishing or Sharawaggi: The Art of Making Urban Landscape," *The Architectural Review* 565 (1944), 6.
38 Michela Rosso, "Rediscovering the Picturesque: Nikolaus Pevsner and the Work of Architects and Planners During and After the Second World War," in *Reassessing Nikolaus Pevsner*, ed. Peter Draper (Aldershot: Ashgate 2004), 195–212; Nikolaus Pevsner, *Visual Planning and the Picturesque*, ed. Mathew Aitchison and John Macarthur (Los Angeles: Getty Research Institute, 2010).
39 Jane M. Jacobs, "The Politics of the Past: Redevelopment in London" (PhD thesis, University College London, 1990), 74.
40 *The Mansion House Square Scheme. A Place for People* (London: 1 Poultry Limited, 1982), in MHSS papers: s. Q, b. IX.

Andrew Demshuk

Preservationism, Postmodernism, and the Public across the Iron Curtain in Leipzig and Frankfurt/Main[1]

Public opinion played a crucial role on both sides of the Iron Curtain in prompting the steady turn away from high modernism after the 1960s. In both Frankfurt/Main and Leipzig, architectural cataclysms on central symbolic sites stimulated massive protests against a perceived "*Baudiktatur*," whose architectural language was modernism. Regime-led destruction of diverse historic monuments prompted Leipzigers to send thousands of letters to leaders at the local, regional, and national levels and to openly demonstrate against plans to demolish the perfectly intact medieval University Church (Paulinerkirche).[2] Regime-led razing and modernist remaking of the space between Frankfurt's Römer and Cathedral and plans to dynamite the opera house ruins and intact historic architecture in the Westend neighborhood prompted Frankfurters to engage in extensive letter-writing campaigns, money-raising efforts, and outright street violence against property speculation that they perceived as supported by local authorities. These broad-based protests toppled a city government in Frankfurt and inspired fear and censure from Leipzig officials. With varying results, the common public conflation of authoritarian governance with modernism forced local governments on both sides of the Iron Curtain to appreciate anti-modernism and historic preservation [*Denkmalpflege*] as a serious motivating force.

After sketching modernist incursions in both cities, this article examines the consequences as they unfolded throughout the 1970s and 1980s: namely the steady trend toward the multivalent and overlapping phenomena of preservationism, historical reproductions, and ultimately postmodernism. Based upon my research in local and state archives, I argue that public unrest due to recent upheavals prompted both cities to create underfunded and understaffed historic preservation offices, whose efforts to preserve and restore local buildings interacted with mistrustful citizens. This initial concession to historic preservation coincided with a growing realization that incipient postmodernist citations and even historic reconstructions were also necessary in order to placate local dissatisfaction with a renewed sense of heritage, even though both of these trends were often at odds with the preservationist precept of "authenticity."[3] Although to varying extents historic preservation, reconstructions, and postmodernism prevailed in both cities after the *Wende* of 1989, preconditions had already been laid on both sides of the Iron Curtain over the preceding twenty years.

Plans and Protests in 1960s Leipzig and Frankfurt

Throughout the 1960s, urban planning decisions in both Frankfurt and Leipzig were determined by a handful of men who largely intimidated other leaders into implementing a sweeping modernist treatment of historic spaces in the urban core against growing pressure from an engaged populace. In both cases, official rhetoric bespoke the utopian maxims of modernity: the creation of an ordered, hygienic future cleared of historicist confections that predated the First World War, all for the greater public good. Whether couched in Frankfurt as democratically based social planning or in Leipzig as "democratic centralism," in neither case was the public seriously consulted before the wrecking ball was already in play.

Throughout this period, both regimes regularly used picture books, newspaper articles and speeches to convey their reasoning that, if the public wanted to see further construction of apartment buildings and infrastructure, they had to allow for the neglect and destruction of cultural treasures. For example, West German Federal Urban Planning and Housing Minister Lauritz Lauritzen asserted that only select historic properties were worthy of modernization due to their "quality" and ability to fit in with the "overall urban plan of the city"; and *Architektur der DDR* chief editor Gerhard Krenz declared that the razing of prewar ruins and even intact structures (euphemistically called "Altsubstanz") proved that "the socialist city is the City of the Future, which is already coming into being today."[4] The biggest difference was that in Frankfurt the authorities generally delivered, whereas the leadership in Leipzig often cleared whole historic ensembles without building anything in their place for years or even at all. Another difference relates to the general freedom of opinion. Whereas both engaged publics saw a democratic deficit in decision-making, Frankfurters enjoyed access to a free press that proffered an open forum for contesting top-town plans, and ultimately a number of polls exerted influence on city politics. In contrast, local planning in Leipzig was heeding more centralized dictates from the *Bezirk* [regional district] or even state level, and the press was merely a mouthpiece for official positions. Whereas in Frankfurt opposition parties – the CDU (Christian Democratic Union) and FDP (Free Democratic Party) – used modernist blunders as political capital for coming elections, in Leipzig the supposed opposition was bullied into voting as the reigning SED had mandated, and although public protest very seldom resulted in any serious punishment apart from increased *Stasi* surveillance, it also had virtually no effect on centralized decision-making.[5]

Frankfurt's stridently modernist regime was spearheaded by urban planning head Hans Kampffmeyer and a succession of modernist-friendly SPD city governments that ended after the tenure of mayor Rudi Arndt. In addition to his support for a modernist remaking of the bombed-out urban core between the Römer and Cathedral, the traditional procession route of medieval Holy Roman Emperors, Kampffmeyer proposed the so-called Three-Finger-Plan that was to replace the Westend neighborhood, Frankfurt's largest surviving collection of *Gründerzeit* historicist homes and villas, with a glass and steel banking district (a move that unintentionally unleashed some of the worst real estate speculation in West German history). Known as "Dynamite Rudi," Arndt had favored dynamiting the ruined opera house and generally backed Kampffmeyer's policies long before he formally took office as mayor in 1972, the same year Kampffmeyer left Frankfurt.

Massive protests throughout the 1960s against the leveling of Westend, the opera, and the modernist remaking of the historic core were supported by a number of cultural institutions and newly founded citizens' initiatives, including the *Aktionsgemeinschaft Westend*, *Kuratorium Kulturelles Frankfurt*, *Arbeitsgemeinschaft der Frankfurter Bürgerverein*, *Aktionsgemeinschaft Dom-Römerberg*, *Freunde Frankfurts*, and the *Polytechnische Gesellschaft*. One flash-point in this rising war of contention was the March 19, 1970 city council decision (41 in favor, 34 against) to construct an ancillary city hall [Technisches Rathaus] atop a parking garage in the middle of the historic procession way between the Cathedral and Römer. A flood of letters swept through state and city offices in protest accusing leaders of adopting dictatorial approaches worthy of the Eastern Bloc. In a letter signed by prominent citizens from the above-mentioned societies, the city council was warned that, after 25 years of discussion, it was inconceivable that the Technisches Rathaus was getting pushed through in a matter of weeks. It urged: "please do not consider the construction of the Technisches Rathaus as a question of the prestige of the parties. Only in the Eastern Bloc is the precept 'the Party is always right' valid." Obliquely referencing Kampffmeyer himself, they concluded: this "realization of the wishes of one department" would be a "pyrrhic victory," as it would destroy the sense that the city council was at all accountable to the people.[6] That the Technisches Rathaus was built anyway, that the wrecking ball danced through Westend despite protest from diverse actors, that the old opera was always on the brink of destruction ultimately compelled "Dynamite Rudi" to transform himself at least superficially into a preservationist, and even this could not save his government from falling to the CDU regime of Walter Wallmann in 1977 (figs. 1, 2).

When Leipzig's intact medieval University Church was targeted for demolition, protests spread across the city and republic. A planning exhibition in fall 1960 had already made known to the population that the fifteenth-century University Church and historic facades of the main university administration building, the Augusteum, were to disappear from the western side of Karl-Marx-Platz (historically and currently known as Augustusplatz), to be replaced by a thoroughly modernist ensemble. Public concern was further heightened by the destruction of the art museum ruin on the southern side of the square, which was replaced by an open green space until the completion of the *Neues Gewandhaus* under Rudolf Skoda with city architect Horst Siegel in 1981. In anticipation of the April 1963 Leipzig city council resolution which called for the demolition of all remaining "ruins" before the city's 800th anniversary in 1965, the local strongman, regional district secretary Paul Fröhlich, met with Mayor Walter Kresse and leading Leipzig planners and city councilmen to emphasize that the "Schandflecke" must vanish from the cityscape.[7] Throughout this meeting, the secretive and authoritarian nature of planning was openly manifest. As Kresse observed, "We will discuss, but not in public. Otherwise, unnecessary unrest will enter in. The shaping of the square has to be prepared internally." To justify this approach, they even asserted that they were taking their lead from West Germany. As Kresse added, "We will not use a public exhibition until we are ready. People in West Germany have also gotten excited that West German architects have made recommendations that are culturally and historically correct. I must say, such architects deserve only praise." Fröhlich was also impressed with Western *Baudiktatur* in Frankfurt, observing: "It's excellent to have the courage to configure a city in such a way," and he called for forging "order" in Leipzig as in other East German cities.

fig. 1 Frankfurt Römerberg, Junkers Aerial Photograph, 1929. ISG-Ffm S7A 1998/1858.

fig. 2 Frankfurt Dom-Römerberg area, Model, Bartsch/Thürwächter/Weber, 1971/80. ISG-Ffm BA S7C 1998/2486.

"Everything has been cleared away in Karl Marx Stadt. No one is keeping us from opening things up," he asserted, concluding: "the people can certainly give their opinion, but we have the sovereign [right] to decide for ourselves."[8]

It was with this Leninist principle of "democratic centralism" in urban planning that the historic Johannis tower was leveled a month later. When the University Church was targeted for immediate demolition in 1964, protests continued to spread. University professors and students, preservationists, religious leaders, and diverse engaged citizens flooded a wide array of city offices (not least those of the mayor and chief architect) with brazen letters, and ultimately compelled the regime to postpone its plans. Silence shrouded the question of the University Church throughout the following years, until quite suddenly on May 23, 1968 the city council all but unanimously voted to demolish it, and the Gothic landmark came crashing down on May 30 in front of thousands of perturbed onlookers, who watched from behind police lines and had spent previous days tossing flowers over the fence and writing of their distress to the authorities.

As in Frankfurt, the replacement of preceding historic structures was a purely modernist ensemble designed by leading architects (in this instance under direction of Horst Siegel and Hermann Henselmann); once completed in 1973, it utterly failed to compensate for the landmarks, which had once stood on such an historic space. However, here the regime had also leveled architectural treasures around which the public had forged strong postwar memories. Neither war-ravaged nor cleared away after the war, the University Church and even portions of the neighboring university ensemble had been intact and in use practically up until the eve of their destruction, and (as in the case of Frankfurt's intact Westend district) this heightened the sense of outrage at their destruction (figs. 3, 4).

Like the controversies in Frankfurt, I argue that the University Church represented a crucial turning point in Leipzigers' relations with their regime; despite continued rhetoric about participation, the disconnect between the regime and populace was now total. Whereas protest had successfully challenged Frankfurt's scandalous democratic deficit and increased public activism, it had not been able to influence any change in the governing structures in Leipzig. Nonetheless, in both cases protests had forced local leaders to recognize that unbridled modernism was not winning public esteem. By the end of the 1970s, each city had adopted at least a symbolic platform favoring historic preservation, and by the 1980s they were both experimenting with a more integrative architectural language in nascent postmodernism.

Official Responses: Historic Preservation and Postmodernism, West and East

Despite serious differences in their approach to public participation, by the 1970s both cities had elected to offer the people an olive branch by founding preservation offices. In Frankfurt, the oft-symbolic and advisory Head of Historic Preservation in the state of Hesse [*Landeskonservator*] was given local support in 1972 by the new office of the young preservationist Heinz Schomann, and citizens' initiatives that had already sprouted up to save the architectural heritage began to influence and even seed the city's political parties. In Leipzig, the equally strapped *Institut für Denkmalpflege* in Dresden

fig. 3 Leipzig Augustus Square, Junkers Aerial Photograph, circa 1929/30. StadtAL BA 1977/1646.

fig. 4 Leipzig Karl Marx Square, Final Version, Siegel/Henselmann, 1968. StadtAL, BCA V, 972, Bd. 1, 59.

was given local support by the new *VEB Denkmalpflege* (1978) and *Büro für Architekturbezogene Kunst* (1975).[9] Underfunded and badly equipped, both the Frankfurt and Leipzig preservation offices had few successes to document by the 1980s, but this was not through lack of trying. This gesture toward preservation was simply incapable of contesting most ongoing modernist projects, which continued to enjoy the greatest private and state financial support – hence, in practice, regime approaches to planning were changing only slowly.

In 1967, chief building officer [*Oberbaurat*] Schubö had already been named as Frankfurt's chief preservation officer, and he struggled to save many monuments that were torn down anyway. By July 1971, the FDP argued that a genuine office for historic preservation had to be founded and heeded, if the regime truly wanted to show that it cared about public interest in architectural heritage.[10] This paralleled a pivotal speech by Hessian Preservation Head Gottfried Kiesow, who asserted that historicist eclecticism from the Wilhelmine period was a worthy style that could and should be renovated to serve contemporary needs, lest Germany continue to suffer from "a loss of history [*Geschichtslosigkeit*] and loss of national consciousness" that was spreading everywhere in faceless modern cityscapes.[11] This was a revolutionary concept, given the global modernist disdain for pre-1914 historicist architecture – a trend especially exacerbated in the German context since 1945 due to the preconception that overcoming the inglorious recent past necessitated constructing a bright modern future.[12] Kiesow's speech was strongly publicized and supported by the *Frankfurter Rundschau*, which cited his comment that, whereas the city of Amsterdam was protecting seven thousand architectural monuments, Frankfurt was failing to save its meager collection of four hundred sixty-nine. Observing regular applause during the speech, the leading newspaper praised Kiesow's opposition to purely economic interests and recalled his slideshow's poignant impression of the "barbaric destruction of culturally valuable objects in Westend." Future generations would hardly be able to grasp how it could be that, in a time of such "affluence," so little had been done for historic preservation.[13]

Appointed as city preservation officer in 1972, thirty-three-year-old Heinz Schomann backed a radical approach that was to become commonplace after 1989: old buildings should be retained and integrated as a contrast with modernist ensembles. As the *Frankfurter Rundschau* observed: "Schomann represents the younger generation, which in a way is newly promoting the neglected old buildings worthy of retention in the cityscape as a logical answer to the leveled similitude [*Gleichmacherei*] we find everywhere in architecture. This is above all a step toward the goal of the "humane city," a city whose appearance cannot be purely oriented toward economic success."[14] Schomann was also critical of the rising trend toward producing historical copies as a cheaper alternative to genuine preservation. He saw it as outrageous that thirty-four million DM were allocated for the historicist reconstruction of the eastern side of the Römer, whereas the 1.5 million DM for historic preservation in 1981 had been reduced to 500,000 in 1983, meaning that many owners willing to restore their homes had to be disappointed. The city was producing a "culture of appearances [*Schein-Kultur*]" utterly disinterested in genuine preservation.[15]

Frankfurt was also on the cutting edge of postmodernism as an aesthetic response to the impossible quandaries created in a historic space like that

fig. 5 Frankfurt Dom-Römerberg area, Stadtvermessungsamt Model, Bangert/Jansen/Scholz/Schultes, 1983. ISG-Ffm S7C 1998/2519.

between the Römer and Cathedral. In some ways, this was a trend "back to the future" of 1950s plans for a modern reconstruction in the general scale of former structures spiced here and there by an historical copy. After all, the immediate postwar years had seen a reconstruction of the devastated Römer and Steinernes Haus from very few architectural remains, and to this day the austere and in-scale 1950s structures on either side of the Römer (almost proto-postmodern) have weathered changing tastes rather well.[16] In like manner, after Rudi Arndt's 1975 poll of the public on the historic zone unleashed a storm of criticism against the Technisches Rathaus, Historisches Museum, and a broad parking garage that was to form the foundation for a Brutalist cultural center, discussions took on a distinctively postmodern flavor. Visiting young architects from TU Darmstadt gave expression to the shifting generational approach to architecture in 1978 when, in place of monumental modernist complexes, they called for "peaceful and idyllic" row houses reminiscent of 1950s construction – a perspective that "conjured more than astonishment" in the newspapers.[17] By the early 1980s, Frankfurt's historic core received one of West Germany's first postmodern masterpieces: the New Schirn Gallery, which represented a humbler scale than high modernism, cited elements from such diverse surroundings as the Technisches Rathaus and excavated archaeological remains of the medieval city, supported wildly postmodern housing on its southern side, roughly occupied and reproduced the space of the medieval "Schirn" alley, and incorporated an historical copy of the eastern

fig. 6 Leipzig's 1981 Third Gewandhaus, Augustus Square, July 2015, Author's Photograph.

side of the Römer, all on the foundation of a parking deck meant to support the cultural center. The aesthetic result found comparatively greater public approval (fig. 5).

As in Frankfurt, Leipzig's city preservationist Hubert Maaß was virtually powerless, and scant money promised for the restoration of historic structures seldom materialized, such that many architectural treasures on historic preservation lists languished and fell down over the coming years. For instance, the city council called for restoring Barthels Hof as "the most important intact bourgeois residential building in Leipzig from the Renaissance" in 1964, but apart from superficial patchwork the historic pedestrian arcade was almost beyond repair by 1989.[18] When the death or retirement of leading party despots by the early 1970s allowed for a shift toward titular preservationism, the newly founded *VEB Denkmalpflege* and *Büro für architekturbezogene Kunst* were just as badly funded as comparable offices in the West. As long-time Leipzig planning administrator Karl-Heinz Blaurock reflected in 2002, "the measure of success became more humble with each year. […] The newly formed *VEB Denkmalpflege* only possessed the necessary reconstruction capacities for a very select number of historic structures." The "Dächer dicht" ["secure the roofs"] initiative of Leipzig mayor Karl-Heinz Müller at the start of the 1980s for securing apartment structures, which was welcomed by the population, dragged on due to an insufficient supply of roof tiles, and newly formed roofing brigades were soon dissolved. Numerous buildings across the city with leaky roofs were getting cleaved down, as floor after floor became uninhabitable.[19]

Although the term "postmodern" was never officially used in the GDR, this global style resonated as a possible solution for Leipzig's popular and aesthetic troubles by the 1980s – even though (as in much of the GDR) such cutting-edge architecture was largely kept to the drawing board. The most significant inner-city exceptions were the *Neues Gewandhaus* in 1981 and *Bowlingtreff* in 1987 (the latter designed by Winfried Sziegoleit and Volker Sieg), both of which cited or incorporated surrounding elements and boasted flashy glass and sandstone facades. Indeed, the sandstone on the *Gewandhaus* was meant to "cite" that of the opera on the other side of the square, and the *Bowlingtreff* was in some ways a recollection of the round panorama that had stood on the same site before the war (fig. 6).

In the GDR's final years, Leipzig's young chief architect Dietmar Fischer called for retaining historic construction and building on a more "humane" scale. Having first inaugurated a new approach to integrate more decorative and small-scale *Plattenbau* apartments into surrounding historic structures, Fischer hosted an international planning competition for the remaking of the inner city in 1988. Along with other Leipzig planners including Johannes Schulze, Wolfgang Müller, and Hubert Maaß, Fischer put out a call for submissions that yielded sixteen models displayed for international visitors when Leipzig hosted the Sixth Urban Planning Research Conference of the UN's Economic Commission for Europe in October. All of this was to inform the city's forthcoming new General Building Plan. As Fischer himself confesses, lack of financial and material support in the dying shortage economy [*Mangelwirtschaft*] consigned all of these plans to oblivion, but the optimistic, ambitious, and cutting-edge postmodern and historicist proposals for new trade fair palaces and passages across the ravaged modernist inner city core were impressive. The intent, in sum, had been to restore much of the prewar streetscape, eliminate ahistorical open squares (such as the 1960s "Saxonplatz", which arose in place of dense old town neighborhoods damaged in the war), and even at times reconstruct the facades of historic buildings (such as the Renaissance gable of Deutrichs Hof, which had been lost amid the 1960s demolitions). From such foundations, both cities widely sought to fashion the humane cityscape on a smaller, more historical-looking scale by 1989. Even in Leipzig, the retention of many pre-1989 planners allowed for significant continuities.

Public Responses to Official Gestures

After the hegemony of modernism, the turn toward preservationism and postmodernism in each city might have rejuvenated a public sense of involvement by heeding general public desire for restoration of the historic cityscape; but perceptions of persisting dictatorial practices at times sustained and even deepened skepticism. Although greater democratic possibilities in Frankfurt led some citizens to get involved in trying to save their city and neighborhoods from the perceived oblivion of modernism, even here continued heavy-handed top-down planning decisions (despite a change in government) sustained some measure of despair and loss from the engaged population. At the same time that citizens' initiatives helped to arrest decay in Westend, bankers and insurance-brokers suddenly realized with what comfort they could conduct their business in the drawing rooms of old Kaiser-era villas. Hence, much as once-threatened edifices now survive in plush form in the shadow of modern towers, Westend is generally a lifeless banking district, whose high property prices have all but totally expelled its former inhabitants to other parts of the city. Far more extreme than the skepticism in Frankfurt, however, Leipzigers felt completely disconnected from city fathers who persisted in ignoring every public critique about the state of the city. As archived protest letters show, even party members were finding it hard to believe in a regime that failed to provide basic repairs to its housing. When in 1977 an apartment owner on Philipp-Müller-Straße asked the *Büro für Architekturbezogene Kunst* for financial help in restoring her historic home, the office delayed for an absurd length of time before writing that, "due to the concrete situation, no reimbursement of costs is possible." While admitting that an historic building like hers *should* qualify for aid, they groused that "funds for preservation don't come from some endless big pot, from which we can reimburse all the demands that arise overnight for great and arbitrary sums." After chastising her for commencing repairs before the bureaucracy could write back, they added that damages which had appeared on her facade nullified any justification for the *Büro* to consider her structure worthy of protection. "Hence, this means that the work you have already carried out fails to correspond with the principles of historic preservation or urban planning."[20] As in countless other cases, the message here was unmistakable: any citizen who dared to believe that preservation was more than empty rhetoric and asked for public financial assistance faced an endless waiting period, in which decay would surely continue; and if the citizen attempted repairs on his or her own initiative, the city's meager preservation offices actually had further grounds to deny reimbursement, even though the city continued to expect that the general public would keep working with them.

In sum, a firm belief in democracy underpinned Frankfurt's citizens' initiatives, and despite many shortfalls these groups refused to bow to the cynical belief that raw power or civic incompetence would rule the day. Lack of even token public influence killed any such optimism in Leipzig before many of the new historic preservation offices were even founded. Both cities had entered the 1970s with a public appalled by an obvious democratic deficit. But whereas in Frankfurt the public's ability to effect some change yielded activism and interaction with newly founded preservation offices and

fig. 7 Leipzig's new Paulinum on Augustus Square, July 2015, Author's Photograph.

postmodern solutions, in Leipzig the public had no interest in the early 1988 architectural competition and resulting exhibition that promised a preservationist and postmodern wonderland; formerly renowned for their civic activism, Leipzigers were stuck in cynicism and disengagement until 1989.

Retrospectives

Since 1989, both cities have seen a construction boom that has remade their inner cores through the widespread preservation of decaying architectural landmarks and a postmodern architectural language that seeks to integrate historicist confections into contemporary ensembles. Leipzig's discovery of a postmodern Gothic in the new ensemble where the modernist university had stood, as well as Frankfurt's ongoing postmodern reconstruction of its old town in place of the demolished *Technisches Rathaus*, offer only two of the most prominent examples (figs. 7, 8). Indeed, in both cities one of the most troubling current trends is the utter neglect and demolition of classical modernist ensembles from the 1960s, to say nothing of the so-called *Betonklötze* [cement blocks] of the 1970s. It is also uncertain whether the pioneering achievements of postmodernism will survive forever – already some have called for the elimination of the Schirn, to be replaced by a fantastic "restoration" of the medieval alleys of Frankfurt's old town; and it is doubtful

fig. 8 Frankfurt's new Old Town between the Dom and Römerberg, November 2015, Author's Photograph.

whether Leipzig's moldering Bowlingtreff will survive proposed plans to one day remake the surrounding Wilhelm-Leuschner-Platz into a monumental square of the 1989 peaceful revolution. In this sense, modernity's impatience with the existing cityscape and its ongoing contortion of prominent sites to serve present memory needs continues, albeit in an ever evolving aesthetic language.

Endnotes

1 I would like to thank the Alexander von Humboldt Foundation for generously supporting research on this article. It touches on initial themes that will find far more detailed treatment in my ongoing book project, which compares architecture and urban planning in Frankfurt/Main, Leipzig, and Wrocław after the fall of the Third Reich. I also wish to thank participants at the conference "Re-Framing Identities: Architecture's Turn to History, 1970–1990" in September 2015. Many thanks as well to Torsten Lange for his helpful comments on a late draft of this paper. Above all, I am grateful to my spouse and intellectual companion Rebecca Mitchell for her support and inspiration.

2 For a monograph treatment of Leipzig's University Church demolition as a means of measuring the relations between regime and public in East Germany, see Andrew Demshuk, *Demolition on Karl Marx Square: Cultural Barbarism in the People's State* (Oxford and New York: Oxford University Press, forthcoming 2017).

3 Although preservationism and postmodernism accompanied each other as a response to modernism, they also often opposed each other, as for instance preservationists generally attacked historical reproductions on principle. Furthermore, although for instance public opposition to modernist property speculation in Frankfurt spurred on historical reproductions and postmodernism, these newer forms have at times proven just as amenable to extreme speculative property incursions.

4 Bundesminister für Städtebau und Wohnungswesen, *Unsere Städte.*

Probleme von heute, Lösungen für morgen (Bad Godesberg: Presse- und Informationsamt der Bundesregierung, Städtebaubericht, 1970), 15–16; for a prominent East German example, see Krenz, "Die Zukunft der Stadt beginnt heute," in *Städte und Stadtzentren in der DDR. Ergebnisse und reale Perspektiven des Städtebaus in der Deutschen Demokratischen Republik*, ed. Idem. et al. (Berlin: VEB Verlag für Bauwesen, 1968), 8–19, (p. 19).

5 At the political/bureaucratic level, East German parties outside the SED were not meant to serve as actual opposition, due to the reigning dogma of democratic centralism and questionable "block party" electoral system; nonetheless, the public was meant to apprehend this oppositional role as real.

6 Aktionsgemeinschaft Dom-Römer an die Stadtverordneten, March 9, 1970, Frankfurt Institut für Stadtgeschichte (ISG-Ffm): V96/99. Author's translation.

7 "Beratung des Genossen Paul Fröhlich, 1. Sekretär der Bezirksleitung der SED Leipzig mit OBM Kresse und Baufachleuten am Sonnabend, dem 20. April 1963," Sächsisches Staatsarchiv Arbeitsstelle Leipzig (SächStAL) SED Bezirksleitung Leipzig Nr. IV/A/2/06/259, 1.

8 "Beratung des Genossen Paul Fröhlich, 1. Sekretär der Bezirksleitung der SED Leipzig mit OBM Kresse und Baufachleuten am Sonnabend, dem 20. April 1963," SächStAL SED Bezirksleitung Leipzig Nr. IV/A/2/06/259, 6, 8, 9–10. Author's translation.

9 The national Institut für Denkmalpflege in Berlin stood directly under the control of the Cultural Ministry. After the dissolution of Länder in the DDR and creation of administrative Bezirke in 1952, subsidiary branches arose across the republic in select cities. Berlin was responsible for the capital, Bezirk Potsdam, and Frankfurt/Oder; Dresden for Bezirk Dresden, Leipzig, Karl-Marx-Stadt, and Cottbus; Halle for Bezirk Halle and Magdeburg; Erfurt for Bezirk Erfurt, Gera, and Suhl; and Schwerin for Bezirk Schwerin, Rostock, and Neubrandenburg. Hence, preservation, scholarly documentation, and artistic advisory roles in Leipzig were first and foremost directed from the subsidiary institute in Dresden.

10 "Frage nach dem Denkmalspfleger. Die FDP drängt eigene Dienststelle unter dem Oberbürgermeister," *Frankfurter Allgemeine Zeitung* (July 19, 1971), ISG-Ffm: Magistratsakten 2.345.

11 Gottfried Kiesow, "Denkmalpflege im Frankfurter Westend," in *Denkmal- und Stadtbildpflege im Frankfurter Westend*, ed. Michael Mrowka and Hans-Georg Wolf (Frankfurt: Aktionsgemeinschaft Westend, 1971), 5–10, (p. 5). Author's translation.

12 For one book among many which discusses the evolving German approach to preservation (also as regards the Wilhelmine architectural legacy) see Rudy Koshar, *Germany's Transient Pasts: Preservation and National Memory in the Twentieth Century* (Chapel Hill: University of North Carolina Press, 1998).

13 "Landeskonservator erhebt schwere Vorwürfe gegenüber der Stadtverwaltung," *Frankfurter Rundschau* (April 5, 1971), ISG-Ffm: V66/104. Author's translation.

14 Margot Felsch, "Er liebt Wasserski, Jazz und Denkmalpflege," *Frankfurter Rundschau* (February 18, 1972), ISG-Ffm: V66/104. Author's translation.

15 Claudia Michels, "Statt Milieupflege nun Neues im alten Stil," *Frankfurter Rundschau* (September 8, 1982), ISG-Ffm: V66/104.

16 By the late 1970s, the general desire for a conservative, restorative aesthetic paralleled a sense that 1950s construction was far more redeemable than what had come later. This is confirmed, for instance, in responses to a 1975 questionnaire which the city had submitted for public response. In addition to archival materials, this is illustrated in Frankfurt/Main Presse- und Informationsamt, *Zur Diskussion: was kommt zwischen Dom und Römer. Das Ergebnis der Fragebogenaktion des Presse- und Informationsamtes. Bericht über die Auswertung des Fragebogens* (Frankfurt am Main: Dezernat Bau und Stadtwerke; Hochbauamt, 1977).

17 "Die Suche nach Ideen für den Römerberg geht weiter. Architekturstudenten: Nicht die Altstadt ist Geschichte, sondern ihre Zerstörung," *Frankfurter Allgemeine Zeitung* (February 23, 1978), 26.

18 Rat der Stadt Leipzig, "Ökonomische Begründung zum Perspektivplanentwurf 1965/1970 für den Aufbau das Stadtzentrum Leipzig," January 8, 1964, Stadtarchiv Leipzig (StadtAL) StVuR 4890, 83–104, (p. 100–101).

19 Karl-Heinz Blaurock, "Territorialplanung – Aufgaben, Erreichtes und Probleme," in *Bauen in Leipzig, 1945–1990*, ed. Joachim Tesch, (Leipzig: Rosa-Luxemburg-Stiftung, 2003), 86–114, (p. 110). Author's translation.

20 H. Schierz, amtlicher Direktor des Büros AKD, an Frau X, "Philipp-Müller-Str. 41a ("Bienenkorb")," August 17, 1977, StadtAL Büro für architekturbezogene Kunst, Nr. 14, 51. Author's translation.

Sebastiaan Loosen

"Le Monopole du Passéisme": A Left-Historicist Critique of Late Capitalism in Brussels

"Nous ne laisserons pas à la droite bourgeoise le monopole du passéisme". This quote – which translates roughly as "We won't leave the monopoly of historicism to the bourgeois right" – dates from 1977 and is a fierce call to arms for traditionalist architecture. But it also epitomizes a particular stance in the history of architecture of a group of Belgian architects in search of a socialist architecture rooted in their Western condition at a time when references to socialism and communism were marked by the European East-West divide.

The quote forms the concluding sentence of a paragraph in which its author, Maurice Culot (born 1937), in advocating a historicist architecture, dismisses contemporary currents of modernism, brutalism and neo-rationalism by means of political arguments. The paragraph, in its turn, concludes a text on the Soviet *avant-garde* of the 1920s that served as the editorial in the eleventh issue of *AAM*, the eponymous journal of the Brussels-based organization Archives d'Architecture Moderne (AAM).[1] Culot's editorial, then, can be positioned in a line of editorial texts in which a discussion took place between him, Léon Krier and others regarding historicist architecture and the form of the socialist city. At the same time, the issue's front cover was illustrated by a postmodern design proposal for the Centre Pompidou inspired by

Ledoux and Boullée (fig. 1). The way in which the starting quote is embedded in its larger textual context already points toward three key notions that pervade this specific episode in architectural history and which are the focus of this chapter: socialism, postmodernism and history.

La Cambre in the 1970s and the Search for a Western Socialist Architecture

The origins of *AAM* and of the organization Archives d'Architecture Moderne are tightly connected with both the Brussels architecture institute La Cambre – which had turned during the 1970s toward a socially engaged pedagogy – and another organization, Atelier de Recherche et d'Action Urbaines (ARAU), which had set up a series of counterprojects voicing a general dissatisfaction with Brussels' urban development. By the mid-1970s, these three actors – ARAU, La Cambre and AAM – had formed a mutually supporting triumvirate with Culot as the pivotal figure, leaving an impact on Brussels through their common critique on the functionalist architecture of their city.

La Cambre served as the host institution, where since the late 1960s the director, Robert L. Delevoy (1914–1982), an art historian inspired by semiology and Baudrillard, had provided institutional maneuvering space for a new generation of teachers including Culot, René Schoonbrodt, Marcel Pesleux and Michel Louis, all of who would contribute to ARAU projects or to *AAM* (fig. 2). Until 1979, when Delevoy's tenure ended and Culot and associated staff were expelled from the institute,[2] La Cambre served as an incubator of creativity where the enthusiasm and eagerness of students could be called upon to test and develop architectural ideas. It was also the institutional backdrop that allowed these people to develop their architectural stance independent of architectural production, and provided physical spaces that could be used for meetings and exhibitions of ARAU and AAM.

The second actor, ARAU, was the activist-populist side of the story. They added a sociologist background to their architectural expertise and were keen on safeguarding close contact with the population. By using student drawings as counterprojects, ARAU managed to garner public support and prevent the implementation of planned projects in Brussels. In the production of these images they gradually turned to a populist historicist architectural language.[3]

The significant role that AAM had in this triumvirate was two-fold: it had an architectural historical ambition that ultimately served the theoretical underpinnings of this group's historicist architecture, but was also a vehicle to be connected to an international network. It did so by generating a fast pace of exhibitions and a steady flow of publications – mainly internationally renowned exhibition catalogues and, from 1975, their own journal.

fig. 1 Cover with design proposal for the rear facade of the Centre Pompidou by Maurice Culot, Jean-Pierre Hoa, Philippe Lefèbvre, Elie Levy, Michel Louis, Daniel Staelens & Anne Van Loo. Source: *AAM*, no. 11 (July 1977). © AAM, Brussels

A second point of important contextualization is the ideological climate. Architectural discourse in Belgium in the 1970s was more a polemic against the excesses of modernism than it was guided by Cold War rhetoric, as in previous decades.[4] In this sense, the general discrediting of Brussels's architecture helped foster La Cambre's strongly articulated political stance. But more importantly, ideology in Belgium was mainly refracted through the lens of pillarization.[5] Combined with the fact that a large part of the Left's intellectuals weren't associated with a specific political party – the Communists were deemed too uncritical of Stalinism, the Socialists too complicit with capitalism[6] – "the political" in architecture became a case of individuals and small groups such as the group at La Cambre, rather than a vision endorsed by a large community.

Nevertheless, since its founding in 1926 by Henry van de Velde, La Cambre had been positioned in the socialist pillar in Belgium, and in the 1970s the Culot group strengthened this ideological positioning and explicitly sought to articulate a form of socialist architecture. In the early 1970s, semiology was the vehicle for this group to translate their political ideas into architecture –

fig. 2 Marcel Pesleux (with beard) and Maurice Culot (right) with assistants Elie Levy, Caroline Mierop, Philippe Lefèbvre and Anne Van Loo, 1977. Source: Robert Delevoy, Maurice Culot and Anne Van Loo, eds., *La Cambre: 1928–1978* (Brussels: AAM, 1979), 390. © AAM, Brussels

undoubtedly the legacy of their patron Delevoy: architecture had to express social relations somehow,[7] resulting in a less articulate architectural language, with mainly the building contours being drawn. But as this approach didn't fulfill expectations, typology gradually became the architectural theoretical tool for translating the group's architectural and political ideas into concrete projects and a more articulate, historicist architectural language.[8] In this regard, the close collaboration with Léon Krier (born 1946) from 1975 on was fundamental.

Socialist Cities of Culot and Krier

After Culot and Krier had met two years earlier, Peter Cook's 1976 Art Net Rally marked the starting point of a fruitful collaboration between the two that spanned the second half the 1970s, and an anchorage in the architectural historical canon as they became known as the Marxist architects, along with Manfredo Tafuri.[9] While Krier brought a solid dose of intellectual rigor into Culot's enterprise, for Krier, ARAU's actions formed the practical pendant to his theoretical ideas.[10]

Culot convinced Krier to elaborate on his 1975 London exhibition *Rational Architecture* – including works by Aldo Rossi, Giorgio Grassi, James Stirling, Oswald Mathias Ungers, Vittorio Gregotti and others – resulting in the publication of the same title by AAM three years later, a manifesto-like book that was a substantial affirmation of a typologically grounded historicist architecture. *Rational Architecture* was Krier's reinterpretation of *Architettura Razionale* by Rossi and others. Their 1973 exhibition had been meant in part to continue the Italian rationalism of the 1920s while omitting its political linkage to fascism; but at the same time to oppose the functionalism of their time by stressing the social aspect of form.

fig. 3 Upper part of first pages of an article by Culot on Spoerry. Source: *AAM*, no. 12 (November 1977): 4–5. © AAM, Brussels

Angelika Schnell has singled out Rossi's inclusion of Halle-Neustadt's Plattenbau, a product of solid socialist-regime engineering, as emblematic of Rossi's politico-theoretical stance.[11] The AAM publication omitted that project, but included an equally emblematic project: François Spoerry's Port Grimaud, a Saint Tropez replica. Though produced by hyper-capitalist real estate action, Port Grimaud would be a recurring architectural model for Culot, who studied its typology and construction details, and would be illustrative of his radically instrumental use of architectural form (fig 3).[12] But he theorized the relation between political convictions and architecture in quite a different way than Krier, which becomes clear in a debate held in the editorial texts of *AAM*, concerned with the form of the socialist city.

A critique on modernism in terms of its alliance with capitalism was never absent from *AAM*'s pages, but an active search for a socialist architecture was initiated by Culot in the May 1976 editorial. Seemingly as a side remark, Culot claims that socialist aesthetics follow a democratic production process and cannot be other than eclectic.[13] In the following issue, Culot was criticized in an open letter by Krier for having a too-shallow interpretation of socialism. A more profound understanding, according to Krier, would shift the problem of architectural form from the realm of aesthetics to that of production: "In an architectural theory and socialist aesthetic, the discussion will have to focus on the question of knowing to what extent a socialist mode of production will become the actual condition of a new architecture."[14] Thus he argues that Culot's style-based approach – giving the people what they like – reduces people to the role of consumers and architecture to a thin cultural facade, hence prone to the same dangers as those that surfaced in the "stylistic orgies" in Stalinist countries.[15]

In the subsequent editorials in this debate, their ideas on the matter are refined, culminating in Culot's populist plea for outright pastiche in order to destroy every grain of "imagination" and "creative genius" on the part of the architect.[16] The form of architecture is emphasized here because it was believed to be the only way to mobilize the population. Krier, on the other hand, remained less interested in the form of the built product than in the actual production process (fig. 4). Each position is Marxist in a different way: while Culot focuses on class struggle, Krier takes up alienation (as a result of a certain mode of production) as his starting point. This starting point can be attributed to his encounter with Marxism through some of Theodor Adorno's works, which Krier deemed salient to his nostalgic mindset.[17] In this regard, his critique of consumer architecture might be read as an attempt to apply Adorno's critique of industrialization to the realm of architecture.

This series of editorials culminated in the ambitious 1978 text "The Only Path for Architecture" by Culot and Krier, which was immediately picked up by *Oppositions* and later anthologized in K. Michael Hays's *Architecture Theory since 1968*. Culot and Krier join hands here, co-authoring the text to prove the existence of a convergent movement of theoretical reflection on an international scale.[18] Though constantly stressing the differences between their approaches –one involved with urban struggle, the other with theoretical reflection – they emphasize that they are pursuing the same goal, which is a more democratic architecture. They take advantage of the unique realm of architecture to imagine ways of gaining social equality by means of a double focus on form and on production process: the retrieval of the constitutive elements of the city that had been ignored by modernist urban planning (the street, the square, the neighborhood, etc.) as well as the reconstruction of craftsmanship. Thus they articulated a speculative reflection on the form of a socialist society.

Though Culot and Krier differ in the details of their socialist architecture, a comparison with Belgium's most famous socialist and modernist architect, Renaat Braem (1910–2001), shows how much they are at odds with their peers. Indeed, Braem didn't shun the explicit connection between postmodern historicist architecture and regression.[19] In his view, old city elements were mainly remnants of an oppression that should make way for new forms. Braem was respectfully criticized on this aspect by his peers at AAM.[20] Emblematic of this critique are the last paragraphs of the monograph on Braem by Francis Strauven (born 1942), an early (and a rare Flemish) member of AAM. In those paragraphs, Strauven frames Braem's socialist projects within the larger politico-economic constellation in which they were formulated: "Also Braem's cult of the new in fact fits better in the Western economy, however much his sincere intentions, which are not being doubted,

fig. 4 Project for the reconstruction of the Brigittines quarter, by Séfik Birkiye, Gilbert Busieau and Patrice Neirinck, 1978. The caption tells of their imagined city: "The inhabitants which have received an artisanal formation in the workshops of the Notre-Seigneur Street make up the spearhead of this popular enterprise … Two artisan-carpenters alter a piece of wood after it was shaped by the new sawmill established on the covered North-South junction. On the opposing pavement, our friend Léon Krier has taken off his jacket and admires, not without astonishment, their regained skills." Source: Annick Brauman, Maurice Culot and Michel Louis, eds., *La Reconstruction de Bruxelles* (Brussels: AAM, 1982), 67. Author's translation. © AAM, Brussels

may run counter to it."[21] Strauven's argument – Braem's cult of the new being unthinkable outside a capitalist framework – points to a political complicity that Culot and Krier are trying to avoid when they call for the reappropriation of the bourgeois legacy. The irony nowadays is that Braem is lauded as a great architect, and one that stayed true to his socialist ideals, while the AAM plea for pastiche is rather associated with the neoliberalization of historicist architecture.[22]

The more substantial architectural argument in Strauven's critique of Braem entailed the latter's unhistorical approach to the city.[23] Originally writing his monograph on Braem contemporaneous with the *Rational Architecture* publication, Strauven stresses the richness of the city, rather than nature or the machine, as the referent for architecture, an argument going back to Anthony Vidler's "The Third Typology," included in the book.[24] Thus Strauven's critique aptly outlines the fundamental difference between these two Belgian socialist architectures.

The search by Culot and Krier for a socialist architecture was kept almost entirely within the West, which contained important strategic consequences with regard to how to match architecture with political ideas. This is evident, for instance, when Culot directs himself towards the international scene and frames the context of their actions as taking place in "a country in which the communists are not candidates for power."[25] Yet they include the East in their rhetoric at one point, and it's interesting to see how.

The Soviet 1920s Avant-Garde and the ~~Socialist~~ Realist Debate

As explained above, the quote at the beginning of this paper is part of an editorial on the USSR's 1920s avant-garde. The corresponding issue of *AAM* contains the transcription of a lecture by Anatole Kopp (1915–1990) held at La Cambre in March 1977, based on his lecture held in Berlin a month earlier (figs. 5, 6).[26] Kopp's visit marked a brief period of fascination with the Soviet avant-garde of the 1920s, not entirely out of tune with the international climate; but whereas their contemporaries were generally positive about the constructivists, the take at La Cambre is more ambivalent, which is perhaps already announced in their placement of the Palace of the Soviets on the title page of Kopp's lecture. This brief period was perhaps the most explicit interpretation of the architecture of socialist countries that the La Cambre group had shown during their own search. The way in which Culot integrates this fascination with the La Cambre narrative of 1970s Brussels is especially revealing of what it meant to advocate a socialist architecture in that setting.

In the midst of the *AAM* editorial debate on the socialist form of the city, Culot reformulated their own position as a continuation of the debate launched by Russian revolutionaries of the 1920s, thus conveniently skipping the Stalinist era.[27] Culot made use of the republications of Russian texts of the era by Éditions l'Âge d'Homme, the Lausanne-based publisher that disseminated Slavic and dissident Soviet writers. Through a 1975 republication of a 1924 issue of the Russian journal *Press and Revolution* [Печать и революция], annotated by Gérard Conio, Culot and others had access to a debate five decades old, which essentially centered on relations between social revolution

U.R.S.S.

1929 - 1931

PROBLEMES URBAINS
ET PROBLEMES DU
MODE DE VIE

par Anatole KOPP

notes et illustrations :
M.Culot et M.Louis

"On ne pourra construire la culture prolétarienne qu'en connaissant exactement la culture qui résulte du développement de l'humanité, qu'en la remaniant."

LENINE

fig. 5 Title page of Anatole Kopp's lecture. Source: *AAM*, no. 11 (July 1977): 5. © AAM, Brussels

and aesthetics – ultimately the same problem they were posing in Brussels.[28] It is most likely in this same book that Culot learned about the quote which he would use as the title of his editorial: "She is good, she is very good, your youth, but what do you teach them!" Again showing their ambivalence, the quote is a remark by Lenin during his 1921 visit to the VKhUTEMAS School in Moscow after he learned that students in their search for new forms put aside the established history of Russian architecture.[29]

Culot explicitly confided to his readers that for them, in European capitalist countries, the thing to do is to continue that debate and bring it to an end in order to start what he and Krier term "the reconstruction of the European city."[30] The way forward would be to recuperate all traditional architectural and urban models, regardless of whether they are of bourgeois descent or not, since – so Culot argues – there is no proletarian culture without tradition. Thus, Culot explicitly parallels his argument to that of Lazar Kaganovich, the Stalinist administrator who had voiced the USSR's departure from constructivism by declaring that "our cities have become socialist at the moment of the October revolution."[31] In other words: no new form is desired. In the same stroke, Culot denounced the socialist merit in architecture not

fig. 6 Anatole Kopp during his conference at La Cambre in March 1977. Photographer: Jean Boucher. Source: ENSAV-La Cambre archives, folder 31.

based on tradition: modernist, or for the same matter, neo-rationalist. For him, the political is something that should be actively seized: the bourgeois *passéisme* should be appropriated for our aims, or so he claimed. Hence the starting quote of this paper.

But what did Culot mean when he urged readers to "continue the debate and bring it to an end"? Two months after Kopp's visit to La Cambre, Culot was more explicit in a discussion with Krier and Bernard Tschumi at Peter Cook's Art Net.[32] There, he confided that he preferred the chaos of Brussels to a definitive image of the socialist city, which was the mistake Russian architects had made in the 1920s. So, Culot preferred chaos, but only as long as it was the result of democratic processes.[33]

Kopp, on the other hand, was a fierce defendant of the modern project and did believe in the power of new architectural forms. He would regularly criticize the stance of AAM, mainly on the crucial point of the intertwinement of form and historical change: if one can only copy from the past, how can one be directed toward a different society?[34]

Kopp would intervene similarly in a contemporaneous debate touching on the same issue of architecture's relationship to society: the realism debate. Kopp's critique targeted Bernard Huet's overt acknowledgement of socialist realism's merits in *L'Architecture d'Aujourd'hui* in April 1977, picking up on two theme issues on realism published by *Archithese* over the two preceding years.[35] Huet argued against an all-too easy alignment of architecture and political merit based on the local regime. As such, some products of socialist realism were placed together with *Tendenza* in Italy in the realist camp, praised for their easily understandable language and their inclination towards typicality. Huet's praise was of course controversial, but also insufficiently understood, since his condensed arguments on realism built on an extensive

fig. 7 Jean Dethier and Bernard Huet at a jury in La Cambre, 1977. Photographer: Hugues Boucher. Source: *La Cambre: 1928–1978* (see fig. 2), 393. © Éditions Trois Arches

debate foreign to France.[36] The realism that Huet was advocating, was set against a formalism that he described as a dogmatic clinging to either side of the form/content divide. The realist position, on the other hand, was not to accept reality as it is, but "to take hold of it, in order to transform it 'politically.'" Huet saw the basis of such a political agency of architecture in common sense or collective meanings, and thus in the use of expected typologies and in the reappropriation of heritage. One such realist approach was recognized by Huet – the intellectual comrade of Culot and an oft-invited speaker at La Cambre (fig. 7) – in Culot's actions in Brussels. The group in Brussels didn't miss the article, as it would serve as the reference point of a set of four texts in *AAM* one year later, by students at La Cambre, in which they would reformulate their personal architectural stances.[37]

The realism debate crossed AAM's path in another way during these years, as it would surface at the margins of Krier's theoretical work of the time. Krier, in a text republished in various forms including in the *Rational Architecture* catalogue and in some of his presentation texts for the 1976 La Villette project in Paris, would point to the political dimension of architecture by briefly evoking the realism debate followed by a denunciation of socialist realism as being focused merely on style.[38] Sometimes Krier would extend the argument and advocate a discussion about realism, which should be centered on "the question of how a socialist mode of production will affect the form of the architectural object."[39] Krier's main preoccupation was of course to critique the alienating aspects of industrialization, but his contribution to the realism debate, which was a rephrasing of the argument presented in the open letter to Culot, nevertheless shows how much the debate in *AAM*'s pages had been informed in dialogue with socialist realism.

Conclusion

As a concluding complication, we can see how much this search for realism and socialism in a Western European society is bound up with postmodernity. In the same context as Krier's evocation of the realism debate, we encounter once more the Centre Pompidou, on the construction site of which the graffiti "The New Is New No More" was apparently painted. For Krier, it attested to the end of an era, a depiction we could interpret as a postmodern weariness with the cult of the new.[40] He would go on to characterize the Centre as "a cultural machine which tries to hide its social emptiness by an ephemeral and prestigious formalism." It's this wish to fill this "social emptiness" that draws us back to the front cover of the eleventh issue of *AAM*, depicting an alternative rear facade to embellish the Centre, designed by Culot and a group of La Cambre associates. This design was published simultaneously in *L'Architecture d'Aujourd'hui*, not coincidentally that journal's "Formalism/Realism" issue.

Thus we find how this chapter's starting quote drags along an intriguing vortex combining elements of a postmodern critique of innovation, an opposition toward capitalism with history as arms, and an embedded nature in international discourse. The La Cambre group's architectural approach was marked by the vivid awareness of articulating it in the political context of Belgium, and shows how the all too rigid East-West divide is refracted by Belgium's pluralist political landscape.

Endnotes

I'm indebted to the various suggestions of Elke Couchez, Rajesh Heynickx, Yves Schoonjans and in particular Hilde Heynen. Discussions at ETH Zurich and at the KU Leuven architectural-theory PhD exchange platform improved the argument. Correspondence with Maurice Culot and with Francis Strauven provided me with much valuable information, though any misinterpretations are the author's. This chapter is the result of research supported by a project grant from the FWO.

1 Maurice Culot, "Elle est bonne, elle est très bonne, votre jeunesse, mais qu'est-ce que vous lui apprenez!", *AAM*, 11 (July 1977), 3–4. In the remainder of this chapter, the acronym AAM stands for the organization Archives d'Architecture Moderne, and when italicized, for the organization's journal.

2 During the 1970s, La Cambre, then a state institution, was divided into a new generation centered around Culot and Delevoy, and an older generation of modernists such as Jacques Wybauw (1925–2005) and Paul-Emile Vincent (1924–2007). Changes in legislation concerning architectural education initiated in 1977 tipped the balance at La Cambre in favor of the latter camp by prioritizing professors appointed before 1976. This eventually led to twenty-four teachers being forced to leave the institute in 1979

and Culot's official dismissal in November 1979. Jacques Aron, *La Cambre et l'architecture: Un regard sur le Bauhaus belge* (Pierre Mardaga: Liège, 1982), 179–188; Geert Bekaert, "Wie over architectuur wil spreken, sta op, en zwijge: Bedenkingen van een buitenstaander, buitenstaanders hebben gemakkelijk spreken," *Wonen-TABK*, 11 (June 1983), 10–27 (p. 15); "L'Invité Maurice Culot," interview by Thierry Paquot, *Urbanisme*, 361 (July–August 2008), 77–86 (p. 81).

3 Isabelle Doucet, "Counter-Projects and the Postmodern User," in *Use Matters: An Alternative History of Architecture*, ed. Kenny Cupers (London: Routledge, 2013), 233–247 (p. 240); Doucet, "Counter-Projects," in *The Practice Turn in Architecture: Brussels after 1968* (Farnham: Ashgate, 2015).

4 Jo Braeken, "Renaat Braem 1910 2001, leven en werk," in *Renaat Braem 1910–2001 architect*, 1, ed. Braeken (Brussels: ASA Publishers, 2010), 14–109 (p. 57).

5 Hilde Heynen, "The Jargon of Authenticity: Modernism and Its (Non) Political Position," in *Constructed Happiness: Domestic Environment in the Cold War Era*, ed. Mart Kalm and Ingrid Ruudi (Tallinn: Estonian Academy of Arts, 2005), 10–27 (p. 22). Pillarization is the far-reaching division of societal organizations (such as trade unions, health services, education) according to political ideology.

6 Renaat Braem, *Het schoonste land ter wereld* (Leuven: Kritak, 1987), 112.

7 Roland Matthu, "Neo-klassieke inspanningen," *A+*, 109 (1990), 28–39 (p. 35).

8 Robert Delevoy, "Diagonal: Towards an Architecture," in *Rational Architecture: The Reconstruction of the European City*, ed. Léon Krier (Brussels: AAM, 1978), 4–22 (p. 15).

9 Robert Maxwell, "Tafuri/Culot/Krier: The Role of Ideology," *Architectural Design*, 47:3 (1977), 186–8. Looking back on this period, Krier describes himself and his contemporaries as "fashionable Marxists" and his own views as an "infantile political outlook" that had yet to mature. Léon Krier, "Looking Back without Anger," in *Exit Utopia: Architectural Provocations 1956–76*, ed. Martin Van Schaik and Otakar Máčel (Munich: Prestel, 2005), 309–314 (pp. 311–313).

10 Geert Bekaert, "'Une mise à nu de l'architecture par ses adorateurs mêmes.' Maurice Culot and Léon Krier: A Forgotten Episode," in *Exit Utopia*, 299–308 (p. 299).

11 Angelika Schnell, "The Socialist Perspective of the XV Triennale di Milano: Hans Schmidt's Influence on Aldo Rossi," *Candide*, 2 (July 2010), 33–72.

12 Maurice Culot, "Portrait de François Spoerry," *AAM*, 12 (November 1977), 4–22. This earned him some mockery from Charles Jencks: "Maurice Culot, a soi-disant Stalinist, even sees [Port Grimaud] as the answer for the communist future, a nice irony of hypertensive capitalism being the midwife of history." *The Language of Post-Modern Architecture*, rev. ed. (London: Academy Editions, 1978), 94.

13 Maurice Culot, "Tout est luxe, calme et beauté," *AAM*, 8 (May 1976), 1–2.

14 Léon Krier, "Lettre ouverte à Culot," *AAM*, 9 (December 1976), 3. Author's translation.

15 Ibid.

16 Maurice Culot, "Le Monoplan de papier," *AAM*, 13 (first trimester 1978), 1–3.

17 "Leon Krier Talks to Colin Davies," in *Drawings 1967 – 1980* (Brussels: AAM, 1980), xvii–xxiv (p. xx).

18 Maurice Culot and Léon Krier, "L'Unique Chemin de l'architecture," *AAM*, 14 (second trimester 1978), 1–5 (p. 3). Trans. Christian Hubert, "The Only Path for Architecture," *Oppositions*, 14 (Fall 1978), 38–53; and in *Architecture Theory since 1968*, ed. K. Michael Hays (Cambridge, Mass.: MIT Press, 1998), 348–355.
19 Braem, *Schoonste land ter wereld*, 178.
20 Tokens of their mutual respect might be seen in La Cambre's recurrent invitations to Braem to take part in the juries, and in Braem's decision to donate part of his archives to AAM, starting from 1974. Culot and Anne Van Loo, eds., *Musée des Archives d'Architecture Moderne: Collections* (Brussels: AAM, 1986), 110–121.
21 Francis Strauven, *Renaat Braem: De dialectische avonturen van een Vlaams functionalist* (Brussels: AAM, 1983), 96. Author's translation.
22 Matthu, "Neo-klassieke inspanningen."
23 Strauven, *Renaat Braem*, 96–97.
24 Anthony Vidler, "The Third Typology," in *Rational Architecture*, ed. Krier, 23–32.
25 Maurice Culot, "The Cambre School of Architecture and Anti-Industrial Resistance," *Lotus International*, 21 (December 1978), 46–71 (p. 49).
26 Anatole Kopp, "U.R.S.S. 1929–1931: Problèmes urbains et problèmes du mode de vie," *AAM*, 11 (July 1977), 5–19.
27 Culot, "Elle est bonne."
28 Gérard Conio, ed., *Le Formalisme et le futurisme russes devant le marxisme: Problèmes de la révolution culturelle*, (Lausanne: Éditions l'Âge d'Homme, 1975).
29 Ibid., 223.
30 Culot, "Elle est bonne," 4.
31 Strauven, *Renaat Braem*, 33.
32 "Postmodernism: Uses of Language in Architecture," Architectural Association video from a discussion between Maxwell, Krier, Culot and Tschumi on May 25, 1977 at Art Net, accessed August 25, 2015, http://www.aaschool.ac.uk/VIDEO/lecture.php?ID=2835.
33 Maxwell, "Tafuri/Culot/Krier," 191.
34 Remnants of earlier, more extensive critiques formulated during lectures in Marseille (March 1979) and Liège (1981) constitute the final paragraphs of Kopp, *Quand le moderne n'était pas un style mais une cause* (Paris: École Nationale Supérieure des Beaux-Arts, 1988). Typescripts of the lectures are kept at the Centre d'Archives de l'IFA.
35 Bernard Huet, "Formalisme – réalisme," *L'Architecture d'Aujourd'hui*, 190 (April 1977), 35–36.
36 Jean-Louis Cohen, "The Italophiles at Work (1984)," in *Architecture Theory since 1968*, ed. Hays, 506–520 (p. 513).
37 Gilbert Busieau, et al., "À propos de 'Formalisme – réalisme' par Bernard Huet, et 'Traditions et luttes urbaines' par René Schoonbrodt," *AAM*, 15 (third and fourth trimester 1978), 95–106.
38 Léon Krier, "Some Ideas on Realism," *Casabella*, 420 (December 1976), 20–27 (pp. 20–21).
39 Ibid.
40 Léon Krier, "The Reconstruction of the City," in *Rational Architecture*, 33–42 (p. 38).

Johannes Warda

Keeping West Berlin "As Found": Alison Smithson, Hardt-Waltherr Hämer and 1970s Proto-Preservation Urban Renewal

On March 18, 1963, Willy Brandt, Governing Mayor of West Berlin, launched one of Germany's first and largest urban renewal[1] projects in Berlin's Wedding working class district, which would entail the demolition of 56,000 apartments in the Berliner *Mietskasernen* (tenement blocks). Brandt, who later became West Germany's first Social Democratic chancellor, sought to accomplish the solution to the "social question". The renewal policy epitomized the Social Democrats' aversion to nineteenth-century housing conditions. This event in March 1963 marked the beginning of a series of similar renewal projects in other parts of Berlin and all over Europe – almost all of which were never executed in their uncompromising final totality. While, from today's perspective, one would credit the preservationist protests at the time for retaining the old city, a closer look at urban renewal practices and the role historic preservation ideas played in them reveals, if not a different, at least a more complex story.

Despite the obvious phenomenological presence of history in European cities today, this essay questions the reading of a turn to history as a formal and ideological tendency in the first place. The citing of history at a particular point in time, I argue, does not necessarily involve history as such. Looking at the agents and undercurrents of this turn, I unravel the multifaceted story of the transformation of the historical monument into a utilitarian materialism, which went beyond the nineteenth-century concept of the monument as a constituent of national identity, or as a matter of arts and aesthetics, towards a broader notion of the building stock as a social and material resource in times of environmental crisis.

To support this reading, I analyze the re-evaluation of historic structures in the city of West Berlin during the 1960s and 70s, drawing on three case studies. Two of them are examples of publicly commissioned research on the building stock in the early years of urban renewal: Hardt-Waltherr Hämer's renewal research projects in the Wedding district, which reveal the mechanisms and effects of what I call "proto-preservation" renewal, and Josef Paul Kleihues's *Berlin-Atlas*, which recorded the image of the renewal areas on the basis of urban history, typology and ornament. The third case concerns design interventions in the existing city proposed by leading architects and theoreticians during a symposium at the *Internationales Design Zentrum Berlin* (IDZ), which took place at the height of heritage awareness during the European Heritage Year of 1975.

Inside the Urban Renewal Laboratory: Berlin, 1963–1987

Right from the beginning, urban renewal in Germany had its "Jane Jacobs moments". The new building complexes in the *Gründerzeit* districts and social housing estates in the urban periphery were met with a wave of criticism from architects, scholars and intellectuals as soon as ground was broken.[2] However, before the idea of keeping the existing city even drew the attention of official preservation institutions, architects and planners were already experimenting with careful renewal alternatives. Paradoxically, the Senate of West Berlin as the organ responsible for initiating the comprehensive urban renewal projects also funded research on the existing building stock, fostering the quest for alternatives to demolition. As part of the Wedding district renewal, the Senate commissioned several reports and planning proposals by architectural schools in West Berlin and West Germany.[3] In 1968, while construction work was already underway on some plots in the renewal area, the Senate commissioned three working groups to redesign the Brunnenstraße/Swinemünder Straße neighborhood, which had originally been slated for demolition. The architect Hardt-Waltherr Hämer headed one of these working groups. Appointed professor of architecture at the *Hochschule für Bildende Künste* Berlin just one year earlier, Hämer set out to shift the focus of urban renewal from demolition to repair and reuse. More than a decade later, his efforts resulted in the so-called *Altbau* (historic buildings) branch of the International Building Exhibition Berlin 1987 (IBA).[4]

Hämer's design proposal, which called for the rehabilitation of the existing apartments, caused the Senate to initiate further research into alternative renewal strategies. By December 1970, Hämer's group presented plans to refurbish three tenement buildings on block 235, Putbusser Straße where it meets Ramler Straße. Keeping the buildings, the group argued, would be more sensitive to the needs of the tenants, especially the many elderly residents, and would comply with the city's beautification and other building codes.[5] The section of Berlin's building code in question here states that the building stock is to be maintained and slightly improved in order to meet changing sanitary and living standards. The reality at the peak of demolition renewal was, however, altogether different. Although Hämer's findings and some of the existing building legislation favored rehabilitation over new buildings, it had little effect on the practice of renewal at that time. Planning procedures and financial tools remained tailored to constructing new buildings until well into the 1970s. As a consequence, Hämer changed the focus of his pre-planning research from spatial analysis of the urban context to the architectural structure itself. The material value, he believed, would be an important factor in bypassing the mechanisms of conventional urban renewal.[6]

Meanwhile, Hämer made the building costs research in the Wedding case one of the first projects at the *Institut Wohnen und Umwelt* (Institute for Housing and Environment) in Darmstadt, of which he was one of the founding directors, together with Egon Eiermann and Alexander Mitscherlich.[7] Hämer's group developed a prognostic tool, which enabled private investors and the public building administration to estimate the rehabilitation costs of the typical Berlin *Gründerzeit* tenements. Based on a thorough building survey, which took into account literally every material component down to the nails, the tool aimed to refute the prevailing general assumption that there was no remaining value in the *Gründerzeit* structures at all. In Hämer's projects, rehabilitation costs ranged between 38 and 112 per cent of the costs of a substitute building (fig. 1). The survey tool eventually became part of the statutory urban renewal regulations of the State of Berlin, providing an early quantitative basis for repair-oriented approaches to urban renewal.[8]

A similar approach to *Gründerzeit* housing was developed in East Berlin only little later, with the well-known Arkonaplatz reconstruction. In the early 1980s, the *Bauakademie* of the GDR established a research center for preservation and rehabilitation. To accomplish the 1973 housing plan promise of 3 million more habitable flats by 1990, rehabilitation was a badly needed option. In 1987, a study introduced a housing management and mainte-

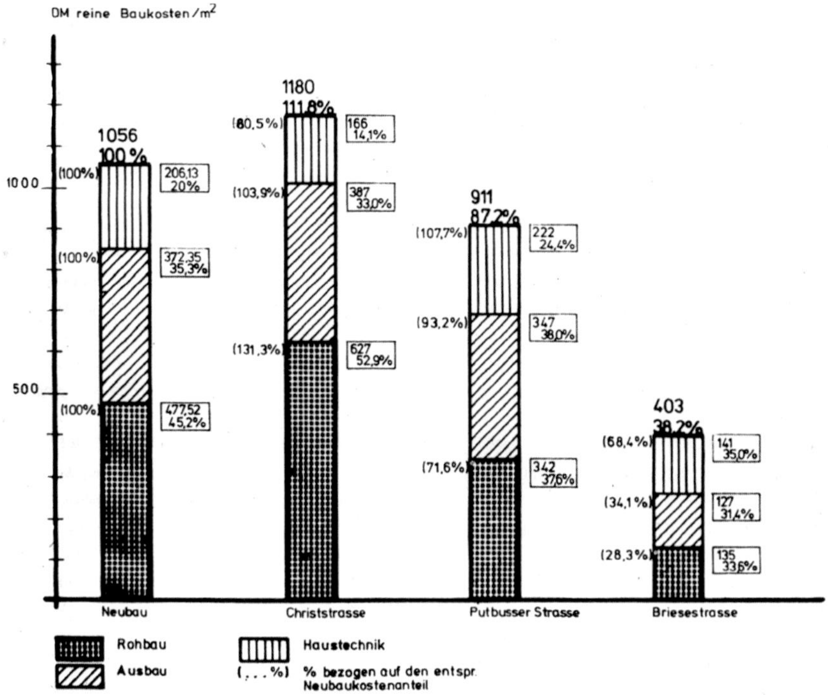

fig. 1 Berlin Wedding urban renewal, comparison of building costs, ca. 1975. Source: Hardt-Waltherr Hämer and Marie-Brigitte Hämer-Buro, *Altbauerneuerung in Sanierungsgebieten. Untersuchung von Modellvorhaben in West-Berlin: Ergebnisbericht zum Forschungsauftrag "Kostenanalyse der Modell-modernisierung von Altbauten"* (Berlin: Arbeitsgruppe Stadterneuereung, 1975), 101.

nance concept under the telling title of planned pre-emptive maintenance, or "Planmäßig vorbeugende Instandhaltung (PVI)."[9]

Another research project that paved the way to careful renewal and keeping the old city in West Berlin was the *Berlin-Atlas zu Stadtbild und Stadtraum.*[10] Commissioned by the Senate of Berlin and published by Josef Paul Kleihues in 1973, the *Berlin-Atlas* contains a thorough evaluation of the facades and streetscapes in the Charlottenburg and Kreuzberg renewal areas. It was intended as a practical tool to complement the existing preservation legislation that, according to Kleihues and the Senate, was unable to meet the challenges posed by the vast number of renewal projects. The *Berlin-Atlas* aimed to record both architectural and socio-spatial qualities.

Framing them historically, the authors compiled one of the few thorough accounts of Berlin's urban history at that time. Most importantly, it presented a set of maps, which provide an evaluation of the morphological and visual qualities of every building and its street facades, recommending either preservation or demolition (fig. 2). Despite the depth of the contextual analysis, the

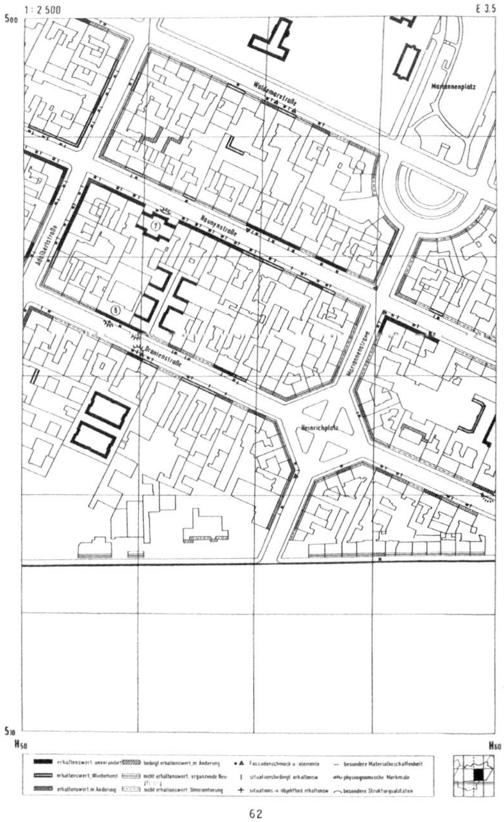

fig. 2 Berlin-Kreuzberg, Luisenstadt, mapping of facade evaluations for Block 77 in Josef Paul Kleihues's *Berlin-Atlas*, 1973. Source: Josef Paul Kleihues, *Berlin-Atlas zu Stadtbild und Stadtraum. Bd. 2: Versuchsgebiet Kreuzberg* (Berlin: Senator für Bau- und Wohnungswesen des Landes Berlin, 1973), 62.

Berlin-Atlas only deemed an average of 30 per cent of the existing buildings worth keeping. It wasn't until the late 1970s that anti-demolition protests and house squatting added a new twist to the discourse on urban renewal, causing the Senate of Berlin to gradually abandon the demolition dogma. Yet how "careful" urban renewal should be was still left to be explored by the IBA. The focus of the initial debates on initiating an IBA was on filling the city's many vacant lots and brownfield sites. By the time the IBA was finally ratified by the parliament of Berlin, more emphasis was put on the existing city – with the twofold approach of new building and urban repair which the IBA became famous for. Kleihues and Hämer as the two IBA directors embodied the dual nature of this enterprise. "Repairing the city," Julius Posener wrote about the IBA, "teaches us how to habituate ourselves to the existing environment and helps to bring about new forms of community life."[11]

Architects in Context: The "Berlin Alt und Neu" Symposium, 1975

Several years before the IBA, and a couple of years after Hämer's Wedding case study, another architectural event marked West Berlin's status as a laboratory for alternative renewal strategies. At that time, in the mid-1970s, the renewal discourse had begun to shift in favor of preservation. Now that the existence of the historic city was no longer threatened *per se*, architects faced the task of designing its revival. This was the overall context in which Heinrich Klotz, then professor of Art History at Marburg University and soon-to-be founding director of the *Deutsches Architekturmuseum* (DAM) in Frankfurt, invited a group of international architects to sketch out their ideas for Block 77 in the Kreuzberg renewal area. The symposium, again, was a publicly commissioned event – by the *Senator für Bau und Wohnungswesen* – with explicit reference to the European Heritage Year and it took place under the label of the *Berliner Festspiele*.

In his opening remarks, Klotz discussed the concept of historicity in architecture as a matter of perception, rejecting the notion of "old" and "historic" as referring to material decay only. The criterion for a building's historicity, Klotz argued, "is its reception by the inhabitants and their ability to recognize it through the times – and evaluate it aesthetically."[12] Another criterion, according to Klotz, was what he called the "visual durability" of the built environment which creates emotional bonds with the city: "even the ugliest building can be more than welcome in a neutral and monotonous environment." Nevertheless, it is clear that a re-appraisal of the historic city had taken place since the mid-60s. As Klotz argued, "architecture today must take into account the meaning of the historic city. [...] The ways in which modern architecture interacts with the old city [...] must be the focus of the *Zweite Moderne* [sic], as a counterpart to the functionalism of the building economy." With this, Klotz set the agenda for the symposium. The schedule of the five-day event reflected his own presuppositions about designing in the old city:[13]

Following excursions to the site of Block 77, there were two days of expert input and three days of designing and discussing the results. André Corboz[14], Christian Norberg-Schulz[15] and the Berlin State Conservator, Hartmut Engel[16], gave theory lectures prior to a design studio phase. Corboz presented a typology of architectural interventions in the existing city focusing on the terms "recycling" and "reanimation," while Norberg-Schulz presented his concept of "genius loci" – that is, that every place has its own innate specific character. Architecture, he argued, is the manifestation of the genius loci and therefore has to be intrinsically "adaptive."[17] Hartmut Engel's input resonated with Klotz's initial remarks and his own understanding of preservation. After

fig. 3 Berlin-Kreuzberg, Luisenstadt, location of Block 77, 2015. Source: mapping by author, not to scale.

fig. 4 O. M. Ungers, facade abstractions. Source: *Lotus International* 13 (1976), 50f.

offering a brief history of the Luisenstadt district and its tenement housing, Engel called for a broadening of the focus of historic preservation from the single object to the "Quartier" in which the life of the community takes place.[18] In short, the symposium took the time to undertake a close analysis of the urban issues in question.

The site of the proposed interventions, Block 77, is a typical situation within the fabric of Berlin's *Gründerzeit* tenement housing (fig. 3). Located in north-east Kreuzberg, in the so-called Luisenstadt neighborhood, it extends to the south into the regular grid of this area. The block's north side borders the Bethanien hospital grounds, and its concave north-east corner shapes part of the Mariannenplatz. The perimeter of the block (in 1975) was formed by tenement buildings, some extending back into courtyards in the block interior, with apartments and workshops, and a dance hall (accessible from Naunynstraße 27) – a perfect example of the so-called *Kreuzberger Mischung*.[19]

At the time of the symposium, 1454 people lived in apartments in the block, and a then state-of-the-art renewal proposal suggested a strategy of *Blockentkernung* – of clearing the interior of the block – which would have slated seventy per cent of the apartments for demolition.[20] The assignment of the symposium was to deal with the buildings on Adalbertstraße 21–23, on the north-west corner of the block.

Despite the preservationist undertone of the symposium, the design assignment produced a variety of approaches which can be roughly clustered into two groups.[21] First, an inductive approach, inferring general design rules

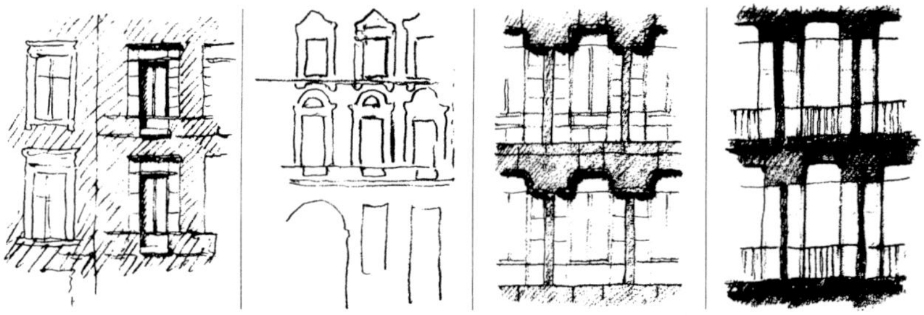

fig. 5 Gottfried Böhm, deduction and interpretations of facade designs for Block 77. Source: *Lotus International* 13 (1976), 34.

fig. 6 Charles Moore, facade designs for Block 77. Source: *Lotus International 13* (1976), 37.

fig. 7 Alison Smithson, north elevation of Block 77. Source: *Lotus International* 13 (1976), 47.

from a close analysis of the site and its characteristics, as applied by O.M. Ungers (fig. 4) and Vittorio Gregotti. Second, a more deductive approach, departing from general assumptions about the found architecture and how to approach it, as applied by Gottfried Böhm, Charles Moore and Alison Smithson (figs. 5–7). Gregotti's and Smithson's design proposals serve as examples of the two approaches:

Gregotti started off with a thorough analysis of the urban context to identify the challenges it poses (fig. 8). He emphasized the importance of the exist-

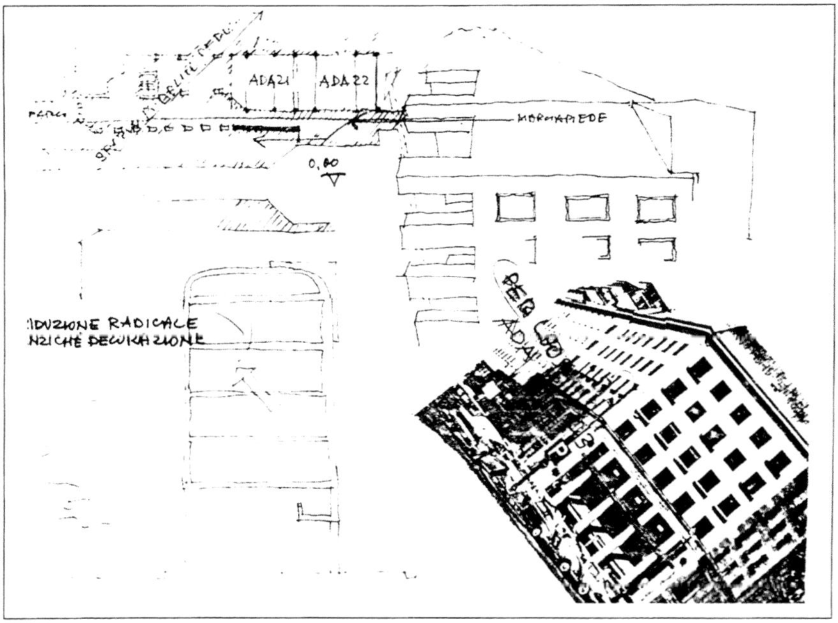

fig. 8 Vittorio Gregotti, concept sketch. Source: *Lotus International* 13 (1976), 43.

ing morphology of the block in terms of its social functions, fostering class diversity and serving as social memory. His intervention was partly guided by a preservationist attitude: keeping the existing structure, but reorganizing the interior of the block and redefining the relationship between inside and outside. In Gregotti's sketch, the buildings on the perimeter of the block become an architecture of facades, which serve only the passing pedestrian, while residential life takes place on the inside. The language of Gregotti's design reflects its social concept: new gateway structures inserted into the perimeter connect the interior with the streetscape. Tube-like skywalks reach out to the adjacent blocks so that Block 77 becomes an urban organism turned inside out, a spatial shell within the fabric of the city (fig. 9). To strengthen the impression of the architectural cohesion of the block, Gregotti removed the Gründerzeit ornamentation from the facades of the preserved buildings.[22]

Alison Smithson's approach is more associative and poetic. Working with the city "as found," as Smithson calls her intervention, she contemplated a historic section of one of the tenement buildings in which she found the secret language of the German Renaissance, its paintings, religious imagery, and the presence of planks and timber.[23] To carry the "as found" forward, she proposed closing the perimeter of the block with a wooden structure reminiscent of Roman viaducts (fig. 7). The viaduct bridges two deteriorated buildings on the block, as if the wooden supporting structure of the block had been stripped of the facades.[24] In her design, the material integrity of the existing architecture does not seem to be important for capturing the spirit and language of the place. Instead, it serves as the point of departure for a new idea – and thus, as a material and cultural resource to work with.

The symposium was widely reported in the media. Most notably, the news magazine *Der Spiegel* published a review speaking of the disillusionment with contemporary architecture and its inability to adapt to the historic city, arguing that even Potemkin would have done a better job. The proposed designs, according to the critic, were far too "sophisticated" for Kreuzberg.[25] And yet the symposium is an important testimony to a tipping point in architecture. It represents a change in attitude towards the old city in which new architecture does not necessarily need the city's physical remains to engage with history, and which employs adaptation rather than contrast. In that sense, the design proposals contrasted with the then prevailing paradigm of so-called *Neues Bauen in alter Umgebung*, which was in line with the general design guidelines of the Venice Charter of 1964.[26] Instead, the architectural dispositions of the symposium presented a picture-book illustration of the discourse on place in architecture, offering insight into the toolbox of *genius loci* design: the architects and theorists that Klotz had invited to consider a *Gründerzeit* block in Berlin defined, through site analysis, history and its abstraction, context as a parameter of new architecture.

Conclusion

Today, the rise in awareness for the historic city in the 1970s is often seen as a victory of historic preservation over urban renewal. But traditional preservation values were not sufficient to defend historic environments against demolition renewal and developers. In 1970s Germany, monuments still referred primarily to churches, castles and town halls. Accordingly, the main concern of the European Heritage Year was to present the old and picturesque city.[27] It was left to emerging grassroots initiatives to eventually expand the heritage concept to architectural typologies and styles of the everyday (one of which was, well into the 1990s, *Gründerzeit* architecture) by pointing out that heritage also referred to a place of residence.[28] In other words, it was the sociopolitical dimension of urban renewal that made people take to the streets. This raises a couple of questions. Firstly, there is the issue of agency: Who turns to history, and why? And secondly, there are formal and topological questions: Which history, and where? What does it look like?

To conclude, I would like to return to my question at the outset concerning the paradigm of reference to history. On the one hand, we can observe

fig. 9 Vittorio Gregotti, view of Block 77 and skywalk. Source: *Lotus International* 13 (1976), 42.

a turn to the physical remains of history and the reappraisal of characteristic architectural features at all scales. With regard to the legacy of the European Heritage Year, one might also think of the re-discovery of the old city (*Altstadt*), the invention of the heritage district (Ensemble), and the victory of careful urban renewal (*Behutsame Stadterneuerung*) over the dogma of demolition. In that sense, the turn to history was a success story. And yet one that turned all too quickly from a preservationist approach into a nostalgic preoccupation with the old city and the urban design practice of "vintage" (as with blue jeans: not old, but aged).

On the other hand, it seems that preservation politics and planning programs such as the IBA 1987 were credited for their careful approach to renewal and site-inspired architectural designs, in which architects and local communities did not necessarily seek to restore the historical, but turned to the (still) existing city for pragmatic reasons, valuing it both as a social and material resource.[29] Finally, alternative renewal concepts, which emphasized building cost savings and material values over historical values, appealed to public and private decision-makers in the capitalist-driven renewal sector – just, as Hämer had shown slightly before the turn to history.

Endnotes

1 The term "urban renewal" refers to the official policy of the Senate and the practice of demolition and reconstruction which is commonly attributed to it at that time. To better distinguish it from alternative forms of careful renewal, the term "demolition renewal" will be used synonymously for the remainder of the chapter.

2 The negative discourse concerning modern mass housing in Germany was fueled by the fact that the main building projects at the periphery of West Berlin in the 1960s and 70s were indeed challenged by technological problems during construction. "Crumbling even before the paint was fully dry," as was reported widely in the rainbow press to *Der Spiegel* magazine. See Florian Urban, *Tower and Slab: Histories of Global Mass Housing* (Abingdon: Routledge, 2012), 59–65.

3 *Anlage I zum Projektvorschlag Stadterneuerung*, UdK-Archiv, Berlin, 115/I/605.

4 *IBA Altbau* brought careful urban renewal strategies to the Kreuzberg district, cooperating with the squatters' movement and grass roots organizations. Alongside Josef Paul Kleihues, who was responsible for the new IBA architecture projects, Hämer as the director of IBA Alt soon went by the name of "saviour of Kreuzberg." Cited in Rudolf Schilling, "Behutsame Stadterneuerung," in *Stadt im Kopf: Hardt-Waltherr Hämer*, ed. Manfred Sack (Berlin: Jovis, 2002), 179. On Hämer see also Helga Fassbinder, "Einleitung," in *Hardt-Waltherr Hämer: Architekt HBK. Behutsame Stadterneuerung*, eds. Michael Bollé and Karl-Robert Schütze (Berlin: Universität der Künste, 2007). For an account of the IBA history see Harald Bodenschatz, Vittorio Magnago Lampugnani and Wolfgang Sonne, eds., *25 Jahre Internationale Bauausstellung Berlin 1987: Ein Wendepunkt des europäischen Städtebaus* (Sulgen: Niggli, 2012).

5 *Modelluntersuchung Rehabilitation Berlin-Wedding, Putbusser Straße/ Ramler Straße*, UdK-Archiv, Berlin, 115/I/610.

6 Hardt-Waltherr Hämer and Marie-Brigitte Hämer-Buro, *Altbauerneuerung in Sanierungsgebieten: Untersuchung von Modellvorhaben in West-Berlin: Ergebnisbericht zum Forschungsauftrag "Kostenanalyse der Modellmodernisierung von Altbauten"* (Berlin: Arbeitsgruppe Stadterneuerung, 1975), 8.

7 *Protokoll der Arbeitssitzung vom 29. Juni 1972. Fallstudie Wedding*, UdK-Archiv, Berlin, 115/I/605.

8 *Modernisierung oder Abriß? Entwurf einer Methode zur Ermittlung der Modernisierungs- und Instandsetzungskosten*, UdK-Archiv, Berlin, 115/I/60.

9 See *Wohnung, Gebäude, Wohnumwelt: Modernisierung von Altwohnbauten der Baujahre 1870–1918, Teil 1* (Berlin [DDR]: Bauakademie der Deutschen Demokratischen Republik, Institut für Wohnungs- und Gesellschaftsbau, 1982), 117.

10 Josef Paul Kleihues, *Berlin-Atlas zu Stadtbild und Stadtraum. Bd. 2: Versuchsgebiet Kreuzberg* (Berlin: Senator für Bau- und Wohnungswesen des Landes Berlin, 1973), 7; 9. The authors' reluctance to apply historic preservation instruments already in place in the 1970s sheds light on the weak position of preservation institutions in the process of urban renewal. Yet why there is no reference to the so-called protected areas (*geschützter Baubereich*), a measure within the *Berliner Bauordnung*, remains unclear.

11 Julius Posener, "Der Schauplatz Berlin – 750 Jahre Städtebau im Zeitraffer," in *Das neue Berlin: Konzepte der Internationalen Bauausstellung 1987 für einen Städtebau mit Zukunft*, ed. Dankwart Guratzsch (Berlin: Mann, 1987), 31. Author's translation. "Repairing" as a term for modernization and restoring a city's urbanity gained both metaphorical and practical meaning in the renewal discourse. While Hämer talks about repair and means just that, Posener was probably also referring to James Stirling's dictum on his Meinekestraße design (1977) which consisted of proper infill and the densification of the dispersed postwar urban fabric. See Heinrich Klotz, "Modelle für eine Stadt," in *Gestaltung einer neuen Umwelt: Kritische Essays zur Architektur der Gegenwart*, Heinrich Klotz (Luzern, Frankfurt/Main: Bucher, 1978). The former was the first article of the so called *Stadtreparatur* (urban repair) series edited by later-to-be publisher Wolf Jobst Siedler in the *Berliner Morgenpost* newspaper. On the use of the term in historic preservation discourse since the 1970s, see Hans-Rudolf Meier, "Stadtreparatur und Denkmalpflege," *Die Denkmalpflege* 2 (2008), 105–117.

12 Heinrich Klotz, "Berlin – Alt und Neu," in *Gestaltung einer neuen Umwelt. Kritische Essays zur Architektur der Gegenwart*, Heinrich Klotz (Luzern, Frankfurt/Main: Bucher, 1978), 103f. Author's translation.

13 Klotz's take on the contested issue of preservation and the European Heritage Year is reflected in the book *Keine Zukunft für unsere Vergangenheit,* which he co-authored with Roland Günter and Gottfried Kiesow and which served as a kind of counter-publication to the well-known official German catalogue of the Heritage Year, *Eine Zukunft für unsere Vergangenheit*. See Roland Günter, Gottfried Kiesow, Heinrich Klotz, *Keine Zukunft für unsere Vergangenheit: Denkmalpflege und Stadtzerstörung* (Gießen: W. Schmitz, 1975).

14 André Corboz, "Re-Animation: Alte Gebäude für neue Funktionen," in *Entwerfen in der historischen Straße*, ed. Martina Schneider (Berlin: Abakon 1976), 20–28.

15 Christian Norberg-Schulz, "Genius Loci," in *Entwerfen in der historischen Straße*, ed. Schneider, 12–19.

16 Hartmut Engel, "Der Rahmen der Aufgabe. Historische Stadtgestalt und Stadterneuerung," in *Entwerfen in der historischen Straße*, ed. Schneider, 29–39.

17 Norberg-Schulz, "Genius Loci," 17.

18 Engel, "Der Rahmen der Aufgabe," 31.

19 See Dieter Hoffmann-Axthelm, "Geschichte und Besonderheiten der Kreuzberger Mischung," in *Kreuzberger Mischung: Die innerstädtische Verflechtung von Architektur, Kultur und Gewerbe*, eds. Karl-Heinz Fiebig, Dieter Hoffmann-Axthelm, Eberhard Knödler-Bunte (Berlin: Verlag Ästhetik und Kommunikation, 1984), 9–20.

20 "Luisenstadt 115," in *Internationale Bauausstellung 1987: Projektübersicht* (Berlin: Bausstellung Berlin GmbH, 1987), 224.

21 The groups, of course, represent an ideal opposition of two poles. During the different phases of the design process, research and design methods constantly switch perspectives, at times being more deductive or more inductive. The classification presented here refers to the final stage of the design proposal, identifying the predominant approach.

22 Vittorio Gregotti, in *Entwerfen in der historischen Straße*, ed. Schneider, 52–65.

23 See Alison and Peter Smithson, "The 'As Found' and the 'Found,'" *The Independent Group: Postwar Britain and the Aesthetics of Plenty*, ed. David Robbins (Cambridge, Mass.: MIT Press, 1990), 201f. The concept of the "as found" is closely connected with the work of Alison and Peter Smithson and was first introduced into architectural discourse by Reyner Banham in the 1950s. At first, "as found" referred to the socio-spatial awareness of the everyday as shown in the exhibition *Parallel of Life and Art*. Banham used the term to characterize the Smithson's early "new brutalist" architecture, which presented the building material rough and bare, just "as found." See Stefania Kenley, "A Shift of Perception in Postwar Architectural Culture," *Nordic Journal of Architecture* (2011) 10–17.

24 Alison Smithson, "Architecture as Found," in *Entwerfen in der historischen Straße*, ed. Schneider, 75.

25 Peter M. Bode, "Potemkin wusste es besser," *Der Spiegel* 44 (1975), 228–232.

26 See Michael Gaenssler, ed., *Neues Bauen in alter Umgebung: Eine Ausstellung der Bayerischen Architektenkammer und der Neuen Sammlung München* (München: Bayerische Architektenkammer, 1978).

27 See Michael S. Falser's critical account of the heritage year: Michael S. Falser, *Zwischen Identität und Authentizität: Zur politischen Geschichte der Denkmalpflege in Deutschland* (Dresden: Thelem, 2008), 99–105.

28 At the forefront of this change of focus were the workers' settlement initiatives in the Ruhrgebiet. Not only did they fight to retain distinctive examples of well-functioning reform housing projects from the heyday of the mining and steel industry, but they also changed the agenda of the preservation bureaucracy, opening the lists and inventories for what is now called industrial heritage.

29 For a discussion of the resource paradigm in historic preservation see Johannes Warda, "Architektur reparieren in der 'Wegwerfgesellschaft': Zur ressourcenökonomischen Dimension des Denkmalbegriffs," in *Knappheit, Mangel, Überfluss: Zum Umgang mit begrenzten Ressourcen. Kulturwissenschaftliche Positionen*, eds. Maria Grewe and Markus Tauschek (Frankfurt/Main: Campus 2015), 309–326.

Tijana Stevanović

Humane Spontaneity: Teaching New Belgrade Lessons of the Past

The last big master plan of Belgrade before the breakup of the Socialist Federal Republic of Yugoslavia was produced in 1972 and contained the projection through the year 2000. Fourteen years later, in 1986, this strictly urban-planning direction of the Institute for Planning the Development of the City of Belgrade, without any other form of socioeconomic planning, lost more jurisdiction and authority in planning. Coinciding with the updated direction of the 1986 decree by the City of Belgrade Assembly was the introduction of the profession of urban planning to a relatively open market.

Subsequently, detailed urban plans and the issuing of licenses for building permission could be obtained from private architecture offices, while the Institute retained dominion only in general urban planning. Between those two historical moments, the postmodernist vision for New Belgrade started taking shape via the Institute's two major projects: the international culture center Home of Friendship (1975) and its aggrandizement in the form of the "Study for the Reurbanization of New Belgrade" (1985), a project published in Miloš R. Perović's *Iskustva Prošlosti* (*Lessons of the Past*) and exhibited widely.[1] In this text, unrealized monumental projects are situated as attempts at restoring authorship of the urban planner as public intellectual, which had been steadily deteriorating due to legal changes. The "Study" of 1985 will be analyzed keeping in mind what had then been a decades-long decentralizing of authorship through self-management policies among Yugoslav workers. Self-management was introduced in Yugoslavia as a critique of so-called state capitalism in the Eastern Bloc and a preventive measure against the formation of a managerial elite, aiming at eventually creating greater equality in the workplace by dissolving the credibility of individual managerial decisions. Nevertheless, the myth of individual genius in architecture seems to have continued unabated, feeding off the contradictions of a political climate favoring freedom of choice yet state decentralizing (fig. 1).

Inventing Tradition

In the bilingual edition of *Lessons of the Past*, Perović, an architect by education and then a head of the Institute's Metropolitan Planning Unit, supplanted his analysis and admiration for historic town agglomerations by casting doubts on the very forms of modern urban planning:

> The abandoning of the traditional constitutive elements of the town led to the spatial disintegration of the town. The strict separation of functions and the reduction of one building to only one function transformed the town into a simple collection of individual buildings. From that time on the town is no longer the living area for a community of citizens, but the living area for a multitude of individuals.[2]

"Individual" is to be both deprecated here for its embodiment of fragmentation and salvaged as a crucial creative subject especially when positioned against New Belgrade's open blocks of skyscrapers and slabs. First, Perović reduces the definition of functionalism to the formal segregation or zoning principles in urban planning. At the same time, the label of functionalism serves to identify and equalize principles in the socialist East and the capitalist West, omitting an analysis of the function the Institute performed until 1974, when its responsibilities were radically reduced.[3] These latter changes aimed to decrease the federal state's importance through the strengthening of self-management policies. But Yugoslav self-management in practice embodied a tension, too: oscillating between rendering individuals as equals free to decide any question of housing community or work organization, while – by such radical negation of the state – imposing an imperative of individual commitment to the betterment of their community as the only way to secure individual freedom. The "Study" for New Belgrade disregarded this state of affairs as a practice of no concern for that "community of citizens"[4] for whom the design aimed to cater. Eliminating one side of history, turning attention instead to the traditional town matrix, the author dabbles in invented tradition, showing for the first time in this context selected drawings and plans from the 1922 competition for *Singidunum Novissima* (New Belgrade)[5] – then in the Kingdom of Serbs, Croats and Slovenes. These mostly neoclassical projects were accentuated as the historical first plans for

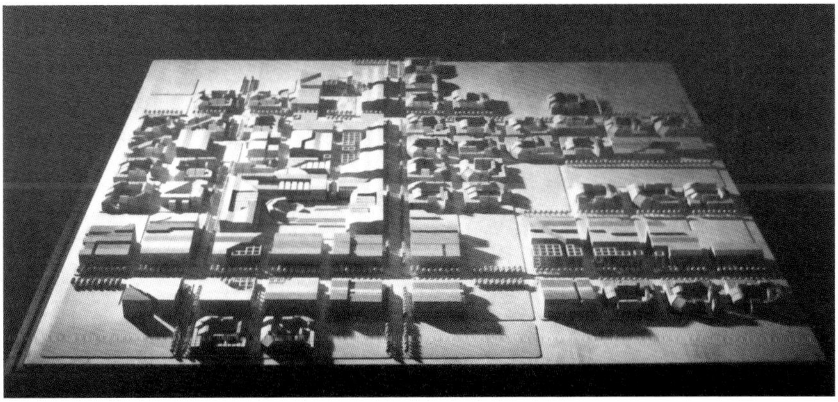

fig. 1 Miloš R. Perović, "Research into alternative urban models, Model C: Proposal for a new urban system," 1981, photograph of the model. Source: *With Man in Mind*: An Exhibition of two Projects from the City Planning Institute / Gradski zavod za planiranje/ Belgrade, Yugoslavia (Belgrade: Cultural Centre Belgrade, 1986), 21

the city of New Belgrade. The second-prize design, by Viennese architects Rudolf Perco, Erwin Ilz and Erwin Böck, still reflects imperial pretexts for Belgrade, at that time newly liberated from the Austro-Hungarian Empire's proximity and thus its influence. Further into the project publication, this archeological operation is blended with an appropriation of Gordon Cullen's idea of "urban warmth."[6] Substantiating it with "ambiance," Perović continues to criticize the functionalism of New Belgrade, which he portrayed as "cold" in comparison to Giambattista Nolli's 1748 survey of Rome in *Nuova Pianta di Roma* and Giambattista Piranesi's peculiar experiments in scale and proportion in his etchings for *Il Campo Marzio dell' Antica Roma* from 1762 (fig. 2).[7] In doing so, Perović spares the reader any cultural or political connotation of Rome or New Belgrade. He employs an opportune optimism that if social background is not mentioned, the cure may also be acknowledged as a formal answer. Though not explicitly acknowledged, Perović's obvious inspiration could have been the "Roma Interrotta" competition in 1978, which used both above-mentioned maps of Rome as provocation for invited architects' renditions of urban development of the city. "Roma Interrotta" omitted the period between the Nolli map's production date and the present moment, as Maarten Delbeke has recently argued; thus this postmodern initiative aimed to get rid of the "embarrassing presence of modern Rome"[8] of the interim period. In similar fashion, Perović disparages the "Oriental mess" the Ottomans left behind in the old-town center and, along with the unrealized historic 1922 *Singidunum Novissima* plan, sees the potential for continuity only with one form of the historic city, while actually existing problems were afforded no attention: neither unplanned growth in the Rome of the nineteenth and twentieth centuries nor the presence of New Belgrade's existing urban structure, built mainly since 1948.[9] Instead, he gives decontextualized, abstract models for reurbanizing "the settlement in the spirit of Athens Charter,"[10] suggesting a universal concept applicable to the entirely different historical and social situation of Belgrade, as compared to Rome.

These models for New Belgrade used techniques resembling Nolli's figure-ground engravings, albeit less so in their form than in their ambition, which was to focus in greater detail on public places for social interaction than on housing, classified as "private" even though the majority of flats in New Belgrade were not privately owned. Perović praises Nolli for allegedly representing "spontaneous growth."[11] What makes his interest particularly obscure, however, is that although it searching for historical examples, his study erases one important part of New Belgrade history. Knowing this, forcing it into the model of an "organic" history may yield ideological biases.

The Universal Scale of Spontaneous Reurbanization

The New Belgrade reurbanization project is readily identified, not with the gradual repair of specific ills Perović found in New Belgrade blocks a mere thirty years old at the time, but with a principal denouncement of the totality of its open blocks, described using an individualistic attribute as "introvert[ed]":

Model B: Settlements built in the spirit of the Athens Charter [...] The residential buildings form a clear geometrical composition primarily artistic in character. At the center of the block there are the local community center buildings, school and nursery and a large non-built-up area for children's playgrounds, sports grounds and green areas. All the buildings form an undefined, vague area and are surrounded by outdoor car parking lots. The entire block is introvert conceived [...] without the need for communication with the identical neighboring blocks, with the result that in essence it represents a small world in itself.[12] Perović accompanies this observation with the bold comparative test of inserting a New Belgrade block – which he calls "inhumane" due to its scale (approx. 640,000 square meters at the base) – within the urban tissue of the old-city center of Belgrade (fig. 3). This seems for the Institute's team of urban designers led by Perović an impossible and destructive effort,[13] which lays bare the "loss of the sense of human scale."[14] But when the same action is performed in reverse – placing a traditional Belgrade block into the modern matrix of open New Belgrade blocks – this appears to them to be plausible. Reviving the traditional urban block in a city district that

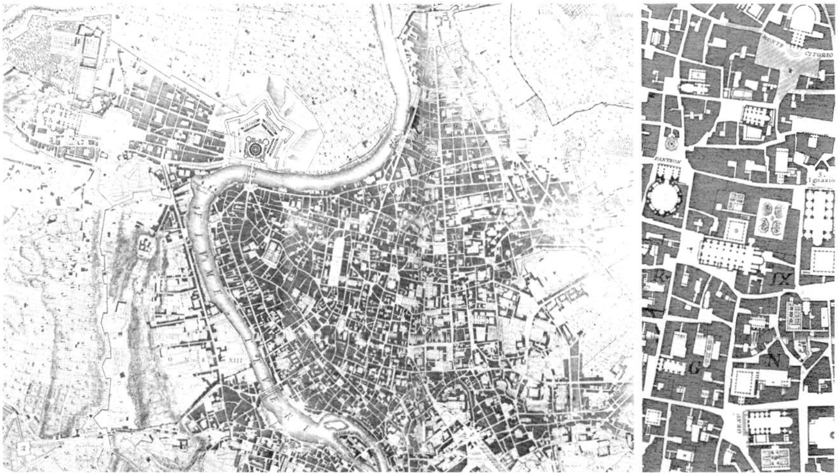

fig. 2 Two details from the engraving Giambattista Nolli, *Pianta Grande di Roma*, 1748, map. Source: Miloš R. Perović, *Iskustva Prošlosti* (Beograd: Zavod za planiranje razvoja grada Beograda, 1986), 150–151

never had a history of such morphology, however, develops a more delicate political position. Followed by the designation that blocks should be built by individually specifying the land allocation for housing, this entirely neglects the socioeconomic planning model introduced in 1961 for the self-governance of housing communes in New Belgrade.

Perović attempts to strip New Belgrade of any specificity, putting it rather into the rubric of universal idealist failures such as Le Corbusier's Radiant City.[15] He condemns previous New Belgrade design as "utopianism," identified as the essence of any functionalist city. By a bizarre interpretation of Iain Boyd Whyte's recently edited translation of the letters of *Die Gläserne Kette*,[16] the author discards any possible accomplishment of the modernist city, qualifying it merely as "reverie."[17] He supports this argument by extracting Lewis Mumford's argument that the functionalist city is much more a suburb than a city,[18] automatically recognizing this as another universal characteristic of New Belgrade's development. By repudiating functionalism as irrational reverie, Perović wishes to establish his design vision as rational and scientific, without diverting from functionalist design means in reaching for the universal answer.

Historical elements of the city – the street, the square and the perimeter block – get a primacy and an absolute positive value over the open block. However, the "scenario for reurbanization"[19] is embodied here in a simply denser design of a more minutely defined collage of block fragments lacking any Belgrade-specific historical reference other than conditioned planning

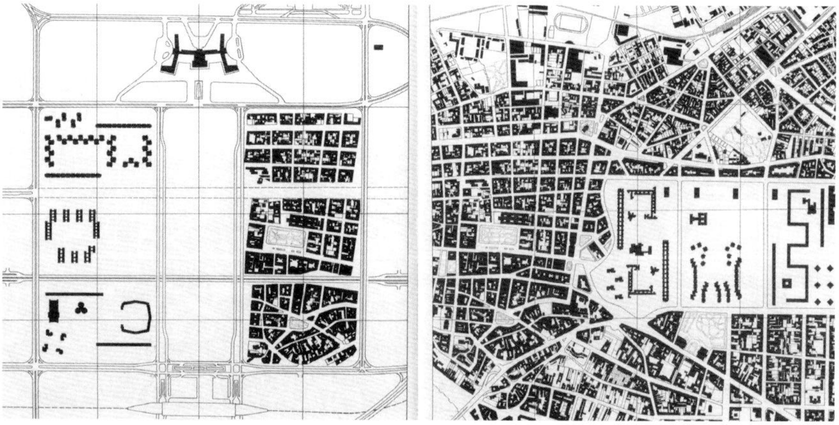

fig. 3 "Loss of the sense of human scale. Implantation of part of the structure of old Belgrade into the urban tissue of the center of New Belgrade" and "Implantation of part of the structure of the center of New Belgrade into the urban tissue of old Belgrade," comparison of plans. Source: Miloš R. Perović, *Iskustva Prošlosti* (Beograd: Zavod za planiranje razvoja grada Beograda, 1986), 62–63

in open blocks. Apart from praise from international professional circles including Dennis Sharp's at RIBA,[20] Miloš Bobić, a Belgrade urban designer who relocated to Amsterdam's Urban Planning Department in 1992, criticized this as precisely what made Perović a conservative planner: "sloppiness in the social base" for the new city of New Belgrade.[21] Yet, a future spontaneous specificity for the place Perović wishes to praise in the project contrasts with his attempts to align with the visionary universalism of the later phase of CIAM and Team 10's critique of functionalist city.[22] Alison and Peter Smithson reflected on "utopianism of the present" in Team 10's principles: [the] architect's responsibility, towards the individual or groups he builds for and towards the cohesion and convenience of the collective structure to which they belong, is taken as being an absolute responsibility. No abstract master plan stands between him and what he has to do, only the "human facts" and the logistics of the situation.[23]

In Perović's attempt to claim humanism as the principle of his plan, those grounded "human facts" become transformed into a lofty plea for "humane scale." Yet he calls this plan a simulation, a theoretical model analysis. This is incidental to the 1972 master plan of Belgrade projecting its development until 2000, for which American experts from Wayne State University were invited to the Institute where they introduced the computer planning models.[24] These models embraced scientific approximation of abstract mapping of large-scale spontaneous growth of a city, rather than strictly suggesting design as the solution (fig. 4).

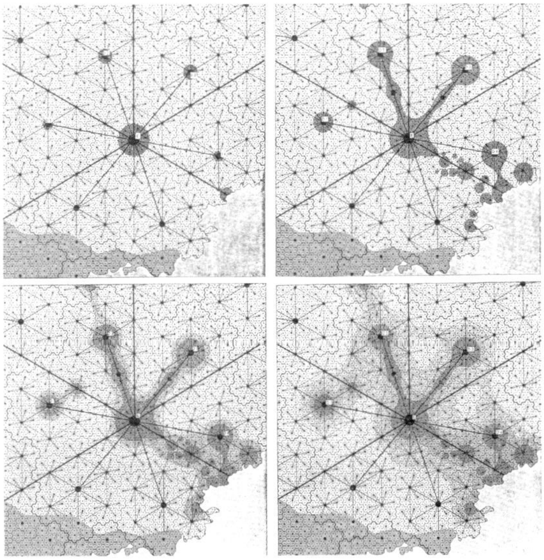

fig. 4 "Corridor theory, Growth and development of region," diagram. Source: Miloš R. Perović, *Iskustva Prošlosti* (Beograd: Zavod za planiranje razvoja grada Beograda, 1986), 128

Architecture critic Peter Krečič reviewed one of the project's iterations and claimed the project's attempt to communicate with the wider audience successful.[25] Yet quantitative computer modeling seems inconsistent with such an aim, while the ideas of natural growth proposed by the planner appear equivalent to the designer's surrendering before the impossibility of planning beyond the individual block. Thus "Study for the Reurbanization of New Belgrade" becomes an indicator for the cancelation of the urban planner's ranking above and beyond the task of the urban designer, due to the ambivalent scale it simultaneously wishes to occupy. In the words of Belgrade architect Milan Lojanica, we should embrace the design's incompleteness as: "The city is a historical creation and the pretension to complete it within one period is senseless [...] the best thing would be to envisage, instead of a finished city, a structure in embryo which will be capable of developing and growing on its own in one process."[26]

However, finality of some aspects of the "Study"'s minute design proposals, like pitched roofs or construction system[27] definition, are as dogmatic as the already-criticized functionalist principles – merely shifting from functionalism to formalism.

An Artistic Demiurge's Enlightened Tyranny

The project stemmed from the Home of Friendship (1975) mentioned above, part of a larger urban-design project Third Millennium, supported, exhibited and published by the Serbian Academy of Sciences and Arts (SANU) in

1985. SANU (famous for housing Serbian nationalists at the time) was entertaining visions for a center of culture in Belgrade, foremost as a flagship site for international Non-Aligned Movement gatherings – the alleged pride of Yugoslav socialists. The federal state was already deeply caught up not only in stark differences in regional development among separate republics but also in disciplinary divisions, similar to what philosopher Jürgen Habermas had already in 1981 identified as postmodern culture's kernel: structures of rationality creating "distance [...] between the culture of the experts and that of the larger public."[28] Far more than the simple assertion of the "unfinished" growth of the city that Perović promoted, the project was closer to that of his contemporary, the philosopher Zoran Đinđić's (a 1980s student of Habermas), and the latter's warning and criticism of Yugoslav self-management as testimonial to an "unfinished state."[29] The tendency of Yugoslavia to decentralize the state and ultimately erase it by encouraging governance by all social strata came into collision in this project with such an elitist state-representative institution as a center of culture. The postmodernist aesthetics that the project adopted are thus not far in intention from the intentions labeled modernist that were directly criticized in the book *Iskustva Prošlosti*. However, the "Study"'s visualization of a happily unfinished future, contradicted by the attempt of the study's authors at coherence in detailing and care for individual buildings, fails to represent the collective dream of the new world and instead reflects more of an artistic temperament. Perović's project traveled from Belgrade to Ljubljana and London's RIBA, relying more on external acknowledgment from professionals than from its own citizens.

This makes Perović no less artistically inclined towards grandeur fiction and no closer to the citizen community than those he says "dreamed a reverie of the functionalist city."[30] *Lessons of the Past*, deriving inspiration from the title of Paolo Portoghesi's theme for the first International Venice Architecture Biannual, "The Presence of the Past" (1980), and from formal and theoretical experiments of the Krier brothers and Colin Rowe and from Oswald Mathias Ungers's writings on the "city as a work of art,"[31] the project uses artistic design, in spite of scientific arguments and statistical data of "wave theory" and "corridors theory," to picture so-called spontaneous urban growth.[32] The latter only served to assert the position of an artistic demiurge. Spontaneous growth here primarily needs to assume a different land-property model from self-managed socialism, and considers it almost natural: "When the land reserves in the town center are exhausted and the intensification of land use in the center reaches a high degree, central activities tend to invade neighboring residential zones." (fig. 5)[33] This is the ground on which Perović's proposal loses mastery. Its function is to persuade us at the same time that

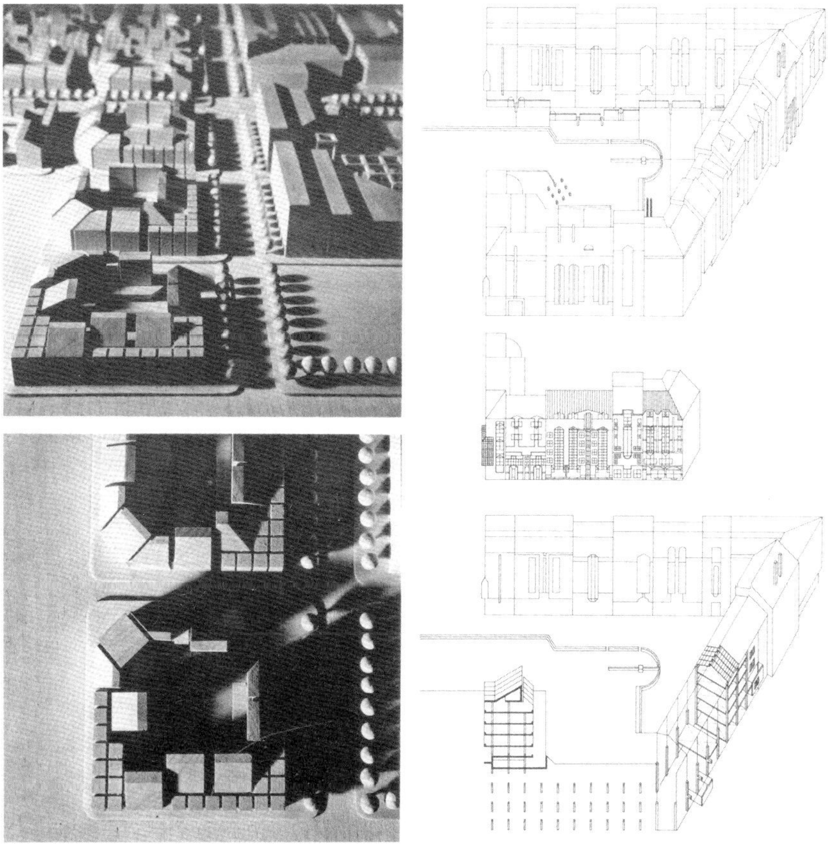

fig. 5 "New urban block, Construction method and system," photograph and axonometric drawings from Miloš R. Perović, *Research into alternative urban models*, 1981. Source: Miloš R. Perović, *Iskustva Prošlosti* (Beograd: Zavod za planiranje razvoja grada Beograda, 1986), 77

New Belgrade will grow spontaneously, and to confirm that urban planners as professionals are still needed for its guidance – even in a development pattern where gentrification presumably leads to urban growth and transformation.

The design for such a reurbanization of New Belgrade could be compared with what William Ellis pinpoints in Colin Rowe's designs for the "Roma Interrotta" exhibition as contradictory fluctuation between "ideals and the community," "type and context," "continuity and change," while not giving up on abstraction altogether[34]:

> Does Rowe's deductive formalism amount to architectural totalitarianism in liberal guise; where is the line between architectural totalitarianism and architectural humanism in these projects; and what is the relation of this deductive approach to actual urbanism?[35]

Comparable to Rowe's ambivalence, Perović attempted to show the design process as both ameliorative and changeable; to embrace both planned and unplanned, by the ambiguity of his creative language. Architectural critic Manfredo Tafuri similarly criticized the ambitions of his postmodern peers, architects, analyzing their favorite quotation of Piranesi's *Campo Marzio* as an example of the "horror vacui of language".[36] Tafuri asserted, through applying both scientific position and encouraging arbitrariness of the "geometric monads," that the loss of a center speaks of deregulation not only of established harmony but of semiological confusion. What Jean-Francois Lyotard characterized as the shift of knowledge production conditioning the appearance of postmodernism as "elimination of the communist alternative and valorization of the individual enjoyment of goods and services"[37] was here occupied by the urbanist's capricious joy in designing a city that ultimately should be left unfinished by design. Thus Perović's project, in its own anticipation of the infinite ways to intervene in the city, which is professed as always already unfinished, created the position from which it was possible – through exposing tensions between continuity and change – to in fact neutralize the effect of its own intention. The "Study" explicitly wanted to denounce any possibility of the architect's creation of the city as a whole, while capitalizing, nevertheless, on the city as an object of the architect's prophecy.

Slavoj Žižek uses the metaphor of the parallax view to analyze how postmodern architecture operates through its discursive tension-making. What Žižek particularly accentuates is the obfuscation of ideology.[38] The simplest explanation of the optical phenomenon of parallax is that the distant object will appear differently from two disparate standpoints. Parallax view exemplifies that the object is inscribed in the subject, only existing through the subject's registration of it. Through this relation, however, the object in itself affects the subject incessantly; the subject can never grasp reality as a whole. In order to claim the object's position, one needs to be viewing it from a specific perspective, which for Žižek entirely marks a postmodern condition. He illustrates this with Fredric Jameson's categorization of American postmodernism, exemplifying how advanced scientific development through a discursive turn can be combined with the other American cultural pole: poverty and waste. In our example, what uniquely constitutes the urban designer's position is a claim that these projects show theoretical models: scientific proposals for formal treatment of what Perović finds a social by-product of functionalism (fig. 6). Much like Perović's peculiar choice of quoting Jacoppo Barozzi da Vignola's seventeenth-century perspectival and analytical experiments and writings, which favor one-point perspective,[39] this project eliminates the possibility of any other subject except that one which constructs

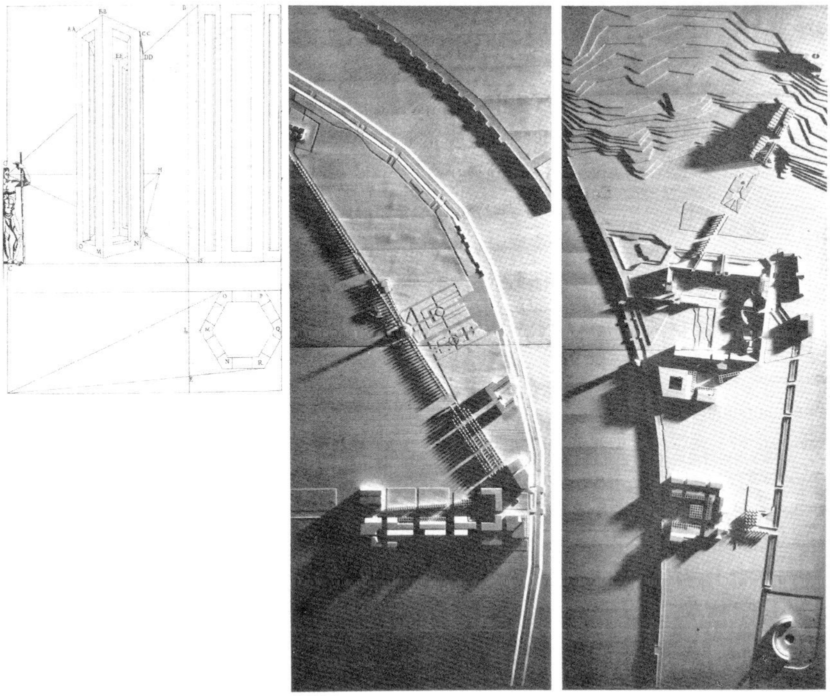

fig. 6 "Jacopo Barozzi da Vignola, Le Due Regole della Prospettiva pratica di M. Iacomo Barozzi da Vignola con i Comentarii del R.P.M. Egnatio Danti, Stamparia oamoralo, Romo, 1583" and "Proposal for the reconstruction of the center of New Belgrade and Sava amphitheater, Focal points and elements lending atmosphere of poetry," image in the catalogue from the traveling exhibition displayed at RIBA London. Source: *With Man in Mind*: An Exhibition of two Projects from the City Planning Institute/ Gradski zavod za planiranje/ Belgrade, Yugoslavia (Belgrade: Cultural Centre Belgrade, 1986), 57

the object, although in the first stance this seems motivated by an aim to represent the multiplicity of standpoints.

These citizens' perspectives, however laudable, remain – in relation to the represented fragmentary models for future development – a mere deregulated collection of monads. Although the powerful postmodern credo of the loss of the center – in accordance with Yugoslav self-management's worker participation in governing – fully potentiates an interaction between producers and consumers that is more than unilateral, here Perović's formal method and abstraction returns to the ostensibly impossible individual standpoint. By accepting that his universal models cannot present "finite" designs, the parallax view reveals that the only spontaneous design feature surfacing here is the "Study"'s embodiment of what it attempts to critique in knowledge-production terms.

Perović edified his project on the criticism of what he had identified in New Belgrade as obsolete CIAM modernist ideas for the functionalist city. In an unexpected turn, the "Study for the Reurbanization of New Belgrade," rather than being diametrically in opposition with modernist ideals of city planning and design, by its scale and ambition aims to partly retain the avant-gardist grand gesture strengthening the architect's creative agency; by the same token, it disguises the sense of impotence, knowing the Institute for Planning the Development of the City of Belgrade's importance has already been diminished. Therefore, through the attempts to marry the concept of the organic growth of the city, made for and by citizens via endorsement of the concept of an "unfinished" project-city, the subject of the architect's knowledge is constructed by limiting and outlining the object of her competence as finished while separating it from the process of his knowledge creation.

The "Study," with its models, attempts to "humanize" New Belgrade blocks by filling them up. In an utterly ideological attempt to erase any political stance by his universal pastiche, Perović further mythologizes the method of his work. While explaining what functionalism means, he fails to explain how his formalism works in demising the zoning. Having used science to legitimize arguments in *Lessons of the Past* and statistical models provided by Branislav Stojanović – his colleague and coauthor of the "With Man in Mind" exhibition – Perović's megaproject still holds a perception which stands contradictory to its aim by embodying a precise, harmonious coherence while advocating "spontaneity" as the basis for thinking of the future projection for everyday life unconstrained by the social planning. The project for the reurbanization of New Belgrade and its claim for ordinary citizens' say and participation in constructing it becomes less persuasive particularly due to its complexity in the detailing of segments and models. While claiming the expression of, and an inclination towards, tending the organic community and a humanizing corrective vision, these designs – in a clandestine turn – elaborate instead the normalization of the individual designer-subject's totalizing ambition through obfuscations of the very tensions contained in the motive for such "reurbanizing" projects.

Endnotes

1 Miloš R. Perović, *Iskustva Prošlosti*, (Beograd: Zavod za planiranje razvoja grada Beograda, 1986), The project and exhibition is largely attributed to Perović although the project had multiple participants with him as the lead designer.

2 Ibid., 57.

3 "Skupština Grada Beograda," July 10, 1974, "Rešenje o osnivanju Zavoda za planiranje razvoja grada Beograda," *Službeni List Grada Beograda*, July 31, 1974, 20, 1359–1360.
4 Perović, *Iskustva Prošlosti*, 57.
5 *Singidunum* is Latin for the old Roman settlement, today's Belgrade castle. This competition was focused on planning land opposite the historic center, in floodplains of the Danube and Sava Rivers.
6 Perović, *Iskustva Prošlosti*, 42.
7 Ibid., 146.
8 Maarten Delbeke, "Roma Interrotta: Baroque Rome as a (Post)Modernist Model," *OASE*, 86 (2011), 74–85 (p. 77).
9 Perović, *Iskustva Prošlosti*, 23.
10 Ibid., 58.
11 Ibid.,146.
12 Ibid., 58.
13 Ibid., 61–62. The urban-design project exhibited at RIBA was done by the team of authors at the Institute with particular input from Branislav Stojanović.
14 Ibid., 67.
15 Ibid., 24–26.
16 Iain Boyd Whyte, Iain, ed., *The Crystal Chain Letters. Architectural Fantasies By Bruno Taut and His Circle*, (Cambridge, MA.: The MIT Press, 1985).
17 Perović, *Iskustva Prošlosti*, 34. Boyd Whyte uses the term reverie to explain early twentieth-century projects' use of surrealist imagination.
18 Ibid., 33.
19 Ibid.,157.
20 Dennis Sharp, "Opening note," in *With Man in Mind*, Miloš Perović (Belgrade: Kulturni Centar Beograda, 1986).
21 Miloš Bobić, "NB – Perspektiva 2000," *Čovjek i Prostor*, 389–390 (1985), 25.
22 CIAM and Team 10 were acknowledged in Yugoslavia, including the organization of CIAM X in Dubrovnik in 1956 and the participation of Yugoslav architects including Ernst Weissmann and Vlado Antolić then Alexis Josić in CIRPAC and CIAM meetings, respectively.
23 Alison Smithson, ed., *Team 10 Meetings* (Delft: Publikatieburo Bouwkunde; Delft University of Technology, 1991), 8.
24 See: Tijana Stevanović. "Review of Le Normand, Brigitte, *Designing Tito's Capital: Urban Planning, Modernism, and Socialism in Belgrade*," H-Urban, H-Net Reviews. August 2015.
25 Peter Krečič, "Urbanistički nacrt za treće tisutljeće," *Čovjek i Prostor* 389–390 (1985), 23.
26 Milan Lojanica, "Genesis of a Concept/Geneza Jednog Koncepta," in Perović, *With Man in Mind* (Kulturni Centar Beograda, 1986), 13–25 (p. 23).
27 Perović, *Lessons of the Past*, 130–131.
28 Jürgen Habermas, "Modernity versus Postmodernity," *New German Critique*, 22 (1981), 3–14 (p. 8).
29 Zoran Đinđić, *Jugoslavija Kao Nedovršena Država* (Novi Sad: Književna Zajednica Novog Sada, 1988), 88.
30 Perović, 47.
31 Oswald Mathias Ungers, "The City as a Work of Art," *Architecture Culture, 1943–1968: A Documentary Anthology* (New York: Rizzoli, 1963), 361–364.

32 Perović "Toward a New Belgrade," in *The Metropolis in Transition*, ed. Ervin Y. Galantay (New York: Paragon House Publishers, 1987), 227–242, (p. 236)
33 Ibid.
34 William Ellis, "Type and Context in Urbanism: Colin Rowe's Contextualism," *Oppositions Reader: Selected Readings from A Journal for Ideas and Criticism in Architecture 1973–1984*, ed. K. Michael Hays (New York: Princeton Architectural Press, 1998), 225–252, (p. 228).
35 Ibid., 234.
36 Manfredo Tafuri, *The Sphere and Labyrinth: Avant-Gardes and Architecture from Piranesi to the 1970s*, trans. by Pellegrino D'Acierno and Robert Connolly (Cambridge, Mass; London: The MIT Press, 1987), 38.
37 Jean-Francois Lyotard, *The Postmodern Condition: A Report on Knowledge*, ed. by Geoff Bennington, Brian Massumi and Fredric Jameson (Manchester University Press, 1984), 37.
38 Slavoj Žižek, *The Parallax View* (Cambridge, MA.; London: The MIT Press, 2006), 17.
39 Perović, *With Man in Mind*, 57.

Maroš Krivý

Quality of Life or Life-in-Truth? A Late-Socialist Critique of Housing Estates in Czechoslovakia

What is architecture's relation to life? Foucault's conceptualization of the biopolitics concept relied on a close reading of architectural, urbanistic and territorial practices.[1] Recent studies have foregrounded architecture's spatial and scalar role in distributing and managing population in the welfare state.[2] While biopolitics attends to bodily aspects of life, what would it mean to consider life incorporeally, as a noopolitics concerned with life's psychological meaning, its quality and authenticity?[3] What is architecture's noopolitical role?

I will address these questions in the case of late socialist Czechoslovakia, considering the architecture of housing estates (*sídliště*). Central to my interpretation will be the critique to which Czechoslovak estates were subjected during the 1970s and 1980s.[4] Such diverse actors as the Communist Party, architecture unions, architects, historians and dissidents held that life in a *sídliště* needs to be critically judged in psychological terms, but they also construed *sídliště* as a living environment. At the heart of such an environmental-psychological critique was the ostensible lack of meaning. The critique prompted the project of humanization aimed at improving the psychological effects of the *sídliště* environment, but also occasioned an interpretation that this environment is intrinsically "inhuman."[5] The underlying theme of the humanization project – addressing the flaws of socialist urban planning rather than the contradictions of capitalist urbanization, as in the 1950s – was a turn to historicity, either as a turn to architectural archetypes in *sídliště* design or as a retreat from *sídliště* due to its incompatibility with history construed in terms of organic evolution (*sídliště* as a historical aberration).

The Meaningful Environment

Architectural historians perused the centrality of cultural meaning to Western postmodernism. Manfredo Tafuri noted that "wherever […] architecture ostensibly poses the problem of its own meaning, we can discern the glimmering of a regressive utopia."[6] According to Tahl Kaminer, "the rise of 'meaning' as a central topic in architectural discourse in the late 1960s […] demonstrat[ed] the manner in which 'culture' had replaced 'society' as the new horizon of post-industrial society."[7] This concern with meaning was expressed in two overlapping registers: communication and experience. Between Robert Venturi and Christian Norberg-Schulz, there was a slippage from semiotic to phenomenological meaning, from the "decoding of diverse levels of communication to an emphasis on the experiential and subjective aspects of architecture."[8]

Such a slippage was also manifested in the parallel process of rethinking space as a place and environment. Kevin Lynch construed city as a Gestalt-like perceptual environment and the Heideggerian influence in architecture transpired as a concern for the (in)authenticity of places. These bypassed the determining role of society by legitimizing place-making and subjective poetics. The semiotic-phenomenological turn to meaning was also a turn to historicity. It manifested as a repertoire of archetypal spatial forms and as a mythology of timelessness, rootedness and organic belonging.

Was there a similar turn to meaning in the East? Philosopher Boris Buden identified the substitution of society by cultural memory with post-communism.[9] But the seeds of the post-communist loss of society were already sown within late socialism. Anna Paretskaya argued that, in the Soviet Union, the Party became "the promoter of new lifestyles, and […] sowed the kernels of more differentiated, privatized, and commodified dispositions" by the 1970s.[10] A similar inadvertent role was played by the Party in Czechoslovakia, where quality-of-life policies were implemented as a way of depoliticizing social conflict after the Soviet invasion in 1968. While critical of these policies, Czechoslovak dissent articulated the critique in terms of life's (in)authenticity, thus cementing meaning (rather than society) as the terrain of struggle.

In architecture, the two registers of meaning – symbolic communication and existential experience – defined the boundaries within which the critique of *sídliště* was articulated in Czechoslovakia in the 1970s and 1980s. The Czechoslovak *sídliště* model dates back to the postwar socialization of architecture by the Communist government, but also to prewar capitalist experiments with architectural industrialization. After the socialist-realist period (1949–1956) that favored modularity and historicist expressiveness, the authorities opted for standardizing entire building units and intensifying the development of housing estates.[11] By the mid-1970s, when the pace of construction peaked, a widespread dissatisfaction with the ostensible monotony and homogeneity of *sídliště* was firmly in place.[12] While the plan (in terms of quantity, speed and densities) continued to define the housing policy throughout the 1970s and 1980s, the considerations of meaning came forward with increasing force in the debates of architects, architectural unions, and the Communist Party.

Semiotic and phenomenological interest in meaning transpired primarily as a critique of the lack thereof and correlated, respectively, with perceiving the *sídliště* environment as being of low quality and inauthentic. Critique of the *sídliště* was inconclusive, legitimizing the improvements of state socialism but also prefiguring its collapse. Architects designed housing estates influenced by archetypal urban forms, researched novel construction systems conducive to historical "iconography" and contexts, and construed meaningful environment as central to socialist personality. They also contrasted the *sídliště* to archetypal forms, deplored its monotony and argued that it is a psychologically harmful environment.

Phenomenology and Postmodernism

Let me begin by invoking a remark by Václav Havel, the well-known dissident and first president of post-socialist Czechoslovakia, who said in 1984 that "postmodernist architecture is a signal [...] that man begins to sense [...] that he cannot understand nor plan everything [...] that he is a part of a mysterious order – the natural world."[13] For Havel, postmodernism was a name for architecture attuned to the natural world (*přirozený svět*), a concept indebted to Czech philosopher Jan Patočka, which is itself indebted to Edmund Husserl's concept of lifeworld.[14] For Patočka, the meaning of life was immanent to the natural world and its loss was brought about by techno-scientific reason.[15] In Havel's reading, the loss of the natural world coincided with the development of industrial society and with the industrialized architecture of the *sídliště*. Whereas the dissident imagined the natural world – and postmodernism as its architectural manifestation – as a preindustrial pastoral, he conceived the *sídliště* as an unnatural and abnormal "contaminated moral environment."[16]

Through a series of conceptual slippages, the phenomenological project, which began for Husserl as an attempt to bracket metaphysics and the "naturalness" of the external world, legitimized in Havel a metaphysics of the natural world ostensibly free from ideology. Conceptual shades of the term "natural" in Patočka were lost in Havel's understanding, which implied a renewed metaphysics of human nature. Resisting post-totalitarian society, but extending his critique to bourgeois-industrial society as such, Havel clung to the metaphysics of life-in-truth untainted by history and ideology.[17]

While Havel knew little about architecture, his association of phenomenology and postmodernism and the idea of an ideology-free architecture concurred with the attentive reception of Western postmodernism in the architectural community. Havel stated the above after a private lecture by Jiří Ševčík in the former's home. While lecturing in "apartment seminars" and publishing in samizdat publications, Ševčík, an architectural historian and a local "operative critic" of postmodernism, was employed as a researcher at the Czech Technical University and was a regular contributor to *Architektura ČSR*, the official journal of the Union of Czech Architects.

Drawing on Kevin Lynch's environmental psychology and Norberg-Schulz's concepts of existential space and genius loci, Ševčík undertook studies of Most (1977) and Prague-Vinohrady (1982).[18] He relied on historic morphological research and made use of residents' mental maps. While the research on the mining town Most – where a *Zeilenbau*-configured *sídliště* was being built while the demolition of the medieval town was ongoing – suggested that the *sídliště* lacked urbanity and was not therefore an authentic city, the latter postulated nineteenth-century block/street configuration as an essence of urbanity. Wandering in Most, a disappearing town doomed to give way to an open-pit coal mine, Ševčík struggled to fuse the scientific and the affective, juxtaposing the mental-map methodology and existential language.[19] Contrasting with the tactical efficacy of the research was Ševčík's conceptual disregard for how power determined the old and traditional. Such mystification of organic urbanism also carved a space for architecture's retreat to the meaning and reframing of history as historicism.

In the face of the *sídliště*, Ševčík reinvented architecture as imagination. Rather than a concrete history, Ševčík was interested in the organic morphological continuity of a concrete place. His understanding of architecture as attending to *genii loci* was predicated on a dilution of concrete history into the abstract historicism of archetypes and timelessness. For Ševčík, postmodernism "does not need a unified linguistic order or a special program [...] because it is firmly grounded in a collective memory, which supplies ever-meaningful formal archetypes warranting architectural permanence and continuity,"[20] and opens a "space for imagination [...] where the world broken into fragments can be united and identity secured even for the price of

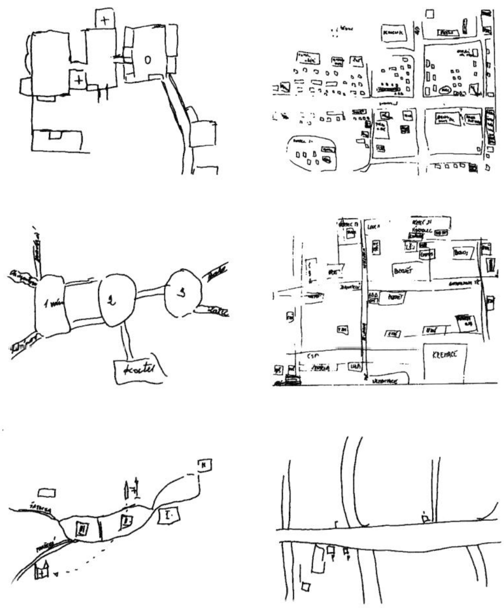

fig. 1 Mental maps drawn by the inhabitants of Most, from the study by Jiří Ševčík, 1977. The old city center is represented in the left column, the new housing estate in the right column. Source: Jiří Ševčík, Ivana Bendová and Jan Benda, "Město Most v obrazu svých obyvatelů: Metoda výzkumu obrazu města a její využití," Acta Polytechnica-Práce ČVUT v Praze 1, no. 3 (1978), 20.

illusion."[21] Such an illusory reworking of timeless archetypes, Ševčík stressed, was guided by an interest in human scale (fig. 1).

Ševčík's study of Most was influential among younger architects, who grappled in the late 1970s and early 1980s to reconcile *sídliště* architecture and postmodernism. Architect Zdeněk Hölzel, while working on the design of the Barrandov housing estate in Prague (1977–1988),[22] translated and published in samizdat Venturi's *Complexity and Contradiction* and Charles Jencks's *The Language of Post-Modern Architecture*, and, together with Ševčík, organized Jencks's visit to Prague in 1979. In the Barrandov project, Hölzel's efforts went primarily into the design of the central pedestrian promenade, conceived as the symbolic heart of the estate. Rather than conceiving sociability in terms of functional concentration, Hölzel defined it through spontaneous circulation. The pedestrian promenade was construed as a timeless urban archetype and a locus of conviviality, where residents find meaning qua human beings, ostensibly outside of any political ideology. It was dotted with primitive brick and metal pavilions and other variations on the primitive hut, signifying an affinity to this timeless archetype but also enacting a minimal gesture of transcendental musing (figs. 2, 3).

Barrandov marked a decisive period in Hölzel's career. After graduating in 1972, he researched modular-construction systems, leading to a publication in 1976 influenced by Metabolist aesthetics.[23] In its wake, Imrich Jankovich, the senior member of the Union of Slovak Architects, prompted Hölzel to rethink residential construction systems.[24] Three strategies suggested by Hölzel were

fig. 2 Zdeněk Hölzel and Jan Kerel, Barrandov housing estate, Prague, promenade, perspective drawing, 1987. The water cascade is titled "Obelisk of The Motion". Source: Zdeněk Hölzel and Jan Kerel, Nový Barrandov: Výtvarný generel (Prague: Pražský Projektový Ústav, 1987), 18.

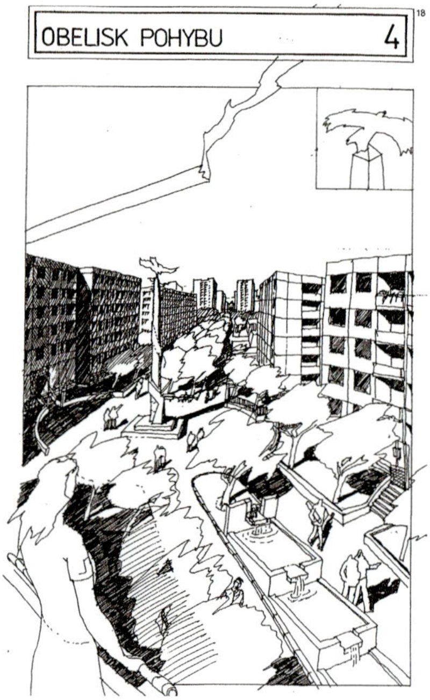

fig. 3 A pavilion at the Barrandov promenade. Photo: author, 2015.

distinguished by the degree of intervention in construction industry they would entail: modifying non-load-bearing elements (windowsills, railings, doorways, etc.), attaching additional structures (loggias, rooftop gardens, ground-floor skeleton constructions, etc.), and "modularizing" the standard types (adding the possibility to recede and protrude individual "cells" while respecting the basic grid).[25] Jankovich stated that the last intervention would be implemented after 1990 (fig. 4).

The encounter with Ševčík and the work on Barrandov redirected Hölzel's interest from modularity to meaning. In 1983, Hölzel commented acerbically on the alleged impasse of industrialized architecture. An ironic accordion book introduced JOTRS, an anagrammatic architectural construction trailer

fig. 4 Zdeněk Hölzel and Jan Kerel, modular construction system, conceptual study, c. 1979. Source: Imrich Jankovich, Výhľady nášho bývania (Bratislava: ALFA, 1980), 103.

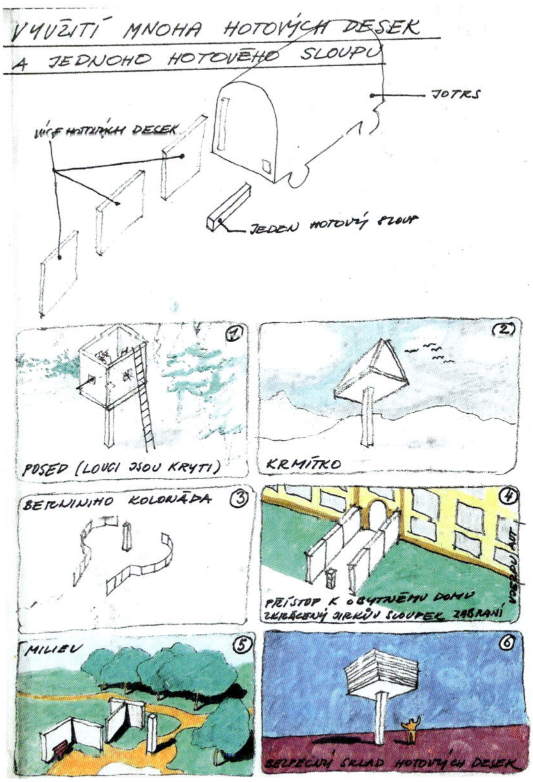

fig. 5 Zdeněk Hölzel and Jan Kerel, JOTRS, 1983. St. Peter's Square is represented as the number three. Source: Zdeněk Hölzel's private archive.

(the title is an anagram of *stroj*, a Czech word for machine). Churning out identical concrete panels and pillars, the architectural capacity of JOTRS was unlimited. It was devised to build roads, walls, milestones, sheds, railway sleepers, fireplaces, victory columns, triumphal arches and prisons; it could also replicate Bernini's Vatican colonnade and put together an "environmen-

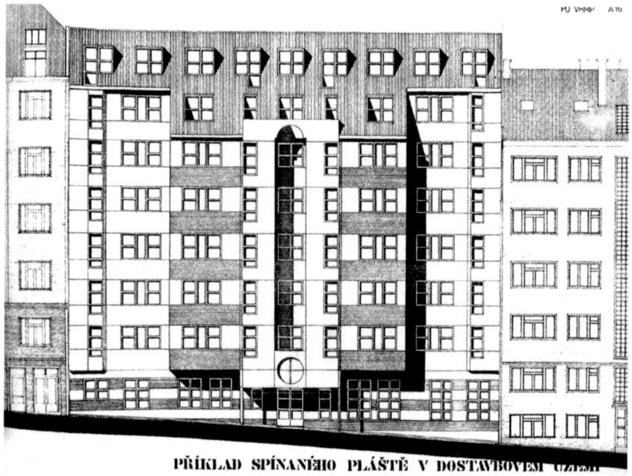

fig. 6 Miloš Pavlík, construction system for infill development, experimental building, elevation, 1986. Source: Miloslav Pavlík, Konstrukce a technologie pro komplexní bytovou výstavbu po roce 1995 (Prague: PÚ VHMP, 1987), 68.

tal milieu." If meaning and historicity entered into Hölzel's perspectives in the 1970s as communicability, they changed into expressions of inauthenticity by the mid-1980s. At first, the pedestrian street archetype informed Hölzel's design strategy; later, the juxtaposition of St. Peter's Square and crude Czechoslovak construction elements informed his retreat strategy (fig. 5).

Postmodernism and Socialist Realism

But modularity and meaning (or industrialization and ideology) were not as incompatible as JOTRS suggested. In the research projects and experimental prototypes of the late 1980s, a new generation of open-construction systems combining the advantages of standardization with historical expressiveness was studied. Miloš Pavlík, the lead author of one such research project, argued that architects should seriously consider that "socialist citizens [...] are attracted towards older neighborhoods that [...] offer more attractive, cultural and stimulating environment, even if technical and hygienic standards are lower."[26] The project – which architects worked on together with engineers, investors and suppliers – introduced a construction system to be implemented by 1995, considering its diverse aspects: technical (compatibility between construction elements from different suppliers, building structure organized according to the lifespan of elements, all while respecting the standard grid), aesthetic (context sensitivity, historical language including facade cladding, entrance canopies, avant-corps, faux pediments, mansard roofs), functional (ground-floor commercial use, rooftop gardens) and urbanistic (atypical plans, infill developments).[27] All in all, the project was guided by a shared conception of the future *sídliště* as a "living street." Pavlík also studied how to regenerate the housing estates of earlier decades, suggesting that an array of historicist vocabulary could be achieved by providing buildings with "second" composite facades[28] (figs. 6, 7).

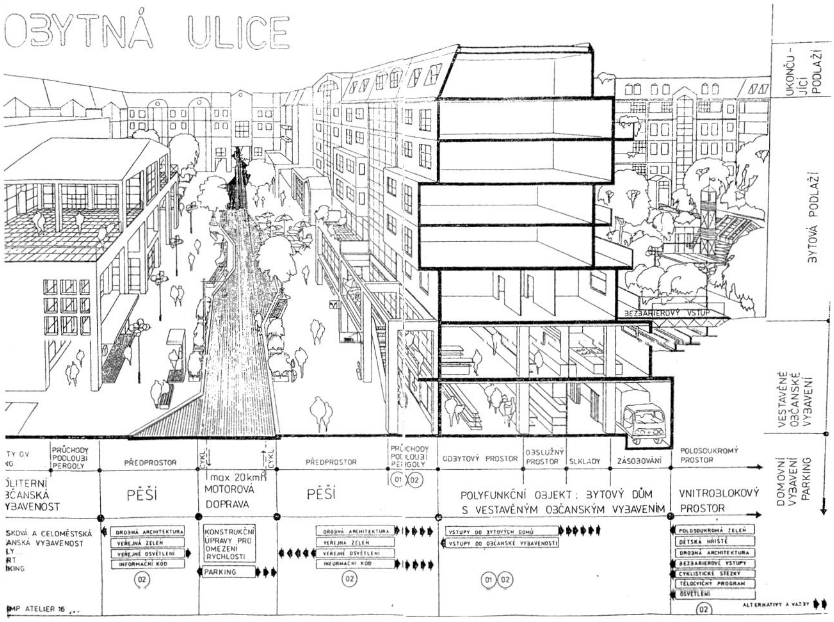

fig. 7 Miloš Pavlík, construction system for infill development, urban concept, perspective drawing, 1986. The drawing is titled "The Living Street". Source: Miloslav Pavlík, et al., Konstrukce a technologie pro komplexní bytovou výstavbu po roce 1995 (Prague: PÚ VHMP, 1987), 7.

The encounter between postmodernist historicism and *sídliště* was not exactly a dissonant one, complicating the narrative of postmodernism as a harbinger of the natural world distorted by ideology. I will proceed from here not by showing how such a narrative is itself ideological, but by illustrating the uncanny proximity of postmodernist historicism to what its proponents would consider as exterior to it: socialist realism. I will rely on the work of architectural historian and curator Radomíra Sedláková, a PhD graduate of the Research Institute of the Theory and History of Architecture in Moscow (supervised by Alexander Riabushin, the eminent Soviet theorist and interpreter of postmodernism) and head of the National Gallery in Prague's architecture collection. Like Ševčík and Hölzel, Sedláková was receptive to postmodernism and critical of the late socialist *sídliště*. Like them, she lamented the loss of meaning and historicity, but framed it as a loss of socialist realism: "a sense of urbanity disappeared with the end of socialist realism," she argued.[29] Sedláková spoke against this disappearance at the international conference "Socialist Realism Reassessed," organized in Poland in 1985, contrasting the *sídliště* of the 1980s and that of the 1950s, contending that the latter had a "sense of scale for human beings [...] who expect that the urban environment will provide enough stimuli for psychological self-development."[30]

Revising post-Stalinist criticism of socialist realism, a critical revival of socialist realism emerged in the 1980s from within the critique of the *sídliště*. What exactly was to be revived from socialist realism? Two competing notions of socialist-realist architecture were a particular style associated in Czechoslovakia with the years 1949–1956 and an architectural method understood as a dialectical synthesis of quantitative and qualitative factors (industrialization and ideology).

In contrast to the Soviet Union, where socialist realism was used in the latter sense in the 1970s and 1980s,[31] in Czechoslovakia, where the term had been introduced only after the war, the meaning was ambiguous. High union representatives who championed the revival of socialist realism had to qualify their agenda. When Zdeněk Strnadel, the outgoing head of the Union of Czech Architects, expressed reservations in 1982 about the late-1950s critique of socialist realism, he was compelled to clarify that the reference was to the method, "pre-empting the fear that we want to return to formalist decorativism."[32] Others in a similar position spoke about the proverbial throwing out of the baby with the bathwater, wherein the baby stood for the socialist-realist method and the bathwater for decorative superfluity.[33]

Yet, in the context of *sídliště* urbanism, the method-style distinction was not very tangible. The late socialist critique of the *sídliště* was inspired by established urbanistic solutions of the 1950s *sídliště*: streets, squares and courtyards. At a 1983 conference dedicated to the work of Jiří Kroha, the most prominent Czechoslovak architect of socialist realism and designer of the town of Nová Dubnica, Ivan Michalec, member of Kroha's studio in the 1950s and head of the Slovak Architecture Union in the 1970s, argued that Kroha's street was already fully socialist. It had a "multifunctional character and pedestrian-level services, […] was well composed and well proportioned" and it "had a human scale and a quality living environment" that made it a desirable blueprint for contemporaneous housing estates, according to Michalec (fig. 8).[34]

In a report on the Polish conference, Sedláková expressed disappointment that Soviet delegates had discussed socialist realism only as method, forgoing the way it transpired as a particular historical style that contrasted with the "style" of 1970s architecture.[35] This contrast was precisely in the human-scale environment that defined the former but was missing in the latter: "thirty years ago houses *made* space, today houses are situated *in* space," Sedláková argued.[36] In her essays, reviews and conference talks written during the 1980s, she repeatedly foregrounded parallels between socialist realism and postmodernism, dissociating their "vulgar" aspects (decorativism, commercial kitsch) from the commendable revival of historical archetypes, classical typomorphology and human-scale urbanism.[37]

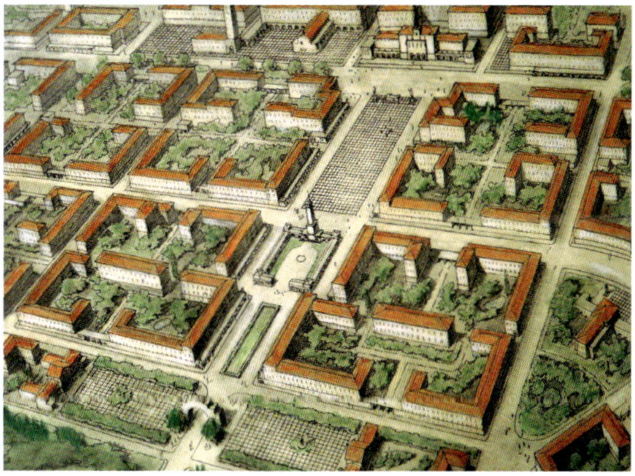

fig. 8 Jiří Kroha, Nová Dubnica, perspective drawing (detail), c. 1951. Source: Museum of the City of Brno.

Sedláková was concurrently interested in the sense of place, ostensibly lost by the 1980s but present in the 1950s. Her attentiveness to regional, national and vernacular architectures related to her support of more flexible construction systems. Echoing Pavlík's research, Sedláková called for modular industrialization conducive to historical language, but legitimized this call by citing Kroha's early 1950s critique: "the standardization of entire building volumes [is…] mechanic and vulgar […and] leads to industrialized anesthetization of the artistic element of architecture."[38] Kroha's pre-emptive critique of "volumetric" industrialization was speaking to late socialist critics of such industrialization and of its ramifications in the *sídliště* environment.

The Spirit of Late Socialism

The attunement of the living environment to residents' psychological life was a regulating idea in the architectural discourse of the 1970s and 1980s. The critique of the *sídliště* stemmed from the ideal of human-scale environment suffused with historically articulated meaning. An apparent paradox is that the same ideal was articulated by those drawing on phenomenology and postmodernism, who wanted to "de-ideologize" architecture, recovering its allegedly natural condition, and those faithful to the dialectic conception of architecture, who wanted to ideologize it, making it properly socialist. Historians of socialist architecture have paid little attention to the ambiguous centrality of the concepts of living environment and psychological meaning in the discipline's challenge to functionalist principles.

In the remaining pages, I will contextualize the architectural turn towards meaning within the broader political and intellectual context of late socialist Czechoslovakia. I want to introduce a hypothesis that this turn was fuelled by a failure to rethink and revive Marxism as a living philosophy and an instrument of concrete political practice in the wake of the 1960s. There are two aspects to this failure: recuperating Marxism as a normative worldview, and ceding the terrain of resistance to phenomenology.

Luc Boltanski and Eve Chiapello identified two critiques of Western capitalism in the 1960s: the social critique of inequality, economic distribution and political control, and the artistic critique of disciplinary regulation as being against the ideals of creativity, self-fulfillment and the authenticity of personal life.[39] By way of integrating the latter critique and sidelining the former, Boltanski and Chiapello argued, the "new spirit of capitalism," developed between the 1970s and the 1990s, legitimized the neoliberal ethos of the entrepreneurial self while undoing welfare-state bureaucratic institutions. A parallel reading can be developed of the new spirit of socialism in Czechoslovakia.

Following the Soviet-led invasion of Czechoslovakia in 1968, sweeping institutional changes were implemented by the reinstated orthodox wing of the Communist Party in 1969 and 1970. In architecture, this included closing down independent studios (such as the SIAL group in Liberec) and the institutional and personal reorganization of the Union of Czech Architects. Historians frequently interpreted these changes through the prism of totalitarianism theory, relying on an ambiguous epistemology of propaganda and indoctrination and a conceptual dualism of opening and closing.[40] The historical dynamics of the critique of the *sídliště* suggest, however, that the relationship between architecture and population cannot be explained in such crude terms.

In Eastern Europe, Marxist revisionism of the 1960s challenged ossification and oligarchic tendencies within the Communist parties. In 1956, Czech philosopher Jiří Cvekl had reintroduced into dialectical materialism the concept of the negation of negation, which had been eliminated in Stalin's version of dialectics. According to sociologist Miloslav Petrusek, "the return of the 'negation of negation' into dialectics heralded a new era."[41] The resurrection of dialectics as a critical method offered new hope for Marxism and socialism. In *Dialectics of Concrete* (1963) and *Our Current Crisis* (1968), Czech philosopher Karel Kosík placed Hegel and Marx in a dialogue with phenomenology, articulating the question of meaning and authenticity of human life as inseparable from concrete political-economic processes – such as the problem of the de-politicization of the working class.[42] Against the unholy marriage of positive dialectical materialism and techno-scientific reason, Kosik called for a rethinking of historical reason in terms of everyday political praxis. He contrasted the system built upon historicist metaphysics and techno-science to the world where political praxis and individual meaning are inseparable.

Revisionist Marxism of the 1960s strived to think of social organization and cultural meaning integrally. But the former was sacrificed to the latter during the early 1970s normalization of revisions. The rise of the critique of the *sídliště* belonged to this process: architecture, reframed in terms of meaning, supplanted society as the object of critique. The normalization process was not simply about repressing the critique,[43] as historians contend, but also about channeling social critique into the domain of private meanings. Although ostensibly antithetical with each other, the Communist Party and dissent concurrently foregrounded the problem of meaning.

The orthodox wing of the Communist Party, reinstated after 1968, curbed demands for political change but gave grounds to the critique of meaning. The historian Paulina Bren argued that normalization policies introduced during the 1970s aimed to depoliticize the 1960s revisions by placating self-realization in the private sphere and associating meaningful life with domesticity. According to Bren, "the message was that a socialist way of life was potentially able to challenge and even surpass capitalism […] by offering an unmatchable 'quality of life.'"[44] Life, measured in terms of quality and quietude, was the life of a private citizen. If it was an attempt to circumvent the "ideology," the "turn toward the domestic," Bren argued, was also "an expression of the quiet life […] as a cornerstone of party policy […] Traditional roles became a model of resistance […] but they were simultaneously reinforced and encouraged by the state."[45]

Dissent embraced the phenomenological liberal themes of life's authenticity and freedom of expression. Charter 77, the most prominent dissent platform in Czechoslovakia, was originally a demand to the party to respect human rights, to which it had subscribed at the Helsinki Accords in 1975. Havel, a founding Charter member, divorced the question of dissensus from left-right politics, arguing that "the problem has no longer resided in a political line or program: it is a problem of life itself."[46] Unlike Kosík, Havel criticized the party in the name of abstract life and humanity: from socialism with a human face to simply a human face. Patočka, another founding Charter member, made meaning the driving force of history: "history differs from prehistoric humanity by the shaking of accepted meaning."[47] For dissent and its phenomenological worldview, meaning determined history rather than history meaning. That dissent largely embraced the idea of apolitical politics (per Havel) testifies to the validity of applying Boltanski and Chiapello's thesis – that the critique of meaning, disconnected from social critique, pioneered the new spirit of capitalism – to state socialism.[48]

Conclusion

The more or less forceful disappearance of social critique in late socialism corresponded to the rise of an artistic critique of *sídliště*. The failure to revise and revive Marxism after the 1960s manifested as a double embrace of the ideal of meaningful life by the Party and the dissent. Terms such as environment, life and meaning supplanted the political critique of society during the 1970s. I suggested that the two critiques of the *sídliště*, judged as offering an insufficient quality of life and being incompatible with life-in-truth, cannot be neatly separated. Both critiques – exemplified, respectively, in the Party chairman's call to architects (in 1982) "to create a living environment conducive to happy family life [...] where people would feel at home"[49] and in Havel's mention (in 1984) of housing estates, prisons and concentration camps in one breath and in contrast to the natural world as a transcendental home[50] – were construed upon the premise that the *sídliště* is a locus in which life is questioned.

Quality of life and life-in-truth were two poles within which architectural practice and discourse oscillated in late socialist Czechoslovakia. Whether architects revisited socialist realism or embraced historicist postmodernism, the noopolitical instrumentarium of phenomenology, semiotics and environmental psychology attuned architecture to the questions of life's quality and meaning and manifested itself in the ideal of the pedestrian street as a locus of urbanity. Nonetheless, this ideal remained restricted to conviviality, culture and consumption. Boltanski and Chiapello suggested that "the artistic critique should [...] reformulate the issues of liberation and authenticity, starting from the new forms of oppression it unwittingly helped to make possible."[51] How the late-socialist critique of *sídliště* played out in the neoliberal urbanization of the post-socialist decades, including the "pacification by cappuccino" of the pedestrian street, is a story that remains to be written.[52]

Endnotes

1 Michel Foucault, *Security, Territory, Population: Lectures at the College de France* (London: Palgrave Macmillan, 2007).

2 See Łukasz Stanek, "Biopolitics of Scale: Architecture, Urbanism, the Welfare State and After," in *The Politics of Life: Michel Foucault and the Biopolitics of Modernity*, ed. Sven-Olov Wallenstein and Jakob Nilsson (Stockholm: Iaspis, 2013).

3 The term is from Maurizio Lazzarato, "The Concepts of Life and the Living in the Societies of Control," in *Deleuze and the Social*, ed. Martin Fuglsang and Bent Meier Sorensen (Edinburgh: Edinburgh University Press, 2006), 171–190.

4 I focus on the Czech part of the Republic.

5 See the debate in Jiří Hrůza, "Humanizace sídlišť," *Architektura ČSR*, 47:6 (1988), 24–27, 30–32.

6 Manfredo Tafuri, "L'architecture dans le Boudoir: The Language of Criticism and the Criticism of Language," in *Architecture Theory Since 1968*, ed. K. Michael Hays (New York: Princeton Architectural Press, 1998), 149.

7 Tahl Kaminer, *Architecture, Crisis and Resuscitation: The Reproduction of Post-Fordism in Late-Twentieth-Century Architecture* (London: Routledge, 2011), 43.

8 Ibid., 45.
9 Boris Buden, *Zone des Übergangs: vom Ende des Postkommunismus* (Frankfurt: Suhrkamp, 2009).
10 Anna Paretskaya, "The Soviet Communist Party and the Other Spirit of Capitalism," *Sociological Theory*, 28:4 (2010), 394.
11 For a history of Czechoslovak housing industrialization see Kimberly Elman Zarecor, *Manufacturing a Socialist Modernity: Housing in Czechoslovakia, 1945–1960* (Pittsburgh: University of Pittsburgh Press, 2011).
12 Such qualities were seen as incompatible with the human psyche. See Michal Beneš, *Monotónie nových obytných souborů* (Prague: VÚVA, 1989).
13 Václav Havel, cited in Jiří Ševčík, "Postmodernismus v architektuře," in *Texty*, Jana Ševčíková and Ševčík, ed. Terezie Nekvindová (Prague: Tranzit.cz and VVP AVU, 2010), 151.
14 Edmund Husserl, *The Crisis of European Sciences and Transcendental Phenomenology* (Evanston: Northwestern University Press, 1970).
15 Jan Patočka, *Heretical Essays in the Philosophy of History* (Chicago: Open Court, 1996), 95–118.
16 Václav Havel, "New Year's Address to the Nation" (1990), http://old.hrad.cz/president/Havel/speeches/1990/0101_uk.html.
17 Václav Havel, "The Power of the Powerless," in *The Power of the Powerless: Citizens and the State in Central-Eastern Europe*, ed. John Keane (London: M.E. Sharpe, 1985).
18 Jiří Ševčík, Ivana Bendová, and Jan Benda, "Obraz města Mostu," *Architektúra a urbanizmus*, 12:3 (1978), 165–178; Jiří Ševčík et al., *Vinohrady. Obraz města 19. století* (Prague: ČVUT FA, 1982).
19 Ševčík stressed the affective side of the fieldwork during an interview with the author, January 14, 2016, Prague.
20 Jana Ševčíková and Jiří Ševčík, "Postmodernismus bez pověr, ale s iluzí," in *Texty*, 82.
21 Ibid., 84.
22 Hölzel collaborated on most projects with architect Jan Kerel. Further references are to collaborative projects.
23 Zdeněk Hölzel, Jan Kerel, *Ocelové prostorové jednotky*, (Prague: GŘ ZLP, 1976).
24 According to Hölzel, personal communication with the author, December 14, 2015.
25 Imrich Jankovich, *Výhľady nášho bývania* (Bratislava: ALFA, 1980), 98–103.
26 Vlastimil Kolář, Miloš Pavlík, "Nová stavební soustava pro Prahu," *Architektura ČSR*, 45:1 (1986), 13.
27 Miloslav Pavlík, et al., *Konstrukce a technologie pro komplexní bytovou výstavbu po roce 1995* (Prague: PÚ VHMP, 1987).
28 Miloslav Pavlík, interview with the author, January 11, 2016. See also Miloslav Pavlík, et al., *Regenerace panelových objektů z 50. a 60.-tých let* (Prague: PÚ VHMP, 1987).
29 Radomíra Sedláková, "Socialistický realismus včera a dnes," unpublished manuscript, 1. This is the original manuscript of the conference talk, obtained from the personal archive of Sedláková.
30 Ibid.
31 See Anatoly Polyansky, "Problemy tvorcheskogo soiuza," *Arkhitektura SSSR*, 50:5 (1982), 1–9. I would like to thank Richard Anderson for this reference.

32 Zdeněk Strnadel, "Za socialistickou architekturu," *Architektura ČSR*, 42:5 (1983), 200.
33 Rudolf Šteis, "Urbanistická tvorba," *Projekt* 25, 2 (1983), 12; Radomíra Sedláková, interview with the author, January 11, 2016, Prague.
34 Ivan Michalec, cited in Eva Hejdová,"Architekt Jiří Kroha a současnost," Československý *architekt*, 30:4 (1984), 4.
35 Radomíra Sedláková, "Socialistický realismus po létech," *Československý architekt*, 32:1 (1986), 1.
36 Radomíra Sedláková, "Socialistický realismus včera a dnes," 3 (my italics).
37 Radomíra Sedláková, "Urbanista bytostně socialistický," *Rudé právo*, 65:256 (1984), 5; Radomíra Sedláková, "Seminář kritiků, tentokrát bez kritiků," unpublished manuscript (c. 1984); Radomíra Valterová, "Postmodernismus-klasicismus-a co dál?," *Výtvarná kultura*, 8:2 (1984), 20–26; Radomíra Sedláková, "Postmodernismus," unpublished manuscript (c. 1984).
38 Jiří Kroha, cited in Hejdová, "Architekt Jiří Kroha a současnost," 4.
39 Luc Boltanski and Eve Chiapello, *The New Spirit of Capitalism* (London: Verso, 2007).
40 See Alexei Yurchak, *Everything Was Forever, Until It Was No More: The Last Soviet Generation* (Princeton: Princeton University Press, 2006), for a critique of applying the prism of totalitarianism to late socialism.
41 Miloslav Petrusek, "Úvahy o dialektice v sociálních vědách," *Teorie vědy*, 33:3 (2011), 402.
42 Karel Kosík, *Dialectics of the Concrete: A Study on Problems of Man and World* (Dordrecht: D. Reidel, 1976); Karel Kosík, "Our Current Crisis," in *The Crisis of Modernity: Essays and Observations from the 1968 Era*, Karel Kosík, ed. James H. Satterwhite (Lanham: Rowman & Littlefield, 1995), 17–51.
43 In 1968, Karel Kosík became a member of the reformed Central Committee of the Communist Party and a professor at the Faculty of Philosophy at Charles University in Prague. In 1970, he was expelled from the Communist Party and from his teaching post.
44 Paulina Bren, *The Greengrocer and His TV: The Culture of Communism after the 1968 Prague Spring* (Ithaca: Cornell University Press, 2010), 185
45 Bren, *The Greengrocer and His TV*, 174.
46 Havel, "The Power of the Powerless," 40. In the same essay, Havel talks about "pseudo-reality" (*pseudoskutečnost*), contrasting it with Kosík's term "pseudo-concrete."
47 Patočka, *Heretical Essays in the Philosophy of History*, 62.
48 Václav Havel, "Politics and Conscience," *The Salisbury Review*, 3:2 (1985), 31–38. This notion cannot be straightforwardly associated with neoliberalism. The problem is rather that Havel identifies political crisis as primarily a "spiritual, moral, and existential" crisis. Cited in Miloš Havelka, "'Nepolitická politika': kontexty a tradice," *Sociologický* časopis, 34:4 (1998), 464.
49 Miloš Jakeš to the 2nd Assembly of the Union of Czechoslovak Architects, in 1982. Miloš Jakeš, [untitled], *Architektura ČSR*, 42:6 (1983), 253.
50 Havel, in Ševčík, "Postmodernismus v architektuře," 150–151.
51 Boltanski and Chiapello, *The New Spirit of Capitalism*, 468.
52 Sharon Zukin, *The Cultures of Cities* (Malden, Blackwell: 2000), 28.

Appendix

Notes on Contributors

Joseph Bedford is Assistant Professor of History and Theory at Virginia Tech. He received his BA in Architecture from Cambridge University; his B.Arch from The Cooper Union; is the holder of the 2008–2009 Rome Prize at the British School in Rome; and received his Master in History, Theory and Criticism at Princeton University, where he is completing his doctorate. He is the founding editor of *Attention: The Princeton Audio Journal for Architecture*, and *The Architecture Exchange*, a platform for theoretical exchange between architecture and other fields. He has worked in practice with offices such as Michael Hopkins Architects in London and Architectural Research Office in New York and has taught architecture at schools such as Princeton University, Pratt Institute, and Columbia University. He is the author of numerous articles in journals such as *Architecture Research Quarterly*, *Log* and *AA Files*.

Andrew Demshuk is Assistant Professor of History at American University in Washington, DC. He received his Ph.D. in post-1945 Central European History from the University of Illinois in 2010. In 2011, he became Assistant Professor of History at the University of Alabama at Birmingham (UAB). Amid many article publications in leading journals and scholarly presentations in the USA, Germany, and Poland, he received fellowships from the Dubnow Institut in Leipzig (2006), Herder Institut in Marburg (2007–2009), German Academic Exchange Council (DAAD) (2007–2008), and Humboldt Foundation (2014–2015). He is the author of *The Lost German East: Forced Migration and the Politics of Memory 1945–1970* (Cambridge, 2012) and *Demolition on Karl Marx Square: Cultural Barbarism in the People's State* (to appear with Oxford, 2017). He is currently working on his third book project titled *Three Cities after Hitler: Urban Reconstruction across Cold War Borders*.

Ruth Hanisch is an independent scholar. She completed her studies in Art History in Vienna with a thesis about the architect Felix Augenfeld, and earned her Ph.D. – also from the University of Vienna – with the thesis "Das Bild des Hafens in der Architektur des 18. Jahrhunderts." She has worked on numerous exhibitions, for example "Visionäre und Vertriebene. Österreichische Wurzeln in der modernen, amerikanischen Architektur" at Kunsthalle Wien in 1995. From 1997 to 2002, she was an assistant at the Institute gta at ETH Zurich. Between 2002 and 2007, she worked on the

AHRC-funded project "Constructing a Modern Architecture of Excellence: The Case of Switzerland" at the University of Strathclyde, Glasgow. From 2007 to 2010, she was research assistant at TU Dortmund. She taught at universities in Vienna and Edinburgh, the University of Strathclyde Glasgow, Bochum and FU Berlin. She has published extensively on Viennese Modernism.

Max Hirsh is Research Assistant Professor of the History and Theory of Architecture and Urban Planning at the Institute for the Humanities and Social Sciences, University of Hong Kong. His research on socialist and post-socialist urbanism interrogates the transition from socialist to capitalist planning principles in a variety of national contexts ranging from East Germany to China. Max is the author of *Airport Urbanism: Infrastructure and Mobility in Asia* (University of Minnesota Press, 2016). His writing has appeared in the *Journal of the Society of Architectural Historians*, *History & Technology*, *Places*, and *Informationen zur modernen Stadtgeschichte*; as well as in edited volumes on architectural history and urban studies.

Judith Hopfengärtner studied architecture at TU Karlsruhe, EPF Lausanne and at the Bartlett School of Architecture, UCL, where she received her Diploma. She taught design at the University of Karlsruhe (KIT) and earned an MAS in History and Theory of Architecture at the Institute gta of the ETH Zurich with research on Aldo Rossi's teachings at the ETH Zurich and his influence on Swiss architects. She was assistant to the Chair for the Theory of Architecture at ETH Zurich 2010–2015 and is co-editor of *Aldo Rossi und die Schweiz. Architektonische Wechselwirkungen* (Zurich, gta, 2011, with Ákos Moravánszky).

Karl R. Kegler is Professor for the History and Theory of Urbanistics and Architecture at the Hochschule München / University of Applied Sciences Munich. From 2011 to 2015, he was postdoc and senior assistant at the Institute gta of the ETH Zurich. Prior to that Kegler worked as a scientific researcher and lecturer at several university institutions, and has co-authored and edited numerous books on the history of architecture and on science and technology studies. Publications and research interests include the intellectual history of planning and architecture, popular culture and literary studies. He has published *Wege zu einer neuen Baukunst* (2000), *Utopische Orte. Utopien in Architektur- und Stadtbaugeschichte* (2004) and *Deutsche Raumplanung* (2015) on the history and theoretical basis of regional planning in Germany.

Daniel Kiss is an architect and urbanist, educated at the TU Budapest and Harvard GSD. Between 2006 and 2008 he worked as project architect with Herzog & de Meuron in Basel, Switzerland and since 2009 he has been senior assistant and lecturer at Kees Christiaanse's Chair for Architecture and Urban Design at the Swiss Federal Institute of Technology (ETH Zurich). He teaches urban design and theory, leads the research platform Urban Breeding Grounds, and is currently finishing his dissertation on the post-socialist urban development of Budapest. Besides his academic affiliation, Kiss is co-founder of the Basel-based design practice XM Architekten.

Maroš Krivý is Professor of Urban Studies at the Faculty of Architecture, Estonian Academy of Arts and postdoctoral researcher at Cambridge University's Department of Geography. He studied sociology and urban studies and obtained his Ph.D. from the University of Helsinki (2012). His research revolves around the "environmental" effects of spatial practices. In addition to the reception of postmodernism in late socialist architecture, he has studied the entrepreneurialization of urban development through culture and the digitalization of urban realms. His publications include "Don't plan!" (*IJURR*, 2013), "Greyness and colour desires" (*JoA*, 2015), "Postmodernism or socialist realism?" (*JSAH*, 2016) and "Towards a critique of cybernetic urbanism" (*Planning Theory*, 2016). He maintains a practice in visual and environmental art. His exhibitions include "New coat of paint" (Hobusepea Gallery, Tallinn, 2013; alternativa festival, Gdansk, 2013) and "Vernacular geology" (with A. Marzecova, Baltic Pavilion, Venice Biennale, 2016).

Torsten Lange is postdoctoral assistant at the Guest Lectureship for the Theory of Architecture at ETH Zurich. He received his Diploma in Architecture from the Bauhaus University Weimar and his Master in Architectural History from the Bartlett School of Architecture/UCL, and earned his Ph.D. with the thesis "*Komplexe Umweltgestaltung* [complex environmental design]: architectural theory and the production of the built environment in the GDR, 1960–1990" (UCL, 2015). His research focuses on postwar architecture and urbanism, especially in socialist European countries, and examines theories of production, labor, and materiality as well as alternative forms of architectural practice. His work has been published in *ARCH+*, *archimaera*, *The Journal of Architecture*, and *East Central Europe*, and in edited volumes such as *Industries of Architecture* (Routledge, 2016).

Sebastiaan Loosen is a Ph.D. candidate at the Department of Architecture at the KU Leuven (2014–2018). His work is positioned in a project on the formative years of architectural theory in Belgium and focuses in particular on the role of publications in the dissemination of architectural ideas in the 1970s and 1980s. He graduated in architectural engineering and in philosophy at the KU Leuven. He is a member of the research groups "Architectural Cultures of the Recent Past" and "Architecture, Interiority, Inhabitation," and is currently co-organizing the international conference "Theory's History 196X–199X. Challenges in the Historiography of Architectural Knowledge," to be held in Brussels in February 2017.

Martin Maleschka is an architect and photographer working and living in Cottbus, Germany. While studying Architecture at Brandenburg University of Technology, he developed a keen interest in photography and architectural art in the German Democratic Republic – a passion that stems from having grown up in the socialist model city of Eisenhüttenstadt. In 2006, he began uploading photos of architectural art on various image hosting websites, and since then has built up the most comprehensive photographic collection of architectural art in East Germany with more than 10,000 images published to this day. His work has been exhibited in a number of solo shows. At the moment, he is working on a guidebook for architectural art in East Germany.

Silvia Micheli is lecturer at The University of Queensland (Australia). Silvia's main research interest focuses on international influence and cross-cultural exchanges in a twentieth and twenty-first century architectural context. Silvia has published extensively on postwar, postmodern and contemporary Italian architecture. She co-authored the book *Storia dell'architettura italiana 1985–2015* (Einaudi, 2013) and co-edited the book *Italia 60/70: Una stagione dell'architettura* (Il Poligrafo, 2010). Silvia's research interests also include Modern Finnish architecture. She is the author of the monographic book *Erik Bryggman (1891–1955): Architettura moderna in Finlandia* (Gangemi, 2009). Silvia has worked with international institutions such as the Alvar Aalto Foundation (Helsinki), Vitra Design Museum (Weil am Rhein), Centre Pompidou (Paris), MAXXI Museum (Rome) and Milan Triennale. Silvia received her Ph.D. in History of Architecture and Urbanism from IUAV, Venice, in 2007 and taught at the Polytechnic of Milan between 2008 and 2012.

Ákos Moravánszky is Professor Emeritus of the Theory of Architecture at the Institut gta of ETH Zurich, where he taught between 1996 and 2016. He studied architecture in Budapest and received his Ph.D. in Vienna. He was a Research Fellow at the Zentralinstitut für Kunstgeschichte in Munich, and the Getty Center in Santa Monica. From 1991 until 1996, he was appointed Visiting

Professor at M.I.T. in Cambridge, Mass. The main areas of his research and publication activities are the history of East and Middle European architecture in the nineteenth and twentieth centuries, the history of architectural theory, and the iconology of building materials and constructions. He is the author of *Competing Visions: Aesthetic Invention and Social Imagination in Central European Architecture, 1867–1918* (Cambridge, Mass., 1998) and *Lehrgerüste: Theorie und Stofflichkeit der Architektur* (Zurich, 2015).

Joan Ockman is an architectural historian, critic and educator. She is currently Distinguished Senior Lecturer at the University of Pennsylvania School of Design and also teaches at Cooper Union and Cornell University. From 1994 to 2008 she served as director of the Temple Hoyne Buell Center for the Study of American Architecture at Columbia University. She began her career at the Institute for Architecture and Urban Studies in New York, where she edited *Oppositions* journal and the Oppositions Books series. Her book publications include *Architecture Culture 1943–1968* (Rizzoli, 1993), *The Pragmatist Imagination: Thinking about Things in the Making* (Princeton Architectural Press, 2000), *Out of Ground Zero: Case Studies in Urban Reinvention* (Prestel, 2002), *Architourism: Authentic, Exotic, Escapist, Spectacular* (Prestel, 2005) and *Architecture School: Three Centuries of Educating Architects in North America* (MIT Press, 2012).

Michela Rosso obtained her Doctorate in Architectural and Urban History at the Politecnico di Torino, where she has been teaching History and Theory of Architecture since 1996. Her main fields of research include the history of architecture (eighteenth to twenty-first centuries) and architectural historiography. On these topics she published the volume *La Storia utile: Modernismo e memoria nazionale: Londra 1928–1951* (Edizioni di Comunità, 2001) and edited the Italian translation of Lewis Mumford's essay *The Culture of Cities* (Edizioni di Comunità, 1999). Among her current interests, research on the relationship between the architectural profession and public opinion occupy an important place. Since the end of 2001, she has been a specialist editor of *Il Giornale dell'Architettura*, to which she contributes regularly. In June 2014, she was general chair of the third EAHN (European Architectural History Network) international conference held at the Turin Polytechnic.

Angelika Schnell is Professor for Architectural History and Theory at the Academy of Fine Arts Vienna. She studied Theatre Science and Architecture in Munich, Berlin and Delft. From 1993 until 2001, she was editor of the architecture theory magazine *ARCH+*. Since 1999, she has held teaching positions in architectural history and theory at the Technical University Berlin, the Academy of Fine Arts Stuttgart, the University of Groningen and the University of Innsbruck. Focal points in her research are the history and theory of modern architecture and urban planning in the twentieth and twenty-first centuries; media and architecture; the relationships between design methods and theories, the arts, literature, and psychoanalysis. Her work has been published internationally.

Karin Šerman is an architect and architectural theorist. She is Professor of Architectural History and Theory and Head of the Department at the University of Zagreb Faculty of Architecture. Her work focuses on modern and contemporary architecture and culture, and current theoretical research. She has written extensively on Central European and Croatian architectural history and the contemporary architectural scene. In 2014, she was the curator of the Croatian entry *Fitting Abstraction* at the 14th Venice Architecture Biennale *Fundamentals: Absorbing Modernity 1914–2014*. She graduated in Architecture from the University of Zagreb Faculty of Architecture in 1989, received her Master in Design Studies degree in Architectural History and Theory from Harvard University Graduate School of Design in 1996 and her PhD from the University of Zagreb in 2000.

Łukasz Stanek is architect and historian of architecture currently teaching at the Manchester School of Architecture, University of Manchester, UK. He graduated in Architecture and Philosophy after studies in Kraków, Weimar, Münster, and Zurich, and received his Ph.D. at the Delft University of Technology. Stanek authored *Henri Lefebvre on Space: Architecture, Urban Research, and the Production of Theory* (2011) and edited Lefebvre's unpublished book about architecture, *Toward an Architecture of Enjoyment* (2014). Stanek also published on the mobilities of architecture between socialist countries and Africa and the Middle East during the Cold War, and he is currently preparing a book on this topic. He taught at the Berlage Institute, Harvard University Graduate School of Design and ETH Zurich, and received fellowships at numerous institutions including the Canadian Center for Architecture (Montreal), and the Center for Advanced Study in Visual Arts (Washington D.C.)

Georgi Stanishev (senior) is a Bulgarian architect and architecture critic, Professor and Chairman of the Department of Theory and History of Architecture at the University for Architecture Civil Engineering and Geodesy, Sofia, where he also studied. He completed his Ph.D. at the Moscow Architecture Institute (MArchI). He was editor-in-chief of *Architecture &*

Society (1982–1987) and further worked as director of the concept feature at the *World Architecture Magazine*, London. Stanishev has acted as curator of many architectural exhibitions, including among others "Iakov Chernikhov Architecture Fantasies" (Sofia, 2000), "Zaha Hadid Architects" (Sofia, 2007), "Bulgarian Young Architects" at the Venice Biennale of Architecture (Venice, 2008), "Foster Architecture" (Sofia, 2008), "Harry Seidler Architecture" (Sofia, 2011), and "Ricciotti Architecte" (Sofia, 2014). He is the editor of two books on Russian contemporary architecture for Thames and Hudson: *Hermitage: The New Art Museum*, and *Studio 44 Architecture*, (London, 2015–2016), and an author of two monographs: *Theory of Architecture in Monologues* (Sofia, 2016) and *Architecture Theory and Criticism* (Sofia, 2016, with Milena Metalkova-Markova).

Georgi Stanishev (junior) is an architect and lecturer at the Ecole Nationale Supérieure d'Architecture de Paris-Malaquais in France. As a practitioner he runs a studio for set design and architecture and has participated in several exhibitions on architectural drawings and representation. The main focus of his pedagogical work are the relations between utopia, ideology and the creative process of the architect. He is a Ph.D. candidate at LIAT research laboratory in ENSAPM and in the department of Theory and History of the Faculty of Architecture in UACEG, Sofia. His research focuses on the evolution and decline of communism during the postwar period and its manifestations within the architectural discourses. He has published several papers on identity in art such as "Adolf Loos against identity" (2015) and "Newness in art and the minor identity" (2011).

Tijana Stevanović is writing her Ph.D. in Architectural Theory and Criticism (Newcastle University). It researches architectural debates on the agency of the architect and the user within the self-managed economy in socialist New Belgrade, and explores why those architectural concerns and projects often need to be situated as containing the contradictory ambitions of both attending to the needs of the individual and the collective. Tijana is a Lecturer at the School of Architecture, UCA and a Teaching Fellow at the Bartlett School of Architecture, UCL. She has published texts in the journals: *H-Urban*; *arq*; *An Architektur*; and has edited the volumes: *Industries of Architecture*; *Pedagogies of Disaster*; *Critical Cities*. She is also engaged in the research toward and enactment of productive/constraining demands of self-management within collaborative art projects: *Overpainting as Temporal Drag* (London, ongoing), *Sick Leave* (District, Berlin, 2015), *A Partial Index* (Baltic 39, Newcastle, 2014), *I am too sad to dissent* (Flutgraben, Berlin, 2013).

Léa-Catherine Szacka is assistant professor at the Oslo School of Architecture and Design (AHO). In 2012, she received a Ph.D. in History and Theory of architecture from the Bartlett, University College London with a thesis on the history of the 1980 Venice Architecture Biennale (*Exhibiting the Postmodern*, forthcoming, Marsilio, 2016). Szacka has lectured and published widely on postmodern architecture and has acted as editor, with Charles Jencks and Eva Branscome, of the 2011 re-edition of *The Post-modern Reader*. Alongside post-modern architecture, Szacka's work focuses on architecture exhibitions. She has contributed to two journals' special issues on the question (*Log*20, 2010 and *OASE*88, 2013), a book (*Exhibiting architecture*, Lars Müller, 2014) and has organized a major symposium at the Centre Georges Pompidou in early 2014 (in the aftermath of which she co-edited a special issue of the *Cahiers du Musée national d'art moderne*, fall 2014).

Alla Vronskaya is a postdoctoral fellow and holds the Guest Lectureship for the Theory of Architecture at the Swiss Federal Institute of Technology (ETH), Zurich. She received a Ph.D. from Massachusetts Institute of Technology and a candidate of sciences degree from State Institute of Art History, Moscow. Her research explores the interest of modernist architects, particularly in Soviet Russia, in experimental psychology and unconscious perception. It has been supported by fellowships from the Getty Research Institute, Dumbarton Oaks Research Library and the Swiss Government, and has been published in journals and collective volumes such as *Architecture and the Unconscious* (Ashgate, 2016).

Johannes Warda is an architectural scholar and teacher working on a wide range of subjects such as sustainability, preservation, the history of ideas, and architectural and design theory. After studying History, American Studies, Political Science and Architecture in Jena, Weimar and Berkeley, he received an M.A. in History. In 2014, Johannes completed a Ph.D. in Architecture at Bauhaus University Weimar ("Veto des Materials: Denkmaldiskurs, Wiederaneignung von Architektur und modernes Umweltbewusstsein"). He is a Fulbright alumnus and has received a dissertation grant from the German National Academic Foundation. In 2015/16, Johannes held the Bauhaus Postdoc Scholarship. His writings appeared in various media, including *Frankfurter Allgemeine Zeitung*, *Merkur*, and *HORIZONTE. Zeitschrift für Architekturdiskurs*. Johannes is member of the Bauhaus Institute for History and Theory of Architecture and Planning at Bauhaus University Weimar and lecturer at the Academy of Fine Arts Vienna (2016/17).

Index